Books by Bil Gilbert

WESTERING MAN: THE LIFE OF JOSEPH WALKER   1983

THE TRAILBLAZERS   1973

CHULO   1973

THE WEASELS   1970

HOW ANIMALS COMMUNICATE   1966

BEARS IN THE LADIES ROOM   1966

Westering Man

Westering Man

The Life of Joseph Walker

Bil Gilbert

University of Oklahoma Press : Norman and London

Text designed by Mary Cregan

Maps by Michael Serrres

Cover painting, "'Bourgeois' W——r, & his Squaw," by Alfred Jacob Miller, reproduced courtesy of The InterNorth Foundation, Joslyn Art Museum, Omaha, Nebraska.

Library of Congress Cataloging-in-Publication Data

Gilbert, Bil.
  Westering man.

  Reprint. Originally published: New York: Atheneum, 1983.
  Bibliography: p. 319.
  Includes index.
  1. Walker, Joseph Reddeford, 1798–1876. 2. Pioneers—West (U.S.)—Biography. 3. Explorers—West (U.S.)—Biography. 4. Frontier and pioneer life—West (U.S.) 5. West (U.S.)—History—To 1848. 6. West (U.S.)—History—1848–1950. I. Title.
[F592.W245G54   1985]   978'.02'0924 [B]   84–22055
ISBN 0–8061–1934–9 (pbk.)

3   4   5   6   7   8   9   10   11   12

TO OUR CHILDREN:
Ky, Lyn, Lee and Kate

Acknowledgments

The libraries and manuscript collections of the following institutions were frequently used: the universities of Arizona, California (Bancroft Library) and Missouri; the Jackson County Historical Society (Independence, Missouri), Missouri Historical Society (St. Louis); the State Historical Society of Missouri (Columbia); Sharlot Hall Historical Society (Prescott, Arizona); Arizona Historical Society (Tucson); U.S. Army War College (Carlisle, Pennsylvania); and the Library of Congress. Staff members at these facilities were without exception cooperative and extremely competent.

Contemporary descendants of eighteenth- and nineteenth-century Walkers made family papers and recollections available. Their specific contributions are acknowledged in the notes. Several editorial professionals and long-time friends, Robert Creamer, Suzanne Hubbell, Patricia Ryan and Jeremiah Tax, read portions of the manuscript and gave useful advice and encouragement. The support and insightful suggestions of Tom Stewart, the working editor of this book, were of great importance. Michael Serres prepared the maps which accompany and enhance the text. Kate, Ky, Lee and Lyn Gilbert; Ruth and Bob Fader; Bill Hamilton; Carol Squires; John Thomson; Margaret, Sam and Tracy Walmer have provided special and significant assistance.

My wife, Ann, is a talented, indefatigable historical researcher, patient editor and discerning critic who was creatively involved from the beginning to the end of this book. During the four years involved she was the only person with sufficient specific knowledge of the subject to speculate about and discuss it intelligently. She also has two natural gifts, the importance of which can be fully appreciated only by those who have been involved in similar exercises. She can read microfilm for hours on end without becoming nauseated. (In contrast, ten minutes

or so of this activity set my head spinning and stomach churning.)
She can decipher crabbed, faded nineteenth-century handwriting
quickly and accurately.

My opinion has been, and is, that Ann's contributions have been so
substantive that they can be properly acknowledged only by formally
presenting this book as a product of joint authorship. However, she
is a person of strong principles and objected to this on the ground that
she did not do any of the actual writing. That is true in a de jure sense,
but it is also true that without her efforts this book would have been
written either much differently from the way it is or not at all. De
facto, *Westering Man* is a cooperative creation, a product of shared
thought, work and pleasure.

Contents

The Frontier Hero 3
The Disposable People 13
The Creek Nation 29
Tennessee 45
Missouri 57
Santa Fe 70
Jackson County 87
The Rockies 103
The Sierra 119
Eden—and Back 139
The Great Basin 153
The Emigrants 174
Frémont 198
The End of the Mountains 217
A Californian 234
Mangas 247
Arizona 267
Manzanita Ranch 278
Addendum: Of Dreams 289
Notes 299
Bibliography 319
Index 331

Westering Man

The Frontier Hero

For 100 years or so, beginning at about the time this Republic did, America produced a class of public figures who as well as anything else might be called Frontier Heroes. They are unique in our history and for that matter in the recent history of the English-speaking people. Frontier heroes were less high and mighty, cerebral and manipulative than presidents, generals or national political figures. (However, because they were so popular, many in the latter classes, including Washington, Jackson and Lincoln, were willing to let it be known that there was a dash of frontier hero in them.) They were leaders, but irregular ones who acted extemporaneously, independent of established authority and sometimes in opposition to it. They were commissioned to lead by popular acclaim and were followed voluntarily because of their common sense, bravery, coolness, ability to shoot straight, ride hard, fight ferociously, bear up and function under formidable hardship.

Commonly they were pathfinders and trailblazers but were not explorers concerned with grand geographical or strategic matters in the fashion of a Magellan, Coronado or Mackenzie. Their problems were discrete, tactical ones: how to find a way from the Valley of Virginia to the mouth of the Tennessee River and then how to get their relatives or companies of followers through the lands they had explored. Nearly all of them had paramilitary experiences, but their soldiering was sporadic and incidental—a matter of eluding or shoving aside British, Mexicans, Indians or whoever stood in the way of their principal business, which was making the continent their own.

When the conditions which required and permitted them to act as they did disappeared, the supply of frontier heroes dried up, and since then we have been unable to find fully satisfying replacements. The

3

gunners and badmen, assorted Wild Bills and Kids who immediately followed, were bold enough but not sufficiently admirable for general consumption. Athletes are entertaining and physically impressive but lack social substance. Astronauts, FBI agents, microbe hunters are too faceless, dry and technical. In consequence, names like Boone and Crockett, Bridger and Carson are still stimulating, and the Frontier Heroes remain perhaps the most generally admired figures of our formal and folk history.

By any objective standard of real accomplishment or influence, a man by the name of Joseph Walker belongs in the front rank of this company. He was born into one of the sprawling Scotch-Irish clans that dominated the American frontier from the early eighteenth to the late nineteenth century. Coming out of Tennessee in 1819 as a twenty-year-old veteran of the Appalachian Indian wars, he emigrated to western Missouri, then the extreme outpost of American settlement. With his brothers and other kin he cleared a farm, built some cabins and then set off for the unexplored (to Americans) southwest as one of the first mountain fur trappers and traders. In 1825 he guided the government party which surveyed and marked the Santa Fe Trail. In 1827 he was one of the founders and the first sheriff of Independence, Missouri, first of the true western boom towns. In 1832 he went to the northern Rockies as a brigade leader in the fur trade and became a principal figure among the mountain men who ever since have so excited the American imagination. In 1833 he led a band of these trappers to California, the first Americans to come to the Pacific through the then unknown Sierra. During the next decade he lived and traded with the Indian tribes of the Great Basin as a kind of white raja. In 1843 he guided the first wagon train to reach California and thereafter was a consulting pathfinder and trail leader for other emigrants, the military, topographical surveyors and railroad builders. He was a California rancher, long-distance stock drover, prospector and enthusiastic archaeological explorer. He ended his field career of five decades in the 1860s, leading the first party of Americans into central Arizona, fighting and negotiating his way through the mountain strongholds of the Apache to find and open the Prescott gold fields.

In terms of durability, Daniel Boone and Jim Bridger were among the few who were active on the frontier for as long as Walker, but their activities were more restricted geographically than his. Meriwether Lewis and William Clark, whose expedition is unquestionably the single most impressive and influential feat of American exploration, were certainly Walker's equals as wilderness leaders, and Clark, like Walker, seems to have been something of an intuitive topographical genius. However, the captains of the Corps of Discovery were in the field, on the frontier, for less than five years.

Jedediah Smith and Joseph Walker are often paired historically as the only mountain men who organized and led true exploratory expeditions, being the first Americans to bring parties from the interior to California over new routes. Again, Smith's was a very short career, for he survived only seven years on the frontier. Smith was a courageous but rash man and at the very least an unlucky leader. He came to California across the Mojave Desert, and before he returned home, twenty-six of the thirty-three men who tried to follow him died. In contrast, Walker followed a more direct but technically difficult route, forcing a passage through the central Sierra. All his forty men survived, and during his career, in which he led hundreds of men, women and children through formidable wilderness areas, only one person is reported to have died while following him.

Though their reputation has come down otherwise, the western mountain men were not as successful or frequent Indian fighters as their Appalachian forebears had been. They had some luck with bushwhacking, but in more or less equal confrontations they were invariably routed. Walker was an exception, being one of the very few partisan commanders who had enough tactical sense and control over his unruly colleagues to win what can be dignified as battles against the Indians. He did so three times, the only occasions in which he engaged in general actions. However, his customary role was that of a peacemaker, trying to restrain bloody-minded and less knowledgeable associates, urging conciliation, patience and fair dealing with the tribes. He often lived with and had great rapport with the Indians and was the only early frontiersman who, according to surviving records, led whites against other whites to redress what he considered an injustice committed against the Indians.

In hundreds of diaries, letters, official reports, newspaper interviews and reminiscences of trappers, traders, emigrants, prospectors, naturalists, military officers, surveyors and others who knew him, Joseph Walker's accomplishments are described with great and consistent admiration. He was so often introduced as the "renowned" explorer, mountaineer, plainsman, guide, Indian fighter or pioneer that it seemed almost to be a title. (In fact, he was usually addressed as Captain. The title was honorary, but in his case it was used respectfully, even by military officers who often were scornful of irregularly commissioned civilians.) The same accounts contain frequent testimonials to his kindness, modesty, courtesy and remarkable wilderness skills.

Also, it seems that Walker possessed great panache. He was a massive, burly, bearded man, gigantic by the standards of the time, standing six feet four inches and weighing more than 200 pounds. As two portraits painted when he was in his prime testify, he was remarkably handsome and well turned out, his dress apparently being one of the few things about which he was vain. Even in the deep wilderness, where most men let themselves go a bit to matted hair, ragged and reeking shirts, travelers who met him were struck by Captain Walker's comparative elegance. One such was an awed fourteen-year-old boy by the name of John McBride. In the summer of 1846 he was traveling by wagon with his family to Oregon. In Utah the McBride party was overtaken by Walker, who, with a small hard-riding band of men, was driving a herd of horses from California to Santa Fe. The riders stopped to talk to members of the emigrant wagon train and give them some advice about the route ahead. Thirty-five years later, when John McBride came to write his memoirs, he recalled the meeting with the great frontier captain as one of the highlights of his trip to Oregon. Allowing for the fact that McBride grew up to be a United States congressman and mastered the florid prose style of that calling, his description still suggests that Walker, then nearly fifty years old, was a most impressive man:

> His dress was a marvel of adaptation to his business, while it was rich and simple. It was of dressed buckskin throughout. A loose fitting coat and pants, richly ornamented with needle-work in silk, trimmed with fur, moccasins that showed all the skill that savage art could muster, California leggings, fastened below the knee and ornamented with thread work of silver and gold wire done by hand, in figures of lilies and a broad sombrero to keep off the sun. Mounted on a noble looking roan horse, of Spanish blood, on a Mexican saddle, with spurs whose rowels were six inches in diameter of polished steel plated with gold at his heels, he was, with his rifle across his saddle bow, as perfect a prince in bearing as I have ever seen. He seemed born to rule the wild spirits around him without effort and they at once acknowledged their leader without discontent or controversy.

McBride went on to say that the names of such as Walker were "in those days, as familiar as are now those of leaders of business and politics."

The evidence of existing records makes it clear that among his contemporaries, Joseph Walker was a celebrity for reasons of both his accomplishments and his character. Historians have generally concurred that he was an important, able and influential frontier figure. There are few works, either academic or popular, dealing with the early trans-Mississippi west in which some mention is not made of his exploits. However, though numerous, the references are usually scattered and fragmentary, seldom connected to give much sense of the man himself. In this respect it sometimes seems that Walker was the frontier equivalent of the mysterious Kilroy of World War II whose name was scrawled from the Aleutians to Assam but who was never met.

Walker did exist, and because of a series of extraordinary accomplishments, he continues to turn up frequently in western histories but, like Kilroy, always in an impersonal, disembodied, name-only way.*

Some ten years ago, while collecting material for a history of early exploration in western North America, I became curious about the personal obscurity of Joe Walker. He had apparently been a dramatic, colorful figure, widely known and very well thought of in his own time, whose accomplishments have been certified by subsequent scholars as being genuine and significant. On its face it would seem he should be one of our most recognizable frontier heroes, at least on a par with contemporaries such as Boone, Bridger and Carson. This is obviously not the case, Walker now being largely unknown except among western history specialists.

With a newcomer's ignorance and arrogance, I felt this was a terrible case of collective negligence and sloth on the part of not only historians but popular mythmakers and keepers. The assumption quickly proved to be false. Long before my interest commenced, many others had been well aware that the life of Joseph Walker—like a challenging, unclimbed mountain—was there and was a prominent phenomenon of western history which should be explored. A good many tried to do so but met with bad luck and not much success.

When Walker died on the family ranch near San Francisco, he was a bona fide celebrity, and in consequence a spate of long obituaries, reminiscences of and sketches about him appeared in periodicals published in California and other western states. They were often more eulogistic than factual, but many subsequent biographical references to Walker (including a fair number of newspaper and magazine features) were summaries or embellishments of these early memorials. The most ambitious effort of this sort was a semifictional biography, privately printed fifty years ago. In it the original obituary material is interlarded and spiced up with passages of turgid description, invented incidents and conversations. It is now a rare book and deservedly not well regarded, except by collectors.

* We have not even been able to remember his name correctly. Since shortly after his death in 1876, he has consistently been referred to in works of all degrees of scholarship as Joseph Reddeford Walker. This is peculiar for two reasons. First, authors who have regularly written of Kit (not Christopher) Carson, Jed (Jedediah Strong) Smith and Broken Hand (Thomas Aloysius) Fitzpatrick have invariably felt obliged to refer to Walker by his full, resounding name. Secondly, it is not the right name. He was Joseph Rutherford, not Reddeford, Walker. It is a small, inconsequential error, but an illustrative one. An explanation of why and how his name, the most distinguishing possession of any man, was garbled appears in the notes section, which commences on page 299.

Otherwise, an excellent master's thesis was prepared at Brigham Young University some twenty years ago by Merton N. Lovell. In it most of the then known published references to Walker were collected. Also, there have been at least five attempts to write comprehensive biographies. None was completed, all five authors dying before their manuscripts were ready for publication.

Nothing suggests that Captain Walker was the sort who would, if such were possible, have put a curse on his biographers. However, he did have habits which made it difficult for those who have tried to be and probably discouraged others from trying. Most notably he was a man of unique and, it seems, principled reticence. As secondhand accounts again indicate, he was, while normally friendly and gregarious, not a casual storyteller. Nor, though he had a better education than was average for his times and class, was he a memoir or even letter writer. Only a few scraps of impersonal, essentially business correspondence survive. That he spent so much of his life in regions well beyond the reach of even the most irregular mails must certainly have been a factor, but it seems that conviction also may have contributed to his relative silence, as the following shadowy incident indicates.

For some years Walker kept a journal. He told members of his family it was an "exact accounting" of where he had been and what he had done. However, in mid-career, while crossing a river, he was caught in the current, overturned and pulled downstream. He and his horse escaped, but he lost the pack which held the journal.

He recalled the happening when he was an old man by way of explaining to several grandnieces and nephews why he tended to be short with journalists, historical investigators and other questioners who then were seeking him out as one of the last living frontier heroes. He said that after losing his exact record, he did not like to trust his memory regarding events which had occurred so many years before. He thought that far too many exaggerated and false stories about the early frontier had already been told, and rather than unintentionally add to them, he preferred to remain silent.

The loss of the notes alone cannot be counted as a critical factor in regard to his historical position or lack of it. A number of frontiersmen who did not and could not by reason of illiteracy make any written records became well known because they found or could not avoid eager Boswells who did some gaudy work without being aided or handicapped by any "exact accountings." In Walker's day there were probably more literary than mineral prospectors in the safer parts of the frontier. All were on the lookout for colorful characters or at least ones suitable for coloring in dispatches sent back to the settlements. The westering adventure was the big story of the time, of perhaps more intense and general interest than space exploration would be a century later. Furthermore, energetic reporters were free to become on-the-scene participant-observers. Many did. Some went west specifically for purposes of publication: Washington Irving, the literary lion of the day; Francis Parkman, the hypochondriac historian who doggedly traveled a few hundred miles of the Oregon Trail suffering from frights, fastidiousness and sick headaches; Rufus Sage, the Connecticut travel writer and moralist; Matt Field, the young new journalist of the old *New Orleans Picayune;* George Ruxton, the British novelist-spy who became the Burton of the Rockies. A greater number were in the West for more pragmatic reasons—to soldier, hunt for gold, emigrate across the plains—but, while and because they were there, decided that they had in them a book, a pamphlet or at least a series of lively sketches which could be printed in their hometown newspapers.

Joe Walker was known to nearly all the literary travelers. He camped with, guided, saved the skins and scalps of many of them, but was of almost no help when it came to supplying raw material for legends: reports of bloody engagements with fierce warriors or passionate ones with their women, duels with grizzly bears or *pistoleros,* descriptions of hidden Spanish treasure, lost gold mines, diamonds as big as the Ritz and the like. Particularly Walker did not tell wild stretchers in which he himself became a half-alligator, half-panther, brother-of-lightning, father-of-thunder champion. This was very unusual, for among the mountain men braggadocio had evolved into something of an art form. In frozen camps, when the ice was too thick to set traps, the snow too deep for traveling, and the whiskey was gone, backgammon, old sledge and yarning were about all that was possible in the way of entertainment. Some of Walker's colleagues—Joe Meek, Jim Bridger, Jim Beckwourth, Bill Craig, Peg-leg Smith—were so talented in this line that after the beaver became scarce, they made what amounted to second careers out of putting on eastern greenhorns and writers with tall stories.

That Walker had so little inclination for this sort of thing, so little apparent need for self-glorification, seemed to many of his contemporaries to be one of his most remarkable traits, and it was often commented upon. Among others who were impressed was a Kentuckian, Daniel Conner. In 1862 Conner was a member of a party that followed Walker through the Apache country and eventually discovered gold in central Arizona. He was the last in a series of younger men—Zenas Leonard, Kit Carson, Joe and Sam Meek, Tom Breckenridge and several of Walker's own nephews—who served frontier apprenticeships under the renowned Captain and thereafter held him in great regard. Conner kept a journal of his adventures, and it provides one of the best and most human portraits of Joe Walker. When Conner knew him, he was sixty-five years old, of an age when a certain amount of garrulousness is expected, but Conner wrote: "We never knew him to relate any exploits of his career though he must have had many. He was dignified, but courteous, talked but little and had small patience with coarse or obscene language."

Not only did Walker refuse to originate glory stories, but he went out of his way to scotch the efforts of others who tried to do so. One who did—several times—was John Charles Frémont, who, whatever his deficiencies as a man of action, was indisputably the great publicizer-romanticizer of the pre-Civil War west. Almost singlehandedly he made a national hero of Kit Carson, who, when they met, was an unassuming young man of no great prominence in the irregular ranks of the frontiersmen. Had Walker been a bit more pliant, the same probably would have been done for or to him.

In the spring of 1844 Frémont was lost, not a rare occurrence for the Pathfinder. This time it was in the southern Great Basin, an area which Frémont had insisted on crossing, though it was unfamiliar to his paid guides. Beyond not knowing how to get to where he wanted to be, which was Washington, D.C., and despite commanding a well-armed party of thirty men, Frémont was jittery about the Ute Indians, who he was certain were working themselves up to a massacre. As it happened, Walker with eight of his irregulars was in the vicinity, headed toward the upper Arkansas River. Riding a few days behind, he picked up Frémont's trail. From the signs he determined that the Pathfinder was in trouble and set off to find him.

By and by Walker caught up and, after some friendly negotiations with a Ute chief who was a long-time acquaintance, led Frémont to Bent's Fort, a large trading establishment located near the present Kansas-Colorado state line. There Walker left the party, apparently assuming that even a captain in the Army Corps of Topographical Engineers could find his way eastward along the Santa Fe Trail, which had become, since Walker had marked it off twenty years earlier, the principal southwestern freight route. Frémont was able to do so and hurried on to Washington to commence work on a book about his latest adventures. When he came to the part about Walker, he was extravagantly complimentary. (The Pathfinder had the literary habit of dropping the names of famous frontiersmen to make it clear that he kept company with heroes.) Frémont worked himself into something of a lather describing the magnitude of the predicament from which Walker had rescued him. "Nothing but his [Walker's] great knowledge of the country, great courage and presence of mind and good rifles could have brought him safe from such a perilous enterprise."

Later Walker heard the story and scathingly debunked it and its author. "The fact is," said the frontier captain, giving his exact accounting of the episode, "the danger was all in Capt. Frémont's fears.

... [I] would have traveled at that time with eight mountain men, well armed, anywhere over the length and breadth of the plains."

With the exception of Frémont, Walker seemed to get on easily enough with touring scribes. They, like Frémont, were invariably enchanted to meet such a celebrity and grateful for the assistance he often gave them. However, none was able to collect him in a literary way. Beyond his adamant reticence, some obvious technical problems made Walker a hard biographical case. Principally, he was a bit too durable, too successful and generally too good to be true or easily made to seem to be true, which is the same thing so far as an author is concerned. It was as if Davy Crockett had victoriously defended the Alamo for fifty years while retaining the high opinion of all witnesses. Walker's life was like a high plain of continuing accomplishment, lacking valleys of defeat and despair which highlight the peaks. Many of the journalists made remarks to the effect that Captain Walker was a fine man, the genuine frontier goods, whose exploits would make a remarkable tale which someday somebody should tell. Regretfully they themselves were not able to do so at the time. They then moved on to men and events that could be conventionally romanticized.

As I suspect has nearly everyone who has tried to become better acquainted with Captain Joseph Walker, I have sometimes wished he had occasionally let down his hair and given a few crackling good dramatic accounts of his exploits, which, as Daniel Conner wistfully wrote, "must have been many." However, on the whole I am glad he did not. If he had, he or a kind of mythic mask of him would be better remembered than is now the case. But if he had, he would not be such an interesting or important man to remember. By all historical and literary rights, he should long ago have become a gaudy, semilegendary figure of pop history, a boon to the toy, T-shirt and TV industries. That he is not may paradoxically be the best and most revealing clue to his unusual personality.

Documentably Walker was proud of many of his accomplishments and contemplative enough to think of himself in relation to at least near posterity. There is no reason to think that he intentionally set out to hide himself from history. However, there is abundant evidence that he wanted to make certain that if anyone wanted to know and remember him, it would be on his own terms for reasons that he, not creators of Wild West romances, thought important. The exploits, after all, were matters of fact and action, the bare record of which should be sufficient to preserve them as great adventures. For example, in the late fall of 1833 Walker led forty men up the eastern slopes of the California Sierra. No Europeans then knew what lay within this range, nor how far it extended, how long it would require to traverse it or if they could traverse it. On very short rations of acorn meal, dried grasshoppers, stringy horse meat and carrion, they struggled for a month through hip-deep snows, roped their surviving horses down slick rock faces, made dangerous, difficult detours and descents of immense canyons. Exhaustion and starvation weakened their bodies. Doubt and fear ate at their minds. The abstract knowledge that they were the first white men to do and see such things—stand on the brink of then unnamed Yosemite Falls and walk through incredible groves of gigantic trees which later were to be called Sequoias—sustained and inspired them. They endured and came down the western slopes into the sunshine and ease of the virgin San Joaquin Valley. If such cannot be recollected as a triumph of human physique, will and curiosity, no amount of purplish Frémont-style prose will help.

It is a reasonable possibility that Walker's flinty refusal to elaborate or exaggerate his acts reflected not unusual modesty, but rather great pride in himself and the westering experience, which he had had as much of as any other American who ever lived. Even in his day, historical revisionists were at work, suggesting that the west had been won at wild rendezvous of drunken beaver trappers, in spectacular cavalry charges, in barroom brawls and shoot-outs around corrals, by psychopathic robber barons, gunslingers, scalpers, braggarts and bullies. There were such events and people. They still make very good copy. But in regard to the main show they were aberrant and often counterproductive. To represent or eulogize them as central factors is to trivialize pioneering.

Walker was no more a typical frontiersman than Mark Twain was a typical journalist. He was engaged in the same line of work as many others, but he was exceptional for his physical prowess, intellect, talents and because of a consistent pattern of decent, principled behavior which only men of great strength and self-confidence can sustain. All available accounts suggest that people of the time who had some direct knowledge of circumstances admired and were proud of Joe Walker because he was such a good—in the several senses of the word—example of what a Frontier Hero could and should be.

The Disposable People

Ingrained in our collective historical consciousness is the notion that the English-speaking colonists, after landing on the Atlantic coast, immediately began flowing westward across the continent like a great river in which the current was so powerful that it could be only momentarily obstructed or deflected. This is invented myth. More accurately the people might be compared in a hydrological way to the waters of a narrow reservoir in which for a long time there was no true current, only an inflow. It took this impoundment nearly 200 years to fill. Then the containing dikes burst, and in the next fifty years the remaining three-fourths of what is now the United States was inundated by a raging flood of people.

A hundred years after the first English-speaking emigrants landed on the Atlantic beaches they, their descendants and newer arrivals had pushed the line of settlement less than 100 miles westward, areas around what is now Albany, New York, Lancaster, Pennsylvania, and Richmond, Virginia, being then on the extreme edge of the frontier. By the early 1700s more than half a million permanent residents were east of this line, but the survival and well-being of virtually all of them depended upon material, cultural and psychic support which they received from England. In 1705, Robert Beverly, a Virginia historian, commented ironically on the situation:

> They [the colonists] have their Cloathing of all sorts from England; as linen, woollen, silk, hats, and leather. Yet flax and hemp grow no where in the world, better than there. Their sheep yield good increase and bear good fleeces; but they shear them only to cool them—the very furs that their hats are made, perhaps go first from thence; and most of their hides lie and rot, or are made use of, only for covering dry goods in a leaky house—

13

nay, they are such abominable ill husbands, that though their country be over-run with wood, yet they have all their wooden ware from England; their cabinets, chairs, tables, stools, chests, boxes, cart wheels, and all other things, even so much as their bowls and birchen brooms. . . .

Beverly was writing specifically about Virginia plantation society, but much the same could have been said about all the settlers of the time. In fact, being almost exclusively agricultural, the Virginians were, if anything, somewhat more self-sufficient than residents of the north. The obvious reason the English had been so unenterprising about advancing into the continental interior was that a formidable geopolitical barrier made it next to impossible for them to do anything but huddle on the narrow tidewater strip. Beyond the fall line of the coastal rivers rose the foothills of the Appalachians. They stood like a wilderness wall, 2,000 miles long and 200 miles deep, parallel to the coastal plains. These mountains were relatively low but topographically very confused and difficult (more difficult, as events would prove, than the Rockies, which a century later frontiersmen, without any spectacular new technology, explored and traversed in less than a decade). They were covered with vast tracts of virgin forest lashed together with an all but impenetrable undergrowth. Simply, the Appalachian highlands supported the most extensive temperate zone jungle existent. Also, they were the homelands of a number of pugnacious native peoples who had no inclination and—during the seventeenth and much of the eighteenth century—no need to share them with whites. Among the Indian nations, two of them, the Iroquois in Pennsylvania and New York and the Cherokee in southern Virginia, the Carolinas and Tennessee, were so puissant that during the first 150 years of their relationship, whites could only bribe, placate and appease them.

The English colonists arrived with no resources or previous experience which prepared them for the Appalachian jungle and its inhabitants. Not until well into the eighteenth century could they even travel in the wilderness without the permission and logistical support of the Indians, and settlement west of the fall line was impossible. Being helpless to get into and stay in the wilderness, they had no opportunity to develop wilderness skills and expertise and remained helpless.

This state of affairs does not seem to have greatly disturbed the Atlantic colonists. A good many of them had emigrated as dissidents—political, economic or religious—but few were rebels against English culture. In the main their ambition was to re-create English society, but in such a way that they might enjoy more of its traditional rewards. The coastal strip was well suited for this purpose, being fertile and relatively easy country in terms of climate, topography, vegetation and Indians. Also, it was surprisingly convenient to the motherland. (In

1725 it would have been far easier, quicker and safer for a Virginia tobacco planter to visit London than it would have been to travel to the present site of Knoxville, Tennessee.) That they could not enter or live in the wilderness did not distress the Atlantic settlers because they did not want to. Initially they did not covet, were not even greatly curious about, the highlands; what they wanted to be was overseas English, not savage frontiersmen.

All this was in accordance with official British policy, which was to maintain the colonies as suppliers of raw materials and as protected markets for manufactured goods which would be returned to them in English ships. Royal administrators made no effort to encourage the colonists to become more self-sufficient and often prohibited them from doing so. The British thought of the western wilderness as being valuable only as a buffer against the French to the north and as a source of furs which could be obtained in trade with the Indians. Policy in regard to it was to preserve the wilderness environment for the beasts and savages in hopes that the former would multiply and the latter would remain agreeable trading partners.

As events of 1776 and thereafter were to demonstrate, the British government would probably have been well pleased if this state of affairs could have been maintained perpetually. However, by the early part of the eighteenth century resident colonials were becoming restive. Coastal populations had grown rapidly. Nearly all the best land had been claimed, and much of it had become less fertile than it had originally been because of exhausting agricultural practices. Large landowners were looking to increase their holdings, and landless men— lesser sons and relatives, new emigrants and former indentured servants who had fulfilled their contracts—were seeking to improve themselves by becoming gentlemen of property. In consequence, for the first time the colonists began thinking about the western wilderness, where if nothing else, there was a lot of virgin land.

Much of the country beyond the fall line was owned in a vague way by a few great men and families of the Penn, Carroll and Fairfax class. They had received it directly or indirectly from the English crown. The grants had been given out in blocks of millions of acres, but casually, since the jungle properties were practically worthless, except that they represented marks of royal favor. However, as land pressure along the coast increased, some of the colonial nabobs began to consider the possibility that their western holdings might become or be made to become commercially valuable. Without exception they were powerful members of the small colonial oligarchy, and thus, their interest became the public interest and policy. This was particularly the case in the middle-Atlantic regions, which were the most populous and where therefore the demand for new land was greatest. Colonies to the north and south were less concerned with western lands because the Iroquois and Cherokee were located directly on their boundaries, making any development projects or even talk of them unwise to deadly.

Though there were eager land buyers and willing sellers, the ambitions of both small and great men in this matter were initially thwarted by the reality that none of them knew how to use the wilderness. Few cared to educate themselves by risking their own lives, those of their families or even valuable servants and slaves in experimental western settlement schemes. As colonial authorities mulled over this problem, it simultaneously occurred to a number of them that what was needed was a kind of disposable people. If such could be found, they could be thrust into the wilderness to break it up a bit, tame it sufficiently so that it could be safely occupied and profitably traded by the upper classes. The present circumstances of these people would obviously have to be low enough so that they could be inveigled into relocating in the mysterious and, it was assumed, very dangerous Appalachian highlands. They should be of a sort whose losses—which would no doubt be heavy—would not cause the English-speaking establishment great sorrow, political or economic inconvenience. But they should be hardy enough to survive at least until their wilderness-breaking work was well advanced.

In the early decades of the eighteenth century, public officials and private entrepreneurs (usually one and the same) began looking about for such stalwart, obliging pioneers. They first invited lowland Germans. Appreciable numbers were willing to come, having suffered religious and economic discrimination at home, but attempts (notably one by Alexander Spotswood, the governor of Virginia) to settle them in the true wilderness ended badly. Generally the Germans preferred to remain in communal groups and in the rolling Piedmont country to the east of the Susquehanna and Blue Ridge. There they prospered, becoming some of the best farmers and most skilled artisans in the colonies. However, like the English, the Pennsylvania Dutch, as they were generally called, showed little enthusiasm for setting off alone to the raw frontier.

As something of a second choice, colonial planners turned their attention to the lowland Scots—the Scotch-Irish, as they came to be known in North America. Admittedly they were not as skilled, industrious or orderly as the Germans; but they were thought to be very hardy, and they were then perhaps the most disposable people in all of Christendom.

Their distant ancestors had been neither Scottish nor Irish (i.e., Celtic), but rather a mixed lot of Danes, Angles and Saxons who had been pushed north by various post-Roman invasions of Great Britain. Not as a unified people but as a collection of refugees they had come

to settle across the narrow northern neck of the island and were identified as lowland Scots more for reasons of geography than race. For
centuries they were caught between the almost perpetually warring
highland Celts to the north and the English to the south. As both participants and sullen bystanders whose welfare was inconsequential to
either side, they were regularly plundered, imprisoned, raped and
massacred. When there were lulls in the conflicts between and with
the outsiders, the lowlanders raided, stole from and killed one another.

Inevitably they became formidable guerrilla fighters, but otherwise,
they developed few social, so to speak, skills. The form of government
they evolved was a primitive feudal one in which obedience was given
to or required by strong partisan captains. The law was regarded not
as an impartial device established for the general benefit, but rather as
a means for the powerful to work their will on the less powerful. The
lowland Scots created very little in the way of art, literature, science,
technology or even crafts. Such require resources and security to master, a certain hopefulness about the future to make mastering them
worth the trouble.

The poverty of the lowland Scots was terrible. The land had not
been richly endowed by nature and was steadily degraded by centuries of war, social upheaval and exploitation by desperate people.
They were bad farmers—seventeenth-century agricultural practices in
the lowlands being not substantially different from those of the twelfth
century—for the same reasons that they were not artists or craftsmen.
There was little incentive to undertake patient husbandry projects
when crops and stock were always in danger of being destroyed or
confiscated. Normal existence was hand-to-mouth, with occasional sur-
pluses being acquired through sporadic acts of plunder. By Eliza-
bethan times the lowlands had been turned into a barren, literally treeless northern desert. The wretchedness of the place was awful even by
prevailing standards, and the reporters, mostly English, who visited it
sent back shocked accounts of the filthy, violent and generally repulsive
people they found there.

The Renaissance largely passed by the lowlands, and conditions of
the Dark Ages prevailed there for much longer than in the rest of
Europe. They began to dissipate in the mid-sixteenth century, the
crucial event being the return of a native son—John Knox—who
brought the Protestant Reformation. Theology aside, the dour, ferociously righteous Knox and the Presbyterian divines who followed him
gave the lowlanders one of their first cultural rallying points, a sense
of and a means for expressing themselves as a people. Among other
surprising consequences the lowlanders, who had long been perhaps
the most educationally backward people in northern Europe, suddenly
became among the most literate. Attached to most of the new churches

was a school in which hard-minded and -handed dominies bullied and beat the children of the congregation until they were at least able to read. General enlightenment and cultural uplift were not the objective. The purpose was to enable the people to comprehend the complex, disputatious sermons which were interminably preached in the kirks and which, circulated in written form, served as political manifestoes.

As scattered bands of rebellious partisans, the lowlanders had long been an annoyance to the English, but their new cohesiveness and Nonconformist fanaticism made them serious political and theological threats. In 1605 James I and his advisers came to a classically British policy decision: to use their lowland Scots problem as a means of settling another—the chronic Irish one. It was decided to establish lowlanders on plantations (similar to those planned for North America) in the north of Ireland. This, it was hoped, would draw off some of the more obstreperous Presbyterians from the northern border. As Ulster pioneers they might subdue or at least counterbalance the Irish, who were nearly as wild and, as Roman Catholics, nearly as objectionable.

The Irish themselves had had a hard history, but they were no match for the Scots. The first wave of lowlanders (about 20,000 came before 1620) displaced the Irish landlords and tenants, drove the resisters into the thickets and bogs to live as outlaw woods kerns. There followed a period of guerrilla warfare not unlike that which was later to take place on the North American frontiers. The last major uprising of the kerns occurred in 1641. Some 15,000 were slaughtered, and for the time being, the Irish resistance movement in Ulster was broken.

The lowlanders prospered in other respects. The land they took from the Irish was more fertile than that to which they were accustomed; they were introduced to better agricultural techniques, and their standard of living improved. Also, with the technical help of Protestant refugees from France they began to establish successful linen and woolen industries. All in all, they did much too well to suit the English, who toward the end of the century found the military and economic power and the continued intransigence of the lowlanders as religious dissenters very alarming. Thereupon the British government took steps to reduce and humble them. Plantation lands were, through punitive taxes, reappropriated and in some cases even given back to the surviving Irish. Presbyterians who refused to recant and accept the authority of the Church of England (and few did) were denied the right to hold political office, serve in the military or bear arms. Their ministers were prohibited from conducting public worship, from performing marriages or other sacramental acts. Stifling regulations and tariffs more or less destroyed the Ulster textile industry, which had become a competitive threat to English manufacturers and traders. By the beginning of the eighteenth century the condition of the lowlanders in

Ulster was as dreadful and hopeless as it had ever been in Scotland. Perhaps they were even a bit worse off, since in Ulster they were aliens vulnerable to both English authority and the lurking native Irish, who had much to be vengeful about.

In 1715 and thereafter, recruiting agents from the North American colonies began circulating among the Ulster Scots and advising them that if they would emigrate to the New World, they would find lots of land, which, if not precisely free (there was considerable dissembling on this point), was at least very cheap and unclaimed. It was not a difficult selling job. In their circumstances any change—even to an unknown wilderness—apparently seemed like an improvement to the lowlanders. In the decade of the 1720s some 50,000 left Ulster, sailing west. (The British put no obstacles in their way, relieved to see them go.) Most of them went first to Pennsylvania, the Quaker colony being more attractive to people who had suffered severe religious persecution than either Catholic Maryland or Anglican, Cavalier Virginia. In attempting to explain and describe the deluge of people, the *Pennsylvania Gazette* sympathetically commented:

> Poverty, Wretchedness, Misery and Want are become almost universal among them; that . . . there is not Corn enough rais'd for their Subsistence one Year with another; and at the same Time the Trade and Manufactures of the Nation being cramp'd and discourag'd, the labouring People have little to do, and consequently are not able to purchase Bread at its present dear Rate; That the Taxes are nevertheless exceeding heavy, and Money very scarce; and add to all this, that their griping, avaricious Landlords exercise over them the most merciless Racking Tyranny and Oppression. Hence it is that such Swarms of them are driven over into America.

One of the officials who first encouraged the emigration was James Logan, who as William Penn's executive secretary had become the most important working administrator in the colony. In 1720 he retrospectively explained his thoughts, which were not unlike those of James I and his associates, who a century before had decided it would be a good idea to move these people from the lowlands of Scotland to Ulster. Wrote Logan: "At the time we were apprehensive from the Northern Indians. . . . I therefore thought it might be prudent to plant a settlement of such men as those who formerly had so bravely defended Londonderry and Inniskillen as a frontier in case of any disturbance. . . . These people if kindly used will be orderly as they have hitherto been and easily dealt with."

Ironically, Logan himself was an Ulster native, but through long association with the Penns and other aristocrats he had become thoroughly English in manner and attitude—so much so that he apparently had forgotten who and what his compatriots were. He was a fussy, bureaucratic man who had a neat vision of what should happen and confused this with reality. After arriving in Philadelphia, Logan suggested that the grateful Scotch-Irish would proceed in a polite, orderly way westward until they reached unoccupied wilderness regions. They would take up small properties, for which they would pay a nominal quitrent (in effect a tax) of a penny an acre. They would, of course, register deeds with the proper authorities, industriously clear these lands, erect defenses against the Indians, build roads and villages so that the wilderness would become suitable for larger landowners and investors. What, in fact, happened was that the Ulster emigrants, penniless and desperate for land, took the first unoccupied properties they found. Asking no one's permission, paying nothing, they squatted on them and refused to leave, exercising what came to be called tomahawk rights, a frontier expression of the long-standing adage that possession is nine points of the law.

Agents sent out by the flustered James Logan to one region infested with squatters were told—before they were driven off by a mob of Ulstermen—"that it was against the laws of God and nature, that so much land should be idle, while so many Christians wanted it to labor on, and to raise their bread."

Logan became quickly and thoroughly disenchanted with the Scotch-Irish whose emigration had been his pet project. Writing in 1724, he called them "bold and indigent strangers," who used as "their excuse when challenged for titles that we had solicited for colonists and they had come accordingly." Later he was to complain in a series of interoffice memos that "the settlement of five families from the North of Ireland gives me more trouble than fifty of any other people," that they were "troublesome settlers to the government and hard neighbors to the Indians."

Some Philadelphians with important real estate interests suggested that the Scotch-Irish be forcibly removed from the lands they had taken, herded east and contained there among the piedmont Germans. Nothing came of these schemes since Pennsylvania had no police or military force able to execute them. The Scotch-Irish were bent on the West, and any attempts to bar their way would have resulted, as one realistic colonial administrator prophesied, in something "next to civil war."

When they left Ulster, most of the lowland Scots were either dispossessed farm laborers or unemployed mill hands and overtly were no better prepared—in fact, in some respects seemed less prepared—

than other Europeans to settle in the North American wilderness. However, though few realized it at the time, certain collective traits of character had been ground into them by their history, and these were probably more valuable in the Appalachian highlands than any discrete skills or expertise. First and foremost, they had been involuntarily trained to endure pain and hardship—both material and psychic—as few ever had been or would be. They had become an exceptionally physical people who admired prowess more than cleverness, were inclined to confront their problems, express themselves, accomplish and take their pleasure through action. When stimulated, they were capable of extraordinary feats of energy, violence and bravery, but they were impatient, easily bored, made indolent and slovenly by routine, repetitious work. With all individual exceptions granted, they were, because their survival had often depended upon their being so, pragmatic, avaricious and pugnacious. They were not overburdened with abstract principles or conventional ethics, but they were mortally stubborn about expressing and protecting their interests. ("Lord, grant that I may always be right, for Thou knowest I am hard to turn," ran a Scotch-Irish prayer.) They had become a very hard or, as some of their critics claimed, even brutal people. But the North American frontier was a hard, brutal place. On it many of the Scotch-Irish traits which gentler Europeans regarded as weaknesses and vices turned out to be strengths and virtues.

For centuries the Scotch-Irish had been more often victims than beneficiaries of political, military, economic and religious institutions. For them, authority had become synonymous with oppression, and they rebelled against it almost reflexively. This made them prickly, problem subjects. But when they came to the frontier, they found the absence of law and order to be one of the utopian attractions of the place. In contrast, people like the English and Germans, more amenable to discipline and more accustomed to security, were frightened and repelled by the anarchy.

The Scotch-Irish were fiercely loyal to, usually only to, their families. (Strangers, anyone of even slightly disparate behavior or blood, were automatically regarded as hostile until abundant evidence to the contrary was accumulated.) These were authoritarian, patriarchal social units in which the development of harmonious and affectionate relationships was a minor—even suspect—concern. These partisan families were inclined to hole up in out-of-the-way defensible places, putting as much distance as possible between themselves and even their distant kin and compatriots. They had the guerrilla's mistrust of cities, towns and even villages as traps-in-waiting, where they could be more easily found, caught and abused. Consequently they had little experience with or regard for community works and pleasures, and the sense of social responsibility—the value of sacrificing self-interest for the collective benefit—was primitive to nonexistent among them. Again, these attitudes, which tended to isolate them from the mainstream of European culture, were to be of practical advantage in the New World wilderness. The prospect of living in fortified clearings, separated by miles of dangerous jungle from not only established communities but neighbors of any sort, did not unnerve the Ulstermen as it did many others. Rather, it struck them as being not only possible but desirable.

Perhaps no other sizable group of emigrants arrived in North America with less baggage, material or cultural, than did the Scotch-Irish. Because of poverty and insecurity, they had acquired few traditional folkways, arts or crafts and almost none they cared enough about to try to bring with them and transplant in the New World. (Presbyterianism was one of their few possessions of this sort, but it did not do well in the wilds of North America. Some of the emigrants held to the kirks, but more turned to exotic native frontier churches or simply decided that religion of any sort was unnecessary and frivolous in the wilderness.) This, too, turned out to be of adaptive benefit for the Scotch-Irish. They wasted little effort trying to re-create European villages, schools, gardens, farms, trades, diets, fashions or social customs. Without nostalgic regret they accepted the reality that they were in a new place where European experience counted for little and could be largely ignored.

Their attitudes and habits did not make it practically easier for them to settle the frontier, but they probably inclined the Scotch-Irish to try and gave them the psychic strength to survive there, as Europeans had previously been unable to do. For seventy-five years—from the 1720s, when the first large groups arrived in Pennsylvania—they endured in the Appalachians. They starved, froze, drowned, were burned out; were stung, poisoned and mauled by beasts; scalped, ravaged, tortured by Indians; went mad, became suicides and drunks, chopped each other up in bloody intramural feuds and brawls. As and because they endured, they began to learn what had to be and could be done to live in the place independent of coastal society. Toward the beginning of the nineteenth century they got the hang of it. When they did, they burst through the Appalachian barrier and in a short fifty years stormed across the remaining 3,000 miles of the continent, making it, all the way to the Pacific, their own.

Initially and during the century and a half after their arrival, the peculiar talents of these people were seldom admired, and their accomplishments not often recognized by polite society. The English and English-minded from the coastal establishment vied with each other in collecting and reporting examples of how loathsome they were and acted. One of the more restrained was Benjamin Franklin, who, after studying the hordes of Ulster refugees, said with a sniff that they were "white savages."

Franklin diagnosed the essential property which made—and continued for some generations to make—these people so alarming to the better classes. They had been a coarse, scruffy lot to begin with, but they were at least of civilized—i.e., European—origin. However, as soon as they hit the wilderness, they were transformed—very willingly, it seemed—into a breed that was not recognizably European except for the skin color. Given civilized frames of reference, *white savage* was a fairly clinical description, but a less pejorative one would have been that these were the first Americans. Before them the name did not apply since the continent was inhabited by Iroquois, Cherokee, Sioux, many other Indian nationalities and Europeans camping out on the beaches.

Being the first Americans, the Scotch-Irish, unlike other emigrant groups, never went through an apprentice period when they had to adjust to and learn the ways of their predecessors. It is true that when they arrived, they were gibed at by coastal colonists, but they quickly left them behind. When they got to the Appalachian foothills, they were immediately and completely in charge of white society since there were no other representatives there. This set a pattern which was to prevail as long as there was and they followed a western frontier.

In comparison with other emigrant groups, the Ulstermen and their descendants left very few overt, material signs of themselves. There are no Scotch-Irish communities, villages or regions, as there are Polish, Chinese or Pennsylvania Dutch ones. There is no Scotch-Irish equivalent of the Italian pizza or Jewish bagel; no style of dress, speech, music or art which is especially Scotch-Irish. There is no distinctive Scotch-Irish style of architecture, as there is English or Hispanic. Since frontiersmen became obsolete, there have been no professions, trades or types of manual labor in which the Scotch-Irish predominate. Paradoxically, the absence of conventional ethnic contributions emphasizes the singular nature of their influence which was substantial, but interior. It is at least arguable that more than any other single happening, their collective response (tempered by their European history) to the Appalachian frontier created our cultural and behavioral norms. Others were to contribute to, alter and decorate it, but the Scotch-Irish laid down the base, to which everyone else adjusted.

The frontier people were not especially cerebral or speculative, but they had a talent for summing up their experience and expressing their convictions in pointed, homely aphorisms: Root hog or die. Fish or cut bait. The early bird gets the worm. A rail-splitter beats a hair-splitter. He who dallies is a dastard; he who doubts is damned. Millions for defense, but not one cent for tribute. To the victor belongs the spoils. Keep your powder dry and your dauber up. Every man for hisself and the devil take the hindmost. Many are drawn from experiences so archaic that they are no longer of practical significance but nevertheless still reflect what has come to be regarded as the unique American set of mind.

Like a descendant from long lines of physicians, academics or soldiers, Joseph Walker, the nineteenth-century Frontier Hero, inherited his calling. He was born in 1798 into one of the first—in terms of both chronology and accomplishments—families of the Appalachian frontier. Most of his relatives for three generations back had been professional pioneers, some of them always living on the extreme western edge of the settlement line. His paternal great-grandparents, John and Katherine Walker, started the family in this direction after they arrived in North America from Ulster in the late summer of 1728.

The John Walkers landed at a Maryland port on the Chesapeake Bay. From there they immediately traveled north to Chester County in Pennsylvania, which was a staging area and something of a displaced persons camp for their compatriots. This was the second substantial migratory move the couple had made. Both were natives of Wigton, a community in the southwestern lowlands of Scotland, which by the time the Walkers reached adulthood was so depressed that people were its chief export. John and Katherine left in 1700 or thereabouts to relocate in Ulster, across the Irish Sea. There they remained until they had enough resources or had become convinced that they must go to America. Few personal records of the couple survive, but since they were lowland Presbyterian Scots living in Ulster, it is almost certain that they were in unfortunate economic, political and religious circumstances and had little hope of improving their situation in the north of Ireland.

Both John and Katherine Walker were said to be large, robust people, and as a matter of record they were very fertile. Katherine had borne four children in Wigton and seven more in northern Ireland. Eight of the children, three daughters and five sons, survived to emigrate with their parents to Pennsylvania. Also in the party were two nephews, sons of John Walker's brother, and a son-in-law, John Campbell, who had married the eldest daughter, Elizabeth. (Campbell's idiosyncratic reason for leaving when he did has been remembered. He was the son and—so the family was thereafter to claim—rightful heir of the Duke of Argyll. He had been banished because of his activities as a religious dissenter, and these may well have included marrying into such a stout Presbyterian family as the Walkers.)

In their size and that of their family, the Walkers also fit the stereotype of the Scotch-Irish, or at least the disdainful one created by the English. On both sides of the Atlantic, fastidious observers invariably commented that these white savages were huge, rawboned, loutish men and women who bred like cattle and were surrounded by herds of unclean, uncouth children. This characteristic was cited so regularly that it probably represented some fact as well as spleen. If so, it is not surprising. The conditions under which they had lived for so long would have given the lowlanders cultural and perhaps genetic incentive to produce quantities of big, durable children. Cattle they might appear to be to those of easier circumstances and history, but they were a herd that had been remorselessly culled of its weaklings and runts.

Of John Walker it was recollected by a grandson that he was "a good and pious man of wonderful physical strength and one that stood high in Scotland as a God fearing man of prayer and good deeds, being noted as an unusually brave man." After his death it was eulogistically noted that among the first frontiersmen, none had left so many descendants who were so well thought of as had he. So far as quantity goes, this may have been the literal truth. When Joe Walker, the future explorer of the trans-Mississippi West, was born, only seventy years after John and Katherine came to America, he was their 254th direct descendant.

Katherine Walker is remembered only as being extremely "respectable," indicating, as the word was then technically used, that she was a staunch church woman. In fact, she was a member of the lowland intellectual and moral elite to the extent one existed. Both her grandfathers, Samuel Rutherford and Joseph Allein, were fiery Presbyterian divines who had become folk heroes for being persecuted and imprisoned by the English for their refusal to be silent about their Nonconformist religious beliefs. (It was Samuel Rutherford who contributed an inflammatory remark which has been remembered as illustrating the unyielding righteousness of the Scotch-Irish. Being hauled off to jail, the loser in one of his confrontations with royal authority, Rutherford is said to have said that he feared God so much that he feared no man, including the English king.) Clusters of other less renowned but very respectable clergy hung from both sides of the Walker family tree.

The historical observation has been made that when the Scotch-Irish began to arrive in America, they were a twice-decapitated people —that is, their migrations first from the lowlands and then from the north of Ireland had deprived them of the classes and individuals that normally provide leadership. Among them were virtually no civil administrators, military officers, judges, lawyers, teachers, established merchants, experienced craftsmen or landowning gentry. The lowlanders had not been able or permitted to produce many prominent citizens, and those who had emerged were disinclined to risk their hard-earned affluence, authority or security by emigrating. This was especially true of the Presbyterian divines, relatively few of whom left their kirks, academies, ongoing theological and political causes, to follow their flocks into the howling wilderness of a new world.

There is no evidence that the Walkers, when they arrived, held any special position of authority among the emigrants, but all of them were literate, and again because of the strong religious ties (*kirk* and *school* being more or less synonymous among the lowlanders), they were probably better educated than most. Two of John Walker's sons and at least three of his grandsons were to become surveyors, a profession which on the frontier usually indicated more formal schooling than was customary.

Economically their circumstances may also have been a bit better than those of many of their fellow refugees. At least they did not have to indenture themselves to pay for their transatlantic passage, and upon landing they did not have to enter this sort of contractual slavery to support themselves during their first years in the New World. (Approximately 100,000 Scotch-Irish came to North America as bond servants prior to the Revolutionary War.) Whatever they worked at immediately after coming to Pennsylvania, they worked as free men. John Walker, his five grown or nearly grown sons, two nephews and son-in-law together constituted a strong labor unit and almost certainly, given the patriarchal nature of Scotch-Irish families, a disciplined communal one.

As subsequent events indicated, the Walkers, like nearly all the emigrant families, had a desperate hunger for land, but by the time they came Pennsylvania was not a good place for satisfying it. Most of the squattable property had already been squatted upon by earlier arrivals from Ulster. Because of them, a smaller but steady influx of Germans and a growing demand among established English colonists, the price of land in Pennsylvania tripled during the 1720s. Also, having been unable directly to control the Scotch-Irish, James Logan and his administrative colleagues had fallen back on a policy of bureaucratic harassment. By making things as expensive and legally difficult as possible, they hoped that the "bold, indigent strangers" might be shooed away to someplace else.

Surveying the situation, John Walker obviously concluded that he and his family could not find habitable, affordable land in Pennsylvania. In 1732 Walker, then in his sixties, started west with some of the younger men of the clan. After crossing the Susquehanna, they came into the Great Valley, called the Cumberland in Pennsylvania and the Shenandoah in Virginia. They began following it toward the southwest. To have gone in any other direction would have been foolish, if not suicidal. To the west and north in Pennsylvania lay a complex of ridges, ravines and forests known as the Seven Mountains. This wilderness was naturally very difficult, but even more important, it lay within the boundaries of the Iroquois empire. If nothing else, the Scotch-Irish were realists when it came to paramilitary matters. They might be strong enough to confound James Logan's land agents and sheriffs, but challenging the Iroquois in their home territory was then out of the question.

In contrast, the Great Valley was relatively open and easy to traverse. Also, it had existed for some generations as a buffer zone between the Iroquois and Cherokee. It was used by hunters and warriors from both these tribes, but neither had been able to make it part of their sovereign domain. A few Indians, mostly Shawnee, lived in it, but they themselves were more or less refugees, having been displaced by the Iroquois and Cherokee acts of war and diplomacy. In consequence western Virginia was one of the few places in the Appalachians which whites could enter uninvited without arousing the immediate animosity of the dominant Indian nations.

The Walkers were by no means the only European explorers and trailblazers of the region—British and French traders had been traveling there during the preceding fifty years—but were among the first whites to arrive with the intention of settling permanently. They were like the first drops of a cloudburst or trickles of a flash flood. During the next fifty years thousands of their compatriots with almost identical motives poured into and down the Great Valley, making it the initial segment in the great pioneering road which was eventually to reach California.

Having passed the last settlements around the trading post-forts on the Potomac and Shenandoah, the Walkers came to the Maury River, a tributary of the James, lying between the contemporary communities of Staunton and Lexington. On the Maury they met Jack Hayes, who was also from Ulster and even then perhaps a Walker kinsman. (Subsequently the Walker and Hayes families would intermarry, neighbor and travel together all the way to the Pacific.) Hayes had been ranging the Appalachians alone for several years, hunting, trading and looking for land. He was to do so for the rest of his life, accumulating experi-

ences and a reputation which would make him the real-life model for
Natty Bumppo, the stalwart Deerslayer of James Fenimore Cooper's
fictions—or so at least Hayes's descendants were to claim for him.

Hayes directed the Walkers to a splendid empty valley which lay
below Jump Mountain. (From this prominence it was reported a
Cherokee maiden had leaped in a fit of Juliet-like passion to save her
Shawnee lover from the vengeance of her family.) The valley was well
watered by a stream that flowed down to the Maury and was set with
a series of open meadows, natural pastures for deer, elk and buffalo.
Beyond these clearings commenced the unbroken virgin forest, in and
beyond which, so far as anyone knew, there were no other white men
to be found short of the Spanish settlements many hundreds of miles
to the south and west.

In one of the meadows was a fine spring which so took John Walker's fancy he decided to end there his quest which had begun in Wigton, Scotland. "Finding," one of his sons was to recall, "the climate
milder, the soil fertile and everything attractive, he concluded to settle
here, cleared off a portion of land, erected a log cabin and then returned to Pennsylvania, expecting to bring back his family."

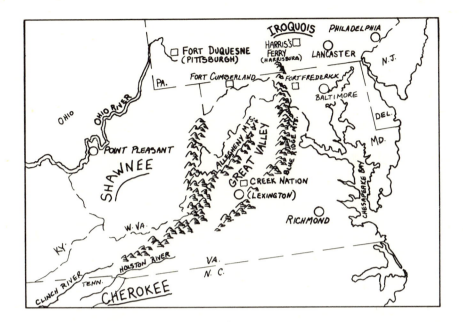

The Creek Nation

John Walker never returned to the Appalachian frontier. He died in 1734 and was buried in Chester County, Pennsylvania, as did and was his wife shortly thereafter. However, he and Katherine Walker had set the family in motion and pointed it west. By 1739 their sons—John, James, Samuel, Alexander and Joseph—their two nephews—John and Alexander—and two sons-in-law—John Campbell and James Moore (who married Jane Walker)—had moved their wives and children to the attractive property below Jump Mountain. Along the way they picked up other Ulster families: the Toomys, Pattersons, Poages, McClellans and Houstons, who, if they were not already, would shortly become relatives. Spreading out from the original cabin site, they made a settlement which for a time was probably the westernmost in Virginia and therefore in any of the English-speaking colonies. They named the stream which ran through the clearings Walker Creek. Soon the place and the vigorous, remarkably reproductive clan itself became known along the frontier as the Creek Nation.

While the sons and daughters of John Walker and the other families were occupying these lands, legal title to them came into the hands of Benjamin Burden (or Borden, as the name was sometimes spelled). He was a minor member of the Virginia Tidewater gentry, a socially adept, hard-drinking, hard-playing young man with good manners and connections but without family means or estate. Looking to improve his fortune, Burden became a real estate promoter and developer. He got his start in a curious way. In 1736 he was employed as an estate agent for the Fairfax family, who held grants for more than a million imprecisely located wilderness acres. Burden went out to the Shenandoah Valley to look at or for some of these lands and there captured a buffalo calf. When he returned to Tidewater civilization, he brought the "shaggy monster" with him, and it created a sensation, being the first buffalo most people in those parts had ever seen. As a promotional gesture, Burden took the calf to a "frolic" being held in Williamsburg and presented the beast to William Gooch, the royal governor of the colony. "The Governor was so pleased with the rare pet," wrote an early Virginia historian, "and so pleased with the donor that he readily acceded to Burden's request for a grant of land."

It was a spectacularly successful evening for Burden. In return for his buffalo (and, as another account dryly suggested, because of "ingratiating himself in other ways") he was given the development rights to 500,000 acres of land between the Shenandoah and James rivers. After the spirit of frolic had passed, Gooch stood by this grand gesture but added some stipulations to bring it into line with public policy— which was to tame the western lands by peopling them. Burden was told that within ten years he must find at least 100 families that would settle in the tract. Once they were in place, Burden was to receive free title to 1,000 acres immediately adjacent to each of the homesteads. Thereafter he could purchase as much of the rest of unclaimed portions of the grant as he wanted at the discount price of one shilling per acre. In the following year Burden traveled to northern Ireland to recruit homesteaders, but before he did, he made a brief exploratory visit to his duchy-sized holdings in the west. There he came upon the outskirts of the Creek Nation. Benjamin Burden was a realist and, according to the one surviving report of this odd encounter, was able gracefully to recognize a *fait accompli*. Burden asked if he could spend the night with the clan and later diffidently explained about his grant but quickly added that he was delighted to see the families there. He in effect wished them long life and prosperity and departed without making any mention of deeds, quitrents or 1,000-acre parcels beside their cabins. Burden was probably genuinely pleased since the Walkers and the others would have accounted for a dozen or so of the families he needed. However, whether Burden was agreeable or not was inconsequential since there were no Virginia authorities with the means for clearing out these hard settlers. In any event, no family or public records indicate that the Walkers ever had any difficulties over ownership of this property.

For the next fifty years the Creek Nation (and a satellite community thirty miles to the southwest near Natural Bridge) was the principal base for the Walker family. They were occupied during this period as others of their sort were in similar clearings all along the Appalachian border—that is, by transforming themselves from Ulster tenant farmers and mill hands into American frontiersmen, women and children. This was an enormous feat of forced education but is seldom remembered as such because the lessons they learned were simple and homely and the things they made were usually crude, cobbled up, seldom durable or handsome. They were not an inventive people in the clever way of the New England mechanics, and they did not have the training or patient temperament of the Pennsylvania Dutch craftsmen of the period. However, using whatever was at hand, making do with very little outside advice or assistance, they adopted old skills and tools and devised a great many new ones suitable for the wilderness environment. By way of nothing more than eclectic example:

. . . The ax Europeans brought to North America was a straight-shafted, light, iron-headed, flat-bladed implement, the design of which had not changed much from Roman days. It served for slow, careful work in European forests, which had been thinned by centuries of timbering. However, it was hopelessly inadequate in the virgin forests of the Appalachians, where the critical need was to make rough clearings quickly without any concern for waste and salvage. Therefore, backwoods smiths designed and forged a tool which has ever since been called the American felling ax. The blade was flared, and a strip of steel, which would take and hold an edge, was set into or welded onto it. The poll was widened and flattened to give weight. The hickory shaft was slimmed down, curved to fit the hands and made whippy so that the heavy head could be in effect slung, very accurately, into the wood. An amazed Benjamin Franklin once watched two white savages working with these new American axes. He reported that in six minutes they felled a pine, fourteen inches in diameter at the cut. Later and farther west, there were to be greater axmen-artists.

. . . With the felling ax, a broadax for roughly squaring timbers, a morticing ax for notching them, and draw and crooked knives for giving them almost any shape, a man and his family could move into the virgin forest and, within a month or so, clear a garden patch, fence it with split rails as protection against deer and for whatever stock they had; put up a one-room cabin, roof it with brush, bark or split shingles, chink it with mud, moss or deerskins; and manufacture the basic wooden utensils and furniture. It was an ugly, not very comfortable or durable place, but it served immediate needs. It was no great loss if it burned or if, after a season or so, the family decided to abandon the whole clearing, move farther into the woods and start again.

. . . A white oak sapling, shaped with a crooked knife, made a good splitting maul. Dogwood made the best splitting gluts. These were used with at least one iron wedge which was driven into the butt, never the small end, of a log. Black oak, honey locust and ash were woods which split well. Once the process was mastered, rail-splitting was still hard, tedious work, but simple enough so it could be left to a "large boy," who, if he were industrious, could make four to six dozen rails a day.

. . . Corn turned out to be the ideal crop for the woodland clearings. The leaves could be pulled and dried for fodder. The ears could be eaten green. Parched flint-hard, the kernels would keep indefinitely. They could be ground into meal, using, if necessary, a hollow stump or even a trough made out of stiff bearskin for a mortar. Also, corn could be converted into, stored and sold as whiskey, one of the few manufacturing processes with which the Scotch-Irish emigrants were familiar. Finally, corn did not require much work. Once enough timber had been cut to use for rails, the cabin and furnishings, it was not necessary to fell the other trees in a potential cornfield. Those still standing were "deadened" by being girdled so that they did not put out leaves, and the seed was planted in between the stumps and trunks. It was a wasteful, slovenly way to farm, but enough of a crop was produced to get people and stock through the winter. However, if the family stayed in a clearing, these agricultural practices could be dangerous. After a few seasons the girdled trees in the field (called a deadening) began to rot and windstorms would bring them down on cabins or people. With this in mind a frontier preacher closed a sermon in a backwoods settlement with a bit of practical as well as theological advice: "Well, men, love God, hate the devil, and keep out of a deadening in time of a thunderstorm."

. . . A man who could kill a bear could chop off all four paws and the head, make one slit along the ventral line, pull off the skin, climb into it and have himself an instant bearskin coverall. He might stink considerably, but he would not freeze.

. . . Turkeys feeding on chestnut and oak mast grew to weigh fifty pounds and were so fat, one frontiersman reported, that after being shot, they would "burst when they fell from the trees." They were also fairly stupid, and it was often not necessary to hunt and waste expensive powder and lead on them. A rough enclosure could be made of brush with a funnel-like opening at one end which led into the center of the pen. Following a trail of bait corn, a flock of turkeys would squeeze into one of these traps and remain there, being unable to find their way out through the small end of the funnel. Thinly sliced turkey breast was called and often used as "bread" on the frontier. A piece of bear, which was real meat, was sandwiched between this "bread."

One reason so much whiskey was drunk was to cut the grease which, because of this carnivorous diet, accumulated on the tongue, on the teeth and in the throat.

. . . The guns available at the beginning of the eighteenth century were manufactured for European battlefields and hunting preserves. They were generally of two types: smoothbore muskets and half-rifled German sporting pieces. The range and accuracy of the muskets were limited since they were designed as infantry weapons to be discharged in massed, aimless volleys. In 1727, the year before the Walkers arrived from Ulster, William Byrd, a Virginia planter, was thrashing around in the Blue Ridge Mountains, trying to locate land claims. His party saw many deer and other game but could bring "none into the Pot," being unable to get close enough to dispatch the animals with their muskets. Byrd and his men were reduced to eating soup made out of items of their leather apparel.

The German Jaguers were somewhat more accurate, but they were too intricate for rough use. Lead balls had to be manufactured to precise specifications and then, to get the proper tight fit, driven down the barrel with an iron rod and hammer. Even men expert in their use did well to fire one shot every fifteen minutes. Also, like the muskets, they were heavy .75 caliber weapons which ate up a pound and a half of lead and powder for a dozen shots. Both types of arms were entirely unsuitable for hunting, fighting or even carrying in the dense Appalachian forests, inferior in many respects to the Indian bow.

By 1730 frontier smiths, borrowing an idea here, making a small invention there, had corrected this situation, coming up with the famous long rifle. The barrel was four feet long with six or eight full interior rifling grooves, but it was nevertheless a slender, comparatively light piece, weighing about ten pounds and varying between .25 and .45 caliber. A pound of lead gave forty to sixty shots, and because of improvements in loading and firing mechanisms, a man could fire two rounds a minute. The parts were simple, and most repairs could be made quickly in the field. While later marvelous stories about marksmen knocking out the eyes of squirrels a quarter of a mile distant may have been somewhat exaggerated, the guns were very accurate at 100 yards and reasonably effective up to 250 yards.

Long rifles were among the few possessions the appearance as well as utility of which was a matter of pride for the frontiersmen. Gunsmiths became perhaps the most admired artists on the border and some of the few whose names remained associated with their work. Among them was John Walker, the original patriarch of the Creek Nation, who was called Gunstocker John to distinguish him from his nephew, Gunmaker John. Until the early twentieth century one of the Walker rifles remained on display in Lexington, Virginia, as a particularly fine example of these beautiful frontier pieces. (Subsequently the gun mysteriously disappeared.)

That the Walkers should have been able to make such apparently elegant weapons is something of a curiosity. The Scotch-Irish became the most notable users of the long rifles, but most of the famous early smiths were German artisans in the vicinity of Lancaster, Pennsylvania. Since it is unlikely that such staunch Presbyterian dissenters would have been able or permitted to become armorers in the lowlands of Scotland or in Ulster, it may be that the Walkers learned their craft during the few years they remained in Pennsylvania prior to settling in western Virginia. However they came by it, there was not a more useful or respected skill on the frontier.

The first public building in the Creek Nation was a fortified blockhouse, located on a cleared knoll 300 yards or so above Walker Creek. It was constructed with black walnut logs, which were laid down, notched and pegged together to enclose a twenty-by-twenty-five-foot area. There was one heavy door which could be barred with crossed timbers, and rifle slits were cut through the logs. A tunnel was dug from inside the compound to a spring fifty yards outside the walls. Similar private forts were built by all the early Appalachian settlers in preparation for the time when, in addition to the wilderness environment and elements, they would have to cope with the wilderness natives, the Iroquois, Cherokee, Shawnee and lesser Indian nations.

Fortunately for the whites the confrontation did not come immediately. Having rather easily cowed several generations of coastal settlers, the powerful interior tribes had formed a low opinion of the hardihood and courage of English-speaking whites in general. As in many racial conflicts, the Indians, initially the dominant party, had difficulty telling whites apart and saw not much reason to do so. The first Scotch-Irish pioneers struck them as being unprepossessing specimens of an inferior race. Except as they provided an additional, though poor, source of European goods, their activities seemed to be of no consequence and certainly not threatening. So far as the first frontier whites were concerned, the Indians seemed exceedingly threatening, and they were careful not to antagonize them.

This peculiar peace based on red contempt and white caution prevailed during the 1730s and 1740s along most of the border. The period of grace gave the whites a chance to dig in, get on with their frontier education and multiply. In 1730 only a few hundred of them were living along the eastern slopes of the Appalachians, but by 1750 there were upwards of 10,000. Suddenly the tribes found that they had in their midst a formidable body of aliens who were becoming almost as resourceful as Indians in getting about and living in the wilderness. Unlike the traders who had been traveling and behaving politely for the sake of furs, these new whites never left and seemed to want only land. Once they had it, they became pugnacious about defending their exclusive rights to use it. As their settlements spread, former tribal hunting and campgrounds were cleared and fenced. Under pressure from these developments and from white pothunters, game became scarce and more wary. Indian gardens and orchards were trampled by cattle and hogs which were turned loose to forage as partly feral animals. Finally the very presence of these foreigners of bad color and worse manners was an affront to Indian traditions and territorial sensibilities. When the new realities of the situation were apparent to both sides, they came, as a later historian remarked, "to understand each other perfectly." The understanding was that both wanted the same lands and would not tolerate the other in them, that one side or the other would be either dispossessed or exterminated.

There followed one of the most bitter and prolonged racial conflicts ever fought in the western world and by far the most serious red-white confrontation to take place in North America. By comparison, though they are now better remembered, later hostilities with the tribes in the western plains were relatively minor engagements. These usually involved professional soldiers—Indian warriors, white troopers and partisans—and the casualties were light. Only about 1,500 American soldiers were killed in all the Indian wars west of the Mississippi, while in one eastern engagement, that in which General Arthur St. Clair was defeated on the Maumee River by a coalition of woodland tribes, 700 American regulars and militiamen were killed during a two-day battle in 1791.

The forest wars engaged all the people on both sides, not simply bands of armed men. Every Indian village and every white settlement were situated in the combat zone, and casualties among civilians were high. Again, by way of comparison, on the basis of innumerable movies, novels and TV films, we have a vision of covered wagon trains struggling west under more or less constant Indian attack, of burning prairie schooners and the prairies littered with white bodies stuck full of arrows. In fact, between 1840 and 1860, when most of the wagons rolled, 362 white civilians were killed by the Plains Indians in all the engagements. On one day, July 4, 1778, the Iroquois rubbed out 360 settlers in the Wyoming Valley of Pennsylvania. (The fighting in the Appalachians was so widespread and records are now so scattered that no body count was or can be made, but as a very conservative estimate, it is likely that 5,000 whites and an equal number of reds died in the forest wars.)

By the time western hostilities commenced the whites were so overwhelmingly superior in numbers and resources that the final result was never in much doubt. The battles were desperate, last stands for the Indians, but only mopping-up police actions for the whites. In the Appalachians the opponents were in the beginning much more closely matched in weapons, numbers and military expertise. Also, the eastern tribes were agricultural people, able to stockpile supplies and therefore conduct long, persistent campaigns. The western warriors were nomadic hunters, seldom with any reserves of rations, vulnerable to being cut off from game and therefore to being starved into submission.

The eastern Indian nations were too few and too technologically primitive to have won a complete victory, but they were strong enough so that the forest wars might have turned out differently. For example, it is possible to speculate that what is now the United States could have become a Balkanized area, occupied by several independent nations of Anglo, French, Spanish, Iroquois or Cherokee origins. Certainly at the time few of the participants regarded the outcome of the forest wars as inevitable.

Lulls, treaties and truces intervened, but essentially the red-white conflict began with General Edward Braddock's defeat by the French and northern Indians in 1755 and ended in 1814, when Andrew Jackson and his Tennessee volunteers destroyed the power of the last major hostile tribe, the Creek. At times, as during the Seven Years' and Revolutionary wars, the border conflict was to be part of larger, European-inspired engagements, and outside soldiers, politicians and diplomats were involved. However, in the main, British and later American authorities left the savages—white and red—to have at each other in places and ways that were strange and repulsive to civilized people. A single incident among many possible ones gives some indication of how and why the forest wars were fought.

In 1759 the British military employed 600 Cherokee warriors, at 100 pounds each, to serve against the French and their Indians. The Cherokee mercenaries were sent north from the Tennessee and Carolina highlands to Pennsylvania, but to get there, they had to fight their way through the white frontier settlers—such as those on Walker Creek—in western Virginia. While these warriors were absent from home, a party of drunken white militiamen raped several of their women. In retaliation the Cherokee killed 23 white settlers and withdrew as British allies. The royal governor of South Carolina then put to death some Cherokee diplomats who were visiting the settlements on a peace mission and offered a 35-pound bounty for every Cherokee scalp turned into the proper authorities. The Cherokee then invested and eventually captured Fort Loudoun, a frontier military post. The commandant, Captain Paul Demere, while still alive was scalped and his arms and legs were chopped off. Before he died, his mouth was stuffed full of dirt and he was told by a Cherokee war chief, "You want land. We give it to you."

The Walkers, being always among the most western of the settlers, were heavily engaged in the border wars. From the 1750s onward there is no record of any able Walker man who did not take part in them, and fifteen members of the family were to be killed or captured by the Indians.

During the first stages of the conflict the most famous Indian fighter of the clan was John, the third son of the original emigrant from Ulster. By 1755 this John Walker was listed in the community records as a ranger—that is, a man detailed to stay more or less permanently in the woods to wait for and deal with Indian raiders.

If not Walker, then men very much like him were in a party that during August 1758 was on patrol looking for marauding Shawnee. One afternoon these rangers came upon and captured five Indians and began making preparations to torture and kill them. However, they were joined by a veteran white hunter and trader by the name of Amos Dunkleberry, who said that these Indians were Cherokees, potential British allies who should be spared. According to one John Echols, who was there and later wrote a report about the incident, this suggestion enraged the men. "They swore," wrote Echols, "that if they were not allowed to kill them, they would never go Ranging again, for they said it was to no purpose to Rang after the Enemy, & when they had found them, not to be allowed to kill them—at that Rate we may all be Kill'd, and never Kill an Indian."

However, Dunkleberry was a forceful man, and his arguments caused enough confusion so that the execution was temporarily delayed. After he left, the Indians were freed and the ranger captain suggested that the rangers "Dog them till night and then ly By till the Brake of Day and then Fall upon them and Kill them. . . ." Some of the men saw no reason to delay the pursuit so long, and thirteen of them, including Echols, started immediately after the Cherokees. "We overtook them at a peach orchard—jest as they were leaving it, we watched our opportunity, and fired at them and followed them up till we Killed 4 of them, and wounded the other—we Skelpt them that we killed, & then followed the other—he bled very much, he went into the river and to an Island."

In addition to ranging, John Walker, along with at least two of his brothers, Samuel and James, fought at Point Pleasant, one of the most crucial pitched battles of the border wars. At the confluence of the

Kanawha and Ohio rivers, some 1,200 white frontiersmen and 900 Shawnee under their war chief, Cornplanter, had at each other for two bloody days in October 1774. Some 200 men on each side were killed, and both the red and white men who fought there later had high praise for the courage of their enemies. However, Cornplanter was finally forced back across the Ohio, and the settlements in western Virginia were spared from what otherwise might have been the worst of all Indian raids against them.

Formidable as he must have been, John Walker became the family's first recorded casualty in the Indian wars. In 1778, when he was seventy-three years old, he and his second son, Samuel, went off hunting or exploring in the Clinch River valley along what is now the boundary between Virginia and Tennessee. There the two men were caught and scalped by the Cherokee. Three years later the war was brought more directly home to the Creek Nation. It was a particularly bad time because the frontiersmen were then, in 1781, fighting on two fronts, against the British in the east and the Indians in the west, and only a few men could be spared for defense of the home settlements. One of those remaining along Walker Creek was Andrew Cowen, who had recently married John Walker's daughter Ann. On a July day, assisted by eleven-year-old William Walker, grandson of the late Ranger John, Cowen was plowing a field on the outskirts of the settlement. As they were attempting to turn the team at the end of a row, a half dozen Delaware braves, who had slipped through the outlying ranger patrols, rose from their hiding place behind a rail fence and began firing at the man and boy. Cowen and young Walker ran for the stockade in the middle of the community, but neither made it. Cowen was cut down and scalped in the field. The boy was captured, as was also, shortly thereafter, his aunt, Cowen's wife. The remaining settlers secured the fort, and after a time the Delawares retired, taking the two captives back to Ohio. Ann Walker Cowen was eventually ransomed by her family, but the boy, William Walker, was sold to the Wyandotte and taken by that tribe to Michigan.

The worst disaster to befall the family involved the children and grandchildren of Jane Walker. The second daughter of the original emigrants, John and Katherine, she married James Moore shortly after arriving in Pennsylvania. The couple then moved south to the Creek Nation. Among their ten children was a son, also named James. This James Moore, like most of the men of his generation, fought against both the Indians and the British, doing well enough to be known, if not commissioned, as a captain. Also, he married Martha Poage, the daughter of one of the related families from the Walker Creek area. In 1778 James Moore determined to emigrate farther into the wilderness to a place called Apps Valley in the extreme southwestern corner of what is now Virginia. With him went his wife and the first three of their children. (They were to have nine.) In the party were two other families, that of his brother-in-law Robert Poage and a Toomy, another of the Creek Nation clan.

The three families soon had Indian trouble. The Poages had scarcely raised their cabin when a small war party attempted to break into it. They were beaten off, but later a hired man named Richards was killed in the woods not far from the clearing. There were no more casualties for several years, but cattle and horses ranging the woods were mutilated and rustled. In 1784 Moore's fourteen-year-old son, also James, was sent off to find a draft horse thought to have strayed into a woodlot some two miles from the clearing. James later recalled that this was a chore he had performed frequently, but on this particular day he had a premonition of disaster. It was shortly fulfilled when four Shawnees, led by a notorious minor war chief named Black Wolf, appeared from behind a windfall. James said that he screamed in terror, thinking at first that he had been jumped by a "wild animal in human shape which would devour me." Perceiving his error, "I felt greatly relieved and spoke out loud, 'It is an Indian, why need I fear'; and thought to myself, 'All that is in it is, I will have to go to the Shawnee towns.' " This was the case, and James Moore was taken to Ohio by Black Wolf.

The kidnapping was too much for the Poages and Toomys, who decided to cut their losses and fled back to better-secured regions. James Moore, Sr., was a more stubborn man, in part because he was more prosperous than the others. By then he had 100 head of horses and more cattle in Apps Valley. Each year he would drive their increase northward, getting good prices, $100 or so for a strong colt, from piedmont and coastal farmers. Moore said that he intended not only to remain in Apps Valley but to expand his holdings there, that no Indians were going to drive him off his place. Technically they never did.

Black Wolf and his men remembered the exposed family and paid it a return visit on July 14, 1786. By dawn thirty Shawnees had hidden themselves around the clearing and lay watching the main cabin, which had been built to serve as a fort. When most of the Moores had gone outside to commence their morning chores, Black Wolf launched the attack. Moore himself was putting out salt for horses in a lick bog. When the Indians appeared, he ran back toward the cabin, passing on the way the bodies of three of his children, William, Rebecca and Alexander, who had been killed while drawing water at the spring. The house was surrounded by Shawnees. Moore ducked behind it and took cover along a section of rail fence. Since the Indians were busy trying to break into the cabin-fort, he might have had a fair chance of escaping. (Two hired men, a William Clark and an "Irishman," who were working in a nearby field were able to do so, fleeing some six miles through the woods to the nearest settlement.) Moore, however, did not run, and survivors later speculated, "When he saw his family about to be massacred, without possibility of rending assistance he chose to share a like fate." If so, Moore did not accept his fate passively. The Shawnees eventually had to shoot him seven times before they could dislodge him from behind the fence and take his scalp.

Inside the cabin, the principal defender was an old man named John Simpson who was living with the family. Simpson was ill and bedridden, but from his shuck mattress in the loft, with a servant girl named Martha Evans to load his guns, he returned the Indian fire until he was shot through the head. Downstairs Martha Moore and her children continued to make what defense they could, and there were also, it was said, "two large dogs who fought like heroes." However, the Shawnees eventually hacked through the door, knocked in the heads of the dogs with their axes and took the survivors captive. After roping them together, Black Wolf headed the party north toward the Ohio. Two of the children, a retarded son named John and an infant daughter, Peggy, who was carried by her elder sister Mary, proved to be nuisances and were killed a day or two later.

On returning to their home village, the Shawnees found a small party of allied Cherokees lying up there. The Cherokees had been out on their own raid but had fared badly, several of their men having been killed and another wounded. They had taken neither scalps nor prisoners and were sore and disgruntled. To cheer them up, the Shawnees turned Martha Moore and her daughter Jane over to the visitors. The Cherokees tied them to stakes and set off fires around them. Eventually the two women were released from their agony by a Shawnee squaw, "more humane than most," who dispatched them with an ax. While being tortured, Martha Moore bore up "with utmost Christian fortitude, expressing great anxiety for the moment to arrive when her soul should wing its way to the bosom of her savior." This was the account of Mary Moore and Martha Evans, the servant girl, both of whom were spared for other purposes by the Shawnees and became the only survivors of the Apps Valley disaster.

The casualties of the Walkers were not exceptional, most frontier families—and, of course, Indian ones—suffering as many or worse losses during the forest wars. When they were over, the majority of whites regarded all Indians with loathing. These feelings were evident as the frontier moved west, and fairly innocuous tribes were dealt with ferociously not so much because of what they had done or could do but because of things which had occurred along the old Appalachian border. The aphorism "The only good Indian is a dead Indian" (or at least a dispossessed reservation Indian) became the common front-stoop, barbershop, trading post, barracks wisdom and frequently the basis for public Indian policy.

There were minority opinions. Far to the east of the frontier, along the Atlantic seaboard and in Europe, were sensitive people who thought well and romantically of the Indians as Innocent Children of Nature. They deplored the mistreatment and misunderstanding of these Noble Savages by the ignoble whites. Their views planted the seeds of guilt-in-regard-to-Indians which were to blossom some generations hence. However, these liberal intellectuals, as they might now be called, had little immediate effect on frontier attitudes or behavior. They were not the kind of people the borderers often encountered or, if they did, admired. When their opinions were heard, they were easily dismissed as coming from sentimental, educated fools who had never had Black Wolf hacking at their cabin doors.

Paradoxically, the other small class in which pro-Indian feelings were likely to be found was made up of men who knew the tribesmen very well, better than did any other whites. Amos Dunkleberry—the trader-hunter who temporarily stayed the execution of the unfortunate Cherokees captured by John Echols and his vengeful mates—appears to have been one of these men. They were generally the boldest wilderness roamers. Often they were also Indian fighters, but more or less professionals, who dueled with the warriors out of self-defense, to travel or trade or because they found it exciting. Very seldom were they Indian haters. To the contrary, they found red culture and customs so attractive that they often lived for long periods as or with Indians. Since they were usually the kind of men most celebrated for their courage and wilderness experiences, their opinions about and behavior toward Indians did have a considerable impact on the frontier psyche.

One of the whites who went native was William Walker, the eleven-year-old who was captured in the Creek Nation by the Delaware in 1781. After being sold to the Wyandotte, he grew up with them in the vicinity of Detroit. Eventually he married Catherine Montour, the daughter of an important French-Iroquois family. Walker became a prominent trader and political agent in red-white negotiations following the War of 1812. At any time after his majority he could have freely returned to his own people but never did. His cousin, James Moore, who was taken by Black Wolf on the first Apps Valley raid in 1784, traveled and hunted for a time with the Shawnee but also ended up in Michigan living voluntarily with a half-breed family. Three years later he was reunited with his sister Mary and Martha Evans, the two captive survivors of the attack on Apps Valley in 1786. James said he found out about the girls from "a Shawnee Indian with whom I had been acquainted." With the assistance of Simon Girty, a white squaw man who has come down through history as a terrible traitor to his race, Moore was able to arrange for the release of the girls and escorted them back to Virginia. They were jubilant, but James Moore was less so. He had fallen in love with one of the trader's daughters, and he later said that if it were not for concern about his sister's safety, he would never have returned to Virginia. After he did, he said he intended shortly to go back to Michigan, but he was dissuaded or became caught up in family affairs and never did. However, he remembered the years with the northern Indians as exciting and agreeable ones.

The experiences and reactions of the two young Walker captives again were not exceptional. Some white prisoners were tortured and killed, and others continued to resist and hate their captors; but there are indisputable records concerning dozens of others who adjusted quickly and found that the new life-style suited them very well. During the forest wars most of these white men who lived with Indians were initially prisoners, the hostilities being so fierce and general that other means of entry into the tribes were difficult. However, later and especially in the west when fairly pacific relations existed between whites and some tribes for considerable periods, a number of frontiersmen voluntarily joined Indians. The reverse—Indians choosing and learning how to live as whites—occurred less often, one reason being that red society was far more racially tolerant than was white. A white man once accepted by Indians enjoyed more or less full tribal privileges, while Indians among the whites usually had a distinctly inferior status.

A fundamental white assumption in regard to other races was that they were, almost as a matter of definition, lewd and lascivious. Therefore, the common "civilized" opinion was that the principal reason white men took up with the Indians was to get at their wanton women. In fact, while whites who adopted Indian ways invariably enjoyed Indian women, it seems that most of them were initially motivated by the prospect of being able to live the life of an Indian man.

From early childhood, Indian boys were encouraged to do more or less exactly as they pleased—self-fulfillment being regarded as far more important and satisfying for a man (but only rarely for a woman) than social service. If they were destructive, violent or headstrong, they were not disciplined since these were looked upon as promising traits of character. So conditioned, Indian men had little interest in any activities except those regarded in their society—and in many others—as the most manly. They played games, made magic, gambled, danced, sang, indulged in prodigious bouts of feasting and drinking, organized religious and fraternal ceremonies, argued about philosophy and politics, boasted about their exploits, told heroic and mythic stories, preened and groomed themselves, courted, made love, traveled as far and stayed as long as they wanted, hunted and explored. Most especially they made war, not as Europeans had come to do, in disciplined armies for strategic purposes, but as European knights-errant once had—for personal glory, plunder and excitement. When they were not otherwise engaged, Indian men recruited their energies and were waited on by mothers, daughters and wives whose social function it was to see that men had the freedom and wherewithal to be men. It is small wonder that some white frontiersmen found this life-style appealing. They discovered that simply by joining the savages, they could live and enjoy themselves as only the richest and most powerful Europeans, the royalty and rulers, were able or permitted to live—that is, with almost total personal freedom.

In part because they refused to sacrifice any of their individual liberties for the sake of collective action, the warriors lost the forest wars and all their freedoms. However, before they were finished, they left a curious mark on the victors by making pseudo Indians out of the greatest of the white heroes—Sam Houston, Kit Carson, Jim Bridger, Milton Sublette, Lucien Maxwell, William Bent, Joe Walker. In fact, virtually all the notable frontiersmen who came from the Appalachian border spent substantial, satisfying periods of their lives as Indians. They seldom were renegades who turned on other whites, but rather were realists who accepted the white conquest of the continent as inevitable. Most of them were leaders in the westering movement that was to bring this about—and very effective ones because of their rapport with their adopted peoples. However, personally and privately they were Indian lovers in many senses of the word. By their actions they made it clear that whatever advantages and rewards white society might have for more tame, collared, harnessed, pussy-whipped men, they themselves found that there was nothing quite so grand and manly as living the life of an Indian.

Fifty years after nine of his kin had been killed by Black Wolf at Apps Valley, Joe Walker made one of his rare trips back from the Rocky Mountains to Independence, Missouri, a community which he had helped organize and in which a good many of his relatives still lived. He was then a renowned frontier figure, and a large party of family, friends and admirers gathered to meet and become reacquainted with him. During the course of things a visiting cousin, an Alabama planter, asked a bit condescendingly if Walker had had enough of the wilderness and was returning to become a settled citizen. Most emphatically not, the frontiersman replied. He was going back immediately "to live with the Indians because white people are too damned mean."

Since it struck at what were assumed to be essential arrangements and purposes of civilized society, this Indianish taint was not (and never since has been) much examined or often acknowledged. Nevertheless, it had a persistent unsettling and subversive influence on the frontier and, therefore, on the American imagination. Working like a chronic low-grade fever, the notion that only a feral man can be genuinely free constituted the most ironic legacy of the forest wars—the final revenge of the Shawnee, Cherokee and Iroquois.

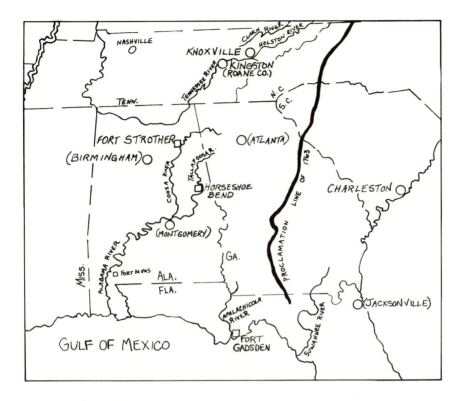

Tennessee

John Murray, the Earl of Dunmore, was the last British governor of Virginia, and few colonial administrators ever had a more difficult assignment. By the time he was appointed in 1771 the eastern, supposedly civilized Anglo section of the state was rife with seditious talk and rebellious plotting. In regard to the Appalachian border, Dunmore was given the task of trying to keep the white settlers east of a boundary running down the crest of the mountains. This had been created by London policy makers following the French and Indian War. Its purpose was to set aside the trans-Appalachian wilderness for the fur trade and for the use of the Indians who were essential for carrying on that business.

The effect of the act had been to turn all parties against the British. In practice, white settlers generally ignored the treaty line but despised it in principle because they saw the boundary as one which restrained their freedom, denied them access to western lands and created a permanent Indian sanctuary from which warriors could freely raid their

45

homes and communities. (These feelings contributed to the fact that when the Revolution came, the frontier people solidly and ferociously supported it.) So far as the Indians were concerned, the stream of illegal settlers who continued to pour across the treaty line was taken as a sign that the British could not or would not honor their obligations.

Dunmore, after a few months on the job, concluded that the boundary line was a ridiculous conceit and the treaty provisions were unenforceable. Exasperated, he wrote a famous minute in which he attempted to explain the realities of the situation to his superiors in London, who were badgering him about why he could not make a rabble of white savages obey British law:

> My Lord I have learnt from experience that the established Authority of any government in America and the policy of the Government at home, are both insufficient to restrain the Americans; and that they do and will remove as their avidity and restlessness incite them. They acquire no attachement to Place: But wandering about seems engrafted in their Nature: and it is a weakness incident to it, that they Should forever immagine the Lands further off are Still better than those upon which they are already settled. . . . In this Colony Proclamations have been published from time to time to restrain them. But impressed from their earliest infancy with Sentiments and habits, very different from those acquired by persons of a similar condition in England, they do not conceive that Government has any right to forbid their taking possession of a Vast tract of Country, either uninhabited, or which serves only as a Shelter to a few scattered Tribes of Indians. Nor can they be easily brought to entertain any belief of the permanent obligation of Treaties made with those People, whom they consider as but little removed from the brute Creation. These notions, My Lord, I beg it may be understood, I by no means pretend to Justify. I only think it my duty to State matters as they really are.

For the next century the restlessness of which Dunmore wrote was to be regarded as a definitive characteristic of American frontier people and continued to confound and exasperate governments. Its causes engaged the analytical interest of schools of social commentators and historians, who have suggested variously that the restlessness was an economic, capitalistic, geopolitical, populist, democratic, psychological, religious or mystic phenomenon. Unquestionably the reasons for the great "wandering about" were disparate and complex, but explanations of its underlying motives and principles tend to be tautological. For 100 years or so Americans were uniquely restless and unruly because they had a unique opportunity to be so.

Presumedly they were vulnerable, as ordinary people have always been everywhere, to common dissatisfactions about how and where they were living. In other times and places these were accepted with some stoicism because there were few alternatives. But along and behind the American frontier, even minor frustrations were magnified and came to be regarded as intolerable because it did not seem they had to be endured. Without much in the way of resources or technology, and especially without seeking anyone's permission, a family or a group could move westward, on foot if necessary. When they came to unoccupied country, they could make new places or positions or at least sustain the satisfying illusion that they were. Since this could be done, the temptation to do so was powerful, and restlessness became a cultural habit.

Just as they were not immediately crafty woodsmen and Indian fighters, the whites on the frontier were not initially wilderness nomads. The first, or at least most clearly remembered, who acquired the skill and confidence to begin roaming in a grand way was a class of young men who came to be known as Long Hunters. Hunting, from the beginning, was an important wilderness occupation, but also a principal pleasure for frontiersmen who found it much more satisfying and manly than the tedious routine of farm work. By the 1760s there were a good many men able and very ready to leave the settlements and their families and wander for months at a time in the western woods. Ostensibly they were working, going off for meat, hides or furs, but essentially they were sports, hunting so that they could continue hunting, to travel farther, see more new land.

Others had done the same in the preceding years, but the first of these groups to be called Long Hunters was a party of forty men from southwestern Virginia organized by a James Knox in the fall of 1770. They set up a base camp in eastern Tennessee and from there in smaller groups ranged into Kentucky, eventually returning to their homes in midwinter. In the spring twenty more men, from the vicinity of Natural Bridge, went off on a long hunt. Their activities were less well memorialized than those of Knox and his men, but they stayed out for nine months and apparently penetrated farther into the southwestern wilderness. Undoubtedly there were Walkers in this group since by then it would have been all but impossible to bring together twenty men from that region without including some members of this family.

When they returned, the Long Hunters were full of themselves and had marvelous travelers' stories about the abundance of game, the fertility of the land and other resources in the places they had visited. "About one hundred acres was principally covered with Buffelowes," reported one Long Hunter about a western meadow he had found. He said his horse could scarcely advance because "the Buffelowes were so crowded in the path." Inspired by these stories, the most restless of the settler families, often with the hunters guiding them, would pick up and move to one of the new paradises. If things went well for them, they sent back glowing reports about their prospects. These in turn would motivate more cautious relatives and friends to follow. This sequence, hunter-explorers followed by the boldest settlers and then settlements, was to occur repeatedly as the frontier advanced.

The westward movements of the Walker family conformed closely to this pattern, which they as much as any others established. John, the ranger, his son Samuel Walker and James Moore were of the right age and temperament to have been among the men who left Natural Bridge in 1771. If not, they were influenced by members of that party, since both the Clinch River and Apps valleys, where these Walkers and Moore were to relocate and lose their lives, were in the wilderness first reconnoitered by the Long Hunters. Thereafter members of the Walker clan were to fan out in two general directions—west and north toward Kentucky and Ohio and southwest toward Tennessee. A catalyst in influencing family movements in the latter direction was Joseph Walker, a grandson of John Walker, the original Ulster emigrant.

Joseph was the next to youngest of nine children of Samuel and Jane Patterson Walker. There is a suspicion that after he grew to be a man, Joseph may not have got along well with his father, who had been a militia captain in the Indian wars and then became a surveyor and prosperous landholder in western Virginia. When Samuel died, Joseph inherited nothing and was not among the children who signed documents having to do with the disposal of their father's property. Whatever the reasons, after service with a Virginia regiment during the Revolution, Joseph Walker did not return to the parental compound. Instead, he made an odd—for one of his family—detour to the east, going to Goochland County, which was in the plantation region. As it turned out, what interested him there was a woman by the name of Susan Willis. She was of English stock, the daughter of a tobacco planter and already a young woman of independent means, having inherited slaves and property from her grandfather.

Susan Willis belonged to a class that did not often associate with or have high regard for Scotch-Irish frontiersmen such as the Walkers. She and Joseph may have met through her brothers, several of whom were also Revolutionary veterans (one of them, William, later joined Joseph on the Tennessee frontier). However they met and whatever their respective families may have thought of it, the couple was married in Goochland County in August 1787. Shortly thereafter Walker set off for Tennessee. He ended up fifty miles west of Knoxville, which was then a fort surrounded by a few cabins. There he took up land along the Emery (now Emory) River near the confluence of that stream, the Clinch and the Tennessee. He cleared it, worked as a surveyor and did some Indian fighting, being, in 1792, one of the defenders of a blockhouse (around which the settlement of Kingston was to grow) against a Cherokee war party.

For the first decade of her marriage, Susan Walker lived permanently, or mostly, in Goochland County. This—a wife's remaining behind in a more secure area while her husband established a place in the wilderness—was not an unusual arrangement. Nevertheless, the couple was obviously together at times since while she was in Goochland County, Susan bore two daughters, Lucy and Jane, and in 1797 a son, Joel. Then the Walkers apparently decided that Tennessee had become reasonably safe, and Susan and the three children moved there permanently. Within a year after they arrived, in December 1798, another son, Joseph was born, in what was shortly to be organized as Roane County. Subsequently three more Walker children, John, Samuel and Susan, were born in Tennessee.

As had been the case in the family for some generations previous, these Walker children were large and vigorous. All seven grew to adulthood. (There may also have been an eighth child named William, or perhaps Isaac, but genealogical records are suspect in regard to his existence.) As for their size, Joe Walker, after he had grown up to be a frontier hero, was known to stand six-four and weigh well over 200 pounds, but his younger brother, whose dimensions were never recorded, was probably larger since in the west he was known as Big John Walker.

In the Emery River-Caney Creek settlement in Tennessee, the Walkers were members of a huge extended family. By the 1800s three of Joseph Walker's brothers, John, James and Samuel, and two of his sisters, Barbara McClellan and Katherine Scott, had moved to Tennessee and were living nearby with their families. Among them they had forty children, who were first cousins of Joseph Walker's children. A maternal uncle, William Willis, also settled nearby, but because he was English or for other reasons, he had only two children. Additionally, a number of other families of various degrees of relationship had come from the Creek Nation country: Poages, Paxtons, Pattersons, Toomys, Coulters, Youngs, Martins, Moores, Houstons and Hayeses. They were connected by blood and marriage to virtually everyone else of importance in Tennessee and—to only a slightly lesser degree— Kentucky. The McClellans, for example, who had been marrying with Walkers for two generations, were also related to Nolichucky Jack Sevier, the foremost military man of early Tennessee, and to the Donelsons, whose daughter married the state's most famous politician, Andrew Jackson.

Aside from the immediate pleasures and advantages of growing up in the midst of a small army of kinfolk, these circumstances influenced the later pioneering careers of the Walker children. Historians have frequently observed that East Tennessee was the seedbed of the nineteenth-century westering movement, providing an inordinate number of the people who proceeded through the Appalachians to Missouri and then to the Pacific coast. This is another way of noting that the first stage of the American migration into the trans-Mississippi west was, to a degree now seldom recalled, an extended family enterprise. The style, tactics and politics of the movement largely reflected arrangements among members of intricately connected clans from the eastern highlands. Among them there was a remarkable homogeneity of attitudes and traditions as well as blood. The Walkers, as they explored and traveled westward, usually dealt with and led people whom they had known or known about all their lives and who were frequently relatives.

So far as formal schooling was concerned, the Walkers received some because later they were to act and be treated as members of the better-educated frontier class, but there are no records indicating how and where they received it. They may have been instructed at home by their mother or by aunts or have attended one of the temporary common schools established on the border as students and teachers became available. They were of the right age and in approximately the right place to have attended one such academy organized by their kinsman Sam Houston after he returned from having lived with the Cherokee as a runaway and dropout from white society. Houston was joshed considerably about setting himself up as a schoolmaster on the strength of a degree from "Indian University," but as a boy he had read well in his father's exceptional library and by frontier standards was a considerable classicist, literary stylist and, competitively, a champion speller. Years later, after he had been the governor of Tennessee, a U.S. senator, a Cherokee again, a raging alcoholic and the president of Texas, Houston was to say that the job he liked best and was proudest of was keeping his one-room school in Tennessee.

Perhaps because of the strong traditions of their grandparents, the Walkers remained Presbyterians for longer than most of the frontier families. Later many of them joined more typically border sects, but in Tennessee they were elders, deacons and pillars of the Bethel Presbyterian Church near Kingston. When they journeyed east to Knoxville, which by 1810 had become a true town of some 1,500 people, they would have been obligated to be instructed by the sermons of the Reverend Samuel Carrick, who had married first one of their Toomy cousins and, after her death, a McClellan aunt. Carrick, regarded as one of the most powerful preachers on the Tennessee border, was generally a man of strong opinions and high temper. He died early one Sunday morning of apoplexy, while putting the finishing touches on a sermon designed to confound members of the congregation with whom he was at theological odds. Following his demise, his widow, Annis, and her two children, William and Barbara, came to live with their Walker-McClellan relatives and later traveled west with them.

Children, especially sons, were economic assets in frontier communities, where most work was labor-intensive. Very early, boys were set to the kinds of tasks—splitting rails, piling rocks, hoeing corn, stoking forges and the like—which grown men found tedious. In consequence fifteen- and sixteen-year-old runaway sons who hated this sort of unpaid labor were common. After Sam Houston had gone off to the Cherokee, his two elder brothers, James and John, who were the heads of the fatherless family, went looking for him. When they found him and told him to come home, Houston refused, saying that he found "the wild liberty of the Red Man better than the tyranny of his own brothers."

The Walker boys certainly would have been put to chores by the time they were eight or nine years old. In the course of carrying, fetching, holding, helping out, they would have learned basic ax, knife, carpentry, butchering, tanning, smithy and distilling work. From their mothers and sisters they learned enough about cooking at least to bake bread, to sew up a pair of moccasins or leggings, and something about home remedies. In the Far West, Joe Walker, for example, was especially adept at finding, identifying and prescribing the use of medicinal herbs.

When Joe and his brothers Joel and John arrived in the trans-Mississippi country in 1819, they were accepted and respected as notable frontiersmen. Joe and Joel almost immediately became leaders of bold, exploratory enterprises. This is not surprising since so far as general wilderness skills were concerned, few boys could have had better instructional opportunities than the Walkers in Tennessee, where they were surrounded by numerous male relatives with extraordinary border experience.

With gunmakers still in the family, the young Walker boys probably received their rifles (the badge of manhood and passport to freedom) earlier than most and were turned loose to hunt, trap and roam in the mountains and forests which began more or less at their back door. Many of the settlers raised and traded horses, cattle and hogs, but the Walkers did so more regularly and on a larger scale than most. The boys presumedly spent a lot of time herding animals in the rough, broken mountain ranges and trailing them up through

Virginia to northern and eastern markets. Again, when he got to the Far West, being beautifully mounted, usually on a big stud horse, became something of a trademark of Joe Walker. Admiring observers said that, despite his bulk, he could ride like a Comanche. Exploring parties he led invariably survived and were successful in part because of his special talent for conserving and getting the most out of horses and mules.

Another assumption may reasonably be made about the childhood of the Walkers. It is that theirs was an unusually affectionate, secure family, of the sort which often produces stable, self-confident adults. As they moved westward, the brothers, sisters, cousins and others remained attentive to and supportive of each other. Though their restlessness was pronounced, they always saw to it that there was a family base, similar to the first one in the Creek Nation, in which young, old, weak, wounded and unlucky relatives could find sanctuary.

Also, no members of the immediate family became—as many did on and because of the frontier—killers, dangerous drunks, brigands, religious or racial zealots, domestic or community tyrants, mean, manipulative people obsessed with accumulating wealth or power. Some, of course, were more able and successful than others, but there is no record of any of them who was not a fairly decent human being. All of which suggests that Joseph and Susan Walker were successful parents.

The last Walker to be lost in the eastern Indian wars was a cousin, Elizabeth, who in the early 1790s, as a very young girl, was kidnapped by a band of Creek Indians and never heard of again. At about this same time Joseph Walker, his brothers and men like them finally subdued the Cherokee in a series of bloody engagements and destroyed the organized military power of that nation. Scattered Cherokee villages survived for a time, and the young Walkers, when they began to travel in the woods, would have certainly met and had some dealings with these Indians. (The village on the Hiwassee River to which Sam Houston had run off in 1809 was within a day's trip of the Walker settlement.) Their relations with the Cherokees in their neighborhood would have been pacific by then, for the forest wars were winding down on the Tennessee frontier and north of it.

Like the Cherokee, the Iroquois, perfectly understanding what an American victory would mean, had fought with the British during the Revolution. As many of their leaders had feared, they were abandoned by their white allies to carry on the western war largely alone and had been finally defeated. Some of the Iroquois had retreated west of the mountains, and there with the Ohio Valley tribes had made a last stand under Tecumseh, perhaps the most able and charismatic of all the eastern Indian leaders. Tecumseh won some notable victories against both American militiamen and regulars but was drawn into the War of 1812, and in 1813 he was killed, and his coalition shattered, at a battle fought near Detroit.

Thereafter the only powerful tribe left in the east was the Creek, who inhabited a sizable territory in southwestern Tennessee, Georgia, Alabama and northern Florida. Though the most numerous Indian nation, they had held aloof from the earlier rounds of the forest wars. They had been able to do so since they were screened from the advance of the white settlements by the Cherokee and were supplied with trade goods from British and Spanish posts along the Gulf coast. However, after the fall of the Cherokee and the subsequent flood of immigrants into the southwest, continued neutrality became impossible for the Creeks.

The war party within the tribe, called the Red Sticks, was led by William Weatherford, whose father and grandfather had been Scotch-Irish traders with the Creeks. With customary provocations and retaliations on both sides, the Red Sticks and white settlers began skirmishing in western Tennessee and Alabama during the first decade of the nineteenth century. In the latter part of 1813, as Tecumseh was going down to final defeat in Michigan, Weatherford's Creeks captured Fort Mims on the Alabama River and killed 500 white soldiers and civilians who had taken refuge there. When the news from Fort Mims reached Tennessee, the state was swept with a fierce desire for immediate revenge. Militia companies began to muster, and a committee of citizens for public safety rode to Nashville to offer the overall command of the campaign against the Red Sticks to Andrew Jackson.

Jackson even then was regarded as an extraordinary man, but of a type fairly new to the frontier. He was neither by experience nor temperament a cabin builder, woodsman or ranger. After the first settlements had been made, he had come to Tennessee as a lawyer, land speculator, gambler, horse breeder and something of a dandy. Though he was later advertised as such, he was anything but a populist, being of the firm opinion that society should be directed by men who had proved their merit by accumulating wealth and land. However, reflecting his own rise, he also supported the principle that any man had the right to try to be a Jacksonian man—that is, without being overly restricted by the laws or traditions, to try to get whatever he wanted by whatsoever means came to hand. This was very much in keeping with the common frontier philosophy. Also, Jackson notably possessed the personal characteristics—raw courage, loyalty to friends and ferocious independence—most admired by frontiersmen. These more than his politics or economics were to make him the hero of the West and eventually president.

When, late in September 1813, the public safety committee came to Jackson in regard to the Creek War, they found him on what attending physicians thought might be his deathbed. He had come there—and was to leave it—under circumstances which were to enhance his popularity among the border people. Two weeks previously, to avenge an insult to his honor, Jackson had set off after Thomas Hart Benton, then a young lawyer (who later as a senator from Missouri was to become the principal orator and strategist of the Manifest Destiny party). Finding him in a tavern corridor, Jackson kicked away Benton's pistol and commenced to lash the younger man with a horsewhip. While he was so occupied, Jesse Benton, Thomas's brother, entered and shot Jackson in the back. With his attacker down, Thomas Benton picked up his own gun and shot Jackson twice more. The Benton brothers then escaped without suffering or giving further injury. Jackson was carried to a hotel room, where his blood "soaked through two mattresses." His left arm was shattered, and a ball remained (for nineteen years thereafter) lodged in his shoulder.

In this condition, propped up in bed, Jackson received the public safety committee. Hearing the details of the Creek uprising he said, "By the Eternal, these people [the white settlers] must be saved." He promised he personally would lead the expedition of retaliation.

Nine days later, his arm in a sling, seldom able to sleep or eat because of the pain and fever from the wounds and a new case of dysentery, Jackson was at the head of 1,500 men marching southwestward, looking for William Weatherford and his Red Sticks. The mountain weather turned cold and wet, bridges and roads had to be built as the troops advanced, but Jackson drove them on at the rate of twenty-five miles a day. During November two sharp engagements were fought with the Indians, but Jackson was unable to catch the main body of warriors. By December 1, with nearly 100 wounded men, the hastily organized white army was virtually without food. Jackson halted his pursuit and encamped at Fort Strother on the Coosa River in northern Alabama. His intention was to wait there for supplies and reinforcements. Because of logistical problems and the fact that there was considerable disagreement between Jackson and officer-politicians from East Tennessee, both the food and the men were slow to arrive. Starving, cold and bored with the inaction, the militia units, despite being harangued and threatened by Jackson, began to disband and head back toward their homes.

In this crisis a lawyer-militia colonel by the name of John Brown, who had already raised one company from Roane County, made a hurried trip back to Kingston to recruit new troops. In January 1814 he organized a regiment of mounted gunmen. Among the recruits were Joel and Joe Walker. They were respectively sixteen and fifteen years old but, by reason of their heredity and training, were probably even then bigger than, and at least as well armed, mounted and able as, most mature men.

By January 21 Brown had his horsemen across the Tennessee River, and he reached Jackson on the Coosa a few days later. Other hastily raised units and some badly needed supplies arrived at about the same time. Twenty years earlier George Washington had commented that frontiersmen were fine fighters but terrible soldiers. On the Coosa, Andrew Jackson learned how astute Washington's observation had been. The new volunteers were on fire to get at the Creek warriors, but they were very green and undisciplined, to the point of rebelliousness. Only after Jackson had a seventeen-year-old, John Wood, executed by a firing squad for having threatened an officer of the day with a rifle was some order imposed upon them.

In early March with 3,000 men Jackson moved out of camp. They finally came upon the main body of Creeks, about 1,000 warriors, at a place called Horseshoe Bend on the Tallapoosa River. This was a peninsula of 100 acres, heavily covered with timber and cut with ravines. The Creeks put up a breastwork of pine logs across the neck of Horseshoe Bend, determined to make a stand there not only because of the tactical advantage it seemed to offer but because they regarded it as a sacred grove. They were assured by their medicine men that on that ground they could never be defeated by white men. It was a false prophecy.

On the morning of March 27, 1814, Jackson began bombarding the breastwork with fire from two field pieces. The balls had little effect on the pine logs and the artillerymen proved to be exposed targets for the Creek sharpshooters. Thereupon in midmorning Jackson ordered 2,000 of his men to storm the barricade, advising them before they left that "any officer or man who fled before the enemy . . . shall suffer death." It was later said that the first of the Tennesseeans to get across the log wall alive was twenty-year-old Sam Houston.

Thereafter the fighting became a hand-to-hand melee. The Creek resisted stubbornly but were slowly pushed back to the tip of the peninsula. Some reached the river and swam across it, but more were picked off as they tried to do so. By nightfall the battle was over. About 800 of the 1,000 Creeks were killed at Horseshoe Bend, and the military power of the tribe died with them. Fifty Tennessee men were killed, and another 150 wounded. Among the latter, the nature of his injuries unreported, was young Joel Walker. Joe came through unscathed, though he must have been among those who stormed the Creek barricade since his brother and all of Brown's company were in this assault force.

That evening a strange incident occurred in the white camp. Somehow having slipped through the pickets, the Creek general, William Weatherford, appeared at the door of Andrew Jackson's tent.

"I am come," he announced, "to give myself up. I can oppose you no longer. I have done you much injury. I should have done you more but my warriors are killed. I am in your power. Dispose of me as you please."

"You are not in my power," said Jackson. "I ordered you brought to me in chains but you come of your own accord. If you think you can contend against me in battle, go and head your warriors."

"Well may such language be addressed to me now," said Weatherford. "There was a time when I could have answered you. I could animate my warriors to battle; but I can not animate the dead. Kill me if the white people want it done."

Andrew Jackson may not have been himself a practicing frontiersman; but he had the panache of the frontier, and also, even in this lawyer-politician-general, there was the taint of the Indian-way lover. He poured out two cups of brandy, drank with Weatherford and ordered that the Creek be allowed to leave the camp freely and safely.

Thus for practical purposes ended the Appalachian wars, which had been fought by three generations of reds and whites. Considering that their own family had been engaged in them since the first days of the Creek Nation, it seems historically appropriate that Joel and Joe Walker were among those who brought down the Creek in the last battle. Also, Horseshoe Bend provided a useful beginning to their own careers as leaders of the advance on the next western frontier.

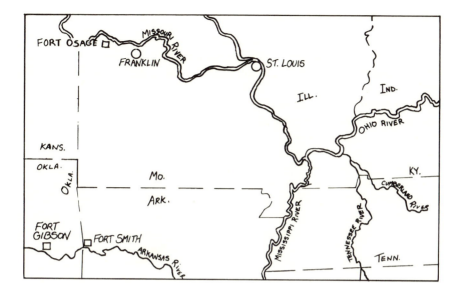

Missouri

Following his victory at Horseshoe Bend, Andrew Jackson imposed a punitive peace treaty on not only the Red Stick warriors but also the members of the tribal peace party that had opposed Weatherford and aided Jackson. The Creeks were stripped of most of their former lands, which became available to white settlers and real estate speculators, among the latter being Jackson. Some of the surviving Red Sticks and other Creek dissidents who were unwilling to live in accordance with this treaty escaped to Florida, where they joined scattered local tribes and bands of escaped black slaves. They came to be called the Seminoles (Runaways). As such, they conducted a long and effective guerrilla campaign. Cornered as they were in the peninsula, they had no effect on the main migratory movements of the whites to their north, but for fifty years they caused the American military considerable expense and more embarrassment.

The first of many commanders to take the field against the Seminoles was Andrew Jackson in 1818. Among the volunteers who followed him to Florida was Joel Walker, recovered from his previous wounds. The Tennesseans skirmished indecisively along the Suwannee River until the Indians disappeared into country where the army did not dare follow. Then the Americans caught a pair of Englishmen, Alexander Arbuthnot and Robert Ambrister. According to the British version, the former was an innocent trader, and the latter a gentleman traveler. Jackson, however, thought they were British secret agents intent on stirring up the Seminoles and hanged both men. After disposing of them and creating a serious international incident, Jackson led his troops west and without bloodshed took Pensacola from the Spanish, making the subsequent annexation of Florida all but inevitable.

Joe Walker may have gone off campaigning with Joel and participated in these actions. If so, neither brother ever made mention of the fact, but given their reticence, this does not prove the matter one way or another. Of the period Joe Walker said only, much later in conversations with acquaintances, that he had spent some time in west Tennessee, Alabama and Mississippi, territories which then constituted the extreme southwestern frontier of the country. Whether or not he was chasing the Seminoles in Florida with Joel or hunting and trapping in these wilderness regions, it is unlikely that after the Horseshoe Bend campaign he would have been satisfied to return to east Tennessee and settle down as a farm boy; his name appears in none of the church or civil records which provide some information about other members of his immediate family still living near Kingston.

He and Joel—then discharged from Jackson's army—both were back in Roane County by at least the late summer of 1819. With other relatives they were preparing to emigrate to Missouri, where Walker may have visited earlier in the year. It was then common for young men to go ahead on scouting missions for families considering relocating in distant western territories. If they thought such a reconnaissance desirable, Joe would have been the logical one to do the job since Joel was with Jackson and the other brothers were still boys. Also, in his later years he told a friend that one of the most enjoyable experiences of his youth was riding on the first steamboat to run up the Missouri into the western part of that state. If he and the man who heard and repeated the story had their facts straight, Walker was in Missouri in the spring or early summer of 1819, when the first steamers came upriver, the *Independence* reaching Franklin in late May and the *Western Engineer* passing that community a month later en route to Council Bluffs.

The first family left Tennessee for Missouri in mid-September 1819. In addition to Joe and Joel, the pioneer company included their younger brother, Big John; their sister, Jane, her husband, Abraham McClellan, and their two sons; a cousin, Annis Carrick, the widow of the late and choleric Reverend Samuel Carrick, and her two children. It is also possible that their widowed mother (Joseph Walker died in 1816 or '17) elected to go west with her children. More kin and retainers may have been in the group, but the only other name of record is that of a slave, Hardy, who made this and later migrations with the family. Eventually Hardy became a free man and ranch foreman with the McClellans in northern California.

Abraham McClellan was in charge of the business end of the move, being ten years older than his brothers-in-law and a much more experienced man of affairs. As were his own brothers, he was a real estate speculator and therefore—the callings being symbiotic in that place and time—a farmer, politician and judge. With both Joel and Joe off either fighting or roaming in the southern wilderness, it was McClellan who had settled the estate after their father's death and sold the property along Caney Creek. During the next two years McClellan was involved in a number of other land transactions, apparently aimed at converting the clan's real property into cash, preparatory to moving west. In September, just before departing, he sold his own place. The 170 acres (and "mansion") brought $2,000, an exceptionally high price at the time. With McClellan's dealing and whatever discharge money or profits from their wilderness adventures the brothers had accumulated, the party was in more comfortable circumstances, so far as cash went, than many emigrants of that year.

They traveled in several heavy southern wagons, Kentucky turnpikers, with the men and older boys driving a herd of spare horses and cattle. Beyond the ordinary clothing and household utensils, they carried at least a good set of tools to equip a blacksmith shop and a bundle of straw-wrapped scions from apple trees. The regions through which they traveled were settled only sparsely, and there were few public accommodations or supply depots even for those who could afford them. Migrants, therefore, carried what they needed and camped out along the way. By then travelers following the Ohio Valley route toward the Mississippi did not often take time to hunt—beyond pot-shooting squirrels—and if they did, they seldom had much luck, for the populations of large-game species had been greatly reduced by white settlement and foraging. Buffalo and elk had disappeared from the eastern woodlands, and even deer were scarce, probably scarcer in 1820 than they are in the same regions today.

Many years later Joel Walker dictated a brief memoir of his life and in it dismissed the family's trip of that fall in a sentence. Even for people less experienced and taciturn than the Walkers, it would not have been regarded then as an extraordinary journey. The roads were bad, scarcely worthy of the name, often being only swaths cut through the woods, still filled with rocks and stump butts, but all the trailblazing had been done. They were jerry-built, leaky and risky, but there were ferries of a sort at most major river crossings. The Indian menace had been removed earlier in the decade, and while there were white toughs like John Murrell (an infamous land pirate of the southern mountains) abroad, these would have posed no threat to such a formidable party as that of the Walkers. Traveling would have been tedious and uncomfortable but, beyond run-of-the-mill accidents and diseases of the road, not dangerous or particularly adventuresome. Also, whatever hardships there were, loneliness and isolation were not among them, for that year thousands of others were on the road, traveling westward.

Between 1810 and 1820 about a million Americans took part in what was justifiably called the Great Migration, passing through or coming out of the Appalachian highlands with the intent of settling permanently in the Mississippi Valley. (Though now better remembered, the subsequent movement across the western plains to the Pacific involved only 300,000 people in the two decades prior to the Civil War—the classic "covered wagon" period.) The Great Migration peaked after the War of 1812, which effectively freed the interior third of the country from both the threat of Indians and British claims. Like water flowing into a hole, the people poured into the newly secured regions, providing a mass demonstration of the national restlessness Lord Dunmore had found so alarming nearly fifty years before. As always, they came for common economic, political and social reasons and for an infinite variety of personal ones, but both the general and particular motives reflected the widespread conviction that if something itched, it could be scratched by moving toward the setting sun. "If hell lay in the West, an American would cross heaven to get to it," was an instructive saying of the time.

If they traveled at the customary pace, the Walkers reached St. Louis sometime in mid-October, still in the company of many others, for Missouri was the Mecca of the 1819 migration season. By word of mouth and through the overt efforts of land speculators the territory was advertised as possessing a marvelous climate in which northern wheat and apples, southern cotton and tobacco and everything in between would grow in soil so fertile that cornmeal sprouted. It was also said of Missouri that it was so healthful, particularly so free of the ague, the chills and fevers, that undertakers had to shoot and kill to get customers.

"The ague"—malaria—which then infected more than half the western population, was one of the great common causes of the migration. Thousands of shaking, enfeebled people moved in panic, trying to escape the disease and the bad air thought to cause it. Missouri in time became one of the worst places for the ague, but the first claims were not entirely false. For a few years settlers did enjoy some relief from the fever, a period of latency occurring while malarial humans infected populations of mosquitoes, which then gave the disease back to the humans in, so to speak, spades. Walker was never reported as suffering from this scourge, which chronically incapacitated many of his contemporaries. Whether it was a consequence of good constitution, environment or luck, his exceptional immunity to malaria must be credited as an important reason for the exceptional length and vigor of his frontier career.

Prospective emigrants—especially southerners who knew that they could bring their slaves to the territory without harassment—responded enthusiastically to the claims about Missouri. As many as 100 wagons a day crossed the Mississippi, and the *St. Louis Enquirer* reported that in September and October 1819, 12,000 "wealthy, respectable immigrants from various states" trundled through the city. Many continued 100 miles upstream on the Missouri and there found lands in the vicinity of the present Jefferson City and Columbia which approximated those of the advertisements and their dreams. This central section of the state was generally known as Boonslick Country, having been named for its most celebrated resident, the venerable Daniel Boone, who had discovered a large, commercially valuable salt lick in the area. Feeling very unappreciated and that rascally newcomers had diddled him out of properties and perks which were rightfully his as the principal pioneer of Kentucky, he had left that state and settled on the Missouri River in 1799, when the area was still part of the Spanish empire.

In 1819 the unofficial capital of the Boonslick Country was the community of Franklin. Now it is a tiny inland community left high and dry by the writhings of the Missouri River, but then it was a busy river port and, with more than 1,000 people, the largest town in the United States west of St. Louis. Among other things, Franklin had 125 log houses, a half dozen warehouses, four taverns, two billiard parlors, a steamboat landing, a $300 courthouse, a two-story jail, a racetrack, brothel, barber, baker and the only newspaper then being published in the trans-Mississippi territory.

The Walkers were among the few pioneers of 1819 who continued westward beyond the Boonslick Country. Twenty miles or so on the far side of Franklin, the settlements petered out and the road ended. Thereafter they had to make their own wagon tracks; even so, the going would not have been especially difficult since a well-worn Indian and game trail, the Osage Trace, ran parallel to and south of the river. It was, according to surviving meteorological reports, a beautiful autumn for overland travel, milder than most in that territory, and so dry that the smoke from numerous prairie fires sometimes clouded the sun. The prairie clearings became more frequent as they proceeded west, but these were studded with groves of big oak and walnut. There were ripening persimmons in the creek hollows and dripping bee trees in all the groves. (The honeybee, imported from Europe, pioneered just ahead of the white settlements and proliferated in the new country, where it had no native competitors for its ecological niche. The extent of the bee range was usually about 100 miles westward of the line of settlement, and so regular was this pattern that the Indians, who much admired it, came to call the bee "the white man's fly.")

Also, this lovely rolling country had not yet been heavily hunted. Deer, elk and black bear were so numerous that the Walkers could, without losing much time, have done some hunting for pleasure and to get welcome relief from cornmeal and salt pork, the staple foods of the road. In November, at the end of this pleasant stage of the journey from Tennessee, they stopped permanently at Fort Osage on the Missouri River, thirty miles downstream from the present site of Kansas City, a community founded 19 years later.

When the Walkers arrived, there may have been a few solitary white hunters camped in the vicinity and perhaps even another family or two, in addition to those stationed at Fort Osage. However, when they finally selected and occupied a piece of land west of the government post, it is likely that they became in 1819 what their grandparents had been in the Creek Nation in 1733—that is, the most westerly permanent settlers of the United States. In fact, they were several miles beyond the point where the United States government officially thought any of its citizens should or could reside.

Following the War of 1812, which gave de facto as well as de jure sovereignty over the vast Louisiana Purchase territory, the American government faced many of the same problems that the British had when they took over the Appalachian and Ohio valley regions after defeating the French in 1763. The American solution, largely devised by John Calhoun, the Secretary of War in the Monroe administration, was very similar to the earlier British one. In Washington an administrative line was laid down on the sketchy trans-Mississippi map. From the Canadian border it followed the Mississippi southward until it reached approximately the present northern boundary of Missouri. There it made a right-angle turn along the Missouri-Iowa state line. It turned south again, passing through Fort Osage, and continued in this direction until it intersected the Red River of Arkansas. Thereafter, angling toward the southeast, it followed this waterway back to the Mississippi. Beyond this line—that is, in what is now western Minnesota and Missouri, all of Iowa, Kansas, Oklahoma and everything west of them—there was to be no white settlement or other activity except for that of fur traders and trappers, and they would be licensed by the federal government to do business with the Indians. Drawn as it was, the boundary made Missouri into a kind of administrative peninsula, jutting toward the west, and thus automatically a logical staging area and jumping-off place for further, if illegal, exploration and migration.

Calhoun sold his plan as one which would solve a number of vexing and interrelated problems. It was thought that keeping the white settlers out of the wilderness would ecologically and politically encourage the American fur trade, just beginning to compete successfully with the British. Presumably, if they were left to themselves and protected from the racial conflicts which white communities invariably created, the Indians would be easier for the furmen to trade with and for the military to control. Also, the scheme gave a place in which the surviving eastern Indians could be relocated. The military power of the woodland tribes had been broken, but a number of them still occupied valuable lands. Besides wanting their property, the majority of whites simply did not like having Indians around them, and very small incidents often turned this dislike into violence. Setting aside the western plains, for which at the moment whites had little use, as a vast Indian nation gave the federal negotiators, who were then trying to cajole the eastern tribes into relocating, another bargaining chip. If this approach failed and they had to be driven out, the military would at least have someplace to drive them to. There was another small advantage. Such a policy could be offered as a humanitarian one—as a means of protecting the reds from the whites—to the small but prominent group of Atlantic coast intellectuals who were complaining that the treatment of Indians was a national disgrace. Finally, setting an arbitrary western limit on white settlements placated a body of opinion—sometimes called the Little America party—which was covertly antimigration. These sentiments were most prevalent among the moneyed and cultured citizens of New England and the Middle Atlantic states, who, somewhat as the British had in colonial times, found the nomadic habits of the lower orders of Americans disturbing and threatening. It was thought that the constant opportunity to respond to any dissatisfactions by picking up and moving west made the masses unruly and allowed them in effect to thumb their noses at their betters. The availability of great tracts of cheap or free virgin land depressed eastern real estate prices, drained off agricultural and industrial workers and kept wages higher than they would have been if laborers had not had an alternative to accepting what employers wanted to pay them.

The Little America view was that if the migrations were at least slowed, the people would become more docile and dependent, and the country could be developed properly, one region being civilized before other, wilder ones were opened. These notions were so contrary to republican dogma and rhetoric that they were seldom openly exposed to the voters, but there were a number of influential Little Americans.

They constituted a political force to reckon with in Washington. Calhoun's western boundary line appealed to them.

Like so many other plans devised by men who did not need or feel the urge to take part personally, Calhoun's had not a snowball's chance in hell of controlling the westering movement. However, for a few years the migration did pause along the politically imposed border. This was largely due to the coincidence that the arbitrary line approximately corresponded to the transition zone between the eastern woodlands, with which the frontier people were very familiar, and the great western plains, about which they knew very little. The migration rolled on only after scouts, such as Joe Walker, went out from Missouri and accumulated information about the western wilderness. During the brief period when the pioneering movement waited, gathering strength at the edge of the plains, the eastern planners had the satisfying feeling that they had indeed come up with a solution to their western problem and proceeded administratively as if they had.

A series of federal military trading posts (called factories) was established from Minnesota to Arkansas for the purpose of conducting and licensing commerce with the Indians, controlling them, protecting them from the whites and vice versa. Fort Osage was the first of these western installations, built even before the Calhoun plan was devised. In 1804, when Meriwether Lewis and William Clark traveled up the Missouri, outward-bound on their great expedition of discovery, the latter had noted this location. There a seventy-foot-high bluff rose directly above the water. In front of it was a long, narrow eddy of navigable water, but beyond was a series of rapids and current boils. Boatmen would have to pass, as the Corps of Discovery did, through the eddy, and a military force on the bluff directly above would command river traffic. Clark wrote in his journal, "This will be a good site for a fort and trading house with the Indians," and kept the place in mind. In 1808, then in charge of Indian affairs for the entire Louisiana Purchase territory, he returned to this bluff and supervised the construction of a post there. With him was George Sibley, one of Thomas Jefferson's bright young eastern men. The fort, four blockhouses connected with palisades, was finished in October of that year. Under the command of Captain Eli Clemson, eighty-one men of the First U.S. Infantry Regiment were posted there as the military garrison. George Sibley stayed on as the Indian agent, to develop good political and commercial relations with the Osage, the strongest tribe in the Missouri, Kansas, Arkansas area.

By 1819, when the Walkers arrived, Fort Osage was functioning only as an Indian post. Except for seven soldiers who provided a work force and honor guard, the military had moved on 200 miles upstream to a new fort at Council Bluffs. George Sibley, however, was still in charge as the official government trader. He was to hold the job for another three years, when—under pressure from the fur lobby—the government factory system was abandoned. (This act marked the official end of the federal effort at conducting the trade with the western Indians. Unofficially it was the beginning of the end of the attempt to control the western migration. Once the private traders were unleashed in the west, the settlers could not be long held back, and any attempt to do so could not be defended even on paper.) After Fort Osage had been closed, Sibley remained in the area for another six years as a private citizen, and he and the Walkers were to have a lot to do with each other.

From a distance in time, George Sibley emerges as a strange but sympathetic figure. For fifteen years he was in essence a frontier viceroy, the most important civilian representative of the U.S. government in a huge territory that stretched west and south into the plains from Fort Osage. He was an intelligent, energetic man and, uncommonly for the times, regarded public service as a high and honorable calling; he was so conscientious that he chronically suffered from sick headaches and other ailments that now would be diagnosed as work-related. He was not charismatic, being a bit pedantic and inhibited, but on the other hand, he was generous and kindly, and there was nothing about his personality that antagonized others.

The strange thing is that with all these advantages of official position and good character, Sibley accomplished relatively little on the frontier and had only a minimal influence on public affairs involving the Indians or later on the white settlers who moved into the territory. The sympathetic thing about him is that though his constituents and neighbors came to ignore or pass around him like a familiar pothole in the road, Sibley kept trying diligently to do the right thing, did not retreat into cynicism, sloth, petty meanness, drunkenness or other forms of escape.

Perhaps as good an explanation as can be made is that Sibley provides a classic example of a round peg in a square hole, of a good man placed in circumstances in which there was not much use for his special virtues and talents. He was a native of Massachusetts, a fact that in itself put him at a disadvantage in the frontier society in which the style was set by men and families from the southern mountains and backwoods. His father was a respected Revolutionary physician, a public servant and a prominent member of the coastal intelligentsia. So was young George, which is what first brought him to the attention of Thomas Jefferson, the most notable member of that class. By association, training and temperament, he was a product of the Enlightenment, but he spent his public career in places and among people about as Unenlightened—in an academic sense—as could be imagined. He was a man who sought knowledge for the sake of knowledge, believed in rational analysis, planning and principled action. He would have made a splendid senior academic or Washington bureaucrat, with junior assistants and file clerks at his command. But he came to a place where pragmatism and empiricism ruled and in which extemporaneous, impetuous, often irrational action generally preceded any consideration of consequences.

An alien in this world, Sibley created his own. He ran Fort Osage like a proper government agency, meticulously collecting information about his bailiwick, forwarding detailed memos to Washington, making thoughtful, abstract suggestions about policy and conscientiously responding to requests and recommendations which came back to him from his distant superiors. In his spare time his pursuits and conduct were those of a cultured eastern gentleman. He maintained a wide correspondence and published thoughtful essays about the natural history, Indian customs and politics of the frontier.

In 1815 he married Mary Easton, the charming daughter of Rufus Easton, an important St. Louis politician and businessman. Mary Easton was a high-spirited, extremely independent girl who had gone east to school and came back to St. Louis with many advanced ideas, including some particularly strong opinions about the rights of women. To protect his bride against culture shock, Sibley built, though it strained his resources, the most stylish house on the frontier, which the couple modestly named Fountain Cottage. Among other furnishings he freighted upriver for his wife a piano with a fife and drum attachment, the only such instrument, it was thought, to be found west of the Mississippi. Along with eastern-style dining and conversation, Mary Sibley entertained guests with musical recitals. Those who could appreciate such things, among them Prince Maximilian of Wied, were astonished by this oasis of culture in the Wild West.

All this struck the Sibleys' Indian, military and settler associates as bizarre and frivolous. Even so, Sibley was treated politely because of his office and also, it seems, because both he and his wife were decent, well-meaning people. However, the local judgment was obviously that they were not the sort to be taken seriously in practical, real-life matters.

Joel Walker recollected that when the family arrived at Fort Osage, they "rented" all the land they could, but this was a euphemism for squatted since there was no land that anybody, even George Sibley, could rent or sell, Fort Osage being beyond the settlement line for whites. By previous treaty negotiation with the Osage, a tract six miles square surrounding the post had been purchased as a government reservation. This was administered by Sibley, and a few hundred acres were sporadically farmed or grazed to raise food for the fort. Also, for a time Sibley used part of the tract for an Indian education project which was dear to his heart and is illustrative of how his administrative mind worked. Thinking ahead about future relations between the races, Sibley concluded that the only hope for his Indians, the Osage, was to adopt white ways and become farmers. He set about organizing a program of instruction aimed at showing the Osage how to become respectable American citizens. It was a perfectly good and humanitarian idea and might have worked to the lasting benefit of both races if the subjects of the experiment had been farsighted, enlightened people on the order of George Sibley. But in fact, they were nomadic, pugnacious, hedonistic horse Indians, who supported themselves and took much of their pleasure by hunting and raiding neighboring tribes.

To advance his plan, Sibley arranged to obtain a shipment of plows, rakes and other agricultural implements. He patiently explained their use to the Osage, then turned the equipment over to the tribe. The Indians were perplexed by the complexity of the tools and disdainful of the heavy, repetitious work that using them seemed to require. However, they shortly figured out how to break up the implements and found useful ways to use the bits of iron around their lodges and in their hunts and raids. Sibley was a persistent man and decided that the Indians had not understood how well they would be rewarded if they farmed and harvested in the white fashion. He therefore directed the men stationed at the fort to plow and plant several fields of corn and wheat. He told the Osage these were to be their crops, and the Indians who came to trade at the post watched with some amusement as the white men sweated away in the fields throughout the Missouri summer. When the grain ripened, Sibley brought together the nearby members of the tribe and formally presented the ready-to-harvest fields to them. Well satisfied, he retired for the day. The next morning, when he went out on a tour of inspection, he found the crops trampled flat by Indian horses. The Osage were essentially a carnivorous people and, having no inclination to collect, store or even eat the grain themselves, had decided that the best thing to do with the gift was to feed it to their ponies. The most efficient means was to bring the animals to the fodder, rather than the other way around.

By the time the Walkers arrived Sibley had abandoned the effort to turn the Osage into Pennsylvania Dutchmen, and in fact, very little farming of any sort was being done around the fort since it was garrisoned by only a skeleton company. In consequence there was plenty of open land in the Six Mile Country, as the whites were to subsequently call the reservation, but it remained legally unavailable for settlement. There is no record from either side of how George Sibley initially greeted the Walkers, but his style would have been first to explain in great detail their status and that of the land, then to take all the names and dates and pertinent facts to be used in a long report which would be sent to Washington to gather dust. It is likely that having done his bureaucratic duty, Sibley, as a hospitable man who probably welcomed having some white neighbors as reasonably respectable as the Walkers, would have pitched in and personally done everything he could to help the family settle.

The Walkers, McClellans and Sibleys did not become close social friends—not surprisingly, given the cultural differences between them. However, during the next ten years there are many indications, mostly found in George Sibley's daybooks, that they became good, cooperative and mutually respectful neighbors. Abraham McClellan traded black-smithing tools and work with Sibley. Joel Walker sold him bearskins. Jane Walker McClellan gave the Sibleys some lessons in how to plant and prune apple trees. Sibley lent Joe Walker $50, and when government contracts enabled him to hire temporary help, he often saw to it that the Walkers and McClellans got these jobs and cash windfalls.

Though there were considerable patches of open prairie in the Six Mile tract, the Walkers picked a small creek valley west of the fort for their first homesite. They did so—as did all the emigrants from the Appalachians who came to the territory in that time—because the hollow was heavily timbered. Not only were they familiar with the construction properties of wood, but the trees, tangles of underbrush and dampness seemed to provide a certain amount of psychic security. (Azubah Chiles was the matriarch of a large Appalachian clan that arrived shortly after the Walkers and during the next thirty years was to be involved in various joint enterprises with them. "This," said Azubah, of the bottomland where the Chiles built their first cabin, "is where I want my home. It looks like Kentucky.")

The nearby prairies had much deeper and richer soil than did the creek bottoms, but the settlers did not discover this for a decade. The prairie sod was too tough to be broken by their light, primitive plows, and initially the mountaineers did not try to do so. Their reasoning was that if land could not even grow proper trees, it was worthless for crops. The Walkers therefore proceeded, as had three generations of their forebears, to hack out a clearing in the woods, using walnut, the predominant hardwood in the Missouri bottoms, for their cabins and fences. During their first few months in the Six Mile Country they would have been glad for any help Sibley and his men could give and at times may have used the fort for temporary shelter. The weather, which had been so mild as they traveled westward from Franklin, turned exceptionally bad shortly after their arrival. On December 12, according to Sibley's records, it snowed, and before Christmas the long eddy in front of the fort froze solid. Blizzards continued until March 1, and all in all, the winter was a very hard one for that part of the country.

Nevertheless, McClellan and the Walkers got their cabin up, the first civilian house other than the Sibleys' Fountain Cottage in the Six Mile Country. Since it was the style universally favored by people from the southern Appalachians, the cabin was probably a double one, the two buildings being connected by a roofed but otherwise open passageway called a dog run. Initially one of the cabins was used for family sleeping and cooking, and the other for stock and storage. Later, when other sheds were built, both parts of the double cabin were taken over as family quarters. The dog run gave a sheltered passageway between them and in the summer served as a kitchen.

In the spring, after completing the building and fencing some stump-filled fields, they put in a crop of corn, planted the apple trees they had brought from Tennessee and set up the smithshop. Having established this base and done their part in providing for the women and children, Joel and Joe Walker left the family in the charge of Abraham McClellan and their younger brother, John, and separately set off to take a look at the much farther West.

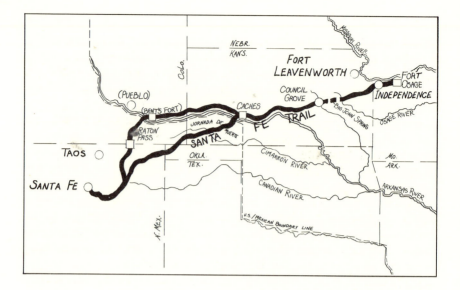

Santa Fe

Joel Walker was not a literary stylist, but he demonstrated a remarkable gift for brevity in the twenty-page autobiography he dictated. After recalling that the Walkers and McClellans put in a crop in the spring of 1820, he explained the next year or so of his life only as follows: "Then I went to Texas, but did not like it and returned to Osage in 1821."

It may have been that the family originally planned to make a temporary stay in Missouri and then move on to Texas, where Moses and Stephen Austin, with the encouragement of the Spanish government, were in the process of establishing a permanent colony of American settlers. However, Joel Walker's single sentence is the only mention any of them ever made of the matter, and if they were contemplating going to Texas, his unfavorable report obviously decided them against it. Most of them remained around Fort Osage for the next twenty years, the original emigrants being joined by the remaining Walker brother, Samuel, and his wife, Barbara (Toomy) and their children; two sisters, Susan and Lucy (who married, respectively, Lucian Ailstock and Ambrose Toomy); a number of McClellans, Toomys, Willises, Pattersons, Hayeses and other kin.

Of this time Joe Walker left even less of a written record than Joel, only—fifty-some years later—instructions that his tombstone bear the line "To New Mexico—1820." However, before that, in conversations with friends, he had elaborated a bit more on his doings in 1820. He said that he joined a party of fur trappers with the intention of going first to New Mexico and then on to California. If so, it was an ambitious plan since at the time no Americans were known to have traveled overland to that Pacific territory, and there were only rumors about the directions, distances and dangers involved.

Walker and his companions, whoever they may have been, were not successful. In New Mexico they were intercepted by the Spanish military and briefly imprisoned in Santa Fe. They were released on the condition that they immediately leave the Spanish territory and return to Missouri. They obeyed, at least to the extent of getting out of New Mexico. This is all that Walker himself is ever known to have said about his first expedition to the far west, but others were to enlarge and embellish, turning it into a campfire story. The first published version was contributed by Washington Irving. Describing Walker as "strong built, dark complexioned, brave in spirit, though mild in manners," Irving wrote: "He had resided for many years in Missouri, on the frontier; had been among the earliest adventurers to Santa Fe, where he went to trap beaver, and was taken by the Spaniards. Being liberated, he engaged with the Spaniards and Sioux Indians in a war against the Pawnees. . . ."

Except for a short VIP tour of government posts in Oklahoma, Irving never visited the west, nor did he meet Walker, but he wrote four books about the region and frequently, if often inaccurately, about the man. The Spanish-Sioux-Pawnee war story was composed in 1836, fifteen years after the events supposedly occurred, while he was in his study in New York and Walker was living with the Shoshoni in Idaho. It has the sound of a concoction, part of the Walker story, fortified with parts of another well-known and much gaudier yarn told and probably invented by one James Ohio Pattie.

Pattie came to Santa Fe with his father in 1824 and wandered about the southwest for the next six years. Upon returning to the States, he wrote one of the great picaresque traveler's tales of American literature and made himself a reputation of being, if not a great explorer, at least the Münchausen of the early southwest. In Santa Fe, Pattie said that like Walker, he was imprisoned. While he was languishing in jail, Comanches raided the territory and among others captured the beautiful daughter of the governor of New Mexico. Immediately James Ohio, his father and three American companions were released and sent off after the Indians. They overtook and routed them, then retrieved the captive beauty. Returning triumphantly to Santa Fe, they were given permission by the grateful governor to trap, trade or do almost anything else they wanted in his jurisdiction. At least in his book, James Ohio had such adventures every month or so, but few of them, including this one, can be documented or were verified by others and have been dismissed as entertaining sketches. However, Pattie's book was published several years before Irving wrote about Walker and would have been available to him if he had felt the need to do some literary embroidery work to introduce his character as a genuine frontier hero. There is the strong suspicion that he did.

If, after being released by the Spanish, Walker returned to Missouri, there are no reminiscences or records of his being there during the next few years. Many of those who have become interested in the activities of Americans in the Spanish Southwest during this period assume that he almost immediately went back to New Mexico or perhaps never left it, having simply gone far enough back into the mountains to elude the Spanish police. The deductive consensus of historians is that he became one of the first of a shadowy band of American adventurers collectively known as the Taos trappers, after the small mountain village in northern New Mexico which they used as a hide- and hangout.

Because they were instrumental in opening both the Santa Fe Trail and the American fur trade in the Rockies, the Taos trappers have intrigued western scholars, but very little is known about what they did or even who they were, for out of necessity they were extremely secretive. Once they left Missouri and entered the territory reserved for Indians, they were non-persons so far as the U.S. government was concerned and received no protection from it. They became illegal aliens when they crossed the Spanish—and after the Revolution of 1821, Mexican—boundaries and proceeded as fugitives, smugglers and dealers in contraband goods. When they could, they avoided the Santa Fe authorities. When they could not, their treatment varied according to the personalities and policies of individual administrators there. Some like Walker and probably Pattie were harassed, jailed and deported. On other occasions, for suitable, under-the-table considerations, they were allowed to go about their fur trapping and trading business discretely, if illegally. In such cases, neither the Americans nor the Santa Fe officials cared to talk much or leave written records about their transactions.

The existence of the Taos trappers reflected the fact that during the second decade of the nineteenth century Americans had grown increasingly interested in the commercial potential of New Mexico, a district which then included all of that present state, plus portions of what is now Chihuahua, Sonora, Texas, Oklahoma, Colorado, Utah and Arizona. The streams in the southwestern mountains had been virtually untrapped by the Spanish and Mexicans and were teeming with beaver. So far as trade went, the prospects were equally good. The two principal communities, Santa Fe and Chihuahua, were a long way from and not well served by either transportation routes or the merchants from Mexico City. Consequently they were starved for manufactured goods, and the closest source of these was Missouri, 800 miles northeast across the plains. Most attractive so far as the Americans were concerned, the New Mexicans had some productive mines and therefore silver with which to pay for anything that could be freighted to them. The difficulty was that the Spanish wanted no sort of free trade with their northern neighbor and, except when bribes temporarily changed the situation, thought consumer shortages in their northern provinces were preferable to Missouri traders bringing goods into and taking specie and furs out of them. During the last ten years of their rule the Spanish authorities in New Mexico were constantly being challenged by Americans who thought the risks of illegal trapping and smuggling were warranted by the potential profits. Some were unquestionably successful, but because they were, little is known about them. Most of the surviving records have to do with entrepreneurs who got caught.

Among them was a party from St. Louis led by James Baird, Robert McKnight and Samuel Chambers, who got into New Mexico in 1812. They were apprehended by Spanish border patrols, held and interrogated for a time in Santa Fe and then sent south to Chihuahua, where they spent the next eight years in prison. In 1815 Auguste Chouteau, a member of the great St. Louis fur trading family, and his partner, Jules De Mun, trapped in the mountains of New Mexico and Colorado but were eventually captured and chained up in Santa Fe. They were held for forty-four days and threatened with death by Pedro María de Allande, the governor and a notable anglophobe. Finally, Allande took all their furs, valued at $30,000, made them kneel before him and kiss the paper upon which was written a record of their crimes, then threw them out of the country with only the supplies they could carry on their backs. All, however, got back safely to Missouri. Chouteau shortly reentered the fur trade, but De Mun had had enough. He emigrated to Cuba and became a successful cigar manufacturer.

Ezekiel Williams was a veteran ranger and Indian fighter from the Boonslick Country, who went to the plains in 1813. He was first captured and robbed by the Kansas Indians and the next year picked up by the Spanish. Perhaps because he had the foresight to cache his furs before capture and therefore had no ransom, he was released and deported after a relatively short stay in jail. Williams was persistent and returned in 1815 for his hidden furs. This time he was successful and returned to Missouri. However, one of his partners in the venture, a M. Champlain, did not. Williams said he had been killed by the Indians, but shortly so much circumstantial evidence to the contrary turned up that Williams, of whom it was said he "loved Mammon more than God," was booked on a suspicion of having murdered Champlain for his share of the furs. A spectacular trial followed, but eventually Williams was acquitted. Almost immediately the widow of another partner brought a suit claiming Williams had wrongfully withheld her share of the profits from the enterprise. This case was settled out of court, whereupon another woman accused Williams of bigamy. These and later litigations kept him off the plains for a good many years.

Despite such difficulties, the Americans kept trying. In 1820, in addition to Joe Walker and his band of trappers, another American, David Meriwether, attempted to reach Santa Fe, and his experiences may also have been confused with and then combined with Walker's for storytelling purposes. Meriwether was a trader working out of the U.S. military post at Council Bluffs on the Missouri River. He traveled to New Mexico with a band of Pawnee. On the border they were surprised by the Spanish cavalry. Thirteen of the seventeen Pawnee were killed, and Meriwether and his black servant were taken prisoner. They were held in Santa Fe but released after their goods had been confiscated. Much later Meriwether got a measure of, if not revenge, at least satisfaction. After his release he went home to Kentucky and in the next twenty-five years became a prominent politician in that state. In 1853 he returned to the southwest as the American governor of the newly acquired territory of New Mexico.

In 1821 rumors about the imminent overthrow of the Spanish by the Mexican nationalists were circulating in Missouri. In hopes that they might be true and that the situation had changed for the better, at least three groups of American traders started out for New Mexico in that year. One was led by Thomas James, a pompous, irascible merchant who floated down the Mississippi to the mouth of the Arkansas and then headed due west through Oklahoma and Texas. The men finally reached Santa Fe but lost most of their trade goods, and James infuriated many of the Indians, Mexicans and Americans he met along the way. A better organized party of better men was led by Hugh Glenn, an Arkansas River trader, and Jacob Fowler, a trapper. They came up the Arkansas and through southern Kansas in the fall of 1821. Fowler kept a journal of the expedition, and it has delighted readers ever since, as perhaps the most orthographically creative of all American literary works. By way of example, Fowler wrote about the commencement of the trip as he and his men rendezvoused with Glenn: "but we Stoped at the trading Hous of Conl Hugh glann about mile up the virdegree Wheare We Remained till the 25th Sept makeing a Raingment for our gurney to the mountains—Heare five of our Hunters Left us and Went Home this Sircumstance much dispereted more of our men—tho We Still determined to purced—and on the 25th of Sept 1821 We found our Selves 20 men in all."

The third Santa Fe expedition of that year was led by William Becknell, a ferryboat operator and sometime manager of the Boone salt lick in central Missouri. Hearing reports about the situation in Santa Fe, Becknell, in August, advertised in the Franklin newspaper for people interested in joining him in a trading venture to New Mexico. Seventeen men showed up for the organizational meeting, which was held at the home of Ezekiel Williams, who was temporarily between court appearances. (Williams acted as a consultant but did not go on the trip.) Leaving in September, Becknell's party struck straight across the plains and were the first of the Americans to reach New Mexico that year, arriving in mid-November. They camped outside Santa Fe while Becknell cautiously went into town to appraise the temper of the place. He found that indeed the revolution had occurred and that the Mexicans were jubilantly celebrating their independence. They invited Becknell to join them and bring his trade goods.

Glenn and Fowler were the next to appear, followed in January by James, who had been saved from the Comanche by Mexican soldiers. The first two American parties did a fine business, but James did not and complained bitterly about how he was mistreated by both his Mexican rescuers and fellow Americans. He probably was, if for no other reason than he had such a wretched personality.

While Hugh Glenn continued trading in town, Jacob Fowler took most of the party into the mountains for beaver. The trapping was good, but the winter was bitter, "the Wind Was So Cold We Scarce dare look Round," wrote Fowler. Even so, Becknell, having got in early and made a killing, decided to risk a trip to Missouri across the blizzard-whipped plains. When he got back to Franklin in February, he and the four men who returned with him (the remainder stayed to trap beaver) made a grand gesture. They untied rawhide bundles from their saddles and threw them down, letting 10,000 Mexican silver dollars roll around on the main street of the town. After the money had been picked up, one local woman who had entrusted $60 to Becknell received $900 in return. Other investors did equally well.

Several Missouri and Santa Fe historians have guessed that Joe Walker and William Wolfskill, another notable Taos trapper, were among those who rode with Becknell in 1821 and 1822. However, this is an unprovable, if reasonable, assumption since the only record of the trip was left by Becknell and he mentioned none of the names of the men with him. Whether he came back with Becknell, stayed in New Mexico or someplace in between, Walker's exact whereabouts then and for the next year cannot now be determined, but in 1823 he made what was in a sense his personal entrance into recorded western history. Fittingly it was dramatic.

Writing to a Maryland physician who was contemplating emigrating to the Fort Osage area, George Sibley devoted several pages to praising the climate, fertility and natural resources of the place. Then he added that frankly there was one serious problem. "*Cash* is a very commanding commodity. It has a preference over any other. Our People are generally poor and want Money to purchase land."

At the time there was a general depression, and money was tight throughout the country, but especially in western Missouri because of its distance from eastern markets. The local economy was largely a subsistence and barter one, and the people lacked cash not only for land but for manufactured necessities and luxuries of all sorts. Therefore, when William Becknell and his men flung 10,000 silver dollars into the streets of Franklin, they touched off a bonanza-type stampede for Santa Fe. Becknell himself stayed in Franklin only long enough to get new trade goods and then started back to New Mexico in May 1822. He led a party of twenty-one men and three freight wagons, the first to travel between Missouri and Mexican territories. For this reason he has rightly been remembered as the founder of the Santa Fe Trail as a formal trade route.

At least two other companies of prospective traders took packtrains across the plains that year. They all did well, and the next spring most of the able-bodied young men in western Missouri were either packing up or trying to find the capital to go to Santa Fe. The first party to leave in 1823 was organized by Stephen Cooper, a pioneer settler in the Boonslick Country, and Joel Walker, back from Texas. There were thirty-one men in the group, all packing their goods on horses or mules. They moved easily until they reached the Little Arkansas River, west of what is now McPherson, Kansas. There they halted on June 1 to rest their animals and hunt buffalo. At dawn the next day they were surprised by Pawnee raiders, who stampeded most of their horses and mules. Joel Walker leaped out of his blankets and, naked as a jaybird, ran for a quarter of a mile across the prairie in pursuit of the Indians. Realizing this was hopeless as well as undignified, he went back to camp, put on his boots and pants, rounded up the horses that remained and with four companions rode off after the Pawnees, but the Indians had too much of a start to be overtaken. The party was left, as Cooper reported, "four hundred miles from home, in a savage country, all afoot, and all our effects in a few dry goods."

Walker, Cooper and two other men took four horses of the six they had saved and, while the remainder of the men stood guard over the Santa Fe dry goods, went back to Missouri to get fresh stock and supplies. They made a fast ride, making the 800-mile round trip in just twenty-two days. With remounts, they rejoined their stranded companions toward the end of June and then moved on to the Arkansas River. Shortly they were in more and worse trouble. Between the Arkansas and the Cimarron they entered the *jornada*, 100 miles of dreadful desert which was to claim a number of Santa Fe traders even after its topography had become better known. Leaving the last water on the Arkansas, they stumbled through the *jornada* for a day and a half under the blazing sun. Then, Walker said, "the men began to give out." He took eighteen of the strongest and went ahead, looking for water. By great good luck they found a small stagnant temporary pond which a herd of buffalo was in the process of drinking and wallowing dry. Five of the men were sent back to bring the others to this hole. Walker and the remainder of his scouts stayed behind to keep the buffalo out of the water.

Two days passed, and Walker decided that the first relief party had lost its way. Thereupon he started off alone, looking for the main company and carrying a water bag made out of the green thigh skin of a freshly killed buffalo. He was in the saddle for twenty-four hours before finding the thirst-weakened men, who gratefully sipped the slimy, stinking water he brought. In the evening it began to thunder and then, miraculously, to rain, an unusual phenomenon for that place and one which probably saved their lives. They caught water in whatever containers they could improvise, saving enough to recruit their strength and that of their horses. However, in the morning it seemed as if they might be in for another very bad, perhaps terminal day, as camp guards spotted a band of mounted men riding rapidly toward them. Joel Walker and another man went out to intercept the strangers, hoping to negotiate with them since their party was too weak and scattered to put up much of a fight. "I kept my eyes on them and *saw*, as I supposed, an Indian with his hair flying up and down. He came up and to my immense astonishment, I saw he was my brother, Capt. Joe Walker. . . ."

Surprised and pleased as the brothers must have been to meet in such a strange place and way, their situation remained precarious.

Between them they had fifty-one men and more horses and mules. All were in urgent need of water. Traveling with Joe Walker was a Comanche, who among the whites went by the name of Francisco Largo. Largo said that he thought he could find a desert water hole, and would ride ahead to look for it. The Comanche set off and shortly disappeared, leaving no trail the Walkers could follow. For the next two days they were thoroughly and seriously lost, the first and last time this is known to have happened to a party which included Joe Walker. Finally, abandoning the search for Largo, they decided that their only chance of survival was to backtrack in hopes of finding the Arkansas before it was too late. At dusk on the third grim, waterless day following their reunion, the Walkers came upon the blessed river. Following their trail, the rest of the men straggled into camp during the night. By morning all except one were accounted for, and the Walkers went back into the *jornada*, carrying water bottles, to look for him. Joel Walker recalled laconically:

> The weather was very hot. After travelling sometime we saw something upon the plains, which upon closer inspection proved to be our man Will Haddard. He had killed a Buffalo and was sucking the blood of the animal to quench his intolerable thirst. When he saw us he inquired, "have you got any water?" We gave him some and put him upon a mule when he said "I had better drink some more blood!" He had crawled into the dead Buffalo and came out a spectacle to behold. He was covered with blood. We got him to camp that night, and next day he was taken to the creek, soaped and washed; had his hair cut, and made him look more like a human being.

Having done what they could for the thirst-demented Will Haddard, the Walkers had a chance to exchange traveler's stories. Joe explained that he had gone out the fall before with a party of Santa Fe traders. They had been caught on the plains by a blizzard and made a camp on the Arkansas upstream from where the Walkers then were. The snows continued, and thinking they could not get through them with their heavily loaded pack animals, they had dug two large pits in the sandy riverbank, lined them with cottonwood bark, put their trade goods in the holes and camouflaged them to hide them from thieving Indians. Then they had ridden on and spent the winter in Taos and Santa Fe. In the spring Walker had gathered together Largo and the others he had with him and returned to the Arkansas for the buried goods. After doing so, he had found signs indicating a white party in trouble on the desert and for that reason eventually came upon his brother. (There being no reason to do otherwise, Walker had left the pits on the Arkansas uncovered, and the empty holes remained for years as a notable landmark along the Santa Fe Trail known as the Caches.)

This was all of the matter Joel Walker reported, the previous history of the party that made the caches being then well known on the frontier. Its organizers were James Baird and Samuel Chambers, two of the men who had been captured by the Spaniards in 1812 and spent the next eight years in a Chihuahua jail. Released in 1821 as part of a general amnesty ordered by the new Mexican government, they had returned to St. Louis. There, hearing about the money to be made in Santa Fe, they had arranged for credit and supplies and, incredibly, considering what they had been through in the previous decade, started back to New Mexico, so eager to get there that they left Missouri in November, after the normal travel season had ended. They paid for their impatience by being caught in the snowstorms on the Arkansas. Since Joel had not previously known his brother's whereabouts, the presumption is that Joe Walker picked up Baird and Chambers and their men someplace on the plains, perhaps when he was on his way back after the fall trapping season of 1822.

The Walkers rested their men and animals for several days on the Arkansas and were rejoined by Francisco Largo, who said he had become worried about them. Thereafter they had easy going. "We went up the Arkansas and reached the Lower Cimeron Springs, and from that place had no more trouble until we reached Santa Fe," Joel Walker economically described the last 300 miles of the trip. Of Santa Fe he said, "The women were all friendly, and told us what was going on. We had two bales of bleached domestic which we sold for Forty five Dollars a bale. We could have sold Calicoes and Cotton for any price asked. A little looking glass worth about ten cents was easily sold for a dollar."

Despite these prices, Joel Walker and Stephen Cooper did not make such a killing as some of the first traders did because their troubles, especially having to return to Missouri in mid-trip and buy more mules and horses, ran up the overhead. However, they did well enough with the friendly Santa Fe women so that when he returned to Missouri, Joel Walker was able to wed Mary Young, the daughter of another family of Tennessee immigrants.

Joe Walker apparently stayed on again in New Mexico, trapping for beaver. Ewing Young, a relative of his new sister-in-law, was doing the same. Also, James Baird remained in Santa Fe as a fur buyer, becoming, despite his previous difficulties, a Mexican citizen. (A year or so later he wrote indignantly to the authorities about the wretched foreigners—that is, the American trappers of Taos—who were undercutting his fur business. As a responsible Mexican citizen Baird demanded that something be done about these illegal aliens.)

In the late fall of 1824 William Becknell came back to Santa Fe and, when his trading was finished, decided to spend the winter in the Green River country, trying his luck with the beaver. He did not have much, as he graphically reported when he got back to Missouri the next spring:

> While at our winter camp we hunted when we could, and the remainder of the time attempted to sleep, so as to dream of the abundance of our own tables at home, and the dark rich tenants of our smoke-houses. . . . Although we were forty days from settlements, the snow three or four feet deep, and our small stock of horses, our principal reliance for effecting a retreat, considered sacred, so that to have eaten them would have been like dining upon our own feet, we still contrived to supply our tables, if not with the dainties of life, with food of the most substantial kind. For instance, we subsisted two days on soup made of a raw hide reserved for soaling our moccasins; on the following morning the remains were dished up into a hash. The young men employed by me had seen better days, and had never before been supperless to bed, nor missed a wholesome and substantial meal at the regular family hour, except one, who was with me when I opened the road to Santa Fe.

Walker fits the description of Becknell's single veteran companion, being one of the few Americans with mountain experience not otherwise engaged. However, Becknell in his brief report did not identify any of the men with him that hard winter. Wherever he spent it, Walker was back at Fort Osage by the early summer of 1825. From there he returned to the plains as a guide and hunter for the government party commissioned to lay out the Santa Fe Trail.

In March 1825 as one of his final presidential acts, James Monroe signed a bill appropriating $30,000 to survey and mark a wagon route to New Mexico and to buy easements for it across the territory of several Indian tribes. The principal congressional sponsor of this legislation, Senator Thomas Hart Benton of Missouri, triumphantly proclaimed that because of it, a grand international highway would soon grace the plains, but this was hyperbole, of which Benton was a master. Even at the prices of the time it was obvious to everyone the appropriation was not enough to build a true road across 800 miles of wilderness. However, the $30,000 was sufficient for making a handsome political and public relations gesture. The act gave formal federal approval to western commerce and expansion, confounded the Little America interests that opposed it, put some Manifest Destiny handwriting on the wall for the instruction of the new Mexican government and, of course, demonstrated to the voters of Missouri that Thomas Hart Benton was a senator with clout.

The field survey was supervised by three federal commissioners. The first two, Thomas Mather and Benjamin Reeves, were appointed principally because they represented political and commercial factions that had supported the bill. The third man was George Sibley, named because he was a career civil servant with long frontier experience. The appointment came much to his surprise and pleasure since at the time he was in the midst of a personal financial crisis and the money he received was a godsend. Sibley commenced the project with his usual bureaucratic diligence, and since the other two men were not as zealous as he about the job, he became, in effect, the executive director of the commission.

The first task for the commissioners was to hire thirty-five men for the field survey party. The pay was only $20 a month for ordinary hands, but this was an attractive salary in cash-short Missouri, "sufficiently lucrative," as the *Franklin Intelligencer* commented editorially, "to enable each of the persons engaged in this service to pay for a tract of land on their return." In consequence there was considerable competition for the public works jobs, and many applicants lined up local political patrons to bring some pressure to bear on their behalf. Sibley, however, warned the other commissioners that life on the plains was hard and that "We do not want a party of Gentlemen Coffee Drinkers, who cannot even cook their own Victuals or Saddle their own Horses." He thought every hand should be a rifleman and should understand that he would not be receiving a "constant and regular supply of bread."

Informally the commissioners divided the appointments among them. Reeves and Mather with a good sense of political reality gave most of theirs to men from more populous areas around St. Louis and Franklin. Sibley was more concerned with merit and held open his final selection until the party assembled at Fort Osage, designated as the official trailhead. There he hired five frontier neighbors who he at least knew were not gentlemen coffee drinkers. Joe Walker and his younger brother, Big John, got two of these jobs. The last man picked was Bill Williams, who was met on the plains and hired as the survey's interpreter.

Having been residents of the same sparsely settled border district and engaged in the same lines of work, Walker and Williams were almost certainly acquainted with each other previously, but the Santa Fe survey was the first time their paths documentably crossed. The two were the most experienced frontiersmen employed by the survey and of its members were to become the most famous figures in western history. They were equals in boldness and as creative trailblazers and survivors but were so different in personality, that if the frontier temperament can be thought of as a coin, they came close to representing its opposite sides.

Williams was famed for his raw physical courage but also for his savagery, being capable of frightening binges of both drunkenness and unadulterated sadism. Whereas Walker seemed to find joy in roaming the west and satisfaction in leading others about it, Williams increasingly became a dangerous loner who escaped into the wilderness for misanthropic reasons and often preyed on others who encountered him there. On later occasions Walker and Williams cooperated, and each may have had a grudging admiration for the abilities of the other; but a showdown between two men of such disparate character was all but inevitable. It occurred, but twenty years later and 1,500 miles farther west.

When he joined the Santa Fe survey in 1825, Williams was already regarded as something of an eccentric, but people were not then—as they would later—calling him Crazy Bill. Like Walker, he was a big man, but grotesque rather than handsome. He had a tall, rawboned, Ichabod Crane frame and sat a horse in an ungainly fashion, long arms and legs, sharp elbows and knees flapping like those of a scarecrow. His gait, taking immense strides but throwing his legs to the side, was peculiar and often commented upon, as were his immense strength and endurance. Sidling on foot or flopping on his horse, often talking to himself, he could keep going long after most men had played out from exhaustion.

Williams was ten years older than Walker, having been born in the North Carolina mountains in 1787. His family were among the very early immigrants to Missouri, settling upriver from St. Louis near St. Charles in 1795. Williams was apparently a farm boy of exceptional intellect and imagination, gifts for which there was limited use and regard in his early environment. In other places and times he might have been a passionate poet, iconoclastic scholar or creative scientist, but in frontier Missouri he became a spellbinding seventeen-year-old preacher with, it was said, remarkable ability to arouse camp meeting crowds. Later several stories circulated about why he left the ministry: that he had been run out by the scandalized and the cuckolded; that he drank and womanized as hard as he preached; that he had been jilted by a highborn beauty and left the settlements in despair and with his rifle and jug.

For whatever reasons, he moved in with the Osage when he was twenty-five years old and married a woman of the tribe. The Osage

called him *Pah-hah-soo-gee-ah* ("The Red-Haired Sharpshooter") and
were very impressed by his abilities as a hunter, warrior and preacher
of drunken, mystical sermons which grew less Christian and more
Indianish as time passed. Williams became the government agent for
the tribe and, to facilitate his work, compiled an Osage-English dic-
tionary, the first such reference in the west. Also, he commenced an
anthropological work having to do with the customs of the plains
tribes. It was eventually lost or destroyed, but companions said that
for some years, in moments of sobriety and serenity, Crazy Bill labored
over this manuscript. In 1824 Williams left the Osage and went off
with a white company to trap in the northern Rockies. He traveled
at least as far as the upper Columbia River but returned in the spring
of 1825 in time to join the Santa Fe survey. Whatever his failings
and idiosyncrasies, Williams was probably the best man the commissioners could have engaged as an interpreter and Indian negotiator.
He was trusted by the Osage, through whose lands much of the northern section of the trail passed and, because of his association with
them, familiar with and to the other plains nations.

The three commissioners and their crew began the field work on
July 17 at Fort Osage and for the next two weeks proceeded steadily
across Kansas. Joseph Brown, reportedly the best surveyor in Missouri, meticulously recorded distances and laid out the route to take
the greatest advantage of local topographic features. Originally, in
keeping with Benton's vision of a great international highway, it was
planned to designate the trail with imposing signs, but in most places
on the treeless short-grass prairie this was impossible. Therefore, the
work crews scraped up piles of dirt as markers. The Walkers and
other hunter-guides foraged ahead for game, scouted the route and
possible campsites. George Sibley contended with the paper work and
his frequent sick headaches. The other two commissioners, Mather
and Reeves, were less directly engaged and treated the assignment as
an interesting summer camping trip.

On the Neosho River, 150 miles from Fort Osage, they came to
a fine grove of trees—some of the last sizable ones they would find—
and decided to halt for a few days to allow their stock to forage in the
good grass. While they were there, Bill Williams rode in with fifty
of the principal Osage chiefs and warriors. After four days of negotiation and conviviality a treaty was made and signed, as official witnesses, by both Williams and Joe Walker. In return for $800 worth
of trade goods, the Osage agreed to let the trail pass through their
territories and never thereafter to molest any white travelers or merchants who might use it.

After the Osage had departed, George Sibley decided that since there was wood at hand, the historic occasion should be commemorated by something other than a pile of dirt. Therefore, he noted in his daybook, he "employed a young man of the party known to be remarkably expert in lettering with his pen knife and tomahawk, by name John Walker, commonly called in camp 'Big John,' in reference to his gigantic size." Sibley said that Big John "executed the order very neatly and substantially," incising a venerable white oak with the message "Council Grove, Aug. 10, 1825."

Except that he was an artist with a knife and hatchet, little is remembered about the personality of Big John Walker, who was to die young. However, perhaps because of his name, he emerges hazily from the past as an appealing figure—a huge, easygoing youngster, whittling away on a white oak trunk, less complex and driven than his more famous brothers, but steady and likable, ready to put his hands and back to whatever anybody needed done. Later he had another moment which Sibley found sufficiently interesting to note. Not far from Council Grove, Big John discovered an excellent prairie spring and brought back a bucketful of the pure water to Sibley, who, as was often the case, was indisposed in his tent. "He asked," reported Sibley, "what name it should have. I directed him to cut in large letters 'Big John's Spring' on a Big Oak that grows near it. He laughed, and with his knife and hatchet soon performed the work in excellent style."

Finding and marking his spring should have assured Big John Walker of a measure of limited immortality. However, seventeen years later a less placid young man, John Charles Frémont, passed by the place. He was a captain in the Topographical Corps, obsessed with his reputation, so the prairie water was renamed Fremont Spring. Thus Big John Walker lost his only formal memorial, but the rights and honors of first discovery remain inalienably his.

Within a week after the survey group had left Council Grove, Bill Williams rounded up the leaders of the Kansas tribe and brought them to the camp to sign a treaty similar to that made with the Osage. Then, without incident, the party continued westward, reaching on September 11 the Arkansas River at a point where, according to the calculations of surveyor Brown, it was crossed by the 100th degree of west longitude. There they halted for nearly three weeks for reasons that now seem comic but that also give a sense of the slow-paced, casual style in which public affairs were conducted in those days.

Despite all the legislative debate and later publicity about the Santa Fe project, and though more than half of the proposed trail ran through foreign territory, nobody had made certain that the Mexicans wanted or would permit such an improvement. Inquiries about the matter had been forwarded through Joel Poinsett, the American ambassador in Mexico City, but since no response was forthcoming, the commissioners had left Fort Osage on the vague assumption that somebody would get word to them before they got to the international boundary line, the conjunction of the Arkansas and the 100th meridian. Since they had no better information there than they had had in Missouri, they waited at the river through September and pondered what to do next. George Sibley was of the bureaucratic opinion that while it would not be right to mark the trail in Mexico without permission, they should proceed to Santa Fe and negotiate directly with the local authorities. Mather and Reeves, who were becoming bored with the field work and anxious to get back to business in the States, were opposed. Reeves said it was his impression that "the Mexican government was somewhat jealous about the little matter of the road," and they would be wrong to continue without definite instructions from Washington. They waited for these until October 1, which both Reeves and Mather agreed was too long. As a compromise, it was decided that Sibley could go ahead to New Mexico with a few men but that the other two commissioners would return with the main survey crew to Missouri. There, if they were able to find out anything, they would try to get a message to Sibley. If not, they agreed to meet again the next summer on the plains.

From the start the homeward-bound party moved slowly because while camped along the Arkansas, a number of their horses and mules had been stampeded by buffalo. They did not reach Council Grove until October 10, and by then many of the men were on foot and all were on very short rations. At this point, Mather, Joe Walker and the ubiquitous William Becknell—who had been hunting on the plains before accidentally meeting the survey—agreed to ride back to Missouri and return with supplies and fresh mounts. This they did. After adding Joel Walker to the rescue column, they retraced their steps from Fort Osage, finding Reeves and the other stragglers on October 21. The three yokes of oxen, horses and beef they brought with them constituted, as Reeves said, "very seasonable relief for us."

Meanwhile, George Sibley, accompanied by Bill Williams and Big John Walker, reached New Mexico. Finding a bivouac for his men in the congenial village of Taos, Sibley continued on to Santa Fe to deal with the authorities there. He was to remain for ten months, while messages slowly passed between that city, Washington and Mexico City. Eventually a kind of qualified permission was granted by the Mexicans, and Sibley and the others returned to Missouri but arrived too late in the summer of 1826 to do any more field work. Moreover, nearly everyone, including the other two commissioners and the Washington planners, had lost interest in the survey, the purpose of which, making a gesture, had already been accomplished. Sibley, however, was a dogged, literal-minded public servant, and while the other commissioners begged off, he went back onto the plains the next summer to recheck parts of the route. He was out only a month, and the survey work was never extended beyond the Mexican boundary. (Sibley alone continued to wrestle with the paper work the project had created until 1834.)

Even before Sibley returned with the final party, the dirt marker mounds they had erected were beginning to erode and disappear. Like these mounds, the physical accomplishments of the federal project were insignificant and impermanent. By then nobody needed to have the trail marked, and those who followed it created numerous private shortcuts which were little influenced by Joseph Brown's careful calculations. However, as Benton and others had foreseen, the symbolic effect of this public work was considerable. By 1831 American traders were grossing $2 million a year, at the rate of about a 300 percent profit on their investments, from the Santa Fe trade, a tenfold increase from 1824, the year before the survey started. Some of the growth might have occurred in any event, but the publicity surrounding the survey and the fact that it legitimized trade between the countries had a stimulating effect on the commerce and attracted many newcomers to it. Also, as again Benton had perhaps hoped, the survey and the trade that followed it served to focus the attention of Americans on the southwest and strongly recommended it as a territory which they were manifestly destined to possess.

Some years later Joe Walker discussed the Santa Fe Trail work with the same acquaintance to whom he described his ride on the first steamboat on the upper Missouri. He seemed to feel that the two experiences were somewhat similar, more interesting because of their historical symbolism than practical importance. Admitting that he and the others on the survey crew had not built a real road to Santa Fe or made the trail substantially more convenient for traders, Walker nevertheless reflected that at least they "broke the crust."

Jackson County

In late May 1827 George Sibley offered both Walker brothers jobs on the crew he took into the field for the last month of work on the Santa Fe survey. Big John went with Sibley, but three days after he was hired, Joe Walker resigned. Having recently been named sheriff of the newly organized Jackson County, he was persuaded that it would be unseemly for the only law officer in the jurisdiction to be gallivanting around the plains. Abraham McClellan was no doubt his chief persuader, appealing to family as well as civic obligations. McClellan remained the head of the clan so far as settlement business was concerned and for the previous two years he had been organizing Jackson County politically. He had made considerable use of his relatives and at that time had special need for his brother-in-law, the sheriff, since the first session of the county court, of which McClellan was president, was to convene on July 2.

McClellan was not by temperament or experience a wilderness man and never showed any inclination to get himself into positions where he had to eat his moccasins or drink buffalo blood. However, he was a good representative of another frontier type: the pioneer entrepreneur and politician. Economic self-interest was a large factor but does not entirely explain the motives of such men, many of whom were affluent before migrating. McClellan, for example, was well fixed in Tennessee but sold out and went west in part for the excitement of the thing. Being the founder of new settlements, commercial enterprises and political coalitions apparently stimulated and satisfied him as trailblazing did the Walker brothers. During the 1820s he pursued various community ventures as energetically and successfully as they did their wilderness ones.

In 1825 a treaty eliminated all the land claims of the Osage in western Missouri, opening the territory, including the Six Mile tract around Fort Osage, to legal white settlement. Thereupon McClellan, his son Mike, Joel, Joe and John Walker and the widow Annis Carrick filed land claims, collectively taking up about 1,500 acres of the best available land. Joel Walker—whose career as a traveler and trader on the plains was cut short by his marriage and the birth of his first child, a son, in 1825—thereafter farmed his own place. However, McClellan supervised most of the combined family holdings because Joe and Big John Walker were seldom available and not much inclined toward this kind of work. In addition to farming, McClellan set up a blacksmith shop and built a tavern and distillery. The three businesses were complementary and prospered as new settlers arrived. The emigration to western Missouri increased rapidly after 1825 because of the treaty with the Osage and changes in the Santa Fe trade which improved the local economy. Previously Franklin in the Boonslick Country had been the center for this commerce because it was the most westerly river port which steamboats could dependably reach with heavy freight. However, in the mid-1820s Franklin suffered a series of floods which damaged its commercial facilities. Also, steamboat pilots became familiar enough with the twisting river channels to run regularly above Fort Osage, twenty miles beyond which the Missouri made a great bend toward the north. The point of this elbow was the closest place on the river to Santa Fe, 100 overland miles closer than Franklin. It was obvious that a new terminal in this region would be convenient and profitable.

Fort Osage, then decommissioned, had become less desirable as a port because of shifts in the river channel. There was a much better place for a new community and trade center fifteen miles to the west at what is now Independence. Early in the summer of 1825, as his brothers and the rest of the survey party passed by on their way west, Joel Walker and his brother-in-law John Young were building the first house on this townsite. Three years later there were nearly 500 people in the community, and Independence was well on its way to becoming the first true western boom town. During the next thirty years it grew to be the largest city in the state, except for St. Louis, and the principal staging area for both the Santa Fe trade and the overland migration to Oregon and California.

The growth of Independence was more or less inevitable because of geographic location, but it developed as and when it did because of the efforts of individuals, especially Abraham McClellan. In 1826 at a "general election" (which seems to have been a cozy meeting of related families and close friends) he and Lilburn Boggs, who had been

George Sibley's assistant at the government factory, were elected unofficial representatives from the unorganized district to the state legislature. The alliance between these two and the Walkers was to be effective and enduring. During the next twenty years McClellan and Boggs were the political overlords of western Missouri, and in 1836, when Boggs became governor of Missouri, McClellan served as the state's treasurer. A little more than a decade later, Boggs and Joel Walker were members of the constitutional committee which organized the civil government of California.

McClellan and Boggs went to the state legislature essentially as lobbyists, with the objective of getting their district separated from Lafayette County, a sprawling one which then administered most of the state west of Franklin. They were successful, and in December 1826 the legislature created the new county, which was called Jackson and included the area now occupied by both Independence and Kansas City, Missouri. Joe Walker was later to say he was one of the principal advocates for naming the new jurisdiction in honor of Andrew Jackson. He would have had little opposition in this matter, for Old Hickory was the universal hero of the West, and twenty counties in trans-Appalachia states were eventually named for him. Among the first county officials, at least the two Walkers and one of the presiding judges, Richard Fristoe, had served at Horseshoe Bend under Jackson.

Once established as a legislative entity, the district was organized by the Scotch-Irish clans from the southern Appalachians according to the principles of cronyism. That system was certainly not invented in Jackson County but was to flourish splendidly there and become something of a political art form by the twentieth century. The first two appointments were made in March 1827 by the governor. He named Richard Todd, who was from the Boonslick Country—but at least a Kentuckian—as the first circuit court judge and Joe Walker as the first sheriff. The initial circuit court session was held in the oldest house in Independence, which had been built by Joel Walker, who at about the same time became the acting justice of the peace for the county. He assumed office apparently by general agreement since there was no election or specific appointment. In this capacity he administered the oath of office to Abraham McClellan, who had been appointed by the governor, as president of the panel of three county judges. (Under the Missouri system these officials acted as county commissioners, and their responsibilities were more executive and administrative than judicial.) McClellan then swore in the other two judges, Richard Fristoe and Henry Burris. They in turn established township lines within the county and made Joel Walker the official justice of the peace of Fort Osage township. Thereafter Joel Walker had no more immediate duties and went off to join the Santa Fe survey party as a substitute for his brother Joe, the sheriff.

These ad hoc arrangements were confirmed at the first local election, held in the summer of 1828. Most of the original appointees won easily, Joe Walker, for example, being returned as sheriff by winning 150 of the 179 votes cast. Only Abraham McClellan had any trouble in this canvass. By then some outsiders and even Yankees had settled in the rapidly growing community of Independence. Many of them had apparently become restive about McClellan's way of doing things since that township voted for his opponent, a local tavernkeeper, by a two to one margin in the race for state representative. However, McClellan carried the county by a single vote, collecting 42 of the 43 votes cast in his home township of Osage. There the polling place was located in the farm home of Joel Walker, and according to the custom of the time, voters walked in and without the benefit of a private booth gave both their own names and those of their electoral choices to a clerk, who certified their ballots.

Walker's handsome majority is good evidence that he had been a popular and probably an effective sheriff during the eighteen months he served before the election. This was confirmed by an anonymous contributor to the first history of Jackson County who commented that as a sheriff Walker was "never a braggart, soft spoken yet capable of maintaining discipline." Based on such records, recollections and the fact that by the late 1820s Independence was attracting hard customers from the Santa Fe and Rocky Mountain fur trade, stories later circulated that Joe Walker was the first of the gunslinging western sheriffs of the Earp-Hickok-Garret type who became such indispensable characters in western novels, TV serials and movie epics. He was not, since—the question of character aside—the conditions which required and permitted lawmen to act in this way did not evolve for another thirty years or so.

During Walker's term of office thirty-three criminal cases were tried in the Jackson County circuit court. More than half were assaults of one sort or another, but none involved gunplay, the absence of which constituted the chief difference between Independence in 1827 and, say, Dodge City fifty years later. In the earlier time it was unusual for a man to bother carrying a handgun principally because the models available were slow to load, inaccurate and inclined to misfire. They were mostly favored by formal duelists, but this was more an interest of eastern gentlemen and their imitators than of western frontiersmen. The latter were just as hot-tempered and violently inclined, but their combats tended to be hand-to-hand ones in which, as one commentator reported, "The acme of accomplishment was to throw one's antagonist down and, catching the fingers under the jaw or in the hair, use this fulcrum to gouge the eyeball out onto the cheek with the thumb. If this could not be done, the fighter tried to bite off a nose or an ear."

In the interior regions of the country the hand weapon of choice was a butcher knife. A popular model was named after the brutal Jim Bowie of Arkansas, who did not invent the style of blade but used it often and artistically. This—and, in the very far west, the hatchet— were considered more manly weapons than a pistol and much more effective for close-in work, say, for grappling with a grizzly, an enraged Comanche or a hotheaded political opponent. This kind of combat produced some dangerous and disagreeable bullies of the Mike Fink sort but had a certain natural restraining effect on the general level of violence. Such fights were seldom quick and clean, and lesser men had an understandable disinclination to provoke opponents who were obviously bigger and stronger. When it came into civilian use after the Civil War, the six-shooter was in a sense a democratic innovation since it offered homicidal opportunities to almost anyone who could afford or steal a gun and had the desire to become expert with it. With their equalizers, demented racists like John Wesley Hardin, the Earps, calculating carpetbaggers and psychopaths of the temper of Billy the Kid became killers and terrorists as they could not and would not have been if they had had to grapple with their victims.

Joe Walker was well endowed for being a sheriff in this time. When he took office, he was twenty-nine years old, but for more than a decade he had been traveling and living with hard men in very hard places. The possibility of anyone's trying to gouge out the eye of or even pull a knife on a six-four, 220-pound, frontier veteran of his sort was remote. As the Jackson County historian suggested, he seems to have had a real knack for keeping "discipline" largely because he had such a commanding presence. There are no records indicating he ever found it necessary physically to overpower anyone while he was sheriff. During the remainder of his long frontier career spent with exceptionally unruly, physical and combative people, there are only three instances of Walker's being directly challenged. On all three occasions the challenger backed down before it came to violence.

As time went on, his reputation, which began growing after he first went to New Mexico in 1820, made confrontations even more unlikely. For example, there was a story, first told in print by George Ruxton, the English author-spy who spent several years with the mountain men and plainsmen. Ruxton may have met Walker but, if so, only briefly and casually. However, like Irving, he obviously heard Walker stories and passed along a particularly bloody one. Walker, wrote Ruxton, was leading a band of trappers camped at an unspecified place in an unspecified year on the Gila River with an unidentified band of Indians. During the evening the trappers turned on the Indians and killed or routed all of them except their gigantic chief. He, despite being wounded, engaged Walker in a duel. Ruxton went on:

> The white [Walker] was a tall powerful man, but, notwith-standing the deadly wound the Indian had received, he had his equal in strength to contend against. The naked form of the In-dian twisted and writhed in his grasp, as he sought to avoid the trapper's uplifted knife. Many of the latter's companions advanced to administer the *coup-de-grace* to the savage, but the trapper cried to them to keep off: "If he couldn't whip the Injun," he said, "he'd go under." At length he succeeded in throwing him, and plunging his knife no less than seven times into his body, tore off his scalp, and went in pursuit of the flying savages.

Ruxton was what now might be called a nonfiction novelist. The two leading characters in his book *Life in the Far West* were admit-tedly inventions or composites, but he used at least the real names, if not adventures, of men like Walker. Since no known incident approxi-mates this campfire knife fight, Ruxton almost certainly invented it or stitched it together from a collection of other stories with the purpose of illustrating that life in the far west was brutal and bloody. Having perhaps seen him and certainly having heard a lot about him, Ruxton may have given his protagonist the name Walker on the grounds that if such a thing had happened, only somebody like Joe Walker could have done it. Throughout the years others were to do the same, though not so dramatically as George Ruxton. The circulation of such stories, apocryphal as they were, would have had the effect of making anyone who encountered Walker in the flesh think long and hard about getting crossways with him.

According to the sketchy court records, Jackson County was a rela-tively orderly place during Walker's term of office, and presumably his presence and reputation were in part responsible for the fact. Cer-tainly its citizens and the traders and plainsmen who passed through Independence were no more pacific than any others on the rough, feud-prone frontier. A year after he left office the community had its first murder, and after that, a quasi-religious war between the Mormons and the Scotch-Irish. The former were brutalized and thrown out of the county but gained some measure of revenge by later shooting—not fatally—Lilburn Boggs in the head. (The animosity which commenced in Jackson County continued as the frontier moved west. In Utah the Mormons used the epithet "Missouri puke" to describe not only resi-dents of that state but, in general, the Scotch-Irish from the southern Appalachians.)

Walker had left Independence by the time the trouble with the Mormons came to a head, and during his term most of his duties were routine. He summoned and paid the expenses of jurors and witnesses and managed the local jail, a log building which was constructed in 1827 at a cost of $150. He held there and perhaps apprehended one cattle and two horse thieves, rustling then being the most common crime against property. Sheriffs were also expected to be on the lookout for runaway slaves and indentured servants, advertisements for whom were often circulated in western Missouri. One of these posted in 1826 described: "Christopher Carson, a boy about 16 years old, small for age but thick-set; light hair." Carson had run away from a Franklin saddler, David Workman, who offered a reward of one penny for his return. He never got the boy back. Carson came to Independence in October and there probably first met Walker, who later was to take an avuncular interest in the young man. William Wolfskill, another Taos trapper, hired Carson as a horse boy and took him to New Mexico that fall.

Keeping order in the court was important and not particularly tame work for western sheriffs of the time. Trials were regarded as social entertainments as well as legal happenings. Judges, lawyers, jurors, witnesses, plaintiffs and defendants were apt to be pugnacious and armed. So were the spectators, who followed the proceedings enthusiastically and rooted for their favorites, like crowds at a competitive athletic event. In a St. Clair County, Missouri, case, Senator Thomas Benton was accused of slander by a political opponent whom Benton had characterized as being no better than a sheep-killing cur dog. The senator's counsel was Waldo Johnson, a renowned frontier orator who in the course of the trial delivered a magnificent, if digressive, harangue about Manifest Destiny, free speech and press and Benton's support for these popular principles. This so excited one spectator that he rose and shouted, "Go it, my little Johnson! Rise and shine, honey; live in the milk and die in the cream." In a Boonslick courtroom another bystander, "a double fisted fellow," rose for reasons unexplained to challenge the bench. "Hell's afloat and the river's risin'. I'm the yaller flower of the forest; a flash and a half of lightning; a perfect thunder gust. Who wants to fight?"

It is an indication of Walker's calming effect that during his term no such incidents were recorded in the Jackson County circuit court, then the most backwoodish one in the state.

A man named Joe O'Conner, frequently drunk, disorderly and assaultive, seems to have been Walker's most regular client. O'Conner was of a temper which in later years might have turned him into a genuine badman, but in Independence he was treated only as a common nuisance whom the sheriff occasionally had to pick up and cool off in the log jail. There was one notable melee during this period. A half dozen young men, sons of good Scotch-Irish settler families, sold a quantity of whiskey to some visiting Osage tribesmen, then got drunk with their customers and started to brawl with them. Selling liquor to Indians, though technically illegal, was a general and profitable business, but doing so within the community and carrying on with the customers were apparently too much. The sheriff, by means unspecified, pulled in the rowdies and restrained them until order was restored. Again it is interesting to consider what might have happened had this brawl taken place fifty years later, when both the lawman and the drunks would have been packing six-shooters.

Nearly all the assault cases which came before the court while Walker was its sheriff involved drunkenness, not surprising since at the time this condition was so general as to amount to a public epidemic. In 1830 the national annual consumption of hard liquor was an astonishing five gallons a head, a tippling rate triple that which prevails today, and in the western districts the general consumption was much higher. There were reasons, other than self-indulgence, for this prodigious boozing. Water and milk were so often contaminated that they were regarded, with justification, as dangerous to lethal drinks. Coffee and tea were dear, and the latter was considered an effete, foreign beverage. Corn whiskey and very hard cider were thought to be, if not wholesome, at least safe. Both were very plentiful and cheap. Particularly in the Mississippi valley regions, shipping bulk produce to eastern markets was slow and expensive. Farmers found it easier and more lucrative to distill their corn and apples, to sell and transport them as kegs of white lightning. In consequence, and for the pleasure of it, Americans drank morning, noon and night. Besotted judges and ministers toppled from their benches and pulpits. Private and public works were disrupted and halted because of the insobriety of laborers, craftsmen and technicians. Families, communities and society in general were unsettled and corrupted by the violence and irrational behavior which was a by-product of the general boozing. Liver diseases, dyspepsia, delirium tremens and terrible hangovers were chronic.

As with malaria, Joe Walker seems to have escaped this other general scourge, drunkenness, which ravaged and incapacitated so many men of his time. He was not a teetotaler, for there are accounts of his mixing a "southern-style toddy" on special occasions. However, there are many testimonials to the fact that he was a very moderate, more or less ceremonial and social drinker. This unusual behavior, beyond helping account for the long years of health and vigorous life he enjoyed, contributed to his reputation as an exceptionally steady and self-controlled man.

Walker discharged his duties as sheriff faithfully and to the apparent satisfaction of the court and public for about a year and a half. The last case he dealt with directly was that of Hanna, a slave who was charged with the attempted murder of her master, Asa Say. The jury found her guilty, and the judge sentenced "The said Hanna to receive on her bare black ass Thirty Nine lashes well laid on, and it is ordered that the Sheriff cause execution of this order immediately."

Hanna was tried and punished late in the winter of 1829. Thereafter, though not necessarily in consequence, Walker seems to have lost interest in sheriffing; he seldom appeared in court and was probably not often in the Independence area. Increasingly the lawwork was handled by his deputy, Jacob Gregg. (This was the brother of the frail Josiah, who a year later joined a Santa Fe caravan, principally seeking better health. He found it, and wrote *Commerce of the Prairies*, one of the finest works of nineteenth-century personal journalism and perhaps the best eyewitness account of the Santa Fe trade and Trail.) Despite his absences, Walker was renominated the next year for another two-year term as sheriff. He adamantly declined to run.

Law enforcement was a part-time job in western Missouri, and even while he was in office, Walker traveled outside the district as a stock drover and trader. This was a calling to which he had been more or less born in Tennessee and to which through his life he would turn during otherwise slack times. After giving over his sheriff duties to Jacob Gregg, he occupied himself in this way for the next year or so. He traded in hogs—which ran semiwild in western Missouri, where they were worth only seventy-five cents a hundredweight on foot—and also occasionally packed along some kegs of whiskey from the distillery Abraham McClellan operated. However, his main interest was—and always would be—in horses. Walker, his brothers and McClellan had a considerable herd pastured in Jackson County, and all along the Missouri Valley he could buy more for $30 or $40 a head. His best customers were army officers stationed at frontier posts in Kansas, Arkansas and Oklahoma. They were always ready to improve their private strings, good mounts being not only a necessity but a status symbol among them. Also, being on the government payroll, they had hard cash in their pockets, and Walker was regularly able to get $100 or $150 for a horse he trailed to their isolated camps.

At this time Walker was in a personal transition period. The nature of his thoughts can only be guessed at—as usual he left no records or comments about them—by working backward from what he eventually did. With the inherent weakness of this deductive method acknowledged, Walker's state of mind at the beginning of 1830 may have been as follows:

In regard to the organization of Jackson County he had done his bit to break the crust, but the responsibilities and restrictions of the settlement had made him restless and impatient to return to wilderness roaming. His problem was to find or devise some means which would enable him to do so in a suitable style. For reasons of temperament and previous experience, his requirements were special, if not unique. Given our advantage of being able to consider his entire life in retrospect, we might conclude that the dislike of repetitive work common in many Scotch-Irish men of the time seems to have been particularly pronounced in Walker. Sheriffing for two years or so was the most regular or routine job he had had since he left his father's farm as a sixteen-year-old. By his standards, this had been too confining and insufficiently stimulating. The obvious vocations open to a man of his background in the far west suffered from the same deficiencies. The Santa Fe trade was booming but was becoming increasingly a mercantile enterprise, exciting perhaps for a bookish Josiah Gregg but not for a Joe Walker. The same held true of beaver trapping. Though Walker has come to be identified in capsule biographical entries in western histories as a notable trapper, he was such only briefly. He became a leader and guide for furmen but, after the first few years in Taos, did very little actual trapping. Despite its being romanticized ever since, this was tedious and restrictive work. The spring and fall seasons were spent alone in icy streams, while the long winters were devoted to cleaning and curing hides and killing time in snowbound camps. The more able and ambitious men, the Sublette brothers, Tom Fitzpatrick, Jed Smith, Jim Bridger, began as trappers—the field hands of the trade—but with the intention of working their way up to management and ownership positions. Those with the business skills to do so found it necessary and desirable to spend most of their time in the settlements, dealing with suppliers, buyers, bankers and government agents. Had becoming a successful entrepreneur been Walker's ambition, it would have been best served by his staying home and becoming more involved with the shrewd Abraham McClellan.

Though it was not a vocation to which a precise name could be put, what Walker wanted was to be a free-lance explorer, a private Meriwether Lewis or William Clark, with sufficient men, resources and freedom of action to travel and live for extended periods in the unsettled and, better, unexplored regions of the west. There had never been many opportunities for this sort of thing and, again in retrospect, only one more of importance was to open up in the trans-Mississippi west. Fortunately Walker was able to find and seize upon it.

The agent of opportunity was a U.S. Army captain, Benjamin Louis Eulalie de Bonneville, stationed at Fort Gibson, then the most westerly post on the Arkansas River. By accident or design, Walker, driving a string of horses, came there late in 1830. It is likely that the two men already were acquainted and, if not, almost certainly had heard of each other, since Regular Army officers and sheriffs were prominent members of the small, gossipy border society. However, if they needed an introduction, there were many who could have performed it. For example, Lieutenant William Montgomery, a regular officer who had served with Bonneville, had become a friend of Walker's while he was stationed at Fort Leavenworth, fifty miles upstream from Osage township. Perhaps their most interesting mutual acquaintance was Sam Houston, Walker's kinsman and fellow veteran of Horseshoe Bend.

After that battle Houston became one of Andrew Jackson's most promising political protégés and allies. However, in 1829 after the never-to-be-explained breakup of his two-month marriage (a happening which Houston said left him "the most unhappy man now living"), he abruptly resigned as the governor of Tennessee and went back to live with his boyhood companions, the Cherokee, who had been driven from the Appalachians and settled in Oklahoma. Eventually Houston recovered his spirits and ambition and went on to organize and become the president of the Republic of Texas. But when Walker arrived, he was living with the Indians near Fort Gibson, serving as an unofficial, and often very drunk, consultant in their dealings with the whites.

However it happened, Walker and Bonneville did meet and agreed upon a joint venture which was to occupy the next four years of their lives and ever thereafter link the frontier captain and the military captain in the formal annals of western American history. The nature of their arrangements requires some consideration of the complicated affairs of Benjamin Bonneville, both before and after he met Walker at Fort Gibson.

Born in Paris in 1796, Bonneville had come to New York as a child, his family leaving France because of the revolutionary turmoil there. The Bonnevilles had good American connections. Their son received an appointment to the U.S. Military Academy and, in 1815, a commission in the Regular Army. He was posted to the western frontier in 1820 and received his captaincy in 1825. Subsequently he was to serve with distinction in the Mexican, various Indian and the Civil wars, rising to the rank of brigadier general. His record does not indicate he was a brilliant officer, but his superiors and those who served with and under him regarded him as a tough, shrewd and competent one. It is an assessment which is meaningful in regard to the portion of his life in which he and Walker were closely associated, since well after the fact, others offered the explanation that Bonneville behaved as he did because he was naïve and foolish.

In 1830 Bonneville conceived, or was made part of, an extraordinary plan: He would take temporary leave of the army, organize and find financing for a fur trapping expedition which he would lead into the central and northern Rocky Mountains. In November 1830, after returning from patrol on the plains, he laid the scheme before his commanding officer at Fort Gibson, Col. Matthew Arbuckle. Arbuckle was noncommittal, but either at this officer's suggestion or on his own, Bonneville later wrote to General Alexander Macomb, commanding officer of the U.S. Army. Bonneville told Macomb that while his planned expedition would be strictly private, undertaken at his own expense, he was certain that so engaged, he would be able to make useful observations about the disposition of Indian tribes, the British in Oregon and the Mexicans in the southwest. These he would be glad to include in formal reports and share with the War Department. Without much delay or apparent surprise, Macomb gave Bonneville a two-year leave of absence, beginning in the fall of 1831, and said that yes, indeed, the military would be interested in hearing from him in a semiofficial way.

Bonneville then headed to New York, looking for financial backers, whom he found rather easily. The records he left are vague on this point, but apparently he got most of the money from agents of John Jacob Astor, then the wealthiest man in America and the corporate head of the American Fur Company, one of the nation's most powerful commercial concerns. The next spring in 1832, Bonneville at the head of an ostentatiously well-equipped company left for the Rockies. Once there, he showed very little interest in the fur trade but spent a lot of time mapping, putting up temporary forts and investigating routes to and conditions on the Pacific coast. He became so engrossed in these activities that in 1833 in a report he sent back to Macomb, Bonneville said it would be necessary for him to remain longer and he was sure that under the circumstances there would be no difficulty about extending his leave of absence.

In fact, Bonneville spent two more years in the far west. As soon as he returned to the Missouri settlements in the late summer of 1835, he found that: (1) the administration of the War Department had changed, that Lewis Cass, a Michigander, had become the Secretary, replacing John Eaton, a Tennesseean and long-time crony of President Jackson, and (2) he had been discharged from the military for being absent without leave for two years. Bonneville seemed not only enraged but very surprised by this latter action and set about getting himself reinstated, as he was able to do, again with remarkable ease. General Macomb supported his cause by saying Bonneville had indeed supplied useful information. Then, in January 1836, Andrew Jackson settled the matter by summarily sending a message to Congress, saying he wanted Bonneville put back on the active duty roster. This was done.

As soon as the details of the episode were known, they began to cause talk and gossip. Many, including a number of field-grade military officers, thought the whole thing most peculiar: that an obscure frontier captain should have been granted a leave to pursue a private commercial venture; that on leave he did not pursue it; that he casually decided to overstay the leave; that he was reinstated quickly through the intervention of the highest authorities. Ever since, scholars of the period have been similarly intrigued and have come to regard Bonneville's activities as one of the outstanding unsolved mysteries of nineteenth-century American military, political and diplomatic history. Many of them have concluded that something more than fur trading was behind the expedition, an opinion succinctly stated by Carl Russell: "The 'adventures' of Captain Bonneville and the related expeditions to California led by Joseph Reddeford [sic] Walker in 1833 were agreed to if not instigated by Andrew Jackson and some of his Cabinet members."

A literary, but associated, happening of the time provided further circumstantial evidence supporting the suspicion that Bonneville had a covert assignment to gather military and commercial intelligence which would prove useful if Americans moved toward either the British or the Mexican possessions. As soon as he returned to Missouri in 1835 and heard about his discharge, Bonneville set off not for Washington but for New York and there spent a weekend at Astor's home. Coincidentally, according to both men, Washington Irving was a houseguest at the same time. Irving was then the most popular and influential man of letters in the country and, after a long stay in Europe, had become interested in the westering movement, particularly the fur trade. (He was completing a two-volume work on Astor's early fur operations.) Naturally, said Irving, he was interested in the accounts the bold Captain Bonneville gave of his recent experiences in the Rockies and, during their stay at Astor's mansion, interrogated him on details.

The next winter Irving was in Washington and again coincidentally happened to meet Bonneville, who, it turned out, was trying to write a book about his expedition. Irving said that surprisingly enough, he had been thinking along the same lines. With great delicacy he suggested that it might be easier for him as a professional author to put the material into shape than it would be for Bonneville, that if he did and it appeared under his name, this would do much to ensure its popularity and sales. Of course, if he were to attempt this work, he would need to have Bonneville's notes, his field diaries and whatever reports he was preparing for the War Department. For these, he, Irving, was prepared to pay the captain $1,000, which he reckoned was more money than Bonneville would get if he wrote and published the book on his own. Without hesitation, Bonneville agreed, packed up his papers and sold them to Irving. The latter took them back to his office in New York. There is no further record of them, though historians have been looking for the documents ever since. Ninety years later a Washington historian said that a colleague told her these papers were stashed someplace in the War Department and had asked about what to do with them. Curiously nothing was done. The informant died, and the historian went off to practice in Australia.

As Irving had predicted, his book, *The Adventures of Captain Bonneville, U.S.A.*, published in 1837, was popular and profitable, deservedly so in many respects. Bonneville was an observant man and a careful diarist, so that working from his notes, Irving was able to give a largely accurate and very readable description of the Rocky Mountain furmen and trade during the early 1830s. However, in regard to the overall conduct of and motives for the "adventures," there is an undercurrent of special pleadings. It is so strong as to raise suspicions that the origins and purpose of this book were not so casual as Irving claimed.

At the time his position was comparable to that of a nationally known contemporary TV newsman, so influential and distinguished as to make him a confidant of the leaders of the Republic, privy to plans and information that were judged unsuitable for public dissemination. These circumstances have led to persistent speculation that *The Adventures of Captain Bonneville, U.S.A.* may have been in part a cover story, that Irving or some of his influential colleagues may have decided he could give a much more politic account of the matter than could an infantry captain, particularly one who considered he had been mistreated by his government. In the book Irving treated Bonneville as simply a bluff soldier who had gone west looking for excitement and to make some money in the fur business. This, however, left him with the problem of explaining why his protagonist did so little and so badly as a fur trader. Claiming sheer incompetence was a possibility, but bunglers make implausible heroes for the kind of high adventure story Irving had in mind. As an alternative, Irving suggested that his captain had been victimized by a trusted lieutenant who, instead of trapping furs, had with forty men wandered capriciously across the unexplored Sierra and then spent three months larking around California, squandering Bonneville's resources. This man was Joe Walker, whom Irving had first introduced as the champion of the Spanish-Pawnee-Sioux battle outside Santa Fe.

To return to Fort Gibson in the early winter of 1830, whatever they may have said or guessed about each other's covert intentions, the ambitions and needs of Walker and Bonneville dovetailed beautifully at that moment. Walker was obviously not looking for a job, business or office since he had either rejected or not pursued a variety of oppor-

tunities in these lines. He wanted an expedition, free-form enough so
that he could spend some time exploring the unknown regions of the
west. Bonneville had exactly such a venture in the making. If only
commerce and sightseeing were his objectives, the army captain needed
a man who could show him the ropes in the mountains and could recruit and manage the irregular troops of a fur brigade. If there was
more to the mission, he needed a steady, close-mouthed man, accustomed to exercising authority, with whom he could share tactical confi-
dences and responsibilities—or at the very minimum, one whose frontier credentials were impressive enough to make the cover story about
fur trading credible. In either case, Walker, by reason of his experience and reputation, probably suited Bonneville's needs better than
anyone available on the border.

Bonneville laid out at least the fur trading part of his proposition
and first asked Walker if he would care to become a stockholder.
Walker declined on the ground that he did not have the ready cash to
risk in this way. (This may have been the case, but on the other hand,
he had access to considerable resources through Abraham McClellan,
who was always on the lookout for good investment opportunities. It
could also have been that Walker had by then put two and two together
and decided that this was not essentially or at all a profit-making
scheme.) Thereupon the two men agreed that Walker would join
Bonneville as his bourgeois or partisan—that is, in the jargon of the
fur trade, as his field commander.

Except for some discussion of logistical details, this may have been
all that passed between them at the time. However, another scenario,
though *absolutely fictitious* in terms of surviving records, is not fantastic. It can be imagined because of what happened later and because
to a degree that is easily forgotten, frontier commercial, political and
military affairs were then conducted through a small, tightly knit good
old boy network. Especially during the Jackson administration, this
was dominated by Scotch-Irish from the southern Appalachians.
Among them the Walkers, McClellans, Toomys, Houstons and others
of their kin were, though operating in the extreme western settlements,
still very well known and connected, better so than a French émigré
army captain. Thus:

"Bonneville still bothers me. He is a good enough little man for a
frog, and ambitious as all sin, but he doesn't make a convincing fur
trader. For that matter, if they get a chance at California, I don't see
him leading a gang of those hillbillies across the mountains, wherever
they are. He's likely to get his French pizzle caught in a beaver trap
and ours with it."

"The senator and I were talking about that. He recommended a
fellow from out there as being a good man for us. One of the first of

those smugglers in New Mexico, part of Benton's boondoggle on the Santa Fe Trail. He's half horse, half alligator, and we're not going to find anybody with more credibility as a mountain man. Keeps his mouth shut, too, I'm told. Name of Joe Walker."

"A Roane County Walker?"

"The same. I also understand that he was on the Tallapoosa with you, General."

"By thunder, I never led finer troops than those boys I had at Horseshoe Bend. I can still see young Sam swarming over Weatherford's pine logs. If this Walker was there, he'll serve us well."

"The senator tells me he's been the sheriff out in Independence—part of the McClellan-Boggs gang. If he handled those Jackson County, you'll pardon the expression, thugs, he's not going to have any trouble with the savages or the greasers, or Bonneville for that matter. Apparently he got bored with court work. Right now he's wandering around selling horses, more or less between massacres. It would be a natural thing for him to stop by Gibson and meet Bonneville."

"Sam is still there playing Indian. By Jehoshaphat, I wish he'd get over that damn woman. But Sam would be the man to give this fellow some private information."

"If he's sober enough to remember it."

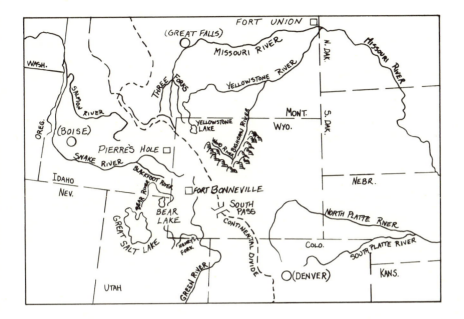

The Rockies

Sometime after Bonneville and Walker talked at Fort Gibson, they brought a third man, Michael Cerré, into the venture. A member of an old St. Louis mercantile family, who had already operated a trading post and made at least one commercial trip to Santa Fe, Cerré was a logical choice, being experienced in the business end of the fur trade, as the other two were not. Bonneville spoke (always with the qualification that his voice was to a large extent that of Washington Irving) of both Walker and Cerré as his lieutenants. Walker, however, referred to Cerré as well as to Bonneville as a partner. Both may have been using the titles figuratively to describe a loose relationship which evolved out of mutual self-interest and was more symbiotic than contractual or hierarchal. A reasonable assumption is that Bonneville had the original idea and raised the money, while Walker and Cerré, for considerations, contributed their frontier expertise and contacts. In the field they cooperated when it individually suited them but acted with great independence when it did not.

In the winter of 1832 Bonneville was in the east, dealing with the War Department and his New York investors; Cerré was in St. Louis, making arrangements for supplies; and Walker was home at Fort Osage, where he recruited men for the expedition. Generally he had to

103

hire green hands because most of his acquaintances and neighbors who had frontier experience were by then either engaged in the Santa Fe trade or connected with other fur companies. He was, however, able to score one recruiting coup, engaging a small party of Delaware Indians.

(After their tribal power had been destroyed in the east, the Delaware, and the Iroquois, played a curious role in the western fur trade. The young men of these nations retained the wilderness skills and aggressive disposition which had made them such formidable adversaries in the Appalachians, but the defeat and dismemberment of their own nations seem to have burned away their racial loyalties. They hired out to British and American furmen and with them roamed the west from the Mexican borders to the Arctic barrens as displaced, mercenary Ishmaels, serving as trappers, trackers and hired guns. Because of their abilities and cold, professional ferocity, they were hated and feared by the western tribes but were in great demand among the fur companies. Walker was lucky to get his Delawares.)

The Bonneville expedition left from Fort Osage in May 1832. It was the most lavishly supplied single fur brigade to leave Missouri, and it included 110 men, each with extra horses and mules, and twenty freight wagons. These were not the first to be taken to the mountains, but no one previously had organized such a large train of them. From Osage they followed what was by then the customary route used by furmen going to the central Rockies, traveling directly west into Kansas and then angling northward to the Platte River valley. This was new country and a new experience for Bonneville, and he was excited by both. "It is not easy to do justice to the exulting feelings of the worthy captain at finding himself at the head of a stout band of hunters, trappers, and woodmen; fairly launched on the broad prairies, with his face to the boundless West," Irving wrote. However, immediately and frequently thereafter he did his best to do justice to these feelings, *The Adventures of Captain Bonneville, U.S.A.* containing a number of fairly lush passages about the grandeurs of the boundless West and the Captain's appreciation of them.

The first Indians they met were some Kansas under a chief named White Plume, who was regarded by both whites along the border and other tribes as a long-winded beggar and petty scalawag. Bonneville, said Irving, found him a capital fellow. He and White Plume ("we are pleased with his chivalrous *soubriquet*") sat in front of the latter's lodge, "in soldier-like communion, the captain delighted with the opportunity of meeting on social terms with one of the red warriors of the wilderness, the unsophisticated children of nature."

As a matter of record, White Plume's permanent residence was a large stone house built for him by the government Indian agency of which he was a very willing and fairly shrewd client. White Plume mostly wanted to commune with Bonneville about the outrageous conduct of white bee hunters, who had begun to roam about the area "without any regard to the ordinance of the American government, which strictly forbids all trespass upon the lands belonging to the Indian tribes." Bonneville-Irving agreed they were a scruffy lot, "generally some settler on the verge of the prairies; a long, lank fellow, of fever and ague complexion, acquired from living on new soil, and in a hut built of green logs."

This was something of a set piece for Irving, who encountered bee hunters during his own brief guided tour of the near prairies and devoted a chapter of his own journal to describing them disdainfully. Like many members of the eastern intelligentsia, he tended to see the residents of the Wild West as existing in a romantic hierarchy. Sharing the top niches were the wild, unspoiled red men, the noble children of nature, and cultured Atlantic travelers who were sensitive to their nobility. Next were genuine and picturesque explorers and adventurers like Bonneville and—at least on first introduction—Walker. They were followed by half-breeds and finally the dull, coarse, unattractive peasantry—that is, the white settlers, who were spoiling the nature of the place.

Walker was presumedly less impressed with White Plume, whom he had known since at least 1825, when they had met at the signing of the Santa Fe Trail treaty. As for the long, lank, sallow bee hunters, these would have been his neighbors, friends and perhaps relatives from Jackson County.

On the North Platte they met wild Indians, a party of sixty Crows who had, with murderous intent, been chasing some Cheyenne raiders. At first alarmed, Bonneville found that the Crows were not then after white scalps and, in fact, were "fine martial-looking fellows, painted and arrayed for war, and mounted on horses decked out with all kinds of wild trappings." Bonneville got together that evening for a party with some of the Crow chiefs, who were "friendly in the extreme." The congenial Indians ended the night bestowing "fraternal caresses" on their white brothers. The captain was less enchanted with them when he discovered that during the embraces the Crows had relieved him and others of their white brothers of their pocketknives, wallets and even some coat buttons.

By July 20 the column was on the Sweetwater River, and the Rockies, the Shining Mountains, became visible for the first time. During the next week they became the first to get a substantial wagon train through South Pass—which in ten years would become the emigrant gateway to the Pacific—and then came down to the Green River, a northern branch of the Colorado. Camping on the Green, in western

Wyoming, near where it was joined by Horse Creek, they prepared to start in the fur business or whatever else they may variously have had in mind.

The Rocky Mountain fur trade had a critical influence on all subsequent aspects of the westering movement. Also, it and the mountaineers who conducted it almost immediately caught and ever since have held the American fancy. Therefore, this is a subject which has probably received more attention, scholarly and popular, than any other phenomenon of our nineteenth-century history, except the Civil War. The literature dealing with the period from 1825 to 1835, the brief heyday of this trade, is by now voluminous and detailed. Only a sketchy summary is needed to indicate some of the problems and possibilities which faced Walker, Bonneville and Cerré when they halted on the Green River in July 1832, a month which commenced the most chaotic and violent year in the history of the fur business.

Though the free-lance Taos trappers had made a good and early start in the southwestern mountains, not until several years later were Americans able to establish themselves in the even richer fur country of the central and northern Rockies. The first efforts were aimed at building permanent trading posts on the upper Missouri and its tributaries and supplying them by water. They were frustrated by logistical difficulties and by hostile Indians, Arikara and Sioux, who made river traffic dangerous. The few who got through found two even more formidable opponents in the mountains. The first was the Hudson's Bay Company, which monopolized the trade from the northern Great Plains and Pacific Northwest to the Arctic Ocean. In what is now the United States the HBC men were permanently established at posts in Oregon, northern and western Montana and Idaho. Their trapping brigades ranged even farther to the east and south, making what mischief they could for Americans by stirring up Indians and laying waste beaver populations.

Secondly, there were the Blackfeet, the most ferocious tribe of the northern Rockies. Ever since their initial meeting—a sharp skirmish— with the Lewis and Clark expedition, they had been virulently anti-American. They were not allies of the Hudson's Bay men, for when it suited their purposes, they would turn with enthusiasm on them, but they disliked them less than they did the Americans. Also, they needed supplies, particularly guns and ammunition from the posts and, because of this, could sometimes be manipulated by the British. The Blackfeet did not suddenly become terrorists after meeting the Americans but had been so for generations previous, preying on other mountain tribes. Therefore, when the Americans did arrive, they were rather well received by the Crow, Snake, Nez Percé and Flathead tribes, largely because these Indians saw the newcomers as a source of supplies and as potential allies to be used against the dreaded Blackfeet.

The first American to do any substantial business in the mountains was William Ashley, a sometime Missouri lead miner, munitions maker, general of the militia and congressman. In both 1822 and 1823 Ashley tried to send trappers up the Missouri but was repulsed by the Arikara. This was a small, semisedentary, but doughty tribe, located on the Missouri in villages along the South-North Dakota line. In the summer of 1823 they killed twelve of Ashley's men who were attempting to force their way upstream. After this debacle Ashley decided that logistically attractive as the waterway was, the Indian problem made it an impossible trade route. Therefore, in the fall of 1823 he organized a packtrain and sent his surviving trappers directly overland to beaver streams in the Wind River and Yellowstone territory. Included in this first group were many of the subsequently most famous mountain men: Jim Bridger, Jed Smith, Tom Fitzpatrick, Edward Rose, James Clyman, Hugh Glass and Bill Sublette.

They did very well trapping in the virgin streams. (In a single season Jed Smith took 668 pelts worth about $4,000). To keep them working in the mountains, Ashley devised what became one of the most famous of all American commercial institutions, the trappers' rendezvous, the first of which was held in 1825 on Henry's Fork of the Green River. Ashley agreed to come out from St. Louis with a caravan of supplies and during the early summer meet the trappers at a designated spot. There he would buy or credit them for the furs they had and sell them supplies for the next year and such sundries, especially whiskey, which they might enjoy while camped at this trading site. The men were encouraged to bring along to the rendezvous, for trade and frolic, any friendly Indians or free trappers they might encounter. Essentially the rendezvous was a floating version of the company store. Ashley and those who succeeded him in middleman roles were the only buyers for the furs and therefore paid off the trappers at rock-bottom prices, giving $4 or $5 for a beaver pelt which might bring twice that amount on the St. Louis market. On the other hand, since they were the only sellers of goods from the settlements, these brought prices marked up as much as 1,000 percent over those that prevailed in Missouri. Generally the trappers left the rendezvous either broke or in debt to the suppliers, but this did not greatly concern them. They had enough supplies to spend another year in the mountains and had the next year's rendezvous to look forward to as a reward.

Ashley got rich, clearing about $200,000 from 1824 to 1827. He then shrewdly concluded that he had made a lucky strike, that the bonanza was likely to draw competitors and that the actual trapping end of the business would subsequently be much less profitable. He was correct in these assumptions. After the rendezvous of 1826 he sold his trapping operation to three of his young fieldmen—Bill Sublette, Jed Smith and David Jackson—for $16,000 but contracted to be the exclusive supplier for the next year's rendezvous, a venture which he again guessed correctly would be less risky and more profitable than trapping. The three new men made some money, but much less than Ashley, and they came to the same commercial conclusions he had. In 1830 they sold out to five of their employees, including Bridger, Fitzpatrick and Milton Sublette. The latter's older brother Bill retained, as Ashley had, the lucrative rights to deliver rendezvous supplies for the new outfit, which called itself the Rocky Mountain Fur Company.

As Ashley had foreseen, news about the killing he had made—and exaggerations thereof—quickly brought competitors into the field. During the late 1820s and early 1830s dozens of individual free-lance trappers and small, badly organized companies of men started for the mountains, hoping to get rich quick in the fur business. More important, so far as the partners of the Rocky Mountain Fur Company were concerned, the American Fur Company decided to enter the mountain trade. This rich, powerful combine, which had been organized by John Jacob Astor in the early 1800s, had come to control 75 percent of the total fur trade—trapping, marketing and exporting—in the United States. Previously it had operated as an absolute monopoly in the Great Lakes and upper Mississippi regions, but the profits made by Ashley and his successors convinced Astor's agents to move into the Rockies. (By then Astor himself had enormous and more lucrative investments in the east and Europe and took only a detached, nostalgic interest in the operations of his fur business.) Making use of the firm's extensive resources and political contacts, the AFC men arranged for federal help in clearing the Missouri of obstreperous Indians. When this was done, the AFC built a large central post, Fort Union, more impressive than anything even the Hudson's Bay Company had in the west, on the Missouri River near the mouth of the Yellowstone. This station was supplied by a company-owned steamboat, the *Yellowstone*. At Fort Union—and a string of lesser posts—the AFC began to woo Indians away from their former suppliers and had some success in this direction even with the Blackfeet. Also, large, well-supplied brigades of trappers directly employed by the company were sent into the mountains for the purpose of not only competing with but ruining the Rocky Mountain Fur Company and all other rivals.

In this confrontation the RMFC had the advantage of field experience, its men being the most knowledgeable about the mountains, but after Bill Sublette had sold out, the company was underfinanced and the partners were deeply in debt. The AFC agents, on the other hand, were backed by almost unlimited financial reserves. These they used to outbid their rivals for the services of good trappers, to lower the price on trade goods and to raise those they paid for beaver, taking temporary losses in the interest of destroying their competitors. Knowingly or otherwise, Bonneville may have been used as a weapon in this commercial warfare. A likely explanation for why he was so quickly and generously financed by Astor's agents in New York is that beyond whatever other results were expected of his expedition, they saw a chance to harass their rivals further by putting another fur brigade into the mountains.

Though the rendezvous system was first used by the RMFC, it shortly became a general trade fair attended by all the competing companies. They gathered for revelry but also to keep an eye on their rivals and try to undercut them by taking the trade of both the friendly Indians and free trappers who came to these gatherings. The rendezvous of 1832 was held at Pierre's Hole on the Teton River. It attracted a crowd of nearly 1,000 whites and reds: 200 men employed or allied with the Rocky Mountain Fur Company; a 175-man brigade from the American Fur Company, led by its two partisans, Henry Vanderburgh and Andrew Drips; some fifty stragglers from a lesser company, Gantt and Blackwell (which had already gone bankrupt); another fifty free trappers, some of whom had come up from Arkansas and New Mexico; a dozen New Englanders, led by a successful but restless young Boston ice merchant, Nathaniel Wyeth, who was in the west to investigate the possibilities of entering the fur trade; 120 lodges of Nez Percés, eighty lodges of Flatheads and a few Delaware and Iroquois mercenaries.

They began congregating in late June, waiting for the arrival of two competing supply trains—one from St. Louis belonging to Bill Sublette, who held the rendezvous contract of the Rocky Mountain Fur Company, and a second, organized by the American Fur Company, en route from Fort Union. Sublette arrived first, on July 8, putting Vanderburgh, Drips and the AFC brigade at a great disadvantage so far as cutting any new deals went. However, they put aside their disappointment and joined in the frolic, which commenced as soon as the trappers got the wherewithal from Sublette to start the serious drinking, gambling, wooing and fighting over Indian women. The festivities continued for nine days and then were violently interrupted by the arrival of 150 Gros Ventres. These Indians were allies of the Blackfoot confederation but also blood brothers of the Arapaho, a plains tribe to which they had been paying a visit on the Arkansas River. Hard as it is to understand, the Gros Ventres seem to have stumbled on the rendezvous site more or less by accident, first encountering a small party of trappers Milton Sublette was taking out of the camp to begin their fall hunt.

Both sides were alarmed and decided to negotiate. Sublette went out to meet some of the Gros Ventre halfway and took with him an Iroquois, Antoine Godin, who was a rabid Blackfoot hater. As the two sides came together, Godin extended his hand to a Gros Ventre chief who took it. Thereupon Godin with his free hand shot and killed the Gros Ventre, who was near enough to a Blackfoot to satisfy the Iroquois.

This ended the peace meeting. The Gros Ventres retreated and took up a defensive position in some marshy thickets. Milton Sublette sent word back to the main rendezvous camp that he had them cornered and with any luck could rub out the lot. Shortly 700 white trappers and their Indian allies, led by Bill Sublette, came boiling out of the camp and surrounded the Gros Ventres who, though outnumbered three to one, put up a stiff fight. Before it was over, they lost twenty-six warriors, including the chief Godin had killed, but they took out thirty-two of Sublette's men. However, their tactical position was hopeless, and in the evening they began to sing their death songs. Mixed in with these dirges were loud conversations to the effect that they regretted their imminent departure from the world of the living, but that their sorrow was eased by knowledge they would be revenged by an army of their Blackfoot allies, who were rushing toward the spot to kill every last one of the whites. In fact, there was no such war party, but the trappers fell for the ruse. Rumors began spreading through the thickets that thousands of Blackfeet were coming up rapidly, that the first of them had already been seen. Shortly, to avoid being themselves surrounded, the trappers ignominiously fled, not stopping until they had run seven miles back to the rendezvous camp. Gratefully the Gros Ventres packed up and escaped.

After tending to their wounds and devising some face-saving stories about the episode, the furmen left the rendezvous, splitting up to begin the trapping year, which among them was measured from rendezvous to rendezvous. The violent tone of it was set by the so-called Battle of Pierre's Hole. For the next eleven months, taking beaver became secondary to skirmishing with the aroused Blackfeet and between rival parties of white trappers. In the wings the Hudson's Bay Company did what it could to harass the Americans.

The day before arriving at the Green River, Bonneville's company had been overtaken by Lucien Fontenelle, an AFC partisan commanding the tardy supply train from Fort Union. Both parties had been on the plains for a month and therefore knew nothing about the happenings at Pierre's Hole. Consequently Fontenelle rushed on, still hoping to get to the rendezvous in time to do some useful business. (He never did.) As he passed, he complained that he and his men had been following for several weeks, and the closer they got, the harder it was for them because Bonneville's hunters and wagons were driving all the game in front of them. Bonneville could now take his own turn at eating little but dust. In response to this challenge, Bonneville, Walker and Cerré picked up their pace, kept the column moving until after dark and got it started before dawn on the next day. By noon they had caught up, finding Fontenelle resting on the Green River because after the sprint his own men and animals were "nearly knocked up by the exertion."

The next morning, when he left, Fontenelle lured away Bonneville's prized Delawares who had been hired at Fort Osage. He did it by offering them $400 for a single trapping season, more than double the going wage scale. It was an effective demonstration of how the AFC was willing to use its superior resources to undercut rivals. Bonneville was shocked at this "first taste of the boasted strategy of the fur trade." Walker and Cerré were probably less surprised since many of the players in this dog-eat-dog game had been their friends, acquaintances and business associates in Missouri.

New as he was to the fur trade, Bonneville did have some information about the mountain country, gained perhaps from existing maps and reports or in conversations with frontiersmen like Walker. Also, he came west with ready-made plans. One of them was to build a substantial military type of fort on the Green River near the confluence of Horse Creek and use this as the expedition's base for the next year. This was apparently the first Walker had heard of the scheme, and it was his turn to be astonished. The frontier captain pointed out to the army captain that the site was a terrible one for a winter fur camp. The Green River valley was wide, exposed to the wind and a notably cold place. In three months it could be expected to be covered with three or four feet of snow, making it impossible, among other things, to find sufficient forage for the horses and mules. Even worse, it was in poor hunting and trapping country. He, Bonneville and Cerré argued the question, but Cerré, whom Walker recollected as "an excellent young man but entirely under the influence and control of Bonneville," sided with the latter. "The majority of partners being opposed" (to Walker), the fort project commenced. It was a considerable work. Fifteen-foot-high foot-in-diameter cottonwood posts were cut along the river and dug in for palisade walls. The inside dimensions were not recorded, but a sufficient area was fenced to accommodate at least 110 men, some of their horses and two blockhouses, which were built at diagonal corners of the post.

When other mountain men saw and heard about this structure, they, for the same reasons Walker did, thought it preposterous and, though its creator grandly named it Fort Bonneville, commonly and derisively referred to it as Fort Nonsense. It was indeed a nonsensical place if it was intended for trappers who had to live off the land with very little outside support. However, it is possible that Bonneville had in mind other things which he kept to himself. He had already demonstrated that the site could be reached by freight wagons. Another sort of outfit, say, a company or so of dragoons who could depend on government issue salt pork, flour and fodder, would not be seriously inconvenienced by the lack of game and winter pasture. In the summer, during the campaigning season, the open meadows provided excellent pasture for stock and ample bivouac room for a small army. (This is exactly why the trappers themselves used the site for six of their subsequent rendezvous. It made a good summer camp and was easily supplied from the east.)

Strategically there was even more to recommend the upper Green River as a base for a military unit. It was centrally located in relation to the most warlike of the Indian tribes in the mountains and on the northern plains. It controlled the passes of the Snake River plateau, which led to and from Oregon and California, and would make an excellent base for any military force that wanted to enter these regions or repel anyone coming from the Pacific side of the Rockies. Later Bonneville was to send a report back to General Macomb at the War Department in which the possibilities of such actions were outlined. When the matter of Bonneville's overstaying his leave came up, Macomb was to say in his defense that the captain had supplied some very useful information, and nobody in the War Department is known to have hooted at his Fort Nonsense.

The anomalies of the place were so apparent that even some of the furmen came to reconsider their first opinions. One of these was Warren Ferris, a subleader of the American Fur Company, who was probably the first to nickname it Fort Nonsense. The next spring Ferris came there for the rendezvous, looked over the installation and thoughtfully commented that the "block houses of unhewn logs are so constructed and situated, as to defend the square outside of the pickets, and hinder the approach of an enemy from any quarter. The prairie in the vicinity of the fort is covered with fine grass, and the whole together seems well calculated for the security both of men and horses."

Unable to stop the building of the fort—and perhaps, in the course of the argument, having been told or guessed that there were other reasons for it—Walker did not take any part in the construction. A few days after it began, he went off to look for a band of free trappers— whom Fontenelle had hoped to trade with or hire—with the intention of engaging them as replacements for the Delawares that the AFC partisan had heisted. He located them and returned to camp with the group of veterans. Bonneville found these mountain men nearly as colorful and interesting as Indians and entertained himself "by observing the habits and characteristics of this singular class of men." He was able to hire some of them and said they provided him with much valuable information.

One of the things the free trappers told Bonneville was that his Fort Nonsense was an impossible place for a winter camp and that he would find a much better one 200 miles to the west on the Salmon River in the Columbia drainage system. Bonneville immediately agreed and took this advice. The alacrity with which he did so, after stubbornly opposing Walker on the same point only a month before, tends to confirm the suspicion that he built the fort for purposes beyond those he openly declared.

The company cached its extra supplies within Fort Nonsense and sent a small party of men and a large herd of emaciated and lamed horses south to the Bear River, where it was hoped they could find good fall pasture. Then the remaining men packed up and moved off to the Salmon. The winter campsite Bonneville selected there does not appear to have been a great improvement, in terms of shelter, available game and trapping prospects, over the one he left on the Green. A few weeks after he had settled in, Warren Ferris stopped by with some of his American Fur Company trappers and remarked, "This miserable establishment, consisted of several log cabins, low, badly constructed, and admirably situated for besiegers only, who would be sheltered on every side, by timber, brush etc."

Walker thought as poorly of the Salmon River camp as did Ferris, remembering that "not a buffalo could be seen in this region and no game whatever, excepting mountain sheep." Also, he had a much different recollection of how the party came there, a move he opposed from the beginning. He said that on the Green River a Frenchman employed by the American Fur Company, "meeting with Bonneville, gave him such a glowing description of the waters of the Columbia, and as the *ne plus ultra* for trapping, etc., that Bonneville determined to go there."

This Frenchman could have well been Lucien Fontenelle, who continued to operate around the Green River area throughout the summer. Considering how the fur game was being played, Fontenelle or any other AFC man would have regarded it as a shrewd and amusing move to send the well-heeled Bonneville off to a place like the Salmon, where he would find few beaver and have his hands full simply surviving. For whatever reasons they had come there, Walker decided he was not going to stay. There is a distinct sense that about this time he had concluded that it was impossible either to educate Bonneville or to figure out what he was up to and that he himself was likely to lose respect among his mountain men acquaintances if he continued to hang around with this peculiar army officer. Two days after arriving on the Salmon, Walker left—a "distribution of forces" occurred, according to Bonneville-Irving. With twenty men he headed northeast to the Madison River, set up a temporary camp there and sent his men after beaver.

With Bonneville out of the way, the two main rivals, the Rocky Mountain Fur and American Fur companies began to have at each other in earnest. Before the untimely breakup of the Pierre's Hole rendezvous, Jim Bridger and Tom Fitzpatrick, the two leading RMFC partners, had offered Drips and Vanderburgh, the AFC partisans, a deal which would in effect divide the trapping territories, giving each company exclusive rights to operate in certain areas. The AFC men refused, an act which amounted to a declaration of commercial war. Immediately Vanderburgh and Drips set off to find their missing colleague Fontenelle. After they had found him and had resupplied their two brigades from the Fort Union packtrain, they began casting around until they picked up the trail of Bridger, Fitzpatrick and their men. Their plan was simply to dog these two RMFC veterans and let them serve as guides into the best beaver country. If during the commotion no pelts were taken, this was of no great concern to the AFC since it could go a season or several without showing a profit, but its rivals were already deep in debt and could not.

Bridger and Fitzpatrick shortly became aware of what was happening and decided that two could play this kind of tag. They did, with a vengeance. Not stopping to do any trapping, they led their pursuers on a wild chase, taking them deep into the heartland of the Blackfoot country. There without much difficulty they lost them and let nature take its course. Drips got his men out safely. Vanderburgh, a brave, intelligent man, a West Point graduate, but new to the mountains, did not. On October 14 he and a small scouting party, including Warren Ferris, were ambushed by the Blackfeet near the confluence of the Jefferson River and a creek which Lewis and Clark had named Philanthropy. Ferris was wounded but escaped. Vanderburgh and another man were killed. When he fell, Vanderburgh was butchered, the flesh stripped from his bones and thrown in the river.

The consensus among the mountaineers was that Bridger and Fitzpatrick had done in Vanderburgh almost as certainly as if they had personally cut him down, the Blackfeet simply being their weapon of choice. However, such was the nature of the fur game at the time that this enhanced rather than diminished their reputations. Bridger at least did not get away scot-free. After eluding Vanderburgh, he too met up with a band of Blackfeet but one so small that they were inclined to parlay. Like the negotiations at Pierre's Hole, these turned to treachery, and in the melee Bridger took two arrows in the back. One head remained there for the next three years.

While all this was going on, Joe Walker and his men were virtually the only ones who did any trapping. By mid-October they had made two or three packs of beaver (weighing 100 pounds apiece by standard mountain measure) on the Madison. With ice beginning to close the streams, they broke camp and headed back toward the Salmon to cache these furs with Bonneville. On the way they had their own encounter with the Blackfeet, who were scouring the mountains for Americans. Camped one evening by a creekside willow thicket, Walker and some of his men brought out the cards and began to deal old sledge, a gambling game for which frontiersmen had a great passion. Play was interrupted by a Blackfoot war whoop coming from a meadow beyond the willows where they had staked their horses. By the time Walker and the others got there some of the raiders had already mounted, but they were forced down by a hail of bullets. The Blackfeet flattened out in the brush, where they held off the trappers and eventually escaped from them. There were no fatalities on either side, and the Indians got away with only two horses; but even in his later years Walker seemed to regard being so inexcusably surprised as the most humiliating experience of his frontier career. As a kind of *aide-mémoire* and penance, he ever thereafter refused to play old sledge.

Walker reached Bonneville on the Salmon in early November but again stayed only a few days, the place having proved as uncomfortable and inconvenient as he had prophesied. According to Bonneville's account, rations were so short at his base camp that wolves, muskrats and bits of root were going into the stewpot, but even with this sort of garbage fare, there were very few days when anybody had a full stomach. To ease the food problems, Walker took an additional twenty men with him when he left. They traveled south and made their own winter camp on the Blackfoot River near its junction with the Snake. Their circumstances were reasonably good, thought Warren Ferris, who, along with Tom Fitzpatrick, visited them on Christmas and spent an unexpectedly comfortable holiday. "We arrived at the quarters of Capt. Walker on the 24th, and passed the next day with this gentleman very pleasantly, receiving the best treatment his—in this country necessarily limited—means would afford. During the last two days, the snow hitherto rare, had fallen to the depth of seven or eight inches."

That Ferris should have been with Fitzpatrick, who only six weeks before had set the trap in which Ferris was wounded and his friend Vanderburgh killed, was not surprising. Their code of conduct was such that when they were not actually engaged in trying to ruin or kill each other, the mountain men got along famously no matter what their commercial allegiances. Ferris and Fitzpatrick traveled together during most of December for companionship and security but were back at each other's throats the next trapping season.

Walker waited out the snows on the Snake River and then went farther south to make his spring hunt around the Bear River and Lake in the home territory of the eastern Shoshoni, customarily called the Snakes. This tribe was more or less continually at war with the Blackfeet and therefore generally well disposed toward American trappers. Through the years Walker was to develop very close ties with the Snakes and that spring he and his men had no trouble with Indians but a great deal with other whites since both RMFC and AFC brigades were working the same area. What went on they themselves never bothered to record, but after talking to Walker a few months later, Bonneville reported: "In fact, in these virulent and sordid competitions, the trappers of each party were more intent upon injuring their rivals, than benefitting themselves; breaking each other's traps, trampling and tearing to pieces the beaver lodges, and doing everything in their power to mar the success of the hunt. We forbear to detail these pitiful contentions."

When the final tally was made at that summer's rendezvous, the Rocky Mountain Fur Company had 62 packs of fur; the AFC, 51; and free trappers dealing directly with Sublette, about, 30. Bonneville's company had only 22½ packs, worth perhaps $15,000, which did not begin to cover the expenses of such a large and elaborately equipped expedition. The poor showing immediately caused talk and ever since has been cited as evidence that this was not principally a fur venture. This assumption is strengthened by the fact that Bonneville and the men who remained with him apparently did almost no trapping. In the 100 pages of Irving's account devoted to 1832–33, Bonneville only once mentions personally trying to make beaver, saying that for two weeks in late May his people set out traps along the Boise River, "with varying success."

He sent out several other groups that perhaps intended to trap but met with very bad luck. The party that had gone south the fall before with the herd of lame horses had four men killed by the Blackfeet, became lost and straggled into Bonneville's camp on the Salmon in late winter. Twenty more men, led by David Adams, had gone to the Crow country. About half these men had deserted, deciding they would rather live and hunt with the Crows. The remainder were robbed of all their horses by the Arikara and then either went to work for other companies or made canoes and paddled back to Missouri. Only Adams returned to the rendezvous. Bonneville did hire twenty-five additional free trappers while on the Salmon, but they had given him an ultimatum that if they were not supplied on the spot, they would go over to another company. Bonneville thought it necessary "to bend wishes." These men, having in effect been paid in advance, stayed in the mountains until the next fall, and whatever beaver they did take would not have been counted at the rendezvous. In consequence all or very nearly all the furs credited to Bonneville must have been taken by Walker. Thus, while the 22½ packs was a wretched total for the entire company, it was very respectable for Walker alone. He had only forty men with him, a much smaller brigade than any of his competitors. Furthermore, many of these were green hands, and with them he had to fend off the veterans of the other companies.

In mid-May Warren Ferris and his AFC partisan Andrew Drips were on the Salt River in Wyoming and met ten men Walker had sent to trap there. From them they learned that Walker was still conducting his hunt in the vicinity of Bear Lake, 100 miles farther to the southwest. Since the trapping season and therefore the field rivalry were ending, the two parties joined forces and continued together to Bonneville's first camp on the Green River, which had been designated as the site for the rendezvous of 1833. Arriving on June 7, they were surprised to find that despite their head start, Walker was already there. After having dispersed his trappers, he was left with only six men. However, on the Bear River a Snake chief had offered to go north to the rendezvous with him and bring along 200 lodges of his people as protection against the Blackfeet. With this formidable escort, Walker and his men had made a quick trip, taking a route through the Salt Mountains which was apparently unknown to either Ferris or Drips. When they met, Walker told Ferris, his former Christmas guest, he had had a good hunt, but it had been marred by the fact that one of the men had been attacked by a grizzly bear and suffered a broken arm.

His conduct and success during this year indicate that Walker was already an experienced furman. Since in the 1825–30 period he was largely occupied by settlement business in Missouri, he could have learned the trade only while working out of New Mexico in the early 1820s, several years before Bridger, Fitzpatrick, the Sublettes or others had come to the mountains. The ease and assurance with which he moved and maneuvered in the central Rockies in 1832 and 1833 also suggest that he may have been there before, either with Becknell on the Green River in 1824 or on another of the shadowy ventures of the Taos trappers-smugglers.

Being the first at the rendezvous site, Walker dug up the caches which he and Bonneville had left at Fort Nonsense and began trading with the Snakes who had come north with him. Bonneville did not appear for another month, having taken a roundabout route through Pierre's Hole. As he approached his fort site, he was alarmed to find numerous and fresh signs of Indians. Therefore, in the late afternoon of July 13 he halted and sent scouts ahead to investigate. They shortly returned with some of Walker's men, who, along with the news that the Indians were friendly Snakes, brought a keg of whiskey. This was broached. "The liquor went briskly round; all absent friends were toasted, and the party moved forward to the rendezvous in high spirits."

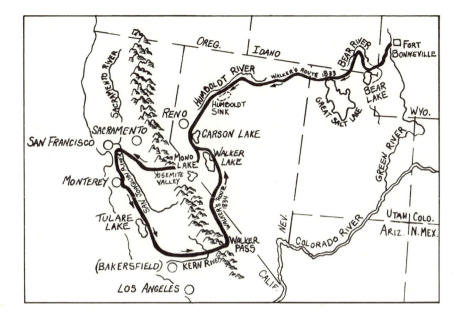

The Sierra

By 1830 attending the summer rendezvous had become for many of the trappers the principal material reward for their work. For a month, which was about as long as even the hardiest could hold the pace, they roistered about in a mountain meadow 1,500 miles west of the last places where there were any laws, police, magistrates, property owners, innocent bystanders, pillars of authority or respectability. They exuberantly scratched their itches with whatever and whoever was handy. After the 1832–33 season, which had been the hardest of all because of their own squabbles and the aroused Blackfeet, the furmen were more than ready to let bygones be bygones and cut loose. They did so with great abandon at what came to be remembered as perhaps the most spectacular of all the rendezvous. In fact, one of the participants, William Drummond Stewart, claimed it "was the last good year, for with 1834 came the spoilers—the idlers, the missionaries, the hard seekers after money."

Stewart himself was a forerunner of people and things to come and of the end of the old ways in the fur trade. Even by then word about these extraordinary bashes of the mountain men had spread through the English-speaking world, inspiring journalists, academics, playboys and, as Stewart said, even preachers, with the desire to attend, to join in the fun, make the acquaintance of the celebrated mountaineers, observe, exploit or pray for them. Stewart, the second son of a British baronet, was one of the first of the tourists, but a very special case. A few years later he became Sir William, the Lord of Murthly, but in 1833 he was one of a sizable cadre of aristocratic half-pay army officers who had been cut loose after the Napoleonic Wars and were wandering about the world like so many Basil Seals, looking for manly excitement while hoping to inherit estates and titles. His background was very different from theirs, but Stewart had skills with guns, knives and women and a zest for hunting and fighting which impressed the mountain men and made them accept him as, so to speak, a deserving peer. About him a mountain veteran said—through George Ruxton— "that ar Englishman. . . . Well, them English are darned fools; they can't fix a rifle any ways; but that one did shoot 'some'; leastwise *he* made it throw plum-center. He made the buffler 'come,' *he* did, and fout well at Pawnee Fork too . . . what he wanted out thar in the mountains, I never jest rightly know'd. He was no trader, nor a trapper, and flung about his dollars right smart. Thar was old grit in him, too, and a hair of the black b'ar at that."

Stewart brought along a few other congenial adventurers, including Benjamin Harrison, whose father, the future president of the United States, had sent him west in hopes of curing his alcoholism. But otherwise, the rendezvous of 1833 was the last which truly belonged to the good old boys. Nearly everyone who had any reputation in the mountain fur trade was there and primed. One of these was a wild, lighthearted, young man by the name of Joe Meek, who said of the beginning of the revels, "when the pie was opened the birds began to sing."

Meek, Stewart and half a dozen others left vivid descriptions of how they sang, drank, gambled, fought, courted and traded for Snake, Nez Percé and Flathead women, all the standard rendezvous amusements. One incident, though unique to 1833, gives some suggestion of the tone of all these gatherings. Needing a place to entertain an Indian girl, William Drummond Stewart kicked out George Holmes, a young New York gentleman, from the tent they shared. While wrapped in his blanket trying to sleep in the grass, Holmes was bitten by a rabid wolf. (These diseased animals replaced the Blackfeet as the hostiles at the 1833 rendezvous. A pack of them hung about the camps and bit, it was reported, a total of twelve men.) Holmes's screams as he was being attacked created more hilarity than sympathy, and someone suggested it would be amusing to stage a midnight mad wolf hunt. Preparations were squelched by Stewart, who interrupted his own recreation in the tent to convince the trappers that the body count—their own—which would almost assuredly result from such drunken sport would not be worth the game.

The next morning, strolling around the camp, talking about the excitement of the evening, Stewart came upon Joe Meek, who was trying groggily to get up from where the whiskey had felled him during the night. Stewart needled him to the effect that Meek was lucky that in his condition he had not also been bitten by a rabid wolf. Even with a bad hangover, Meek was quick with a comeback and replied, "It would have killed him sure [that is, a wolf who bit into such a booze-soaked carcass as his] if it hadn't cured him."

Whiskey did not save the unfortunate Holmes. He sickened, died and was buried in an unmarked grave along a stream that then had not been named.

The 1833 rendezvous drew about 350 white trappers, traders and tourists and 500 Indians. Their various camps were strung out for ten miles along the Green River and Horse Creek, with most of Bonneville's company located around Fort Nonsense at the northern end of the strip. Bonneville himself was no Stewart and, though he left a good clinical report of the festivities, did not carouse with the men. Temperament aside, he had a lot of business that needed attending. Michael Cerré was getting together a packtrain to take the beaver Walker's men had trapped back to the St. Louis market. In addition to helping with these preparations, Bonneville was composing a report to General Macomb at the War Department. This, Cerré had agreed to hand-carry to Washington.

In it, Bonneville casually mentioned that it would be necessary to overstay his official leave. He went on to offer some general observations about the fur trade and some specific ones about the fighting strength of the Pawnee, Sioux, Crow, Arapaho, Cheyenne, Snake and other principal tribes of the region. He also included notes on the British positions along the Columbia and a recommendation of sorts:

> The information I have already obtained authorizes me to say this much; that if our Government ever intend taking possession of Origon the sooner it shall be done the better, and at present I deem a sub-alterns command equal to enforce all the views of our Government; altho a sub-alter[n]s command is equal to the task, yet I would recommend a full company, which by bringing provision to last till June could then live upon the salmon which abounds there during the summer and fall and farming for themselves for the next year could subsist themselves well.

Walker apparently spent more time at the other bivouacs along the river than at Fort Nonsense. Most of the men in the camps along the Green were friends and acquaintances, and among them he was a considerable figure, having enhanced his reputation by his performance the previous spring and winter. He had the almost inbred Tennessee passion for good horses and made a point of showing up at this and other rendezvous with some big, fast studs, which he ran, bet on and usually won with at the impromptu races which were daily occurrences. Otherwise, there are no stories about Walker's being involved in celebrative high jinks. He was too reserved to be a rendezvous cutup on the order of Joe Meek; nevertheless, in 1833 he was the center of attention and made most of the nonorgiastic news at the gathering. After the various parties had assembled, Walker passed along the word that he wanted to recruit at least forty good men for an expedition from the Green River all the way to California. The response was enthusiastic. Though there was still a great scarcity of facts about the place, California was already rumored to be the warm, golden, natural Eden of the continent.

Among the first men Walker engaged was a clerk (in the fur trade this was an executive position, second in administrative authority only to that of the partisan), a twenty-three-year-old Pennsylvanian by the name of Zenas Leonard. It was a fortunate choice, not only for Walker at the time—because Leonard proved to be a brave, steady man—but also for all those who later became interested in the history of the period. For his own satisfaction Leonard kept a journal, one of the best ever compiled by a genuine mountain man, and when it was published a few years later, it gave the only detailed account of the California expedition, the most successful exploration ever undertaken by furmen.

Leonard had grown up in the jungly Seven Mountains region along the West Branch of the Susquehanna River. On his twenty-first birthday, in 1830, he told his father that he could make his living without picking up rocks on the hardscrabble family farm. His father informed him that he was "at liberty" to leave. He did, taking only his rifle and what he could carry on his back. He traveled down the Ohio and then to St. Louis. There he eventually got a job with a small fur company which had been organized on a shoestring by John Gantt, an ex-army officer who had been cashiered for misappropriating government funds, and Jefferson Blackwell, about whom very little is remembered. In the spring of 1831 Gantt and Blackwell sent a party of seventy poorly provisioned men, with Leonard serving as their clerk, into the mountains. There, so far as logistical support went, they were more or less abandoned, the two partners going broke within the year. As part of this ragtag, leaderless brigade, Leonard had as hard a two years as any mountain man ever experienced. On several occasions he was within a day or two of either freezing or starving to death, was badly lost for weeks at a time, was captured by the Arikara and took a Blackfoot arrow in the side. In the spring of 1832 Leonard and two of his mates finally made a respectable beaver hunt but then were robbed of their 150 pelts by a band of eighteen free trappers that included some of their original Gantt and Blackwell companions. Leonard never exaggerated his predicaments or glorified his own responses to them. He confessed to being frightened, lonely, bored and occasionally very homesick for his Pennsylvania farm, often berating himself for having foolishly left it. He wrote that he was sometimes done in by his own carelessness, inexperience and stupidity and was admiring of braver, shrewder veterans.

Leonard's style is illustrated by his account of the "Battle" of Pierre's Hole. There he took up a position in a rifle pit directly opposite the Gros Ventre and held it while many of the others who later had better stories were milling around in the rear. After dragging a wounded friend to safety while under fire, Leonard returned to the front lines. He said he did so to gain "a little glory," but mostly because he did not want the others to think he was a coward. When all the trappers began running to escape the nonexistent Blackfoot relief party, Leonard stated flatly that he ran with them. When it was over, he offered the opinion that the Indians had proved themselves the smarter and braver men and deserved to win. Such passages make Leonard's journal one of the most human and convincing firsthand accounts of the fur trade.

After having had so much trouble during his first two years in the mountains, Leonard was pleased to join the apparently well-organized expedition to California. "Mr. Walker," he wrote after signing on, "was a man well calculated to undertake a business of this kind. He was well hardened to the hardships of the wilderness—understood the character of the Indians very well—was kind and affable to his men, but at the same time at liberty to command without giving offence— and to explore unknown regions was his chief delight."

Leonard was an observant, thoughtful young man, who was with Walker almost constantly for the next two years and remained a friend for the rest of his life. His phrase "to explore unknown regions" was probably the most insightful comment that anybody ever made about the character of his leader. If Leonard's simple explanation for what made the man tick was not true and crucial, then most of Walker's motives and activities will always remain rationally inexplicable.

For the expedition, Walker recruited some of the boldest and most experienced of the mountain men but also some of the most unruly and difficult to lead. Among those who went with him, in addition to Leonard, were: Bill Williams, whose peculiarities and savagery had become more pronounced since his days on the Santa Fe Trail survey; Levin Mitchell, a big, florid-faced, red-headed man (sometimes called Colorado because of his coloring) who was a crony of Williams and with

him and on his own was to become a notable frontier horse thief;
George Nidever, reputed to be one of the best rifle shots in the west;
probably Powell (later called Pauline) Weaver, who together had
fought their way up the Arkansas River into the Rockies, losing
thirty men of their company of forty-eight; Bill Craig, who fled from the
States after having killed a man; Joe Meek, the rendezvous gay blade
who had run away as a sixteen-year-old from Virginia because he had
thrashed a schoolteacher; and his older and even tougher brother,
Stephen Hall Meek. That hardiness and wildness often went together
would have been a common-sense reason for the selection of these and
similar men. Needing those with the first characteristic, Walker was
willing to take his chances at being able to control this crew sufficiently
to get the job done.

The opportunity to go to the Pacific coast seems to have been the
principal attraction for the recruits. Making such a trip would be "a
feather in a man's cap," said Joe Meek, who was always interested in
such adornments. Also, like Leonard, the others were impressed with
the organization of the expedition. Each man, according to Leonard,
was "provided with four horses, and an equal share of blankets, buffalo
robes, provisions, and every article necessary for the comfort of men
engaged in an expedition of this kind." Finally, Walker's own character and credentials contributed to the enthusiasm of the men. George
Nidever, for example, had a comment which was somewhat similar to
that of Leonard: "He [Walker] was one of the best leaders I have ever
met, a good hunter and trapper, thoroughly versed in Indian signs and
possessed of good knowledge of the mountains. He could find water
quicker than any man I ever met."

In regard to the preparations for and destination of the expedition,
the account of Leonard and the recollections of the others were straightforward. There would be no reason to question them except that three
years later, in his book about Bonneville, Washington Irving published
a much different and very peculiar version of the story. He said that
Bonneville said that he had decided to send a party to explore only the
"unknown regions" of the Great Salt Lake:

> This momentous undertaking he confided to his lieutenant,
> Mr. Walker, in whose experience and ability he had great confi-
> dence. He instructed him to keep along the shores of the lake, and
> trap in all the streams on his route; also to keep a journal, and
> minutely to record the events of his journey, and everything
> curious or interesting, making maps or charts of his route, and
> of the surrounding country.
>
> No pains nor expense were spared in fitting out the party, of
> forty men, which he was to command. They had complete sup-
> plies for a year, and were to meet Captain Bonneville in the ensu-

ing summer, in the valley of Bear River, the largest tributary of
the Salt Lake, which was to be his point of general rendezvous.

All this may have sounded plausible and grand to eastern readers
with only hazy ideas about western geography and exploration but
would have struck the few then acquainted with frontier conditions as
preposterous. So far as Americans went, the Great Salt Lake had been
discovered at least as early as 1825 by Jim Bridger and others from
Ashley's fur company. Since then trappers had regularly worked
around and beyond it, and Bonneville, as other passages in the book
indicate, was well aware of their activities. Also, had he wanted to collect additional information about the lake, he had no need to go to the
"pain and expense" of equipping forty men for a year's field trip since
it lay only two weeks' travel from the Green River encampment. That
the expedition was planned to go much farther, as Zenas Leonard
plainly stated, was generally known at the rendezvous. Nidever, Craig
and Walker himself were to leave brief recollections about the matter,
and all agreed with Leonard that when they left, California was their
destination. It is beyond belief that somehow Walker could have kept
these intentions secret from Bonneville. He had no need to do so since
Bonneville knew exactly where he was headed, a fact emphatically confirmed by a document that apparently escaped Irving when he was
scooping up the rest of Bonneville's papers.

In January 1832, while he was in the east making preparations,
Bonneville visited the State Department in Washington. There he ap-
plied for and received a passport (number 2567) made out in the
name of Joseph R. Walker and later obtained a visa for it from the
Mexican consul. Under the arrangements of the time, these papers were
sufficient for not only Walker but also men under his command to
enter California legally. Bonneville made no other passport application,
for either himself or anyone else connected with the venture. (The
copy of Walker's passport in the State Department files bears the nota-
tion "B. L. E. Bonneville, Capt. Army," a curious one since Bonneville
was supposedly not then on active duty.)

Therefore, certainly before they started west and very likely during
their first conversations at Fort Gibson, the two men had agreed that
Walker, and only Walker, would lead a party to California. Given his
long-standing interest in making such a trip, this may have been a
major reason why he joined forces with Bonneville. It is unlikely that
either through conversations with Bonneville or in reading his private
papers, Irving did not learn about the California reconnaissance, which
was the most ambitious exploratory venture of the entire expedition.

There seems to be only one explanation for why Irving ignored this
interesting matter and, in fact, created a bogus destination for Walker.

At this point in the story he needed to set up an explanation which, without making his hero appear a fool, would cover Bonneville's lack of success as a conventional fur trader. He did so by stating that Walker had set off with forty men and a year's supplies to find and look about the Great Salt Lake. With this established, he later could—and did, in shocked detail—describe Walker as an insubordinate incompetent who wandered off to California and thus wasted the resources of the trusting Bonneville. Logistical and topographical realities, the recollections of men who were there and the existence of Walker's passport provide clear evidence—as a trout does in a milk pail—that for reasons that can now only be guessed at, Irving, with or without Bonneville's help, intentionally invented this part of his narrative.

Since Walker had first tried and failed to reach the coast in 1820, several overland parties had succeeded. Two of the original Taos trappers, Ewing Young and William Wolfskill, had taken men across the Sonoran Desert and reached the Los Angeles area by 1829. So had Peter Skene Ogden, a Hudson's Bay Company partisan also traveling by the way of the western Great Basin and southern deserts. Of more importance to the trappers in the central Rockies was an expedition led by Jedediah Smith. He had left the Green River area in the summer of 1826 with fifteen men. They had worked their way along the eastern rim of the Great Basin (which Smith called Starvation Country), coming finally to the lower Colorado and crossing into the Mojave Desert at about Needles. Often lost, suffering exceedingly from lack of food and water, they dragged, fifteen days later, into the Mexican settlements around San Diego.

Smith was one of the few northerners and puritans among the early furmen. He was born in New York State, was a Bible thumper and had, it seems, the personality of a self-righteous YMCA secretary. In San Diego he did little to ingratiate himself, having some very hard things to say about the corrupt Latin culture and the shocking behavior of the women. He and his men were put under house arrest as illegal and undesirable aliens. They remained for a month until an American sailing captain, whose ship was anchored in the harbor, intervened on their behalf with the local authorities. They were paroled on the condition they would immediately leave California. They did not do so but went north into the San Joaquin Valley and trapped beaver there. In May, leaving the others to guard their furs, Smith and two companions made the first west-east crossing of the Sierra and returned to the summer rendezvous, held that year at Bear Lake. Smith stayed only a few weeks before heading back to California, this time with eighteen men. They followed essentially the same route he had taken in 1826 but had a harder trip. At the Colorado crossing some of his men got into an altercation over women with the Mojave Indians. The warriors fell on the trappers, killed ten of them and seized most of their supplies. Smith and eight companions escaped into the desert. However, he could not find the trail he had made the year before and, after another period of suffering, came out of the wilderness near Los Angeles. There Smith was immediately picked up not only for illegal entry but also as a felon and fugitive who had broken the terms of the parole granted in 1826. This time he and all his company were jailed but again were released in response to pleas entered for them by American merchant seamen. Smith went north again, picked up the men and furs he had left there and continued on up the northern California coast toward Oregon. On the way they were surprised and overwhelmed by the Kelawatset Indians. Only one man at the camp and Smith and two others, who were out fishing, escaped. In all, Smith took thirty-three men with him on his two trips to California; twenty-six were killed and two others deserted.

Smith and the other survivors were rescued by agents of the despised Hudson's Bay Company but did not return to the Rockies until the rendezvous of 1829. Smith then sold out his interest in the Rocky Mountain Fur Company and returned to Missouri, where, in partnership with Bill Sublette, he decided to take a fling at the Santa Fe trade. The trail to New Mexico, which Sibley's crews had surveyed five years earlier, had by then become something of a milk run for wagons, but it was a new country and environment for Smith. He became lost in the *jornada* between the Arkansas and Cimarron rivers, just as had the Walker brothers when they were blazing trails there seven years before. Smith, however, was not able to save himself as they had. Scouting ahead of the main party, he came on a water hole and, kneeling down to quench his terrible thirst, was found and killed by some wandering Comanches.

Walker and his men left the Green River on July 27, 1833. Four days later they reached the headwaters of the Bear River, where Walker had trapped in the spring and which he knew was at the western edge of the buffalo range. The company halted there to make meat, staying almost a week, until every man had at least sixty pounds of jerky in his pack. Simple and obvious as this may seem, many of the mountain men did not have the patience or foresight for such preparation. In this respect they had become Indianish and were inclined to gorge themselves when they made big kills and starve when they could not. Also on the Bear River, Walker increased his strength by adding fifteen or twenty more free trappers who were camped there and enthusiastic about joining the California column. Among them was Joe Meek, who had apparently played out and left the Green River rendezvous crapulent and early.

The brigade, then numbering about sixty men, was just north of the Great Salt Lake in mid-August. During the next week they made a thorough reconnaissance of the western shores of this body of water, looking, Walker said, for the outlet of a large river which was marked on an old map in his possession. Rumors of this river, the Buenaventura, had been circulating for some time, and on many early maps it was marked as flowing from the lake directly to the Pacific. Walker, of course, found no trace of it and included this negative information in a topographic briefing he gave to Bonneville on his return the next year. Bonneville therefore eliminated the Buenaventura from the maps, excellent ones, he later drew. Thus Walker and Bonneville had the distinction of doing away with the last major mythic geographical feature in the country.

After this exploration the expedition encountered a hunting party of Bannocks, a Shoshoni people, heading east for buffalo. Ever since Jim Bridger had first met members of this tribe and found them to be a predatory race, given to "murder and thievery," the Bannocks had a bad reputation among the mountaineers. However, at least on this occasion Walker seems to have got along well enough with them, and as was his lifelong custom—again not common among the white trappers —he camped with them to exchange small trade goods for topographical information. On the basis of what the Bannocks told him, information from some of his own men (at least Leonard and Nidever had trapped in this territory the previous winter) and his own intuitive sense, Walker decided to strike directly west through the salt desert. They came in a few days to the upper reaches of the Humboldt River, which Leonard was to name the Barren, on about September 1 and followed it downstream, taking it easy on their horses and themselves. One afternoon they camped early along this shallow stream, and there occurred the only truly comic incident involving Joe Walker which was ever reported. It was described by Bill Craig and is still best told in his own words, or at least those attributed to him many years later by an Idaho journalist:

> The waters of the Humboldt river are of a milky cast, not clear, so one afternoon while camped on the said stream and being the first to strip, I started for the swimming hole and was just about to plunge in when I got a hunch that things were not as they should be and I had better investigate before taking a dive. I did so and found the water was about a foot and a half deep and the mud four, this condition being in the eddy. So I waded to where there was a current and found the water a little

more than waist deep, no mud and good smooth bottom. In looking towards the camp I espied Joe Walker coming and he was jumping like a buck deer, and when he arrived at the brink he says to me: "How is it?" "Joe," I replied, "it is just splendid." With that he plunged head-first into that four and a half feet of blue mud.

Fearing trouble and not being interested in the subsequent proceedings, I made myself scarce by hiding in the brush on the opposite side and in so doing I ran into some rosebrier bushes and scratched myself some, but I was so full of laughter I did not mind that. I peeped through the bushes just in time to see him extricate himself from the mud. He then washed the mud off as well as he could, returned to the tepee, put on his clothes, shot his rifle off, cleaned it, then reloaded it and hollered at me and said: "Now show yourself and I'll drop a piece of lead into you," which I failed to do as I did not want to be encumbered with any extra weight especially at that time. I was compelled to remain in hiding nearly the whole afternoon. Before sundown I was told to come into camp and get my supper and leave, that I could not travel any further with that party.

I was very glad of the permit for it was rather monotonous out there in the brush with nothing but a blanket around me and nobody to talk to and my pipe in camp. I soon dressed myself and then it was time to chew. Our company was divided into messes and each mess was provided with a dressed buffalo hide. It was spread on the ground and the grub placed upon it. When supper was announced we sat down. I sat opposite to Walker and in looking at him I discovered some of that blue mud of the Humboldt on each side of his nose and just below his eyelids, and I could not help laughing. He addressed me in an abrupt manner and said: "What the h--l are you laughing at." I told him that gentlemen generally washed before eating. With that the others observed the mud and they too roared with laughter in which Walker joined, but he threatened if ever I played another such trick on him he would kill me as sure as my name was Craig.

Craig was to tell and retell this story, largely, it seems, as a means of proving he had been such a hell-raising young buck that he had dared play a prank on the great Joe Walker. For this purpose he may have stretched the facts a bit, but even so, it stands as the only light, joky story anyone ever told about or on Walker. Zenas Leonard never mentioned the incident, perhaps because he thought it would make Walker, whom Leonard admired to the point of hero worship, seem undignified.

Along with such high jinks the party also made a few beaver as they moved along the Humboldt. However, as they went farther downstream, they began to lose traps to the Paiutes, who in increasing numbers commenced following them and lurking around their camps. These were another western Shoshoni people who generally were horseless and supported themselves by poking about with sticks for insects, lizards and roots. They seemed such a poor, scruffy lot that whites came to speak derisively of all the related desert tribes of Utah, Nevada, southern Idaho and eastern California as Diggers.

Walker's party may have been the first whites these Paiutes had ever met, and their own technology being a stone-and-stick one, they were fascinated by the foreigners' equipment. Shortly they became adept at pilfering it. "The great annoyance we sustained in this respect greatly displeased some of our men," wrote Leonard, "and they were for taking vengeance before we left the country—but this was not the disposition of Captain Walker. These discontents being out hunting one day, fell in with a few Indians, two or three of whom they killed, and then returned to camp, not daring to let the Captain know it."

There probably were very few men in this company who would have refrained from such an act on principle, but Bill Williams, Levin Mitchell and Bill Craig had particularly murderous reputations. There was also a man named Frazier who is said to have been slightly wounded by the Paiutes. Leonard went on: "The next day while hunting, they repeated the same violation—but this time not quite so successful, for the Captain found it out, and immediately took measures for its effectual suppression." Leonard did not describe what disciplinary action Walker took, but as he noted, it stopped the casual killings. However, the damage had been done in regard to relations with the Paiutes. At the end of the first week of September the party came to the Humboldt Sink, an area of marshes and shallow lakes. While camp was being made, Walker surveyed the country through his spyglass and found that on all sides of them there were Indians, who, said Leonard, "we readily guessed . . . were in arms to revenge the death of those which our men had killed up the river."

A breastwork, made out of their packs, was thrown up around the camp, and the horses were brought inside it and tied to a picket line. Before this work was finished, 800 or 900 Paiutes (according to Leonard; 400 or 500, as recollected George Nidever) emerged from the brush and reeds and began moving toward them. They halted about 150 yards in front of the breastwork, and five chiefs advanced to make medicine. Through signs, they asked if their people might come into the camp to smoke and parley with the white men. Walker said they could not but offered to meet with the chiefs and any of their counselors halfway between the two parties and there continue the negotiations. The chiefs went back to confer with their warriors, and shortly a number of them came forward, indicating that they intended to come into the camp, with or without invitation. Walker then put a dozen riflemen on the breastwork and signed that if any of the Indians advanced farther, they would be killed. This made the Paiutes laugh, and they asked how the white men could possibly carry out their threat from that distance.

At this point it occurred to Walker that the primitive tribesmen had never seen and did not understand the properties of guns. He set about trying to instruct them. A flock of ducks was floating on a small pond near the camp, and he had his marksmen pick off several birds. This, wrote Leonard, "astonished the Indians a good deal, though not so much as the noise of the guns—which caused them to fall flat on the ground. After this they put up a beaver skin on a bank for us to shoot at for their gratification—when they left us for the night. This night we stationed a strong guard, but no Indians made their appearance, and were permitted to pass the night in pleasant dreams."

The next morning Walker got his men moving before dawn, hoping the shooting exhibition had given the Paiutes some pause. However, when the sun came up, Indians could be seen converging from all directions. Shortly groups of the bolder warriors began cutting in front of the column with the intent, the trappers decided, of delaying them until the entire Paiute fighting force could gather and surround them. Leonard described what happened next:

> We now began to be a little stern with them, and gave them to understand that if they continued to trouble us they would do it at their own risk. In this manner we were teased until a party of eighty or one hundred came forward, who appeared more saucy and bold than any others. This greatly excited Captain Walker, who was naturally of a very cool temperament, and he gave orders for the charge, saying that there was nothing equal to a good start in such a case. This was sufficient. A number of our men had never been engaged in any fighting with the Indians, and were anxious to try their skill. When our commander gave his consent to chastise these Indians, and give them an idea of our strength, 32 of us dismounted and prepared ourselves to give a severe blow. We tied our extra horses to some shrubs and left them with the main body of our company, and then selected each a choice steed, mounted and surrounded this party of Indians. We closed in on them and fired, leaving thirty-nine dead on the field—which was nearly the half—the remainder were overwhelmed with dismay—running into the high grass in every direction, howling in the most lamentable manner. Captain Walker then gave orders to some of the men to take the bows of the fallen Indians and put the wounded out of misery.

All the other firsthand witnesses who reminisced about this bloody incident left accounts which substantially agreed with Leonard's as to how it began and what happened. However, Washington Irving, when he came to write his *Adventures of Captain Bonneville, U.S.A.*, had an entirely different version of the fight, even though his principal second-hand informant was a month's travel to the north when it occurred and the author himself was in his study in New York City. Irving reported that the Paiutes were a "timid and inoffensive race" and that the trouble had begun because a white "ruffian" had taken "a horrid oath to kill the first Indian he should meet" and, coming upon a Digger peaceably fishing by a stream, had fulfilled it and "flung his bleeding body into the stream. . . . [T]he only punishment this desperado met with, was a rebuke from the leader of the party."

After that, said Irving, the Indians began appearing in numbers but were "always pacific. . . . The trappers, however, had persuaded themselves that they were making their way through hostile country. . . . At length, one day they came to the banks of a stream . . . which they were obliged to ford. Here a great number of Shoshokoes [another name for the Paiutes] were posted on the opposite bank. Persuaded they were there with hostile intent, they advanced upon them, levelled their rifles, and killed twenty-five of them upon the spot. The rest fled a short distance, then halted and turned about, howling and whining like wolves, and uttering the most piteous wailings. The trappers chased them in every direction; the poor wretches made no defence. . . . We feel perfectly convinced that the poor savages had no hostile intention, but had merely gathered together through motives of curiosity."

In truth, what occurred can be called a massacre, for only Indians were killed. Also, it may have been unnecessary and Walker may have been mistaken in how serious the threat was. On the other hand, there is no other record of a white leader's going to such lengths to avoid hostilities. As for the man who started the trouble by first killing an Indian upriver, being, as Irving scathingly wrote, only rebuked by his leader, the mores of the time and place were such that a man who killed a strange Indian for whatever reason was invariably congratulated for the act. That Walker was outraged by this murder and disciplined the man who committed it was, against this ethical background, a surprising and unconventional response.

What could and should have been done on this bad day at the Humboldt Sink came down to a matter of judgment, and Irving was in a weak position to criticize Walker's. He was not there, but more important, he had never been and never would be in a position where his own well-being depended on making a quick, accurate estimate about the intentions of 500 or more very excited Indians. Inferior as they were in arms, the Paiutes, if they were hostile and had been allowed to get close to the whites, would have very probably overwhelmed them by sheer numbers. Almost as if in rebuttal to Irving (and perhaps it was, since his narrative was published several years after *The Adventures of Captain Bonneville, U.S.A.*), Leonard observed, "The severity with which we dealt with these Indians may be revolting to the heart of the philanthropist; but the circumstances of the case altogether atones for the cruelty. It must be borne in mind that we were far removed from the hope of any succor in case we were surrounded, and that the country we were in was swarming with hostile savages, sufficiently numerous to devour us. Our object was to strike a decisive blow. This we did—even to a greater extent than we had intended."

Finally, there was the matter of the ax that Washington Irving was so persistently grinding. Whatever the facts or circumstances, the more villainous and bloodthirsty Walker could be made to seem, the more convincing he was as Bonneville's scapegoat.

Questions about the morality and necessity aside, Walker accomplished the end he had in mind with this preemptive strike. After the terrible morning of instruction about the capabilities of rifles, the Paiutes disappeared. Free from their teasing, the party crossed to the west side of the Humboldt, ferrying their supplies on rafts they made by lashing together bundles of tule rushes. Then they began traveling westward through regions no white man was known to have previously visited.

Since there were no named points of reference, Leonard's journal for the next six weeks is only an approximate guide to their route. However, from the occasional descriptions he gave of prominent topographic features, it seems that they traveled in a southwesterly line from the Humboldt, passing by first Carson and then Walker Lake. From there they probably followed what later was to be named the Walker River toward the mountains. The hunters fanned out from the main party to scour the sagebrush flats and gullies for game. They found nothing larger than jackrabbits, but one day they surprised a few families of Diggers encamped near one of the desert lakes. These Indians had perhaps already heard something about these white strangers and prudently fled at their approach. In one of the abandoned brush lean-tos, the hunters found two rabbitskin bags full of what they judged to be pieces of dried fish. These they took back to camp, and the contents were emptied into the supper stew, then served up again the next morning. However, a good many of the trappers lost their breakfast when Walker, becoming curious, dissected some of the fish bits and found that in fact, they were worms, insect larvae, that the Diggers had rooted out with their sticks.

North of Mono Lake they caught their first impressive glimpse of the east wall of the Sierra, halted for a day and sent out scouting parties to look for a pass. Walker and Leonard went together and in the brush startled two Indians, who fled, unfortunately, in the direction of George Nidever. Nidever said that as he watched them running toward him, he thought about letting them go, "but the death of my brother, so treacherously murdered by these red devils, was too fresh in my mind." (Nidever's brother Mark had been rubbed out three years before by Arapahoes in Oklahoma.) So Nidever shot and killed both of them. However, on the way back to camp his fit of revengeful rage passed, and he told Walker he was sorry for what he had done. Nothing resembling a pass was discovered, but by then they had very few options. The jerked buffalo and other supplies of food they had carried were virtually exhausted, and they knew they were a month's hard, dangerous travel west of any place where they could expect to replenish them by hunting. Therefore, they had no real choice but to go into the forbidding mountains and hope that they could find a way through them and that if they did, California would be as bountiful as rumored. They left the next day, October 1 or thereabouts, following a narrow Indian and game trail to the west and up.

When they had climbed high enough on the mountainside to provide a lookout over the Nevada plains, Leonard said the experience was "awfully sublime." So was the entire next month of their lives, spent trying to find and force a passage through the Sierra. This was a veteran party, and probably not a man in it had not previously been very cold and hungry and at times lost; but none had experienced physical and psychic hardships on the scale they found in the Sierra. In fact, this was one of the very few times that any of the frontiersmen had to do any sustained mountaineering, as the term is now technically used. In consequence they learned and invented techniques as they proceeded. Shortly they were above the snow and often the tree line, trying to cope with snow-filled crevasses, icy rock walls and cliffs down which they had to rope themselves and their horses. They struggled ahead on half rations, making many camps where they spent a freezing night without either food or fire, huddled in their blankets and wet buckskins. The fear of avalanche and rock slides was constant.

After a week or so Leonard said the horses began to grow "stiff and stupid" from the numbing cold, exhaustion and starvation. So, too, did some of the men, who staged a brief rebellion, demanding that Walker turn around and lead them back to buffalo country. He tried to reason with them, pointing out that they had neither the supplies nor the strength to reach the familiar plains. When this did not convince them, he frightened them into their senses by saying they could go back if they chose, but he would not let them take any of the expedition's horses or ammunition. Not daring to demand these absolutely essential possessions from their formidable Captain, they continued to follow him. As a conciliatory gesture, Walker, after this matter was settled, permitted the men to butcher two horses. "This," wrote Leonard, "gave our men fresh courage, and we went to bed this night in better spirits than we had done for a long time. Some of the men had fasted so long, and were so much in want of nourishment, that they did not know when they had satisfied the demands of nature, and eat as much and as eagerly of this black, tough, lean, horse flesh, as if it had been the choicest piece of beef steak."

These were the first of seventeen horses that were to be eaten in the next several weeks. Without them Walker and his men would almost certainly have died, but even so, Leonard, who was a sentimentalist about animals, found the choice hard. "It seemed to be the greatest cruelty to take your rifle, when your horse sinks to the ground from starvation, but still manifests a desire and willingness to follow you, to shoot him in the head and then cut him up and take such parts of their flesh as extreme hunger alone will render it possible for a human being to eat."

Leonard's journal for this period is not much concerned with topographic detail but rather is a strange, surrealistic diary, in which nightmarish vignettes about their efforts and hardships are mixed with peculiarly brilliant descriptions of scenic grandeur. All in all, it is a moving account of men who were terrified that they would never get out alive from this "awfully sublime" place but day after day continued trying, calling on their final reserves of strength, cunning and courage. As best as can now be determined, they reached the main ridge of the Sierra northeast of Tuolumne Canyon, where they found themselves in a maze of cols, peaks and boulder fields which fell away precipitously to the west. Not able to find a way down through these formations, they turned south and traveled along the crest. Leonard complained that they could make no more than eight or ten miles a day, but this seems like an exceptional pace, given their situation and the fact that they were constantly making probes to the west, looking for a descent route.

Continuing in this direction, they came on about October 20 to one of the great natural marvels of North America, being the first whites to reach the brink and look down into the Yosemite Valley. Walker, to the day he died, was to remember the moment. Leonard described it for the first time:

> Here we began to encounter in our path, many small streams which would shoot out from under these high snowbanks, and after running a short distance in deep chasms which they have through the ages cut in the rocks, precipitate themselves from one lofty precipice to another, until they are exhausted in rain below. Some of these precipices appeared to us to be more than

a mile high. Some of the men thought that if we could succeed in descending one of these precipices to the bottom, we might thus work our way into the valley below—but on making several attempts we found it utterly impossible for a man to descend, to say nothing of our horses.

Unable to climb down into the Yosemite Valley, they began to follow its rim westward along the ridge which separates it from the almost equally impressive Tuolumne Canyon, of which they also caught glimpses. The going was still very difficult, and they were becoming weaker and more dispirited almost by the hour. However, on the twenty-sixth they came to an outlook where they could see plains to the west. Walker studied them and told the exhausted men that he thought the Pacific lay just beyond the range of his telescope. He was overly optimistic, but the men were encouraged, for they had during the previous three months come to trust their Captain, "who was a man well acquainted with geography."

His reputation was further enhanced when the next day they discovered a well-used Indian trail going down the ridge to the west. In the afternoon, following this path, they killed a deer, the largest game they had taken since the buffalo north of Salt Lake. They stopped, cooked and ate the animal on the spot, "in less time," Leonard noted, "than a hungry wolf would devour a lamb." The descent was slow and difficult, but from that moment on, the pages of Leonard's journal reflect the soaring optimism of men who knew they could make it out of the mountains alive. The snow depths began to decrease, and they came into some green oak scrub, where the hunters brought down two large black-tailed deer and a black bear, "all very fat and in good eating order. This night we passed more cheerful and in better heart than any we had spent for a long time. Our meat was dressed and well cooked, and every man felt in good order to partake of it."

Sitting around a fire, stuffed and warm, they began, a few nights later, to talk about with certain nostalgia their crossing of the Sierra. While it was true they had as yet earned no profit from the expedition and had lost a lot of equipment and horses, nobody had died and, recorded Leonard, "every man expressed himself fully compensated for his labor, by the many natural curiosities which we had discovered."

There were more of these to come. On October 30 they found "trees of the red-wood species, incredibly large—some of which would measure from sixteen to eighteen fathom round the trunk and at the height of a man's head from the ground." (They had passed through and again became the first whites known to have seen one of the stands of giant sequoias—probably the present Merced Grove.) Thereafter they were in the cream. They traveled easily along the Merced, marveling at the white water rapids and the beautiful, deep eddies of clear water. Coming to the San Joaquin, they began trapping beaver and found some Indians with whom, after "calming their terror," they smoked and traded for good horses. Leonard reported that camped along the river on the night of November 12, "our men were again thrown into great consternation by the singular appearance of the heavens. Soon after dark the air appeared to be completely thickened with meteors falling towards the earth, some of which would explode in the air and others would be dashed to pieces on the ground, frightening our horses so much that it required the most active vigilance of the whole company to keep them together."

They had a very good vantage point for watching one of the spectacular celestial happenings of the nineteenth century. This meteor show was visible and caused great excitement throughout the United States on the evening of November 12, 1833. It was later estimated that in certain places 200,000 shooting stars were visible between midnight and dawn. The display was "altogether a mystery to some of the men," and at least one of them was terrified by it. Dragging Walker from his blankets, the mountaineer demanded the leader protect them against "the damndest shooting-match that ever was seen." Leonard wrote that "after an explanation from Captain Walker, they were satisfied that no danger need be apprehended from the falling of the stars, as they were termed."

It would be interesting to know what sort of astronomical lesson Walker gave them and where he came by his own information, but it is apparent that by that time the hard-bitten trappers had come to have an almost childlike faith in his wisdom and turned to him as a soothing authority. They were to appeal to him as the natural history authority once again while traveling down the San Joaquin. Leonard wrote:

> This night we encamped on the bank of the river in a very beautiful situation. Soon after the men went to rest and the camp had become quieted, we were startled by a loud distant noise similar to that of thunder. Whilst lying close to the ground this noise could be distinctly heard for a considerable length of time without intermission. When it was at first observed some of our men were much alarmed, as they readily supposed it was occasioned by an earthquake, and they began to fear that we would all be swallowed up in the bowels of the earth; and others judged it to be the noise of a neighboring cataract. Captain Walker, however, suggested a more plausible cause, which allayed the fears of the most timid. He supposed that the noise originated by the Pacific rolling and dashing her boisterous waves against the rocky shore. Had any of us ever before been at the coast, we would have readily accounted for the mysterious noise. The idea

of being within hearing of the *end* of the *Far West* inspired the heart of every member of our company with a patriotic feeling for his country's honor, and all were eager to lose no time until they should behold what they had heard. We felt as if all our previous hardships and privations would be adequately compensated, if we would be spared to return in safety to the homes of our kindred and have it to say that we had stood upon the extreme end of the great west.

Eden—and Back

Walker and his men followed the San Joaquin to Suisun Bay, reaching salt water on November 13, 1833, the day after the great meteor shower. Having received general directions from local Indians, they decided to find the Spanish (as frontiersmen customarily called the Mexicans) settlements on the coast. The company struck out to the southwest, skirting San Francisco Bay, and a week later "the broad Pacific burst forth to view." This improved their morale tremendously, and thereafter Leonard's journal gives a sense that these hard mountaineers were constantly pinching themselves to make sure they had not died and gone to heaven.

They made their first seaside camp on the beach at Año Nuevo Point by a spring of "delightful water." They found the carcass of a beached sperm whale and were astonished by the monster. Almost as much a wonder were the gardens of nearby coastal Indians, who were growing, even though it was December, splendid "corn, pumpkins, melons, etc., the soil being so very strong and mellow that it requires but little labor to raise good crops." They spent two days playing around in the sun and sand and often simply staring out, fascinated by the sea. On the third day they saw distant sails and began waving blankets to attract the attention of the ship's lookouts. The vessel anchored and sent in a boat party to investigate. The ship turned out to be the 292-ton *Lagoda* from Boston, commanded by John Bradshaw, who was trading along the coast for cowhides and tallow, the chief exportable products of Alta California. Bradshaw asked Walker and his men to come aboard, "stating that he had a few casks of untapped Coneac. This was an invitation none of us had the least desire to refuse," wrote Leonard, "and accordingly forty-five of us went . . . leaving the remainder to take care of the camp, etc. When arriving on the ship Captain B., had a table spread with the choicest of liquors and best fare the ship would afford, which was immediately surrounded with hungry captains, mates, clerks, sailors, and greasy trappers—after eating, the glass was passed around in quick succession, first drinking after the fashion of brave Jack Tars, and afterwards in the mountain style, mixed with something of the manners of the natives, in order to amuse the sailors."

Poor Leonard became sea or otherwise sick and had to be rowed back to camp, but his mates kept going until dawn. Then all hands piled into boats, came ashore and continued the frolic. The mountaineers were able to provide venison, and the sailors "appeared perfectly satisfied with the reception they met with from us, as it was a long time since they had tasted any fresh meat, or anything but salted victuals; and theirs was the first bread, butter, cheese, etc, that we had seen for more than two years."

After everyone had somewhat recovered, Bradshaw said they were about seventy miles north of Monterey, the Spanish capital, and advised Walker to go there directly to present his credentials. Then the seaman explained something about the international situation: that because of the weakness of Mexico, the British and Russians were encroaching from the north, establishing posts which seemed to him more military than commercial. Bradshaw, Walker and the others who took part in the discussion were all, according to Leonard, of the opinion that the U.S. government "should assert her claim by taking possession of the whole territory as soon as possible—for we have good reason to suppose that the territory *west* of the mountain will some day be equally as important to a nation as that on the *east*."

The next day, before the *Lagoda* pulled anchor, Bradshaw told Walker he would meet him in Monterey and promised to assist him in dealing with the governor. The mountaineers then started south through the marshy coastal meadows, still traveling easily and eating well. One day they killed ninety-three deer and a few wild cattle, from which they took hides to make themselves new moccasins. Along the way they met some friendly Spaniards, "fine portly looking men," who guided them to the ranch of John Gilroy. He was a Scotsman and the first English-speaking settler in northern California, having remained there since jumping a British ship in Monterey in 1814. Gilroy also proved very hospitable and, when his guests were ready to leave, directed them to the mission of San Juan Bautista, the principal settlement in the area. This had been established in 1797 and had grown into a commune of twenty priests and some 1,000 Indians, who received instruction in religion, domestic and agricultural crafts. After they had got over their suspicions about the papish taint of the place

("Everything in this station is under the control and management of the priests"), the Americans were able to admire the architecture, industries, well-tilled fields and vineyards.

Walker conducted himself much more diplomatically than had the pious Jed Smith (who earned a reputation in California as a disagreeable land pirate) and with much better results. At San Juan Bautista "Captain Walker deemed it prudent to halt for a few days, in order to ascertain the disposition of the people, and make further inquiries with respect to the country, etc., lest we might be considered as intruders and treated in a way that we would not much like." After talking to the missionaries, Walker decided that because of the difficulty of finding food and forage, it would not do to ride into the coastal settlements with the entire party. Therefore, he left for Monterey accompanied by only two men. As he had promised, Captain Bradshaw was waiting in Monterey Roads and, after Walker arrived, arranged for an appointment with the governor of Alta California, His Excellency José Figueroa. The meeting went very well. Figueroa told Walker that he and his men were welcome to stay all winter, to travel freely, to kill as much game as they needed and, if they wished, to trade with Mexican citizens. However, they were not to brawl with or molest any residents and were prohibited from trapping on Indian lands or trading with Indians. Finding these conditions reasonable, Walker agreed to them and went back to San Juan Bautista. In the open country beyond the mission he selected a site for a permanent winter camp, moved his party to it and made it clear to his men that he expected them to behave themselves according to the arrangements he had made with the governor. After settling these matters, Walker proposed to Leonard that the two of them take a sightseeing "tramp" through the country. "This," wrote Leonard, "was precisely what I had long been wanting." The Captain and his clerk set off on their tour the week before Christmas and spent the holiday at the warm, sunny mission of San Jose, "employing our time in watching the proceedings of these Indians in their devotional exercises. The manoeuvres of those who have been lately converted to the Christian religion (being of the Catholic faith) is something very singular." They continued on to Monterey, where they were joined by some of the others from the camp, who had come to town with the packs of beaver they had made on the San Joaquin. These were exchanged with Bradshaw for powder, lead and other supplies. After the business had been concluded, they had a bang-up New Year's party on board the *Lagoda*. Among others attending was the governor, and he, Walker and Bradshaw, the three ranking men, apparently got along like a house afire. On New Year's Day the Missouri trappers invited their new friends ashore and put on a demonstration of sharpshooting, "which terminated by conclusively convincing the sailors that if they could beat us in telling 'long yarns,' we were more than a match for them with the rifle."

Returning to their base camp, Walker and Leonard found everything in order except that one of the men, Philips, while out hunting had been surprised by a grizzly. His arm had been broken, and he was "most shockingly cut and mangled," but he recovered. This seems to have been the most serious injury suffered by any man during the entire expedition, a remarkable record considering what they did. For the next month the mountaineers, except for the convalescent Philips, enjoyed themselves hugely as California tourists and had, it seems, great social success after the Californians decided these big, wild-looking Americans were not going to break up their homes or communities. They went out riding and hunting with the Mexican cowboys, and for many of them this was their first experience with the lariats used for roping cattle, horses and even bears. At the big ranches in the neighborhood there were dances and other entertainments. Also, there were women, dressed, as Joe Meek—who had a keen eye for this sort of thing—said, in "gowns of gaudy calico or silk, and a bright colored shawl, which served for mantilla and bonnet together. They were well formed, with languishing eyes and soft voices; and doubtless appeared charming in the eyes of our band of trappers, with whom they associated freely at fandangoes, bull-fights or bear baitings." Meek added that during their stay in California, "a land of sunshine and plenty," he and his mates "were mad with delight." This may have seemed to him about as close as he could come to describing the winter with propriety to the lady historian who years later interviewed him and wrote his biography.

As for Walker himself, he was not a fandango type on the order of the uninhibited Meek but, on the other hand, was not a puritan like Jed Smith, who had felt himself obliged to lecture the Californians about their morals and Roman errors. Also, it seems that Walker made a very good impression on California officials because he was able to control the white savages he had brought out of the mountains. Following their New Year's celebration the governor took Walker aside and made him an extraordinary offer. Figueroa said he would give the American outright title to 30,000 acres of whatever unoccupied land he found most desirable in northern California if, in return, Walker would undertake to establish a colony of fifty American "mechanics of different kinds." Under Walker's direction these men and their families would be free to develop the land in whatever way seemed best and most lucrative to them. From Figueroa's standpoint it was a sensible and politically shrewd proposition. The colony would provide California with some badly needed artisans, could be expected to help hold the local Indians in check, would serve to frustrate British and Russian incursions from the north and, though out of politeness it was not mentioned, those of less desirable Americans from the east.

Walker was well aware of what he might gain. He told Zenas Leonard that he listened carefully to the governor because he "was well pleased with the country, and . . . had no doubt he could in a few years amass a fortune, and be the head of a rich and flourishing settlement." No doubt he could have, for he was being offered his choice of some of the best lands on the continent. However, he politely turned down the opportunity. Privately he told Leonard that his "love for the laws and free institutions of the United States, and his hatred for those of the Spanish government, deterred him from accepting the governor's benevolent offer."

Leonard, or the editor who first prepared his journal for publication, may have laid it on a bit thick with these Fourth of July sentiments. However, the incident again impressed on Leonard that so far as motives and ambitions went, his leader was a puzzling and exceptional man. The Austins in Texas, Daniel Boone in Missouri, later John Marsh and John Sutter in California were to trade, if not their souls, at least their citizenship and in several cases religion for proprietary grants which if anything were less desirable than those offered to Walker. It is unlikely that in his shoes, many or any of the other early frontier figures would have done as Walker did. Beyond adventure, they all were looking for good deals—ranches, farming land, mineral deposits, trading post sites and other commercial opportunities. When they found them, they seized them and settled down. Already, in regard to the opening of the Santa Fe trade and the development of Jackson County, Walker had demonstrated how little appeal this sort of thing had for him. The rejection of Figueroa's offer was another, if particularly impressive, example, of a consistent trait. "He was not," wrote a journalist who became acquainted with him fifteen years later during the California gold rush days—and was perplexed about how little this bonanza interested Walker—"wantonly prodigal with gold, but he was never so fond of it as to make its acquisition the aim or end of his lifetime pursuit."

After refusing Figueroa, Walker began making preparations to pursue what Leonard thought was his "chief delight": the exploration of unknown regions. Specifically he gathered the men for their return trip, during which he intended to find a new and better way through the Sierra. Understandably some of the men were not enthusiastic about going back into those mountains. Six of them decided to remain in the golden country. One of these was George Nidever, who was an able cabinetmaker and had found that there was a great demand for his craft in California. (Nidever later moved to the coast and prospered as a sea otter hunter.) Though they all were sorry to leave these companions, who, Leonard said, had become closer than brothers, Walker was apparently understanding about their feelings, and they parted on good terms.

On February 14, 1834, the company, then numbering fifty-two men, left the vicinity of San Juan Bautista. They had with them 315 horses, 47 head of cattle and 30 dogs. The latter were more durable and no less palatable reserve rations than horses or mules. They traveled southwest up the San Joaquin valley, roughly paralleling the Sierra, while making local inquiries about passes through it. In the vicinity of the present Bakersfield, they turned eastward up the Kern River and there came to a village of Tübatulabel (Pine-nut Eater) Indians. They made the tribe a present of a cow, a dog and a little tobacco. Then the chief "brought a hearty and good-looking young female to our captain and proposed to give her in exchange for an ox. Captain Walker very prudently declined the offer, telling the chief that we had a great distance to travel, and would probably be without meat half the time."

Further upstream on the Kern they came to another Tübatulabel village and had better luck in obtaining topographical information. This chief said that indeed, there was a fine pass through the Sierra and allowed Walker to engage two of the tribesmen as guides to it. Following the Indians, they were the first whites to travel through this pass, which was to be named for Walker and would become an important gateway for California-bound emigrants a decade later. (The summit of Walker Pass is almost exactly a mile above sea level, but it is far enough south in the Sierra so that overland travelers could count on its being snow-free until at least early winter. Also, it provided an alternative to continuing farther south and then having to cross the Mojave Desert.)

The Tübatulabel guides led them down the eastern slope of the mountain to a good spring in the Owens Valley, where the party camped on about May 1. There the Indians were paid in tobacco and small trade goods and departed for their home. At the same place a dozen or so of the free trappers who had joined Walker on the Bear River the fall before decided to strike off on their own to the Gila River in Arizona and from there to New Mexico. Again, their departure caused no hard feelings since they had come along as volunteers and had been at liberty to leave whenever they chose. Bill Williams (if he had not already left or been discharged from the expedition), Bill Craig, Levin Mitchell, a Delaware named Mark Head and Stephen Meek were probably in this group. Joe Meek certainly was, for he gave the only account of the adventures of this band.

One reason for their leaving may have been that they were growing restive under the tight discipline imposed by Walker. Once they were released from it, they more or less ran amuck. Eventually they came to a Moqui (Hopi) village near the Little Colorado in Arizona. These people, said Meek, were a "half-civilized nation." They were much more than that, having been a peaceful, cultured agricultural people when the ancestors of the lowland Scots, for example, were still practicing human sacrifice. In their high, isolated villages the Moqui had had few white visitors, but those who had come their way had been treated very hospitably. This band of trappers, perhaps feeling they had been behaving themselves for too long, stormed into the village and began stealing from the Indian orchards and melon patches. When some of the Moqui objected, the whites gunned down fifteen or twenty of them. This was too much for Joe Meek, who, though wild and violent, was never a mean, sadistic young man. "I didn't belong to that crowd," he protested. "I sat on the fence and saw it, though. It was a shameful thing."

Thereafter, Meek said, he met Kit Carson and several others in New Mexico, and they decided to go to the Arkansas River, where they were jumped by 200 Comanches. According to Meek, he, Carson, Mark Head and three other trappers stood off the war party, killing forty-two of its members. Carson later said that he could remember only two dead Indians and that the whole thing happened in another year. Wherever he was, Meek came back to the rendezvous on the Green River that summer, saying that on his way the only other happening of note was that a companion had been struck and killed by a bolt of lightning.

After Meek and the others had departed, Walker and his men began traveling north, skirting Death Valley and the Nevada barrens while following the eastern foothills of the Sierra, where they were able to find tolerable water and pasture. It was a safe route, and they reckoned that by following it, they would sooner or later cut the trail they had made the previous fall while traveling from the Humboldt Sink into the Sierra. When they did, they would simply backtrack up the Humboldt and from there to Salt Lake. However, since the Sierra tends toward the west, this was a long way around. Walker reasoned they could head into the desert on a diagonal northeasterly course and eliminate a corner of the rectangle they would otherwise travel. The men, being impatient to get to the rendezvous, initially agreed to try this shortcut, and on May 10 they turned away from the Sierra into the desert. On the first night they camped by a small, stagnant puddle, but the next day not even Walker could find water. By the third day the men were mortally thirsty, frightened and rebellious. Most of them demanded that they turn back to the Sierra and, if they could get there, continue on their previous course, which, however long, at least had water.

> Captain Walker, who never done anything by halves, with a few others [Leonard does not make it clear whether he himself was one of them] were of the opinion that we were half way across, and could as easily proceed as return. On all such disputes, on all former occasions, the majority decided on what steps should be taken; but when our Captain was in the minority, and being beloved by the whole company, and being a man who was seldom mistaken in anything he undertook, the men were very reluctant in going contrary to his will. The dispute created much confusion in our ranks; but fortunately, about midnight the Captain yielded to the wishes of his men, and as it was cool, and more pleasant traveling than in the day time, we started back towards the mountain.

The two days and nights which followed were bad ones, during which they were reduced to drinking the blood of some of their cattle, but they got back to the Sierra and found water before any of them died. Thereafter they stayed along the mountain and came to the Humboldt Sink on June 8. The marshes were again swarming with Paiutes, more of them, Leonard thought, than they had met there the previous September. They were so numerous that some of them must have been present at the former encounter. If so, they were very slow learners. Again they began to press in around the whites, who again "used every endeavor that we could think of, to reconcile and make them friendly, but all to no purpose." Presents were given, and Walker even inquired by sign to determine if the Paiutes had tribal enemies. If they did, he told them, he and his men would fight with them as allies. The Paiutes showed no inclination to be either pacified or bribed and continued what seemed to be preparations for a battle. Remembering how effectively (and perhaps satisfyingly) they had previously dealt with the Paiutes, "some of our men said hard things about what they would do if we would again come into contact with these provoking Indians."

This comment by Leonard indicates that Walker was by then having considerable difficulty controlling his men, who were now on a known trail and perhaps felt less dependent upon and intimidated by him. "Our Captain," wrote Leonard of the situation, "was afraid that, if once engaged, the passion of his men would become so wild that he could not call them off, whilst there was an Indian found to be slaughtered." There followed a ghastly replay of the events of the past fall. Again Walker gave the order to charge. His men did, this time killing fourteen of the Indians. Three of the whites were slightly wounded. However, after this quick strike Walker was able to call off his troops. As Leonard suggested, this was perhaps the only way he could avoid something worse, a truly terrible massacre of the Paiute women and children who had gathered beyond the warriors. While the second fight at the "Battle Lakes" seems less defensible in terms of self-protection than the first, Walker may have been even less responsible for the bloodshed on this occasion. He had repeated his exceptional efforts to avoid hostilities. However, at the second encounter not only the Paiutes but his own men were determined to have at each other, no matter what he said or did.

Thereafter the company experienced no special hardships or risks. They continued up the Humboldt without further Indian trouble, crossed over to the Snake and then went to the Bear River, looking for Bonneville. They found him in July, a year after they had left for California.

Bonneville had much less to show for his year than had Walker and his men, having neither made a good haul of furs nor accomplished any notable feats of exploration. Certainly his winter had been much less pleasant and interesting than theirs in sunny California. On Christmas Day he had left his main party at a winter camp on the Portneuf River, near the present site of Pocatello, Idaho, and with three men had set off on "a reconnoitring expedition . . . to penetrate to the Hudson's Bay establishments." (Throughout his stay in the west Bonneville was especially interested in the activity of the British. On this occasion his intention was to look at some of their posts on the lower Columbia.) In February bad weather and lack of supplies forced the small party to stop at a Nez Percé village on the Imnaha River, where "they fairly begged some fish or flesh from the hospitable savages." The Indians were not unfriendly, but they had very little extra food, and to get some of it for himself and his men, Bonneville exercised his ingenuity during his three-week stay at their village. Having no regular trade goods, he cut up his plaid poncho and, from the pieces, sewed colorful hats for the Indians. "A man-milliner," he ironically referred to himself. Also, he found that taking off his own hat and exposing his head, which was bald as a billiard ball, amused his hosts and kept them in a charitable mood.

In March with the Nez Percé he went to Fort Walla, a small up-country HBC post made of driftwood and garrisoned by only half a dozen men. He was politely received but was refused supplies and left, noting in his report that he had learned enough at this place about the

British methods to make it unnecessary to visit their larger posts in western Oregon. Following a circuitous route, he returned to the Portneuf, but the men he had left there were gone. They had very nearly starved at this site and, shortly after Bonneville's departure, moved to Walker's old winter quarters on the Blackfoot. Bonneville continued on his way and eventually found some of the missing men. Together they traveled to Bear River, which had been designated as the rendezvous site for their entire expedition. There they found or were found by Walker.

Bonneville had said that during the spring he was sometimes "destitute," but Walker some years later was to recall his situation more vividly and with some mockery. He said he found Bonneville, wearing rags, "in camp with nothing but a squaw." If so, this was a temporary situation, for Bonneville had some men with him, and the party was trying to build up its stores by hunting on the Bear River. Even so, Walker's fairly testy remark, the only derogatory one he was ever known to have passed about Bonneville, is understandable. By the time he made it he had had a chance to read *The Adventures of Captain Bonneville, USA*, in which Washington Irving had a number of very hard things to say about Walker. Specifically he wrote that after Walker began to describe the details of "this most disgraceful expedition" to California, Bonneville was "so deeply grieved by the failure of his plans, and so indignant at the atrocities related to him, that he turned, with disgust and horror, from the narrators. Had he exerted a little of the Lynch law of the wilderness, and hanged those dexterous horsemen in their own lasos, it would have been a well-merited and salutary act of retributive justice. The failure of this expedition was a blow to his pride, and a still greater blow to his purse. The Great Salt Lake still remained unexplored; at the same time, the means which had been furnished so liberally to fit out this favorite expedition, had all been squandered at Monterey. . . ."

Irving went on to say that Bonneville then sent the disgraced Captain Walker back to St. Louis, convoying their packs of furs in company with Michael Cerré. Where they got these packs is something of a mystery. Walker had sold his beaver to Captain Bradshaw in California, and Bonneville's journal gives no indication that he did any trapping that year.

In general, Irving's description of the scene on the Bear River—the ragged Bonneville, with only his squaw for support, dressing down Walker in front of his California veterans, suggesting that hanging was too good for him and then sending him back home like a disobedient child—is beyond belief. No great attempt has to be made to believe this version, for it seems to be almost entirely a fiction. The Great Salt Lake was explored. On the basis of the information Walker gave him,

Bonneville included with his report an excellent map, the best drawn to that time, of the area. As for the overall results of the expedition, it had been most successful in accomplishing what Bonneville and Walker had apparently previously agreed on as its principal objective: finding a route to California and making a reconnaissance of the Mexican territories.

No doubt both men were disappointed that along with the exploration the party had not also been able to take some furs. However, given the personalities of the two men and their future relations, it seems improbable that this was a cause for criticism or hard feelings. A conversation may be imagined which at least seems more plausible than that created by Irving:

"Marvelous, marvelous. I'd love to have been there—but no beaver, eh?"

"Good God, man, we're lucky to be back alive."

"No offense, I'm sure, Mr. Walker. I understand. It was a magnificent reconnoiter, and I am sure they are going to be very pleased to hear about it in Washington. I was simply expressing the thought that it is a pity that our—shall we say?—material rewards will not be great."

As for Irving's report that Walker was dismissed from the expedition and sent back to Missouri, this is also pure fabrication. From Irving's standpoint, it was necessary. Having defamed Walker as a bloodthirsty, extravagant fool, he could not very well let him continue as a friend and business associate of Bonneville's. However, that is what the two men remained—cordial partners. Fortunately Zenas Leonard was still there and still keeping his journal, in which he described what transpired between them during the next year. (Walker's name never again appeared in Irving's book.)

When they finally were reunited on the Bear, Bonneville's and Walker's brigades waited together until July 20, when Michael Cerré came out from St. Louis to resupply them. Cerré stayed ten days and then returned to Missouri. In the meantime, Walker and Bonneville had worked out their plan of operations for the next year. Leonard, who as a clerk would have probably been part of the discussion, reported: "Captain Bonneville was left to make his fall hunt on the headwaters of the Columbia River and the adjacent country with fifty men, and Captain Walker with fifty-five men, being the balance of our force, to cross the Rocky Mountains to the waters of the Missouri River, and then continue hunting and trading with the Indians until the month of June, 1835, when Captain Bonneville with his men would join us on the Bighorn River, at the mouth of Popoasia [Popo Agie] Creek." In accordance with these arrangements, they left their rendezvous site on the last day of July, and Leonard saw no sign of animosity between either the men or their two leaders. "After the usual ceremony of parting on such occasions, which is performed by each one affectionately shaking hands all round—we separated, each division taking off in a separate direction."

Leonard went with Walker, and after crossing to the eastern side of the Rockies, the party trapped, "very successfully," Leonard said, on streams in the Yellowstone and Bighorn drainage system. This country was called the Absaroka and was the wild and beautiful homeland of the Crow tribe. In late October Walker divided the brigade, taking most of the men to a site on the Wind River, where, sixty or seventy miles east of the Continental Divide, he established their winter camp and a temporary trading post. Leonard, in charge of a small detachment, remained temporarily behind to continue trapping and trading while living in a Crow village. He was very pleased with the assignment. "I now found myself in a situation that had charms which I had many times longed for. Ever since I engaged in the trapping business, I had occasional intercourse with the Indians, but never resided with them until now; which would afford me every opportunity to minutely observe their internal mode of living."

The Crows were an interesting people with a reputation for cleverness or treachery, depending upon whether the observers benefited from or were victims of their activities. Individually and collectively they had considerable need to be quick-witted, for they were a small nation surrounded by larger and pugnacious neighbors, the Blackfeet to the north, Sioux to the east, Cheyenne and Arapaho to the south and Snakes to the west. The Crows fought well and enthusiastically when they liked the odds but were also adept at playing their enemies off against each other, making and breaking alliances as suited their self-interest. They had used these traditional tactics when dealing with the Americans and therefore had a mixed reputation among the trappers, some regarding them as being as bad as the Blackfeet, and others claiming they were as good as the Snakes or Nez Percé.

Very early the Crows adopted two of Ashley's men, Edward Rose and Jim Beckworth—both coincidentally mulattoes—into the tribe as advisers and liaison agents to the traders. It was also the Crows who had taken in some of Bonneville's men who had gone out on the plains in 1832 with the ill-fated party led by David Adams. On the other hand, the tribe was not opposed in principle to using and preying upon the whites when it was to its advantage. The Crows were talented thieves who boasted about being such. They specialized in rustling horses but often were successful in lighter larcenous work, as, for example, they had been when they picked Bonneville's pockets and buttons. At the time the Crows claimed they had never murdered a white man, but if not, they had treated some of them very roughly. In 1834 they had caught Tom Fitzpatrick and a band of his trappers, robbed them of all their goods, horses and furs, and left Fitzpatrick stripped of everything but his pants. The RMFC men were certain that the Crows had been put up to this by the American Fur Company as a means of gaining some revenge for Fitzpatrick's part in the ambush of Henry Vanderburgh. The Crows later more or less admitted that they had been hired for the job as hit men, and such a role was certainly in keeping with their general style.

Because it was in their mutual interest, Walker, Leonard and the Crows got along very well in the winter of 1834–35. Leonard left an excellent set of ethnological notes about the tribe and found them to be a hospitable, extremely individualistic, competitive, humorous and a strangely sentimental people. He remained with them for about six weeks and then, in early December, went to the base camp on the Wind River, where he found Walker and the others "in good health and spirits," in an area which was alive with buffalo and other game and was "one of the most beautiful formations of nature. It [the Wind River valley] is upwards of twenty miles wide in some places, and is as level as a floor, with the margin of the river evenly ornamented with thriving cottonwood."

It may not have been up to their previous one in California, but they had a good winter in the Absaroka. They ate well, stayed warm because of the abundance of firewood and traded regularly with the Crows for buffalo robes, "which they would bring into our camp as fast as they could dress them."

One band of Crows who stayed around the post for several weeks brought with them, in a litter, a man of their tribe who had apparently suffered a stroke. His companions said that this affliction had occurred suddenly four years previously. After a battle against the Pawnee they found the man dead, or so they thought. However, while they were preparing to give him an honorable funeral, he had shown signs of life. They had then nursed him, and he survived but had never again been able to speak, and the left side of his body remained paralyzed. Because he had previously been a brave warrior, the others had carried him about with them ever since, but they had grown tired of the job, the Crows told Walker. When they left the post, they left the helpless man with the whites to do with as they chose.

In early March Walker began to break camp in preparation for a spring hunt on the Bighorn. When he was ready to leave, "Captain Walker went to the palsied Indian and told him that we were about going and were not able to take him with us. The poor Indian then, not being able to speak, made imploring signs to us to leave him as much provisions as we could spare. This we did with cheerfulness, but it only consisted of the carcass of a wolf [the buffalo herds had moved on in the late winter], which we placed within reach of him, when he requested that we would fasten the cabin door so as to prevent the entrance of wild beasts."

After trapping along the Bighorn, Walker met Bonneville, as agreed, on Popo Agie Creek. According to Leonard, the meeting was again cordial, and they were still cooperating in a business way. Bonneville was finally going home and took Walker's furs with him. Also, the army captain said that perhaps he would come out the next summer with more supplies. (He started to do so but never met Walker; it is unlikely that the two ever saw each other again.) No record was left as to how many furs Walker and his men made in the Absaroka. However, Leonard indicated in several of his journal entries that they did well. Also, when Leonard, who went east with Bonneville, got back to Missouri, he had, once his account was settled, $1,100. This, for those days, was an impressive sum for a year's work, and he must have made most of it in the final season since his previous ones had been anything but profitable. On the other hand, it was not much for the four hard years Leonard had spent in the wilderness.

By way of a brief epilogue in regard to Zenas Leonard: From Missouri he traveled to his home in Pennsylvania and was joyfully received by his family, who had given him up for dead, having had no word from him in more than three years. His stories about the Wild West and particularly California were the sensation of the neighborhood. Eventually D. W. Moore, the publisher of the *Clearfield* (Pennsylvania) *Republican,* printed Leonard's journal as an eighty-seven-page book. This first edition is now one of the rarest volumes of Americana. However, since then the *Adventures of Zenas Leonard, Fur Trader* has been reissued four times, most recently in 1959, and remains generally available.

Leonard returned to Missouri in 1836, settling in Fort Osage township in the midst of the remaining Walkers, McClellans and their relatives. Almost certainly he benefited from introductions and recommendations provided by his old field leader. He married a Harrelson girl, of a family connected with the Walkers, and bought an interest in a country store. The business prospered, and he became a leading citizen of the area. Though he died at a relatively young age, in 1857, taken, it seems, by cholera, he led a very full, good and honorable American life. In retrospect it was one of more than ordinary importance because of the intelligent, keenly observed report he made about the places he went, things he did and people he met during his adventuresome youth. Without it, our historical record and sense of heritage—who we are and how we got this way—would be more imperfect than it is. Subsequent generations, whether they have remembered his name or not, have been in the debt of the stout-hearted, level-headed Zenas Leonard.

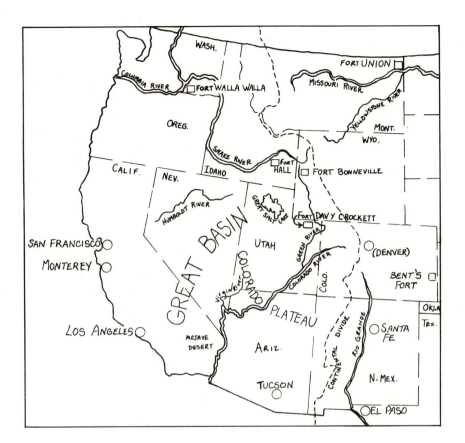

The Great Basin

Leonard and Bonneville were among a number of furmen who left the mountains for good in 1835, and this exodus continued during the remainder of the decade. By its end there were only fifty to seventy-five white trappers left in the far west, whereas there had been 500 or 600 of them at the beginning. A principal reason for this reduction was that in the early 1830s there were more mountain men earning more money than the economics of the fur trade justified. They had been attracted by the bonanza reputation the business acquired after Ashley's first success. They were kept there by the bitter, sometimes childish rivalries of the fur companies. These in effect subsidized wages and fur prices and maintained both at artificially high levels. The competition also devastated beaver populations so that increasingly more men were hunting fewer animals.

153

The bubble collapsed in the mid-thirties. Fashions changed in the civilized parts; beaver fur became less desirable, and its price therefore dropped from $7 or $8 a pelt to less than $5. Small fur outfits on the order of Gantt and Blackwell went broke immediately, and in 1834 even the famous Rocky Mountain Fur Company was too deep in debt to continue business. Some of its partners continued alone, and others hired out to their hated rival, the American Fur Company. Even that giant concern changed drastically. Astor, whose business sense proved stronger than his nostalgia for the fur business in which he had made his first fortune, sold the company division by division. The western operation was purchased by a combine of old-line St. Louis merchants, who kept the original company name. They had neither inclination nor—after the demise of many of their competitors—need to continue the extravagant practices which had prevailed in Astor's day. Increasingly they depended on the Indians and their own employees, to whom they paid only subsistence wages, to bring in the furs. They would still take pelts from the remaining free trappers but, because it was a buyer's market, turned the screws on them by upping the price of supplies and lowering that paid for furs. Essentially the same practices were followed by their only major competitor, the Hudson's Bay Company, which improved its position in the mountains by buying Fort Hall from the Boston ice merchant, Nathaniel Wyeth.

As the number of trappers, the competition for and the price of furs declined, so did the rendezvous system, which had been a boomtime phenomenon. In the last years of the thirties various St. Louis entrepreneurs continued to send out rendezvous supply trains, but these grew increasingly smaller and less profitable. The last of these gatherings was held in 1840, again on the Green River near the remains of Fort Nonsense. In comparison to the grand frolics of the past, it was a poor thing. "Times was certainly hard no beaver and every thing dull," recalled Doc (Robert) Newell, who, along with his long-time companion in hardship and revelry Joe Meek, was among those who showed up for the final rendezvous. When it was over, Newell said to Meek, "Come, we are done with this life in the mountains—done with wading in beaver-dams, and freezing or starving alternately—done with Indian trading and Indian fighting. The fur trade is dead in the Rocky Mountains, and it is no place for us now, if ever it was." Meek agreed. Along with Newell, Bill Craig and (for reasons to be considered shortly) Joel Walker, his wife, Mary, and their four children, he headed for the settlements in Oregon.

Newell was right about nothing being left in the mountains for a trapper such as himself, but he was wrong about the fur trade being dead. It had simply changed. The Ashley system of big brigades, expensively supported with supplies obtained at rendezvous, had brought men like Newell and Meek into the mountains and allowed them to have their fun. But that system had outlived its usefulness. It was replaced by less glamorous but more flexible ways of doing business in which individual white trappers were not of great importance. After, and to some extent because, many of the old-style trappers left, the fur trade not only continued but improved somewhat. When the pressure from large, fiercely competitive trapping brigades was removed, beaver populations recovered. While this fur was never again so popular as in the beaver hat days of the first quarter of the century, a demand for it continued, and with fewer suppliers the price stabilized. Small furs, such as otter and mink, continued to be valuable. New markets for buffalo robes opened up, and by the 1850s these had become the principal items of trade. Finally, as the number of whites roaming the mountains and plains decreased, so, for those who remained, did hostilities with the Indians. Perhaps the biggest improvement—from the white standpoint—in racial relations came about by dreadful accident. In 1837 smallpox, brought up the Missouri by steamboat crews and passengers, struck the Blackfeet in epidemic proportions. It diminished and dociled this fierce nation as the trappers and other tribes had never been able to do.

In addition to the American and Hudson's Bay companies, a handful of independents were able to adapt to the changed circumstances. For a brief time after the passing of the violent brigade and rendezvous fur trade and before the coming of the settlers and soldiers (approximately 1835–45), they lived well in the truly Wild West, came to know and savor it in ways that had been impossible before and would never again be possible. Prominent members of this small group were William Bent, Jim Bridger and his sometime partners Louis Vasquez and Henry Fraeb, Kit Carson, Jim Beckwourth, Bill Williams and Joe Walker.

They and a few others were scattered over an immense unsettled territory, extending from the central plains and upper Missouri to the Sonoran deserts and the Sierra. They had various styles of life and business but shared at least one characteristic. Each had a special rapport with one or more of the important Indian nations. For purely economic reasons these connections were essential. After 1835 or thereabouts there was not enough money to keep white trappers in the field, except those who worked virtually as indentured servants of the American Fur and Hudson's Bay companies. With the Indians it was a different matter because they did not have to be expensively supported by supplies brought in over long freight routes. Therefore, the tribes replaced the trappers of the 1820s and 1830s as the fur harvesters. With few exceptions, the only whites who remained and did well were those who established good commercial relations with the Indians and bartered with them for pelts.

William Bent, his three brothers and their partner, Ceran St. Vrain, built a great adobe castle-fort at the headwaters of the Arkansas River and from there traded and traveled among the Cheyenne and Arapaho. Kit Carson, a sometime employee of Bent, and Tom Fitzpatrick (who after abandoning the old-style fur trade came to the southwest as perhaps the most effective and sympathetic of all the government Indian agents) associated with these same tribes. Bridger, Vasquez and Fraeb, after unhappy experiences as American Fur Company employees, built and operated posts in Utah and Wyoming among the Shoshoni. To the north, in the Absaroka, Jim Beckwourth became a member of the Crow nation. Bill Williams was a blood brother of the Utes. Even the two large remaining companies, though they continued to buy from free-lance white trappers, tended more and more to cultivate Indians. The Hudson's Bay specialized in the Nez Percé, Flathead, Bannock, northern Shoshoni and lower Columbia River tribes, while American Fur dealt largely with the Sioux, Pawnee, Crow and northern Cheyenne. The remnants of the pox-decimated Blackfeet were split between the two.

Walker was more of a generalist than the others. He made his base among the Snakes (eastern Shoshoni) in the Green and Bear River country but traveled extensively from rim to rim of the Great Basin. By the 1840s he was generally acknowledged to know this vast tract of wilderness better than any living white or red man. He was acquainted and able to trade with not only his own people, the Snake, but also the Crow, Bannock, Paiute, Apache and Navajo. He sold the furs and robes he collected from them wherever was the most convenient and prices were best. Virtually alone among the remaining white traders, he made repeated trips to California and dealt directly with Los Angeles merchants. A young Kentuckian, Thomas Breckenridge, was with him in Utah and Nevada for a few months in the 1840s and learned something about his peripatetic business methods. Walker, said Breckenridge, "would go to the coast and trade with the Mexicans for Abolona shells, a shell highly prized by the Indians, especially by the mountain tribes, then he would start east and go from tribe to tribe trading for other trinkets, furs and skins until he was again loaded for the Eastern market. And perhaps turn up at Taos, New Mexico, or at Ft. Bent or perhaps farther east. . . . Capt. Walker never seemed to have any trouble with the Indians on these trips, they always seemed to be at peace with him."

His relations with the Hudson's Bay and American Fur companies were unique. Generally these two giant firms insisted that traders deal with them on an exclusive basis and blackballed those who did not. Walker, because of extensive connections within the tribes or by force of personality, was an exception, buying for and selling to both outfits. Joe Meek, among others, had reason to be grateful for his leverage in this regard. In 1838 Meek was under contract to the American Fur Company but, having made a good hunt on the upper Missouri, decided to try to bootleg his furs at Fort Hall, the Hudson's Bay post. On the way he met Walker, who bought the beaver packs on the spot, saving Meek the trouble of a trip. Later Meek was called up before some American Fur Company partisans who, suspecting trickery, interrogated him angrily about why he had not delivered his quota of furs. Meek said he put a stop to their "threats" when he told them he had sold them to Walker and produced a receipt as proof.

In the sense that all transactions aimed at turning a profit are, the relationship between these white traders and the Indians was exploitative. (On the other hand, the tribes had come to regard some of the goods they received in exchange for furs as necessities, or at least very desirable luxuries, which is why they cordially received the traders they trusted.) However, the activities of many of the independents strongly suggested that more than greed was involved, that they also stayed in the trade because it gave them a means of living in places, in styles and among people they found admirable and stimulating. The best of them showed genuine concern for the welfare of their tribes. More because it was their friends who were being debauched than for purely commercial reasons, the Bents despised the fly-by-night whiskey merchants who came out on the plains from Missouri and had some success at frustrating them. Even the irascible, antisocial Bill Williams, who was in a very poor position to moralize about the evils of strong drink, had protective feelings. Camped with a party of Cheyennes who were being drugged and cheated by Jim Beckwourth, Williams reacted directly and with characteristic savagery. Calling out Beckwourth, using only his bony fists, he beat him to a bloody pulp.

Walker was involved in a more complicated episode of the same sort, which contributed to the legend about him. It commenced with a sad encounter with Joe Meek—also an instructive one since it provided an example of how hard times had become for whites who tried to stay in the mountains simply as trappers. In 1839, Meek's last full year in the mountains, he was broke and went out to trap early in September, leaving his Nez Percé wife and their first-born son with the British at Fort Hall. When he returned in mid-October, he found that his wife and child had left with his sidekick Doc Newell for Fort Davy Crockett in Brown's Hole on the Green River. Though Meek had not made enough beaver to buy much in the way of provisions or even clothing, he started out alone and on foot on the 200-mile trip to Crockett. On the way he met one of the oddest of the early western tourists, Thomas Jefferson Farnham. A Vermont lawyer, Farnham had come west with the ambition of establishing a wilderness commune for the pure-minded, something on the order of a Brook Farm or New Harmony colony. He had left that spring from Independence with nineteen true believers, but fourteen of them had become disenchanted with him and his scheme and had turned back.

Such was the celebrity of the mountain men that even the other-worldly Farnham recognized Meek, saying he had seen a wax statue of him in a St. Louis museum. In the flesh, almost literally, Meek was a far less glamorous figure than he was in the waxworks. Farnham noted that the mountaineer "was evidently very poor" and had "scarcely enough [clothes] to cover his body." Those he had were worn so thin that "the frosty winds which sucked up the valley, made him shiver like an aspen leaf."

After leaving Farnham, Meek had a stupid but nearly fatal accident. He fell and smashed the hammer on his rifle. Thereafter he went on with no food, growing increasingly weaker and colder, its then being mid-October, early winter on the Snake plateau. Only fifteen miles from Fort Davy Crockett he had had enough and lay down along the trail "to rest" for a time. In his condition, he probably would have frozen to death on the spot. However, fortunately, Walker and a companion named Gordon came by, having been doing something some-place to the north. Meek's obvious first question was did they have food. "Walker replied in the affirmative," according to Meek and his biographer, "and getting down from his horse, produced some dried buffalo meat which he gave to the famishing trapper. But seeing the ravenous manner in which he began to eat, Walker inquired how long it had been since he had eaten anything.

" 'Five days since I had a bite.'

" 'Then, my man, you can't have any more just now,' said Walker, seizing the meat in alarm lest Meek should kill himself.

" 'It was hard to see the meat packed away again,' said Meek in relating his sufferings, 'I told Walker that if my gun had a hammer I'd shoot and eat him. But he talked very kindly, and helped me on my horse, and we all went on to the Fort.' " (The horse was obviously a spare belonging to Walker.) At Fort Davy Crockett, Meek found his wife and child, who had arrived safely under Newell's protection.

Fort was more or less an honorary name for this establishment. It was a low one-story building of wood and clay with three sheds attached. However, there was good water, pasture and hunting nearby, and this post and the surrounding Brown's Hole area had become a favorite winter camp for the remaining trappers and traders. That winter fifty or more were in the vicinity. Most were impoverished and were also in a great commotion when Walker, Gordon and the wobbly Meek arrived. Sometime prior, a Sioux war party had raided the area, driving off 150 horses. Thereupon Philip Thompson, a twenty-nine-year-old Tennesseean who had come to the mountains in 1835, Levin Mitchell, a big, rowdy redhead who had gone with Walker to California in 1833, and ten other men rode off to get more mounts. Wisely they made no effort to chase the Sioux, who were out in force, but instead raided a peaceful Snake village. When they returned to Davy Crocket, they had forty horses, all stolen.

Walker was enraged by the thievery from his Snakes, explaining that "under Indian law when one of a tribe offends, the whole tribe is responsible." He organized a posse of thirty men to go after the white rustlers. Included were Newell and Kit Carson and at least two of his California veterans, Meek and Bill Craig. They caught up with Thompson and Mitchell on the Green River. There on an island another so-called fort had been built. It was abandoned at the time; but the palisades around it still stood, and the thieves had driven the horses into the enclosure, the Green being frozen solid. Walker wanted, if he could, to avoid spilling white blood and therefore, according to Meek, "made an effort to get the horses off the island undiscovered. But while horses and men were crossing the river on the ice, the ice sinking with them until the water was knee-deep, the robbers discovered the escape of their booty, and charging on the trappers tried to recover the horses. In this effort they were not successful; while Walker made a masterly flank movement and getting in Thompson's rear, ran the horses into the fort, where he stationed his men, and succeeded in keeping the robbers on the outside."

Thompson did not give up easily. A traveling party of Ute warriors, traditional enemies of the Snakes, were camped nearby, and Thompson offered to split the herd if they would help recapture it. The Utes were interested enough to come to the river and look over the situation, but "On his side, Walker threatened the Utes with dire vengeance if they dared interfere. The Utes who had a wholesome fear not only of the trappers, but of their foes the Snakes, declined to enter into the quarrel. After a day of strategy, and of threats alternated with arguments, strengthened by a warlike display, the trappers marched out of the fort before the faces of the discomfitted thieves, taking their booty with them, which was duly restored to the Snakes . . . and peace secured once more with that people."

Beyond the threats of force and his own reputation, Walker had another lever with the Utes that Meek did not mention and perhaps did not know about. He had obtained it in a previous incident, where again he acted somewhat as if he still thought of himself as a sheriff, not just of Jackson County but of the entire Great Basin. Returning from a trip to the Crow country, Walker came upon a Snake raiding party that had taken three Ute captives, two women, one with an infant at her breast. The Snakes planned to put the three to death when the proper ceremonial occasion occurred, but Walker negotiated and was able to purchase the women and the child. Though he himself was going in the opposite direction, he gave the women directions and an introduction to his old friend Warren Ferris, who, he knew, was starting south into Ute country on a trapping-trading trip. The women found Ferris and traveled with him until, somewhere south of the Great Salt Lake, they were restored to their people. At that time Ferris discovered what perhaps Walker had known from the beginning: that one of the women and infant were the wife and son of Con-mar-ra-nap, or, as he was also called, Walkara.

Walkara, already a prominent chief, was to become the most famous and feared red leader in the southwest. The Ute warriors who rode with him constituted the best light cavalry west of the Sioux and Cheyenne, and with them he raided and fought from Colorado to California and deep into Sonora and Chihuahua. He was a man of personal charm and magnetism with a genuine flair for guerrilla tactics. Because of his style and success, some whites who did not have to deal directly with him found him romantic and called him the Desert Napoleon. A Sagebrush Captain Kidd would have been more like it. He was not a racial leader on the order of a Tecumseh or Sitting Bull, fighting in the interests or defense of his people. More often, Walkara rode against either whites or Indians—and often with the former—for personal gain and glory. Even some of his own Ute people found his methods excessive. His specialties were stealing horses and raiding other Indian and Mexican communities for their women and children. Those he did not wish to keep for his personal use he sold in Chihuahua, Santa Fe and Taos, where the slave trade flourished until well after the American Civil War. Navajos, Paiutes, Zuñi and rural Mexicans were the principal victims of this traffic. Walkara's greatest exploit (of which more later) was organizing a massive raid in which he rode to the outskirts of Los Angeles and there stole at least 3,000 and perhaps as many as 5,000 horses. Even the lower figure appears to stand as the American rustling record.

Since he was reported to have had at various times thirty of them, Walkara may not have placed much intrinsic value on the single wife rescued by Walker from the Snake tribe. However, he had a Bedouin sense of honor, as well as life-style, and felt obligated for the favor. Thereafter he frequently and openly demonstrated his high regard for Walker. Beyond question he was a good friend to have. Throughout Walkara's domain, Walker traveled and traded among the wild Utes in peace and security.

There was another odd consequence of this incident. Whether as a means of showing his admiration for the mountain man or because of the similarity in names, Walkara often went among the whites as not only Walker but Joe Walker. This may have been a mark of honor at the time, but it had an adverse effect on the historical reputation of the white man. Beginning with some stories of George Ruxton's, the two were confused in subsequent fictions and careless histories, some gaudy exploits of the red Joe Walker, especially his large-scale rustling raids, being assigned to the white Joe Walker.

There were occasions when the behavior of other resident white men was comparable to Walker's when he aided the paralyzed Crow warrior, returned rustled horses to the Snakes and Snake captives to the Utes. There was an element of self-interest in such actions since they enhanced the reputations of the traders and put potential customers in their debt. However, men like Walker, the Bents and Bridger also cared for the tribes because they were their own people. Ironically, these frontier figures are often remembered only as bloody killers. They did kill and fight but often with their own Indians against tribal foes. Even as enemies, they acted as warriors, in ways the tribes found comprehensible and honorable. They might take scalps, but unlike the whites who came later, farmers, ranchers and soldiers, they had no reason to destroy the independent Indian nations or drive them from their lands. Others, generally far removed from the scene, sometimes found Indians admirable and romantic and became exercised in cerebral ways about their mistreatment. But it was this small group of men who came to the mountains and plains in the 1820s and remained there who provided nearly all the visceral Indian lovers in the American westering movement.

With very few exceptions, resident whites took Indian wives, not in such bestial and predatory ways as was often imagined in the east, but as was proper according to the customs of the tribes. If nothing else, this was good for business. "Men in charge of trading posts like to marry into prominent Indian families," wrote Edwin Denig, who was the bourgeois of Fort Union, the AFC's citadel on the upper Missouri. Denig was a well-educated, cultured man of many civilized attainments. However, like nearly all the company and independent furmen of the time, he had an Indian wife. She was Deer Little Woman, the sister of two leading Assiniboin chiefs, in her own right a woman of exceptional beauty and character, of whom Denig was very proud. "By such connection," Denig went on, "they increase their adherents, their patronage is extended, and they make correspondingly larger profits. Their Indian relatives remain loyal and trade with no other company.

They have the further advantage of being constantly informed through their association with the former as to the demands of the trade and the village or even the tent where they can immediately find buffalo robes stored away."

Again, there was much more than commerce involved. The white men who came early into the far west found the native women one of the great attractions and rewards of the place. They were fascinated by their beauty, style, liveliness, erotic and domestic behavior. This interest was so pronounced that after having had a chance to observe the behavior of furmen coming up the Missouri, an Arikara chief asked one of them with fine irony, "I was wondering whether you white people have any women amongst you. One might suppose they [the trappers] had never seen any before."

For those who did not have the money or inclination for more, there were whores, often with male relatives acting as enthusiastic pimps, who congregated at rendezvous and established trading posts. However, substantial and permanent men like Walker, Denig, Andrew Drips, William Bent and many others sought the pleasure, convenience and respectability of more regular unions. Mores varied from tribe to tribe. The Cheyenne and Sioux placed a high, in some cases almost psychopathic value on premarital chastity—for women—while the Crow and Arikara found this of little concern. But in general, sexual relations were much freer, easier and more permissive than in the fairly inhibited and still puritanical society from which the white men came. The traditions of romantic love and related displacement activities had not evolved among the western Indians, but neither had notions that sex was something shameful that had to be dealt with secretly. Individuals openly expressed their physical interest in members of the opposite sex, and courtship rituals were neither long nor elaborate. In some tribes couples announced they were man and wife simply by commencing to live and travel together as such. More often marriages—which seldom involved much ceremony since mating was generally thought to be a natural, nontheological phenomenon—were arranged and took place after a would-be groom had made suitable payment to the family of his intended.

Almost anywhere in the plains or mountains a marriageable woman was worth at least one horse, and in some nations and circumstances an attractive bride cost a dozen horses or their equivalent ($500 to $1000) in trade goods. To steal such a valuable possession was grand larceny, and to damage it was very malicious mischief. Any man who committed this sort of rustling could not live peaceably or at all in the tribal territories since a father and brothers were within their rights to hunt him down as a felon. White men who wanted both a woman and to stay in the country accepted these customs and paid the going price. There is no record of any who took their wives by force.

One of the things that most astonished and delighted the white men was the manner and mood in which their Indian wives discharged their domestic duties. According to numerous testimonials, they made not only interesting lovers but marvelous lodgekeepers, home economists and mothers. In this regard their behavior reflected the fact that in almost all the Indian nations the roles of men and women were, by tradition, clearly defined and mutually exclusive. First and foremost a man should be a brave warrior and, as a hunter, raider, extortionist or trader, a good provider. Religion, fraternal ceremonials, politics, diplomacy and travel were suitable secondary masculine interests. These were such noble pursuits that it was unseemly for a husband to be distracted or wearied by lesser ones. Therefore, all other work of the tribe or family was performed by the women. This included not only ordinary domestic chores but making and maintaining the supplies and equipment men needed in their business. The work was to be done cheerfully and unobtrusively so that the men would be rested and in a good frame of mind for their ventures. If a lodge leaked, a woman was to patch it before her husband had reason to complain. For her to nag him about the job as a frontier white wife might about a rotten cabin roof was unthinkable, a serious domestic offense justifying a sound beating. "Women," said Walter McClintock, a white man who spent some time with the Blackfeet after the power but not the traditions of that tribe had declined, "considered it a disgrace for men to do any of their work—put up lodges, tan skins, cook food at home or look after the provisions; all this was woman's work in which they were trained from childhood, and they resented any interference from the men."

Indian men took these arrangements for granted, but whites found them almost utopian. Beyond satisfying them sexually and caring royally for their other creature comforts, Indian wives provided them with entrée into the tribes, served when needed as interpreters and guides and performed all manner of miscellaneous chores—tanning beaver, drying meat, foraging for herbs, making moccasins and leggings, tending, raising and moving camp—which allowed a man to live well and prosper. Not surprisingly, the important furmen who were able to marry well within the tribes regarded their Indian wives as not simply available substitutes for white ones but as far superior, being prettier, cleaner, more stylish, seductive and much more useful than white women. Some said as much, and many others indicated that this was their opinion by keeping their Indian wives even when they moved back to the settlements.

As for the other side, what Indian women thought about white men, none of the hundreds who lived with them left a formal record of their feelings. However, their behavior indicated they were equally pleased. For many white men the problem was not finding an Indian wife but diplomatically selecting one from among numerous eager candidates without giving offense to the rejected women or the fathers and brothers negotiating on their behalf. The vision of shy, trembling maidens being dragged from their families and friends and delivered into the clutches of terrifying white devils is pure fiction. To the contrary, a good many girls who caught a white husband put on great airs and bragged insufferably to their less fortunate sisters about their success. One reason for this attraction was that foreignness in itself often seems to have an aphrodisiac effect on both sexes. As the furmen were aroused by the exotic dress, manners and color of the native girls, the women apparently found white skins, blue eyes and flowing beards erotically stimulating. Also, while the early plains and mountain men came, as a rule, from the hardest and least sentimental classes of white society, they were, in comparison to Indian men, Lotharios and Lochinvars so far as romantic sensibilities were concerned. Kit Carson and Joe Meek, notable ladies' men, both fought duels over girls—an Arapaho and Shoshoni respectively—with whom they had fallen in love and then married. From the Indian standpoint, to become so emotionally befuddled by a woman was astonishing, but the girls found it titillating. For the same reason, the romantic tradition in their culture, white men made safer, more considerate husbands than did Indians, disciplining their wives less harshly and generally being more indulgent.

Most important, the sort of men who wanted wives appeared, by Indian standards, to be very rich. This automatically certified them as good men—that is, valiant warriors, energetic hunters and shrewd traders since in the tribal frame of reference wealth came from success in these activities. For an Indian woman an affluent husband not only made her life easier and materially more secure but was also the ultimate status symbol, indicating she could attract, keep and support a great man. The wealth of whites obviously recommended them highly to the male relatives of marriageable women. Most agreeably they discovered that white men were strangely soft-headed in these negotiations. In consequence fathers or brothers were often able to get two or three times more from whites than that which an Indian suitor would pay for a daughter or sister. The greatest fleecing ever recorded in such a transaction was perpetrated by Comcomly, a Chinook chief who sold his daughter to Duncan McDougall, the bourgeois of a British trading post. The marriage price was fifteen blankets, 2½ feet wide, fifteen guns and "a great deal of other property." Another trader, Alexander Henry, who witnessed the deal, was shocked by it and commented, "This Comcomly is a mercenary brute, destitute of decency."

The brides were flattered by the high value white men placed on them and after marriage were delighted to discover that their foreign husbands were exceptionally willing to continue to spend extravagantly. To please and honor his first wife, the Shoshoni Mountain Lamb, Joe Meek, when he was still flush, blew almost the entire proceeds of a year's trapping by buying her a $300 horse, $150 saddle, $50 bridle and about $200 worth of boots, blankets, beads, a blue broadcloth skirt, scarlet blouse and leggings. These were Meek's figures, and he was generally shaky about large numbers, but in this case he may have been nearer the truth than usual. Mountain Lamb was one of the great beauties of the west, and he was much in love with her.

The romantic white men were open-handed to begin with, and their wives insistently cajoled, manipulated and goaded them to be more so. Benjamin Bonneville was of the opinion, wrote Washington Irving,

No sooner does an Indian belle experience this promotion [becoming a mountain man's wife], than all her notions at once rise and expand to the dignity of her situation; and the purse of her lover, and his credit into the bargain, are taxed to the utmost to fit her out in becoming style. The wife of a free trapper to be equipped and arrayed like any undistinguished squaw? Perish the grovelling thought! In the first place, she must have a horse . . . the most beautiful animal she can lay her eyes on. And then, as to his decoration: headstall, breast-bands, saddle and crupper, are lavishly embroidered with beads, and hung with thimbles, hawks' bells and bunches of ribands. . . . As to her own person, she is even still more extravagant. . . . Her riding hat is stuck full of parti-colored feathers; her robe is of red, green, and sometimes gray cloth, but always of the finest texture which can be procured. Her leggins and moccasons are of the most beautiful and expensive workmanship, in the way of finger-rings, ear-rings, necklaces, and other female glories, nothing within reach of the trapper's means is omitted. To finish the whole, she selects from among her blankets of various dyes, one of some glowing color . . . vaults into the saddle of her gay, prancing steed, and is ready to follow her mountaineer "to the last gasp with love and loyalty."

Though the passage was included as a kind of light ethnological aside, Bonneville may have been reporting from personal experience and some pique. Among other things Irving emphatically did not make clear—and in this case may not have known about—is that the little French captain was a notable Don Juan who cut a great swath among the mountain ladies. There were reports that he bought at least six "belles," including the one who was with him on the Bear River in the spring of 1834, when Walker, returning from California, found the couple destitute. Given the high price of women, Bonneville's sexual adventures may have contributed more than was ever acknowledged to his lack of commercial success.

In addition to a number of chronological gaps in his precise activities and whereabouts, there are three substantive mysteries, by now probably unsolvable, about the life of Joe Walker. The first two—what he did and where he went as a Taos trapper in the early 1820s and what was his true relationship with Benjamin Bonneville—are the most important in regard to his professional, so to speak, career and historical influence. However, the third—who his Indian wife was and what their feelings for each other and their family were—if it could be solved, would provide more information about what kind of man he really was.

Walker was married more than likely in 1836 after his return from the Crow country, but certainly by the spring of 1837, when a white journalist was first introduced to his wife. They traveled and lived together from then until at least 1846, when they were last seen, according to surviving records, as a couple. She was with him longer and almost certainly knew him more intimately than any other single person who was associated with him on the frontier. Yet not even her name in now remembered.

The woman was a Snake, and this is not surprising. Since the time when Lewis and Clark first met and admired Sacajawea, white men had had very high opinions of the beauty, personality and conduct of Snake women. They were thought less greedy than the Cheyenne, more chaste and faithful than the Crow, and whites married them more often than women of any other single tribe. Beyond her nationality, some reasonable assumptions can be made about the kind of woman she was. To the Indians, Walker would have been one of the greatest matrimonial catches. He was a notable leader of men, a feared warrior, and among the most affluent of the mountaineers, far better off than an ordinary trapper like Meek or Carson. Though it was of little consequence to their male relatives who were negotiating for them, prospective brides no doubt were also attracted by the fact that he was a big, handsome man of temperate habits and a good disposition. For such reasons, the girl he finally selected was almost certainly well connected within the Snake tribe to important warriors and chieftains and had received a good tribal education in the womanly arts. That she was a beauty is a matter of record, for oddly, considering how little else is remembered about her, we still know what she looked like.

In 1837 William Drummond Stewart, the first tourist of the Rockies, was back in the mountains. He came with a considerable retinue which included a talented young Baltimore artist, Alfred Jacob Miller, whose function it was to memorialize Stewart's trip and enhance its cultural significance. The rendezvous was again held that year on the Green River, and there Stewart introduced his artist to Walker, with whom he had been acquainted since 1834. Miller made the preliminary sketches for an individual portrait and another of Walker and his wife.

Miller had been trained in Paris and steeped in the romantic tradition. This influence shows strongly in the portrait of Walker alone. The face, when compared to photographs taken in the last years of Walker's life, appears to be exceedingly fine and delicate, as though Miller had put an idealized English lake poet or Parisian *boulevardier* into buckskins. The joint portrait is stronger, more naturalistic and interesting. There are at least two versions since, as was the custom of the time, Miller made copies of his popular western paintings after returning to Baltimore. However, in both Walker and the Snake woman are on horseback, against a background which suggests they were emerging from a Monet-like mountain pass. She is the lesser figure, riding, according to the perspective, fifty feet behind. The position, Miller noted in his commentary, "exhibits a certain etiquette. The Squaw's station in travelling is at a considerable distance in the rear of her liege lord, and never at the side of him."

Walker was then in his prime, a burly, poker-faced man, with hair flowing to his shoulders and cavalier mustaches sweeping down into his beard. The girl—for though she is more than a child, she is a very young woman—is in full feminine flower. She is modestly robed and sits her horse demurely, but in the small, pretty face there is a look of repressed mirth, as though she were holding in a bubble of laughter which she will let out when she gets her "liege lord" alone and quizzes him about, and gives her own observations on, the strange white man with his bits of paper, pens and brushes. Both are dressed to the nines, suitably for an important warrior-trader and his lady. Probably they spent considerable time on their costumes, for Walker was always proud of his wardrobe, and Snake women had the reputation of being great clotheshorses. All and all, they make an exceedingly handsome couple, but such an exotic one that it is difficult now to remember that this is a likeness of as truly an American husband and wife as any who ever sat for their portrait.

A few years later Miller's sketch was filled out and confirmed by Adolph Wislizenus. He was a German-born physician, naturalist and essayist who emigrated to the United States because his liberal political views got him in trouble at home. After practicing medicine for a time in Illinois among German farmers, he grew bored and went to the Wild West. His journals are in the classic style of Teutonic travelers, a bit heavy and pedantic but full of hard facts and meticulously recorded observations. In 1839 he met Walker and Andrew Drips, the veteran AFC partisan, who were traveling in the Wind River mountains "accompanied by their Indian Wives [Drips had married an Oto woman] and a lot of dogs. The two squaws, quite passable as to their features, appeared in highest state. Their red blankets, with the silk kerchiefs on their heads, and their gaudy embroideries, gave them quite an Oriental appearance. Like themselves, their horses were bedight with embroideries, beads, corals, ribbons and little bells. The bells were hung about in such number than when riding in their neighborhood, one might think one's self in the midst of Turkish music. The squaws, however, behaved most properly. They took care of the horses, pitched a tent, and were alert for every word of their wedded lords."

Later in the summer, traveling homeward and trying to find the North Fork of the Platte River, Wislizenus came upon the Walkers again. He was gratified since the party he was with was somewhat lost, on short rations and nervous about grizzly bears and hostile Indians. Working their way through some streamside brush, their leader, a French Canadian of apparently less than first-class talents as a guide, "suddenly exclaimed, 'Indians!' . . . We listened, and heard to one side Indian speech. We approached carefully, and found a little party, consisting of Captain Walker, who we had met at the rendezvous, and some trappers and Indians, who had come here some days ago to get dried meat. Captain Walker is an original among mountain loafers," wrote Wislizenus, who was inclined to find everyone who was not a German university man somewhat irregular. "He has roamed through the mountains, chiefly on his own hook, in all directions, and has made a side trip to California. He has taken such a fancy to this life that it is unlikely that he ever returns to civilization."

On this occasion Wislizenus had nothing directly to say about the wife, but he caught Walker in a domestic situation that indicated she was surely there. "We found him [Walker] with pipe in mouth, and clad with nothing but a blanket, for which he excused himself to us, because his shirt was in the wash. He had sufficient fresh buffalo meat, and invited us to the rib of a fat cow."

Beyond being a lodgekeeper, groom and laundress, Walker's wife was, in the style of her people, an artistic young woman, a bit of information also preserved by Alfred Jacob Miller. In his notes about the portraits the painter wrote that Walker "had the kindness to present the writer a dozen pairs of moccasins worked by this squaw—richly embroidered on the instep with colored porcupine quills. He [Walker] did him also the favor to have some Indian dances exhibited, that he

[Miller] might have an opportunity of seeing them—so he [Miller] did not care to risk his friendship by questions touching his famous and recherché feast."

(The "recherché feast" Miller coyly mentioned had to do with another of the famous campfire stories circulated about Walker. Neither Miller nor any of the other authors who published it could provide hard facts about dates, places and people. The tale was more than likely apocryphal, but it was often repeated and became part of the Walker legend. Since it can be assigned to no particular year or locality, it is as well retold here as in any other place.

(Miiler's version was: Walker had been "victorious in a battle with a tribe, and the Indians, finding themselves worsted, proposed to bury the tomahawk and invited him to a feast and pipe smoking. Of course the worthy Captain was ready to make friends and smoke the pipe of peace, for no matter how hard you may pound in battle, you must of necessity receive some pounding in return, and the Captain felt sore from the loss of some of his men,—but horror of horrors! in a short time they had let him know that he had partaken of a meal composed of his own men! Only fancy his blasphemy, rage, and disgust.")

Walker's marriage, like that of most of the prominent furmen, was not a back-alley affair, and as the session with Miller indicated, Walker was not shy about acknowledging or presenting his Shoshoni lady even to cultured whites from the east. In 1838 he had a chance to introduce her to the most respectable company that had as of that time been seen in the west. In the early summer of that year three couples of Presbyterian missionaries had left Missouri under the protection of the American Fur Company supply caravan. Their intention was to do good work among the savages in Oregon. The Reverend Cushing Eells, one of the three divines, was accompanied by his wife, Myra, who kept an excellent diary which gives one of the first and best feminine impressions of the Wild West. Myra Eells was alternately awed by the grandeur of the wilderness, curious about its odd residents and shocked by their roughness and brutality. She was also enraged because the ungodly white, red, and half-breed furmen who traveled with them persisted in hazing her husband, who was a much less adaptable person than his wife. On one occasion a band of these rowdies, very full of liquor, came cavorting around the Eells's tent, shouting bawdy songs, banging pans and doing Indian dances in a kind of malicious shivaree. Among other things they demanded that the Reverend Eells join them in a sing-along. He apparently kept well back in the tent and a dignified silence, but Myra shooed them away and said that they looked like "emissaries of the Devil worshipping their own master."

On the Wind River the caravan was intercepted by Walker, who, with a small band of his own men and his wife, was trailing a herd of

200 or 300 horses, which he intended to trade at the fur posts. Myra Eells was pleased to meet such decent people and invited the Walkers along with Captain and Mrs. Drips to dinner. She made no mention of how the evening went, but it must have been reasonably successful, for on two afternoons, when the men were otherwise occupied, she entertained "Mrs. Walker" and two other Indian wives of fur partisans at parties for ladies only. At one of these sessions the women cut patterns and stitched on dresses. Mrs. Walker, the fashionable and talented Shoshoni, would have shown off well in this strange sewing circle.

Several years later (for reasons of which more shortly) Walker made his first trip, since he left in 1832, back to Missouri. He took his wife with him, and she was properly introduced to his remaining family and friends. On a spring Sunday he escorted her into the very bastion of Jackson County respectability, the Six Mile Baptist Church, the first and most prestigious one in Fort Osage township. Given the attitudes and fantasies about white men and women of different colors, there may well have been some malicious gossip behind fans and curtains, but the only account of that day—a secondhand one—indicated that Mrs. Walker made a favorable impression on and was politely received by the Six Mile Baptists. This was contributed some years later by a woman, G. Poe Smedley, who had grown up in Jackson County and in her maturity wrote a romantic novel about the good old days there. She said that both her grandmother and a great-uncle well remembered the visit the Walkers made to Jackson County. The uncle, Maxwell Shepherd, of a family that had settled early in the area near the Walkers, was there on a Sunday when the famous frontier Captain brought his wife to church. He said that she was very presentable, "always clean and smelled clean, which was an anomaly for an Indian."

Smedley also heard from her elderly relatives that Captain Walker did not want his wife associating with any of the local Indians. This was understandable, for by then all that was left around Jackson County were detribalized, pauperized, debauched Osages and Wyandottes. Any attempt to bring or segregate them and the highborn Snake woman together, on the ground that they all were Indians, would have insulted both the Captain and his lady.

The years between 1835 and 1845 may have been the best of Walker's life in terms of personal pleasure and satisfaction. It was the only time when he had the regular companionship of a woman. Toward the end of the period there were children, though their number or sex was never identified in the journals and memoirs of those who met them. Everything about the man suggests he would have been a proud and good father. Also, during this decade he had almost absolute freedom to seek the delight he found in exploring unknown places. Both before and after that time he was almost continually engaged in planning and leading risky ventures in which he was responsible for the welfare and lives of others and therefore somewhat restricted by their abilities and ambitions. But between 1835 and 1840 his line of work and rapport with the Indians permitted him to roam the wilderness as he pleased without being beholden to anyone. He made good use of the opportunity.

In 1837, after leaving Stewart, Miller and the others at the Green River rendezvous, he headed southwest with a veteran trapper named Jack Ralston. There may have been several other men in the party, including Pauline Weaver, and presumedly they were accompanied by their wives, for no matter how difficult the trip, the Indian women did not slow travel but rather made it easier and more pleasant. Thomas Breckenridge wrote, "Captain Walker always took along with him on these lonely trips his squaw."

They spent most of the winter in northern Arizona along the upper Gila, Little Colorado and Mogollon Rim, being, it is now thought, the first whites to see many parts of this territory. The route they followed and what they did on their return trip to the Green River country are conjectural. However, George Ruxton was to tell as true a story about a band of mountain men under Walker's leadership which fits the circumstances and time frame of this expedition. Ruxton said that after leaving Arizona, the party went east and in central New Mexico encountered sixty Navajos returning from a successful raid on Socorro, where they had taken a number of horses and women and children for the slave trade. Walker and his men fell upon and routed the Navajos. The stolen horses and people were returned to their grateful owners and families. As a reward the mountaineers kept fifty of the horses and continued north toward the Green.

In Ruxton's stories it is almost impossible to determine how much, if any, fact was mixed in with the fiction. In this case none of the details is verifiable, and since he included in the account of the trip the story about Walker's bloody duel with a giant Indian chief, it seems likely that he invented much of it after having heard that Walker was in about the right area at the right time for his narrative purposes.

It is true that when Walker came to the Wind River in 1838, he was trailing horses, but 200 or 300 of them, according to Myra Eells, rather than the 50 Ruxton mentioned. Beyond being an infinitely more accurate reporter, Mrs. Eells had the advantage of actually seeing the animals on the spot, as Ruxton did not. It is possible, of course, that Walker had waylaid three or four other groups of Indian rustlers and built up the herd in this way or traded for the extra ones in Santa Fe.

On the other hand, there were many more and cheaper horses available in California, and having been only a few hundred miles distant when they were in northern Arizona, the party may have gone there for the animals.

Walker remained in the Snake and upper Columbia country during the winter of 1838–39, but the southern Great Basin and Colorado Plateau, which then contained most of the unknown country in the west, was much on his mind. In the fall of 1839 at Fort Davy Crockett, after the ruckus with Philip Thompson and his rustlers, he discussed the geography of the unexplored west with Willard Smith. Smith was a New York architect who had taken a year's sabbatical from his profession and as a tourist had come to the Green River under the guidance of Andrew Sublette and Louis Vasquez. In the party of these two veterans, the New Yorker wintered at the Brown's Hole-Davy Crockett camps. There, said Smith, Walker was trying to recruit a party to start out the next spring in boats on the Grand River and ride them down through the canyons of the Colorado to the Mojave crossings, from which they would strike overland across the desert to California. At the time the course of the Colorado, how it got through the great plateau, was the outstanding unsolved mystery of western topography. Walker said that he had come to the edge of some immense canyons, noted that the river in each place seemed much the same and deduced that it might be possible to go by water from Utah to the California border.

That spring the boat party never got beyond the talking stage, which was probably fortunate. Neither Walker nor any of the mountaineers he might have taken with him had the experience or equipment to cope with the great canyons of the Colorado. Nevertheless, the hope of making this expedition remained with Walker for some time. Three years later he talked about it again to Theodore Talbot, a government surveyor whom he had occasion to guide around the Great Basin. Talbot noted in his journal that Walker had "often endeavored to raise a party to descend Green River, but with no success. He thinks that the cannions of that River are in a country of high table lands." Not until thirty years later, when John Wesley Powell and his ten men first ran the length of the Green and Colorado, was anyone able to make the great canyon trip Walker began thinking about in the 1830s.

However, so far as exploring went, 1840 was by no means a wasted year. In the spring, with a dozen men, Walker left Brown's Hole for the southwest. They stayed on the north side of the Colorado, traveling from Sevier Lake to the Virgin River, becoming the first whites to make this crossing of the Utah-Nevada desert. Walker was later to describe that country as "torn all to pieces with canyons," generally "so repulsive" that "nothing could induce him to enter it again."

They were also the first Americans to see the upper Virgin. Descending along it, Walker investigated a series of falls and side canyons which, in contrast with the desert they had just crossed, he thought were extraordinarily beautiful, "grand beyond description." They continued down the Virgin, riding through country now deep below the surface of Lake Mead, to its junction with the Colorado, and then struck across the Mojave, entering California in the late fall or early winter of 1840. Either here or sometime earlier on their trip they were joined by Henry Fraeb, a former Rocky Mountain Fur Company partner who that year with Jim Bridger had organized a new trading firm.

They trapped along the Virgin or other streams and had 417 pounds of beaver pelts when they arrived in Los Angeles. These Walker sold for about $1,200 to Abel Stearns, a Massachusetts-born merchant who had established himself in that Mexican city as a storekeeper and exporter.

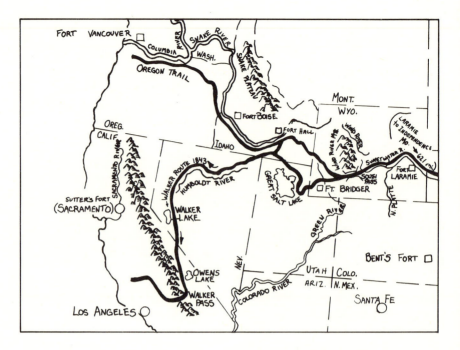

The Emigrants

The year 1840 makes an appropriate time to turn again to the affairs of Joel Walker. In the summer and fall, while his brother was exploring the Virgin River, Joel, his wife, Mary, their four children and his sister-in-law, Martha Young, emigrated overland in covered wagons to the Pacific coast. They were the first of some 300,000 American pioneers who were to make this trip during the next twenty years. Among many others, the life of Joe Walker would be substantially affected by this migratory endeavor which the Joel Walkers commenced.

After returning from his hard, trailblazing trading trip to Santa Fe in 1823, Joel Walker married and settled down as a farmer in Fort Osage township. There is no indication that he was anything but a good husband, father and responsible citizen, but it would be understandable if there were times when he felt nostalgia for the style of life he had so abruptly abandoned. By the fall of 1839 Joel Walker had had enough of being a Missouri farmer. In the winter he sold his land and the other property he could not carry. When the snow melted, he began getting his wagons ready, improvising and inventing as he went along, since nobody had ever previously prepared for the kind of over-land haul he had in mind. However, he had some company and con-sultants as he planned and tinkered, there being forty other people in the neighborhood who said they were going to make the trip with Walker. But "when the time for starting arrived," Walker dryly re-called, "there was not one of them ready except myself and family."

Had Joel and Mary Walker not teamed it to the coast in 1840, some others would have within a year or so. By then the increase of popula-tion and the pressures this created in the Mississippi Valley and the accounts, such as Irving's and Leonard's, about the wealth and wonders of the Far West had made the emigration as inevitable as a happening which has yet to occur can be. However, that the Walkers were the first to respond to these circumstances is not surprising. There were few families in which the westering tradition had been so strong for so long as it had been among the Walkers and Youngs. Both had near relatives, Joe Walker and Ewing Young, who were already famous for having led exploratory expeditions to the Pacific. Even if their kins-men had not directly encouraged the couple to make the move, the reports of their activities gave the Walkers more than average interest in and information about the coast. In his youth Joel had been a fron-tiersman the equal of his brother, Ewing Young or anyone else. This may have made him particularly restless and also more confident than most about facing the risks and hardships of an overland trip. The women, because of their own family history or personal restlessness, appear to have been as eager to go as Joel and certainly behaved with as much boldness. Mary Walker was pregnant when they left Missouri that spring, and had she not wanted to make the crossing, her condition gave a powerful excuse for postponing or canceling it. Her sister Mar-tha was unmarried, had no obligations to any man, and therefore must have decided to go because it personally suited her.

The Walkers packed their belongings into two light wagons and joined an American Fur Company caravan which left Independence on April 30, 1840, bound for the last rendezvous on the Green River. From there Joel Walker planned to go it alone, making his own wagon trail to California. The AFC train was under the command of Andrew Drips, who had with him some forty men, sixty pack mules and thirty two-wheeled carts. Traveling with this brigade, with some pack mules and carts of their own, were Jim Bridger and Henry Fraeb. In addition to the furmen and the Walkers, there was a mixed religious party that had joined the column for guidance and protection. Three Congrega-tionalist ministers—Harvey Clark, Philo Littlejohn and Alvin Smith—each with a wife, were intending to go to Oregon to set up an indepen-dent church among the Indians. Several other groups of missionaries and their wives had previously crossed to that territory, but they had been sent or called there for professional reasons. None intended, as Joel and Mary Walker did, to take up land as permanent settlers.

Joel Walker said that he talked some to Clark and found him reasonably congenial but made no comment about the other two. (As a rule, these Protestant preachers were not well liked by either the furmen or border settlers because they were helpless in practical matters and prone to criticize frontier manners and morals.) The other divine in the party, Father Pierre Jean De Smet, a Belgian-born Jesuit, was an exceptional man who, before his career in the west was completed, traveled 125,000 miles in the interest of the Indian tribes of the Rockies and western plains. Because of his grit and good nature, the frontiersmen generally thought him to be an admirable foreign tourist, the religious equivalent of Sir William Drummond Stewart. Of De Smet, Kit Carson once remarked, "I can say of him that if ever there was a man that wished to do good, he is one. He never feared danger when duty required his presence among the savages and if good works on this earth are rewarded hereafter I am confident that his share of glory and happiness in the next world will be great." Joel Walker was less effusive but found the Jesuit more praiseworthy than the Congregationalists. He said that De Smet was a "heavy set, fine looking man, and a Frenchman. I became well acquainted with him and liked him."

In June Walker carved his name on Independence Rock, the natural tower which marked the gateway to the Rockies, and became first of some thousands of emigrants who signed these stones so as to leave a record of their overland passage. Shortly thereafter he met a band of Snake Indians and traveled with them for the next several weeks. It is not clear from his memoir whether he did so alone, leaving his family with the fur caravan or whether all of them went with the Indians; if so, they probably met some in-laws among them. In any event, the Walkers arrived without difficulty at the rendezvous site on the Green River on July 30. There they were met by "one of my brother's men," Bill Craig. In fact, Craig was then nobody's man so far as the fur business was concerned, he, Joe Meek and Doc Newell having decided to leave the mountains. These three, all of whom had been employees and to a certain extent protégés of Joe Walker's, undertook to lead Joel and his family and the three missionary couples to Fort Hall on the Snake River. Joel was still planning to go to California, but on the way to Fort Hall, Craig and Meek must have told him enough about the passage of the Sierra they had made in 1833, following his brother, to have convinced him that it would be suicidal to attempt the trip with wagons and only two women and four small children to help. At Fort Hall, Walker changed his mind and decided to go to Oregon with

Meek, Newell, Craig and several other ex-trappers, including a French Canadian, Jandreau. All of them were intending to settle there with their Indian wives and children. The missionaries, however, had had enough. Deciding the Indian souls could wait and "being more wearied than the others, [they] stopped to spend the winter" at Fort Hall.

Still with their wagons, the first from the States to go beyond Boise, the party entered the Columbia Plateau. Somewhere in it they had Indian trouble, for the Walker children were to remember their mother, by then five months pregnant, wading with them into a shallow river and keeping them on a sandbar while the fight was in progress. Later, on the basis of this experience and several others he was to have in Oregon, Joel Walker compiled a formal set of safety rules for those traveling among the tribes of the Northwest. A copy of these was received by James Clyman, who transcribed them into his diary:

DIRECTIONS BY MR. [JOEL P.] WALKER
Be carefull to never camp in the timber if it can be avoided. Be carefull to never Let any Indians come amongst you Never Lit the Indians have any amunition on any account Keep careful watch both day and night Never neglect camp guard on any account

Never Fire a gun after crossing the Umqua mountain untill you cross the siskiew mountain perhaps Five days travel Keep yourselves close as possible in traveling through the Brush

Never scatter after game or [make] any other division

Keep your guns in the best firing condition

Clyman had been in the first group of trappers engaged by William Ashley and sent to the Rockies in 1823. Thereafter he had become one of the most expert and well traveled of the mountain men. That he should have thought so well of these instructions is a good indication that even among the veteran trappers Joel Walker was not regarded or patronized as a greenhorn.

The party arrived on September 13, a Sunday, in the Willamette Valley, where they intended to take up land. All had made it safely through the mountains, but it had been a hard trip, especially for the children. The first settlement they came to was a Methodist mission, where the first overland pioneers received a cool reception. The Methodists told them that since it was the Sabbath, it would be sacrilegious to give them dinner but that they were welcome to attend an evening prayer session, where they could "partake of a meal of spiritual food." The families withdrew and made a rough camp in the open. However, they were entertained by Jandreau, an ebullient young man who staged his own religious service, a hilarious charade in which he mocked the manners of the preachers. Joel Walker in his usual laconic way said only, "The Methodist mission was not much liked at that time."

The feeling was mutual. The Methodists and other early missionaries had come to Oregon in hopes of establishing godly communes where they could tend, undisturbed, to the spiritual needs of the child-like Indians. They looked on other whites with disfavor, despising the mountain men for their profane ways and fearing that even respectable American emigrant families might not appreciate or support the theocratic order they were attempting to establish. It was a reasonable suspicion, for in their splendid isolation some peculiar, fairly medieval devotional practices had developed among the missionaries. For example, at the Methodist compound where the Walkers had first stopped, one of the pastors, the Reverend Asahel Munger, became determined to work a miracle for the edification of the savages. Acting on this passion, he nailed his hand to a fireplace mantel. So impaled, he roasted to death on the mission hearth.

Later in September Walker went to the Hudson's Bay post at Vancouver and found the British factor, Dr. John McLoughlin, far more helpful than the American preachers had been. McLoughlin advanced him credit against his next year's crops and immediately gave him supplies he badly needed to commence farming. Returning to the Willamette Valley, Walker selected land and sowed it in wheat. There he also received assistance from Ewing Young, his wife's relative. Young, the old Taos trapper, had settled in Oregon in 1834 and had done so well hunting sea otters, trading horses and ranching that he had become the most prosperous American in the territory. He hired Joel and his eldest son, John, to do occasional farmwork, paying $1 and 75 cents per day respectively, and bought a few beaver and possum pelts from them. He also engaged Martha Young to sew shirts and do his washing. Joel Walker said that with all this scratching around, the family made "just about a living" during their first winter.

On January 14, 1841, the fifth Walker child, Louisa, was born near what is now Salem, the first American baby to come into the world in Oregon. Louisa Walker made her first migration when she was seven months old, her father having decided to see if the prospects were better in California. Traveling by ship, they arrived in San Francisco in September 1841, adding to their historical records by becoming the first American family to reach that state. They continued up the Sacramento, where Walker became the manager of John Sutter's farm and also did some stock trading on his own. The family stayed for a year and a half and then went back to Oregon because, unlike California, there were English-speaking schools in that territory. Walker, his son John, and some other wranglers returned by the overland route, driving 1,200 cows, 600 sheep and 200 horses. On the way, said Walker, "We were met by a large number of Indians who pretended to be friendly, but killed a good many of our horses. The next day we returned the favor by killing a good many Indians."

Walker claimed 640 acres of land in Yamhill County and farmed it with good success for the next four years. Then he sold out and in the fall of 1848 again moved to California. There he shortly met his old political ally from Missouri, the ex-governor Lilburn Boggs, and the two of them served as delegates to the California Constitutional Convention in 1849. Thereafter he settled down and prospered on a ranch in what is now Napa County, finished with the westering movement. Some years later Walker dictated his brief memoir, calling it "Pioneer of Pioneers." Nobody, excepting his wife, Mary, and his sister-in-law, Martha, has ever established a more legitimate claim to that title.

It is likely that Joe Walker knew about his brother's plans well before the family started its overland journey in the spring of 1840. Among others, Andrew Sublette and Louis Vasquez had come out from Missouri in the fall of 1839 and spent part of the winter at Brown's Hole, where Walker and his men camped. If they brought no personal messages, they would certainly have heard the news about Joel—with forty people planning to join him, his activities must have been a matter of common knowledge and general interest in western Missouri—and related it to his brother.

Bill Craig, Joe Meek and Doc Newell all wintered with Walker and were making their plans to leave the mountains for Oregon. By asking Craig, and probably the others, to look out for his brother and family, Walker gave some practical assistance. Had he changed his own plans, specifically so that he could meet his brother, he could not have done much more for him than these three veterans did. Also, beyond being unnecessary, this might not have been a diplomatic thing to do. The overland trip was Joel's show, and he does not seem to have been a man who would have reacted well if he had thought he was being hovered over and patronized, especially by a younger brother whom he had introduced to the frontier twenty-five years earlier. In any event, the brothers went their separate ways and, knowingly or not, missed by a few weeks seeing each other on the Green River.

Walker had news about the progress of his family's overland journey, at least by the time he himself reached California in the fall of the year. The messenger was Henry Fraeb, Bridger's partner, who had traveled with the Joel Walkers in the fur caravan from Missouri to the Green River. After staying only a few days at the last rendezvous, he hurried on to overtake Joe Walker and caught him east of Los Angeles. In California Walker had trouble with the locals just as Joel had at about the same time in Oregon. Reaching the first settlement after having crossed the Mojave, the party was stopped by a Mexican border patrol and interrogated by the local prefect of justice. They were allowed to proceed but with the understanding that Walker would present himself to the secretary of state in Los Angeles for further questioning. To ensure compliance, the prefect forwarded a report about the matter to that official:

> They have presented in your office Joseph R. Walker and two other individuals, Americans, in charge of twelve individuals of the same nationality, a United States passport viséed by the Mexican Charge d'affairs Don J. Maria Montoya in Washington. They inform us that other strangers are on their way with the object of purchasing horses and remaining in the area two months and they [Walker and group] propose that their government [the American] be informed of the robbery that took place in the department last year by the *chaguanosos*. That he [Walker] offers to take the communications with him when he departs, then he also desires to obtain security in the establishment in which he lives called *el Deposito*.

The apprehensions of the Mexican authorities about the party were understandable. For the previous several years Walkara, the Ute chief who was Walker's namesake, supported by bands of out-of-work white trappers, had been raiding southern California for horses. Only a few months earlier these rustlers, the *chaguanosos* as the prefect contemptuously referred to them, had staged a raid of such proportions that it amounted to an invasion. Prominent among the white *chaguanosos* had been Bill Williams; a crony of his, Peg-leg Smith; and two of the men, Phil Thompson and Levin Mitchell, whom Walker had driven out of Brown's Hole the fall before because of their attempted theft of Snake horses.

These and others entered southern California in small, inconspicuous groups during the early spring of 1840. In May, in a series of quick strikes coordinated with the arrival of Walkara's warriors, they had hit half a dozen big ranches between the outskirts of Los Angeles and San Luis Obispo, taking at least 3,000 horses, including some of the best broodmares and stallions in the state. Then they had started running the animals east. A hastily organized posse of thirty ranchers under the leadership of a Don Ygnacio Palomares set off in pursuit and caught one of the bands of rustlers in the vicinity of the present community of Barstow. However, Palomares was not only defeated (two of his men were killed) but humiliated. All his own horses were either killed or taken from him, and he and his surviving men were forced to walk home. This was a touch about which Bill Williams was to brag considerably in later years. Other military and vigilante units took up the chase, but none of the rustlers were caught by the Mexicans. However, they were punished by the desert, 1,500 of the stolen horses dying in the Mojave from lack of water and forage.

Given those recent events, the border patrol, when they found Walker and his fifteen hard-looking men coming from the east, were in no mood to let them pass unchallenged. However, because he had a valid passport—a document seldom carried by rustlers—and perhaps because he could provide character references from responsible local citizens with whom he had dealt previously, Walker convinced the California secretary of state that he was on a legitimate business trip. Thereafter he sold his furs to Abel Stearns and entered into an arrangement whereby the merchant would act as his agent in Los Angeles. In this capacity Stearns wrote a note to Don Juan Bandini, one of the largest ranchers in the area: "Don José Walker tells me that he has received from you two horses at $45 which are to be charged to his account. He also tells me that he wishes to buy some mares or horses from you. . . ." Stearns went on to say that Walker had deposited sufficient beaver to give him an excellent credit rating. Later Walker had some commercial difficulty with Bandini and again turned to Stearns for assistance, writing (this is the longest letter in Walker's own hand which survives) to him: "I had misunderstood Mr. Bandini when I was trading with him the first time. He now says he wants the cash for his Horses. I therefore make the reduction of 50cts on the pound [on the beaver he was using for collateral] . . . you will please settle with him and oblige."

This was done, and Walker eventually acquired 100 mares and an unspecified number of mules, paying $2 each for the former and $12 for the latter. After purchasing beans, coffee, sugar, soap and some liquor from Stearns, he, Fraeb and the others left California in mid-April, driving the herd with them. They spent no time exploring new country and probably followed the Old Spanish Trail, the main caravan route to Santa Fe. They were back in the vicinity of Brown's Hole in late June or early July. There Walker apparently stopped with the Snakes to see his wife, who had not gone to California, and to recruit his horses after the long, hard trip. Fraeb, however, continued on to meet his partner, Bridger. There was no rendezvous that year, but many of the remaining trappers were milling about along the Green, either out of habit or because they had not understood there would be no supply train. Mingling with the last of these old westerners were some very new ones, a caravan of fifty men, women and children headed for California. If Joel and Mary Walker are thought of as representing the very first drops, this party was the first true wave of the overland emigration.

The wagon train was theoretically commanded by John Bartleson, a prosperous Missouri farmer. He had been elected to his position principally because he had brought seven or eight hired hands with him and said that if he could not be the leader, he and his men would withdraw from the enterprise. However, Bartleson proved to be incompetent and hateful. He was reduced to following the others, some of whom, before the trip was over, could scarcely bring themselves to speak to—or even of—the man. When it was organized, there had been no one in the party with frontier experience comparable to that of Joel Walker, and therefore, they had a much harder trip than his. But they had reached the Green River safely, mostly because their real leader was Tom Fitzpatrick. After having retired from the fur trade in the mid-1830s, Fitzpatrick had gone east, perhaps as far as Ireland to pay a visit to his relatives. However, he was back in St. Louis in the spring of 1841. There he had been engaged by the peripatetic Father De Smet to guide him and some of his Jesuit associates to the Flathead and Nez Percé tribes. Upon encountering the Bartleson company in Independence, both De Smet and Fitzpatrick were agreeable to having the emigrants join them and benefit from the services of the veteran mountain man. "It was well we did," said one of the overlanders, John Bidwell, of Fitzpatrick's employment, "for otherwise probably not one of us would ever have reached California, because of our inexperience."

Another member of the party was an eccentric sixty-four-year-old Methodist preacher from Indiana by the name of Joseph Williams and with a personality of the sort which had given his profession a bad name. He had set off alone to improve the moral climate of the Far West but fortunately, before he was lost or scalped, encountered the emigrant caravan and joined it. By all accounts, he made an unpleasant addition. He did not like De Smet because he was Catholic and did not like Fitzpatrick because he "is a wicked, worldly man, who is much opposed to Missionaries going among the Indians." Since he was guiding De Smet, the most prominent Indian missionary, and was to become a good friend of the priest, what Fitzpatrick obviously opposed was a man like Williams going among the Indians. In fact, the Methodist never got at the tribes but continued on to Oregon.

Fitzpatrick, as he had agreed to do, led the Bartleson party as far as Soda Springs in southern Idaho, where he and De Smet left them to go north to the Nez Percé. Before departing, Fitzpatrick told the overlanders that he had no knowledge about routes from there to California and suggested that the only man who did was Joe Walker. Since they were mostly from western Missouri, many in the party probably were acquainted with Walker. One of them, a young man named Joe Chiles —the son of Azubah, who had picked her home along a creek bed in Fort Osage township because it "looked like Kentucky"—had been a next-door neighbor. Having learned perhaps from Henry Fraeb, whom they had met in late July on the Green River, that Walker was someplace between there and Bear Lake, the emigrants looked for him, but with no success. Some of the party therefore abandoned the idea of going to California. They continued with Fitzpatrick to Fort Hall and from there to Oregon, following the route Joel Walker had taken the season before.

However, thirty of the people decided they would find the way to California on their own. Very green and without a guide, they underwent dreadful hardships and certainly did not make an artistic passage, but in the annals of the American westering movement, their trip stands as a monument to the powers of human endurance and determination. In Nevada they either lost or abandoned all their wagons and most of their animals. By the time they came down on the western side of the Sierra they were on foot. Nancy Kelsey, the only woman who was still with them, was without shoes and carrying her infant daughter in her arms.

Had they found him, Walker could have given the Bartleson party advice about the trails which would have made their trip somewhat easier. However, it is doubtful that he himself would have guided them west, for by then he had made plans to visit Missouri for the first time in ten years. After returning from California, he stayed with the Snakes only long enough to tell his wife they were going back to see his people and to allow her to pack for the trip. After the preparations had been completed, he, she, perhaps some of their relatives and a few white mountaineers started east with the herd of California horses. They stopped first on the edge of the plains along the present Colorado-Wyoming-Nebraska border for the purpose of making buffalo meat. Since, like Walker, he had had no chance to lay in winter provisions while traveling back and forth to California, Henry Fraeb, with forty-some men, was in the same area, doing the same thing. If the two parties hunted together, it was not for long, because before the end of August Fraeb and ten or so of his men were killed by a combined party of Sioux, Cheyenne and Arapaho. At the end of a running battle the whites forted up behind the carcasses of their dead horses. It was in this enclosure that Fraeb finally went down. One of the survivors reported he made "the ugliest looking dead man I ever saw, and I have seen a good many. His face was all covered with blood, and he had rotten front teeth and a horrible grin. When he was killed he never fell, but sat braced up against the stump, a sight to behold." None of those who left accounts of this engagement mentioned Walker, as they probably would have if he had been with them. Walker himself later made a casual reference to the fact that at that time he had a brush with the Sioux. Some of the same warriors may have been involved, but it seems to have been a different incident, certainly one which ended better for Walker than it had for his California trail companion, Fraeb.

There is reason to suspect that the fight started because Fraeb made a bad mistake in judgment. Bartleson, the failed leader of the emigrant caravan of that season, had left home with the idea that he might be able to make some money en route to California. In his wagon he hid a number of kegs of whiskey. (When he found out about this cargo, John Bidwell said he was very surprised because there had been no drinking among the Bartleson hired hands while they were crossing the plains.) On the Green, after first cutting the booze with water, Bartleson began looking for a buyer. Eventually he got in touch with Henry Fraeb, who took it off his hands. Since he left almost immediately on the buffalo hunt, Fraeb must have had the kegs with him. It was John Bidwell's opinion that he used the whiskey in an attempt to befuddle the Sioux and Cheyenne—who were not his Indians—to get cheap buffalo robes from them. If so, the plan backfired fatally. Fraeb, a veteran, should have known, and probably did, that this was risky business.

The difficulties Walker and Fraeb had with the Indians were two among a series of violent incidents on the plains during the summer of 1841. Before attacking Fraeb, the Cheyenne had made a pass at the emigrant train, the first they had ever seen. They might have taken scalps there except for Tom Fitzpatrick's able negotiations and bluffing. Later in the season the Cheyenne fought a pitched battle against the Pawnee, killing seventy. The Sioux harassed a party of traders under the leadership of Lancaster Lupton and also struck a settlement of mission Delawares in Iowa, where they took fourteen scalps. A band of Osage, returning to the Missouri from a hunting and trading trip to Texas, brought two white girls with them. They had purchased the pair from Comanches, who the Osage reported had a number of other white captive slaves for sale. Neither interracial nor intertribal violence was new, but from that summer on, the amount of it increased and its character changed. There were many secondary reasons and excuses for this, but underlying them was the fact that the manner in which Indians and whites lived and lived together on the plains and in the mountains was altered suddenly and drastically. As an arbitrary date, 1841 serves perhaps better than any other as a year which separates two eras of western society. Prior to that time the interior regions of the trans-Mississippi west were dominated by independent Indian nations. The only whites they met regularly were connected in one way or another with the fur trade. Conflicts occurred sporadically, but generally the two races got along well because it was in their mutual self-interest. The whites were so numerically inferior that they had to be at least tolerated by the tribes to live and trade with them. The Indians did tolerate some of them because they were useful as a source of the marvelous goods of European civilization. Neither side was a threat, in a racial or territorial way, to the other. Individually many of the whites and reds came to admire each other as humans.

After 1841 the trappers and traders were a small minority among western whites, and their influence was greatly diminished. They were displaced by, or became agents of, the emigrants and a variety of others—the military, government surveyors, contractors, sutlers and private enterpreneurs—who came west essentially because the emigrants did. With only a few exceptions, the new classes had no use, in both senses of the word, for Indians. They regarded the natives as obstacles and problems, often as varmints, who, like wolves and snakes, had to be controlled or eliminated. If they were truly human—and the point was seriously debated—they were so lowly that the legal and ethical restraints which prevailed between civilized men did not apply in their case. Aside from the open hostilities which predictably followed from these racial attitudes, the coming of the emigrants, even those with the most pacific intent, had an enormous impact on the tribal cultures. For example, when Walker, Bonneville and Cerré had taken twenty wagons across the plains in 1832, Lucien Fontenelle, traveling in their wake, had complained that they scared the game and made hunting and therefore eating difficult for his brigade. By the mid-1840s thousands of emigrants were trundling across the west during the seasons when meat had to be made. Just their presence— and to a lesser extent the hunting they did—had a disruptive effect on game populations, particularly the buffalo herds. The difficulties Fontenelle had had to endure for a week or so became chronic for the Indians, whose economies were almost exclusively based on hunting.

As game became scarcer and spookier, the Indians were more inclined and had more need to harass whites, for reasons of retaliation and as a means of seizing badly needed livestock and supplies. Also, as hunting grounds changed and became less productive, tribes had to travel farther and into different areas. When they did, they infringed on the territories of their neighbors, who in turn had either to resist or to

trespass elsewhere. Traditional alliances and arrangements were overturned; old animosities were intensified, and new ones created. All this
further weakened and demoralized tribal societies.

The emigration and its support elements constituted a massive
military, economic and cultural invasion of the Indian nations, mounted
by a much more numerous and powerful people. By 1841 it was irre-
versible, and it is difficult, even with the advantage of hindsight, to
imagine how the racial conflicts which followed might have been
avoided or ended in any way appreciably different from the way they
did. The emigration and the conditions it created made the Indian way
of life insupportable. As a minor and incidental matter it had the same
effect on the life-styles of the few white men who, like Walker, had
established symbiotic relationships with the tribes as they had been.
By 1841 the new West was obviously beginning, and the old one ending. Though they might hang on and resist for a time, the residents of
the latter, red and white, had to adjust, surrender or be rubbed out
by those of the former.

After having made sufficient meat and standing off or eluding the
Sioux, Walker, his wife and a few others traveled to Missouri over
the route established by the fur rendezvous suppliers. They remained
the winter and part of the next spring in Jackson County, but beyond
the fact that they were there and attended the Six Mile Baptist Church,
not much is remembered about how they spent their time. However,
after an absence of ten years, Walker had many social demands on
his time. Besides his brothers John and Sam, a sister and Abraham
McClellan, there were a number of nieces and nephews who had been
either very small children or unborn when he left the States in 1832
with Bonneville. Also, there was the young son of a former neighbor,
William Adams, whom he would have visited if for no other reason
than that the little boy was named Joseph Rutherford Walker Adams.

There were other old friends in the county, including Zenas Leonard, by then proprietor of the principal store in Fort Osage township.
(The old fort had fallen into ruins, but a village fittingly named Sibley had been founded on the site.) No doubt Walker spent a good
many winter afternoons sitting around the stove in Leonard's store,
yarning with his friend and former clerk, within a circle of very attentive listeners. He was famous, a local man whose name could be found
in books published in the East, one of the very few people who had
firsthand information about how to get to California and Oregon and
what those places were like. These were topics of general and very
serious discussion, for by 1842 the westering fever was of epidemic
proportions through the Mississippi Valley. As an indication of how

this interest grew, in 1840 forty people had been thinking about making the overland trip, but only Joel and Mary Walker had actually done so. The next year a Western Emigration Society with 500 members was organized. Out of it came the fifty members of the Bartleson party. In 1847 nearly 4,500 overlanders reached Oregon and California.

Nowhere was the westering fever more virulent than in western Missouri. It infected not only would-be emigrants but local entrepreneurs who had hopes of getting rich by supplying and gouging them. By the mid-1840s Independence—and St. Joseph, sixty miles up the Missouri—were port cities to the prairie oceans of the west. In them, emigrants made their final preparations: attempted to dispose of belongings they had already found superfluous and to buy supplies they had forgotten to bring from home or had not known they would need. Local merchants bought from the travelers at rock-bottom prices and sold at ones which were marked up in the traveling season by several hundred percent. Swarming around the pioneers were outfitters, livestock traders, itinerant blacksmiths, mechanics, wheelwrights, life insurance and guidebook salesmen.

Travel agents of various sorts were among the most numerous and interesting of these hustlers. Some had fairly straightforward propositions, offering to sell a seat on a mule or wagon in an already organized caravan. Others had more bizarre schemes. An Independence resident who became known as Wind Wagon Thomas equipped a prairie schooner with a mast and sails. He began booking seats on this craft with the understanding that it would carry passengers west at the steady speed of fifteen miles per hour. However, on a trial run Thomas lost control of his machine, and he and it smashed up in a ravine. The Wind Wagon was later displayed as a curiosity but never sailed. The most astonishing invention, or at least prospectus, was that of Rufus Porter. He designed and then built a model of a 1,000-foot-long propeller-driven balloon which was to be powered by twin steam engines. With this model he toured eastern cities, advertising that, when built, the balloon would carry 200 people from St. Louis to San Francisco in as little as twenty-four hours. However, to avoid any future complaints about the schedule, Porter warned that if the aircraft encountered strong headwinds, the trip might take as long as five days. Even if there were such delays, the travelers, Porter promised, would not be uncomfortable because both meals and wine were included in the price of their ticket—$50 one way. However, it seems that he encountered technical difficulties, and the steam balloon was never built. Discouraged, Porter lost interest in the emigration and became the founder of *Scientific American* magazine.

Porter did not announce his airline plans until 1849; but by 1842 the emigration was well advanced, and it was generally assumed that the movement would increase dramatically in the following years. During his stay in Jackson County Walker was ideally situated to observe the migratory commotion and ponder its implications. Shortly thereafter he displayed—as he had in regard to the Taos and Santa Fe trades in the 1820s and the Rocky Mountain fur business and Pacific explorations in the 1830s—his remarkable knack for catching the mainstream westering current.

Walker left Missouri in the late spring of 1842 and, so far as surviving records are concerned, disappeared for a year. The presumption is that he returned with his wife to her people and spent the period trading with the Snake and other tribes. He did a good business, emerging from the mountains in June 1843, driving a packtrain loaded with fur. His traveling companion was Louis Vasquez, who had replaced the late Henry Fraeb as Bridger's partner. On the Platte River Walker and Vasquez paid a social call on an old friend, Sir William Drummond Stewart, who was making his last hunting, rough-riding, hard-drinking tour of the West. He had with him a group of sixty-some spirited gentlemen thrill seekers and their servants. Bill Sublette was serving as trail guide and recreation director for the party. Walker met Stewart and the playboys in the forepart of July but stayed only a day with them. Then he and Vasquez rode on to sell their furs at Fort Laramie. There he picked up his first emigrant party. During the next several years his movements are fairly easy to determine since he was often working with overlanders, many of whom were inveterate diary keepers.

Almost certainly Walker had previous information about the plans of the emigrants he met in July 1843 near Laramie since the caravan was composed of people from western Missouri among whom he had visited the year before. In the company was his nephew Frank McClellan, the twenty-five-year-old son of Abraham. Also, the train had been organized by Joe Chiles, the Jackson County neighbor of the Walkers and McClellans. Chiles, after his first, very hard overland trip with Bartleson, had returned to Missouri in 1842 and set himself up as an emigration agent and authority. He continued in this work during the remainder of the decade, the caravan of 1843 being his first venture. Whether by prearrangement or chance, Chiles and the others were delighted to find Walker and engaged him to pilot the wagon train to California for a fee of $300.

In the 1843 season 913 emigrants made the overland trip, but only 38, those Walker guided, reached California. The remainder went on to Oregon. There were several reasons for the greater popularity of the latter territory at this time. While Oregon did not definitely belong to the United States, its possession was at least a matter of dispute with the British. The society there was Anglo-American, and the language was English. California, in contrast, was unquestionably a foreign country. Also, at least until Walker finished his trip in 1843, there was no California wagon trail, and about all that was known of the route—mostly from the awful experience of the Bartleson party in 1841—was that it was extremely difficult. Finally, because of the presence of the Protestant missionaries, Oregon had the reputation of being a more respectable place than California, the general impression of the latter being that it was full of wild Mexican cowboys, roistering sailors and Catholics.

There were two principal officers in most of the overland wagon trains, a captain and a pilot. Captains were either men, like Chiles, who organized a caravan back in the States or were elected to that office after an emigrant company had been formed in Independence or St. Joseph. Their functions were administrative and to an extent judicial, involving such things as establishing the order of march, drawing up rosters for guard duty and settling quarrels, which in nearly all the caravans were numerous and often bitter.

Pilots (or guides) actually led the trains once they started westward and made the day-to-day tactical decisions. In some respects their duties were similar to those of a senior counselor taking children on a wilderness outing. Unlike Joel Walker, most of the members of the Chiles party and subsequent wagon caravans were very green. Generally they were midwestern farm families who had seldom been beyond the settlements. In consequence pilots were responsible for showing the overlanders not only where to travel but how to do so: how to make camps, guard livestock, ford rivers, hunt, make and mend equipment, deal with Indians and generally survive in the west. Also, since they were usually the only veterans in the companies, pilots were often obliged to soothe the fears and boost the morale of the newcomers.

Because they were so inexperienced, the overland travelers often got lost, set themselves and their wagons on fire, were kicked by mules, died from eating bad food, drinking poisonous water, being crushed under wagons, and at least one of them scalded himself to death in a natural hot spring. Many emigrants suffered greatly because of the lack of water in the arid west, but ironically, the most common cause of accidental death was drowning, which occurred when they attempted to ford rivers. During the twenty years between 1840 and 1860, when wagon travel was at its peak, 300 pioneers lost their lives in this way. Their physical sufferings were compounded by psychic ones. Most of

the overlanders did not expect to encounter such hardships as they did
—in part because of the glowing accounts circulated by emigration
promoters. Consequently they were often shocked by the real difficulties of the trip and inclined to feel sorry for themselves. To make an
overland crossing, wrote one who did, "a man must be able to endure
heat like a Salamander, mud and water like a muskrat, dust like a toad,
and labor like a jackass." Journals kept by members of the Chiles party
—who, in fact, had an easier time of it than many—were filled with
complaints and descriptions of their miseries: "Cold wind from the
north," "our clothing and blankets wet," "an uncomfortable night without fire, dinner or supper," "the first cooking done with buffalo manure,"
"road very bad," "teams gave out," "Oh the mosquitos," "Misery loves
company."

In fairness they also had some good times, were inspired by the
beauty of the new country and elated by their sense of adventure. Pierson B. Reading, a young man with Chiles, made an ecstatic entry in his
diary about prairie flowers, "surpassing in beauty those cultivated by
the hand of man," found the meat of wild sheep "the most delicious of
any I ever ate," was very proud that he had spent the Fourth of July
swimming in the Platte River as he helped the family men get their
wagons across, was pleased that in the Chiles party there were "some
very handsome young ladies, accomplished and intelligent."

Having since childhood heard stories about bloodthirsty savages,
many of the travelers were hysterical on the subject. When Indians
were met, pilots had to keep a close eye on their own people to see that
they did not do something foolish. In the very first wagon train, the
Bartleson company of 1841 for which Tom Fitzpatrick served as pilot,
there was a case of this sort. A young man named Nicholas Dawson
wandered away from the main body and was picked up by the Cheyenne. He was in such a panic that the warriors were amused by him
and brought the boy back to Fitzpatrick unharmed. Later he was to
become a prominent settler, but he was never able to live down this
early incident, being called, for the rest of his life, Cheyenne Dawson.

The fears of the emigrants about Indians proved almost as dangerous as the Indians themselves. To protect themselves against the red
menace, the newcomers usually left Missouri armed almost literally to
the teeth. One caravan of seventy-two wagons which made the crossing
in 1846 carried, for example, 155 rifles, 104 pistols, 1,672 pounds of
lead and 1,100 pounds of powder. "Perhaps," wrote a student of the
emigration, "there was never, at any other time, so great a number of
firearms per capita among a civilian population, as was to be found on
the overland trail." A California traveler who left Missouri with twenty-five men said of his party, "When we first crossed into the Indian
territory above St. Joseph, every man displayed his arms in the most

approved desperado style, and rarely thought of stirring from the train without his trusty rifle. But no enemies were seen. By degrees all were abandoned except a knife, and sometimes a pistol, which might be seen peeping from a pocket."

With such arsenals in the hands of nervous people, many of whom were relatively inexperienced in their use, accidents were inevitable. The first occurred, again, in the first overland caravan, the Bartleson company. Despite the hardships this party experienced, only one of its members was killed, a man with the ironic, as it turned out, name of Shotwell. Shotwell died as a result of trying to remove his rifle from his wagon muzzle first. Some current opinions to the contrary, the rifles of the emigrants did little to win the West, but according to journals of the overlanders, half a dozen or so of them lost their lives each year through mishaps similar to that which did in Shotwell. By way of comparison, thirty-four pioneers died between 1840 and 1847 because of Indian attacks. (This figure is distorted by the fact that twenty-three of these fatalities occurred in a single massacre when a tribe struck an emigrant company that had finished its trip and was in Oregon.) During the twenty peak years of the emigration, prior to the Civil War, the two most frequent accidents, drownings and gunshots, killed 350 overlanders, almost exactly the same number as were rubbed out by Indians.

A more generalized but also sometimes fatal source of self-inflicted difficulty was cantankerousness—the refusal of the emigrants to co-operate with one another and the quarreling that went on within nearly all the caravans. "The 'American character' was fully exhibited," sar-castically wrote Lansford Hastings of the company with which he made his first crossing in 1842. "All appeared to be determined to gov-ern, but not to be governed." Hastings was to have reason to ponder this trait. Four years later largely on his recommendation, given for reasons of venal self-interest, the Donner party took its fatal route. For his part in the affair Hastings has been remembered, with some justification, as a great scoundrel. However, among all the emigrant caravans, few others had so many bickering, contentious, hubristic people as did that of the Donners. Their inability to get along with each other had as much or more to do with their deaths as did Hast-ings's bad advice.

The Chiles party had set out from Missouri with only fifteen or sixteen people. On the trail, stragglers and defectors from other cara-vans were recruited. When Walker took over as the pilot, there were about fifty members in the company, still determined to go to Cali-fornia. There were two couples with five children between them and two unmarried women. The remainder were single men such as Frank McClellan.

One of the couples, Mr. and Mrs. Julius Martin, came from a family that had lived near the Walkers in east Tennessee and relocated in Missouri shortly after they did. Another member of the party was John Gantt, the cashiered army officer who had been a partner in the short-lived fur company which had first employed Zenas Leonard. Gantt had acted as an unofficial pilot on the plains. However, he had no knowledge of the country beyond Laramie and, after Walker arrived, rejoined the ranks, but he must have been a useful man, being one of the few who had any real frontier experience.

On the plains two of the men traveling with the loosely organized company had died—one of malaria and the other of "brain congestion." The party had suffered the usual hardships and done their share of squabbling. However, Walker seemed to settle them down, perhaps because so many of them knew him or simply because of his ability to establish and maintain discipline. Without incident he brought them from Fort Laramie to Black's Fork of the Green River. There, a few months earlier, Jim Bridger and Louis Vasquez had built a "post," a few rough cabins and corrals from which they intended to sell supplies and services to the emigrants. However, when Walker brought his column to the site on August 13, neither of the partners was there and the few buildings they had put up were in ruins. Bridger had left earlier in the summer to visit Sir William Drummond Stewart, and after he had departed, a war party of some seventy-five Cheyenne had raided his establishment, killed one of the hands he had left there and taken several prisoners from among a band of Snakes camped nearby.

Nevertheless, there was still good pasture and water, so the party halted to recruit their mules and horses and to build up their stock of provisions, which was low. Walker kept the emigrants hunting and drying meat for nearly two weeks. The delay and tedious work started some of them grumbling. John Boardman, one of the diarists, noted in his entry for August 25 that "many are dissatisfied with their style of living: [dry meat and coffee] and talk of trying some other way of going to Fort Hall." Impatiently some of the party argued that by waiting, they were running the risk of coming to the Sierra, "the California mountain," late in the season. It was their understanding that the snows commenced very early there. As well as anybody in the west, Walker was aware of how bad travel could be in the Sierra in the fall, but he was also familiar, as none of the others were, with the Nevada-California desert and the fact that once in it, they would find little in the way of forage for either themselves or their livestock. Therefore, the hunting continued. Though this was normally a good area, it did not go as well as Walker hoped; the Cheyenne had scattered the game, and '43 was a severe drought year. Also, part of the meat they did make was lost because of greenhorn carelessness. One evening Walker sent in some 300 pounds of elk with his hunters. John Boardman, who was among those remaining in camp, said they made a good supper and then set aside the remaining meat to pack the next morning. However, they cached it under some canvas on the ground and found upon arising that "the Indian dogs, d——— them, had eaten nearly the whole of it."

About the first of September the company started toward Fort Hall on the Snake River. Since the trail to that Hudson's Bay establishment was well marked, Walker rode ahead to see if he could secure additional supplies at the post, where he had frequently traded in years past. After he left, the party was joined in a melodramatic fashion by another single young woman, remembered only as Miss Eyers (or sometimes Ayers). She had been traveling with or near the Chiles group all summer in company with her mother and father. The Eyers were an English couple, and the husband-father had earned a reputation as being a disagreeable, terrible-tempered man who often beat his wife and daughter. The others had previously ignored these outbursts, but on the way to Fort Hall, such a violent quarrel occurred that William Baldridge could no longer restrain himself. (Baldridge was thirty-one years old and had been born in east Tennessee. His family emigrated to Missouri when he was eight years old, only a year after the Walkers and McClellans.)

"When," Baldridge recollected, he "saw a sweet-faced, innocent girl subjected to brutal treatment of a father with a vicious and capricious temper, [I] resolved to liberate the girl from the abject bondage." Baldridge went to Mrs. Julius Martin and asked her, if he were able to liberate Miss Eyers, would she let the girl travel with her and her family to California. The Martins agreed. Miss Eyers, "only too glad to escape the outbursts of her father's wrath," secretly transferred her belongings to the Martin wagons. She was assisted in her escape by her mother, "who was left to bear the brunt of rage, which evidently welled up in torrents when the father discovered what had taken place." Eyers and his unfortunate wife separated from the Chiles party and went on to Oregon. Baldridge commenced calling Miss Eyers his "prairie flower," but his intentions toward her were very pure. In California he acted as her guardian for a time, then married her off to a rancher, John Sinclair, who had first come west ten years before as a clerk for the Boston iceman, Nathaniel Wyeth.

While this was going on, Walker reached Fort Hall. He was cordially received by the British factor, Richard Grant. Grant, in fact, arranged a dinner party at the post to honor Walker and another American, Theodore Talbot, a member of a government surveying party led by Captain John Charles Frémont of the U.S. Corps of Topographical Engineers. (When Walker was at Fort Hall, Frémont was looking about Salt Lake. Talbot, Frémont's principal civilian aide, had come ahead to the Snake River with the bulk of the party.) Walker and Talbot, who were to see much more of each other in years to come, spent the evening discussing western geography. It was during this conversation that Walker gave Talbot his views on the course of the Colorado River and told him about his repeated efforts to organize a party to explore it by boat. After retiring to his quarters, Talbot noted in his journal: "Walker is an agreeable companion and possesses much knowledge of the country, Indians and also indomitable bravery." As for their host, Talbot wrote, "Grant is a good looking gentlemanly man [who] talks of the country as British, the Indians in it, as serfs of the Hudson Bay Compy, and soforth, in the same strain."

Though the urbane Richard Grant was delighted to give a dinner for two prominent American explorers, he was not eager to help American emigrants traveling into what he considered British territory. According to Talbot, Walker later made inquiries about buying provisions for the wagon party which was approaching and Grant "refused to sell, even at the most exorbitant prices." When Joe Chiles came up, Walker explained that in his opinion their supply situation was critical and that if they were not able to improve it, he was not going to take the responsibility for leading the people farther. Finally, the two men were able to cajole four head of cattle and a few other provisions from Grant. However, these were not considered sufficient, so they made a decision to split the party. Chiles would take thirteen of the strongest men and on horseback proceed to Fort Boise, the next Hudson's Bay post to the west. There they hoped they might have better luck bargaining with the British. Even if they did not, the mounted men could travel faster and were in a better position to forage for themselves than those who remained with the wagons. Also, by leaving, they increased the provisions available to the others. From Fort Boise Chiles would take his men to the Truckee River and then directly across the Sierra to Sutter's Fort. There he would obtain supplies and attempt to get them back over the mountains to the wagon party.

While Chiles was so engaged, Walker would take the wagons south from Fort Hall to the Humboldt Sink and wait a time for the relief party. He warned Chiles that he could not stay long, for by his calculations he had to get the people from Fort Hall to California within sixty days. If it took longer, he feared the draft animals and the emigrants themselves would begin to fail from hunger and exhaustion. From the Humboldt Sink, with or without additional supplies, Walker said he would proceed south through the Owens Valley to the pass he had discovered in 1834—which would come to bear his name. Though nobody had done so previously, he thought that by this route he could get wagons into California. Events were to prove that splitting the party was an excellent decision, but the plan involved serious risks. Chiles needed to take the best men and riding animals with him if his group was to make a fast trip to California. Walker was left with one man, Major (a given name) Walton, who had been with Chiles to California in 1841. The other twenty-three people were, beyond what they had learned that summer, very inexperienced. Ten of them were either women or children. There had been and would be no other emigrant parties which were as dependent on their pilot, not only on his judgment and information but also on his physical strength and skill. Fortunately, as George Stewart, a principal historian of the California Trail, was to write, "Walker was a host in himself."

They left Fort Hall on September 16 with six mule-drawn wagons, trailing some animals to be eaten, including Richard Grant's four cows. Despite the planning, Walker was still worried about the supply situation. He halted the company a few miles beyond the fort, far enough removed so that the others would not be involved if trouble started. Then he sent back two men to make a final attempt, using more or less any tactics they could, to get more provisions from Grant. For the job he selected Julius Martin and his own nephew Frank McClellan. They both were well motivated—Martin because of concern about his family and McClellan because he wanted to show well on the first independent mission he had been given by his uncle. Outside Fort Hall the two met some of Talbot's men and explained their intentions. The surveyors were sympathetic and said that if it came to shooting, they would fight with them against the British. It fell just short of that. Martin and McClellan confronted Grant and succeeded in "frightening him into terms." It was very close to being an outright robbery but also was close to being justifiable. The two men could not have carried much in the way of supplies, but the situation with the wagon train was to become so critical that what they did take may have saved lives two months later.

The next morning the party split according to their plan. Walker led the wagons up the Raft River to Goose Creek and from there to the Humboldt Sink, which they reached on or about October 22. They halted there, hoping to meet the relief party. It did not come, though, as they were to learn later, Chiles and his men had made a heroic effort to aid them. The riders had been unable to obtain supplies at Fort Boise but had been given a map, not, as it turned out, a very good one, showing the route from that post to the Sacramento River. Following it, Chiles had made a long, looping swing through southern Oregon and eventually reached Sutter's on November 11, having ridden nearly

800 miles in forty days while living off the land. Immediately Chiles had organized a small packtrain and sent it east to find Walker. However, the Sierra passes were filled with snow, and it had to turn back.

Even had the relief column been able to force its way through the Sierra, it would have done little good, for having waited as long as he dared, Walker left the Humboldt Sink about November 1. By then, though they were only halfway to California, forty-five of the days allotted for the trip were gone. Rations were cut, and Walker pushed them along as rapidly as he judged the animals and people could stand. They were constantly tired and hungry, but even so, their position was not as grim as that of the Bartleson party in 1841. Their supplies were short, but they still had the wagons and some of their livestock. Most important, because of Walker, they knew where they were going and something about the nature of the country ahead. These certainties were a source of psychic strength.

Beyond Carson Lake one of the men, Milton Little, who was on night guard duty, was wounded with an arrow delivered by a Paiute lurking about their camp. (Though they were generally regarded as an inferior lot, these Indians of the Nevada desert consistently gave Walker more trouble than any others in the west.) However, the attack was isolated, and no others followed. Coming to the next big lake, which a few years later was to be officially named Walker, they got some welcome aid from the Indians, trading horseshoe nails to them for fresh fish. When they entered the Owens Valley, they became the first to bring wagons into California and, except for the drought, might have succeeded in taking them all the way to the coast—that honor was to belong to a party that came the next year. However, lacking forage, the draft animals had become too weak to pull any farther, so at Owens Lake the wagons were unloaded and abandoned. Among other things, a full set of mill irons, including three sash saws, which had been carried all the way from Missouri, were cached in the desert. With much less baggage, at least the women and children were able to continue riding. On December 3 they reached the summit of Walker Pass and, though there was six inches of snow on it, crossed without difficulty. They had cut it very thin so far as time went, for an exceptional blizzard closed the route a few days later. Had they been there then, they would have either been marooned in the snow or left with virtually no food on the desert side of the pass.

As soon as they descended, some of the party were hellbent on striking directly north toward Sutter's Fort, but Walker restrained them, pointing out that because of the very dry year, they would still have trouble finding game. He had not taken them that far to see them starve in California, and he kept the party together, leading it across the coastal mountains, another hard, hungry, dry three-day journey. However, all survived it and, coming down on the sea side of the range, suddenly found themselves in well-watered meadows, teeming with deer and elk. They spent Christmas in Peachtree Valley, resting, rejoicing and feasting on "finest haunches of venison." Thereafter the company separated, its members going to various places and fates in California.

So far as Walker was concerned, getting the wagon train into California was in some respects a more difficult expedition than that of 1833, when he made the first passage of the Sierra with his fur brigade. The overland caravan had done no true exploring but had laid down 500 miles of what was to become the California Trail. The physical hardships and dangers were less severe than those met in the Sierra, but the emigrants were less experienced and able than the trappers had been. To a far greater degree than was the case with his veterans of '33, Walker had been personally responsible for the lives of everyone in the wagon party. During the course of the overland passage he seemed to have developed considerable admiration for the spunk of these greenhorns, particularly for Mrs. Julius Martin, one of the first white women with whom he had been closely associated as an adult. Years later a member of the Walker family was to tell not a sentimental story but rather to pass along a single suggestive, sentimental sentence. "Captain Uncle Jo" (which is how some members of the clan still refer to their famous ancestor) "always told people he thought Mrs. Martin was more than a little bit alright."

Frémont

In February, after the emigrants had dispersed, Walker rode to Monterey, where he presented his passport. He received permission to stay and do business in California and agreed to be responsible for three companions: Lewis Anderson, Tom Cowie and Fleurnaye Dawson. The three had been among the single men in the overland caravan, and with their help Walker immediately began assembling a herd of horses and mules to drive east. He left the Los Angeles area in mid-April with the livestock and an eight-man trail crew. They followed the Old Spanish Trail—a packtrain route between Santa Fe and southern California. Near the present Las Vegas, Nevada, they found signs that another party had left the trail heading into the Ute country. Walker guessed correctly that Captain John Charles Frémont of the U.S. Topographical Engineers and members of his expedition had made the signs. Since Walker had met and dined with Theodore Talbot, Frémont's civilian assistant, at Fort Hall the previous September, this company had been wandering about in Oregon and then in California, and its progress was a matter of general interest. Curious about what the Pathfinder was doing, Walker rode after them.

Frémont at the time was certain that he was being dogged by hordes of "marauding savages," among whom "there was manifestly a consultation and calculation going on to decide the question of attacking us." He consequently was delighted when Walker caught up on May 12, and this was the occasion which caused him to write later that nothing but Walker's "great knowledge of the country, great courage and presence of mind, and good rifles could have brought him safe from such a perilous enterprise [that is, finding Frémont]." Frémont suggested that Walker had fought his way through "a gantlet of desert robbers, killing two and getting some of the horses wounded."

Walker never made mention of such heroics and in fact, as previously noted, declared sarcastically, after reading Frémont's account of his rescue, that the danger had been mostly imagined by the army captain. That this was a reasonably accurate assessment is supported by the fact that Frémont had with him at the time Tom Fitzpatrick, Kit Carson and Alex Godey, the last being one of the veterans of the expedition Walker had led across the Sierra in 1833. Unless he had completely ignored these three, Frémont could not have been in any great difficulty, and none of them ever had anything to say about perils of the magnitude their leader described. (Fitzpatrick was the chief guide, while Carson assisted him and also served as a kind of personal aide to Frémont.)

As it turned out, Walkara, the red Joe Walker, was behind the Indian trouble Frémont had been having or fearing. The white Walker sought out his Ute namesake and smoothed things over with him. Saying that he knew almost all the Utes and thought them "good sorts," Walker introduced the Desert Napoleon to the topographic captain. Frémont was pleased, saying that the "chief was quite civil to me." Thereafter nothing more was heard about the "marauding savages." Frémont wanted to go north to the vicinity of Utah Lake and immediately engaged Walker ("who has more knowledge of these parts than any man I know") to join the expedition as the chief guide for this part of their trip. Tom Fitzpatrick relinquished the title willingly and without resentment. At the time he and Walker were probably the two best-informed Americans about the general geography of the West, but the Great Basin had become Walker's specialty. Since his own credentials were enormous, Fitzpatrick, a confident, commonsense sort of man, had no need to dispute Walker's. Beyond that, the two had been friends since at least the winter of 1832, when they spent Christmas together on the Blackfoot River.

Since the book he was later to write included a number of Walker stories—about the Humboldt River, the Sierra, salmon fishing in the Columbia, eating insect larvae in the Nevada desert—Frémont apparently spent considerable time questioning his guide about his western experiences. There was plenty of opportunity for this, since the combined parties—Walker still had his own men and California horses with him—made a leisurely and uneventful tour of the Great Basin. However, when, a year later, Frémont published his report, the men with him, and the entire nation, were to find out they had in fact been on a death-defying exploration in wild and unknown places. The passage about Walker's ride through a "gantlet of desert robbers" was a fair but small sample. A larger one had to do with the Search for the Mysterious Buenaventura River.

Frémont suggested that a principal objective of the 1843–44 expedition was to find the Buenaventura, which he said was reputed to run from the Great Salt Lake directly to the Pacific. That he truly thought it was there is very hard to believe. Benjamin Bonneville's map which eliminated the Buenaventura had been published six years before, and other cartographers had accepted his negative information as conclusive. If for some reason Frémont, a trained topographer, had neglected his homework and was unaware of this, Walker, the man who had supplied Bonneville with his data, was riding at the Pathfinder's side. All in all, it seems probable that Frémont was not seriously looking for the Buenaventura, and had he suggested as much in the company he was with, he would have been a laughingstock. On the other hand, writing that he was looking for the Buenaventura would sound very well when his book was read by people 2,500 miles to the east. Whether this was his purpose from the beginning—that is, collecting and arranging for experiences which could be shaped to serve his literary and promotional needs—or if he concluded, after he had sat down to write, that a mysterious river, like "marauding savages," would make a good touch is a question nobody but Frémont could answer. Walker, Fitzpatrick, Carson and the others had no way of knowing that their major function was to serve as a supporting cast in a kind of living pageant: John Charles Frémont, Intrepid Explorer. Therefore, they treated their employer, who invariably made a good first impression, as if dealing with a somewhat jittery version of William Drummond Stewart—a vigorous tourist who for reasons of his own wanted to see a bit of the Wild West and had the wherewithal to pay for the experience.

In late May Walker brought the expedition to the upper Sevier. There one of Frémont's men accidentally killed himself while attempting to draw his gun muzzle first. After he was buried, they proceeded to Utah Lake, which Frémont was later to describe as a "southern limb" of the Great Salt Lake. Any of the mountain men present could have disabused him of this false notion, if, in fact, he actually entertained it. However, again, linking the two bodies of water sounded well. Frémont, who had visited the northern portions of Salt Lake during the previous fall, could then claim to have made a complete circuit of the Great Basin when he reached the southern shore of the Salt-Utah Lake. From there Walker and Fitzpatrick took Frémont through Colorado to Bent's Fort on the upper Arkansas. During this part of the tour the two guides were following trails with which they had been familiar for twenty years. But Frémont was to suggest that again they were in the howling wilderness, writing after they reached Bent's Fort: "We were now in the region where our mountaineers were accustomed to live; and all the dangers and difficulties of the road being considered past, four of them, including Carson and Walker, remained at the Fort."

They parted company in early July, and Frémont, on his own, hurried east along the Santa Fe wagon trail and on to Washington. There he began work on his book, which was to have a far more significant influence on the westering movement than anything the expedition had discovered or accomplished in the field.

Though it was narrower in scope, the nineteenth-century version of American Manifest Destiny was based on major premises very similar to those of the Marxists. Supporters of the doctrine were convinced that its triumph—in this case occupation of the continent by Americans—was inevitable and would occur as the people, their government aside, responded to natural and social laws. This is how things worked out, for Manifest Destiny was preeminently a grass-roots movement in which the flag generally followed the people.

Walker, Zenas Leonard and John Bradshaw, sitting on the beach at Año Nuevo Point in December 1833, discussing the need for the United States to seize Oregon and California, not only were talking pure Manifest Destiny but represented what might be called its gestative stage. In themselves they could not directly, even in a sacrificial way, accomplish its objectives. They were single men engaged in private, irregular ventures, the risks of which were obvious. If anything happened to them, it would not provide sufficient excuse for formal action by their government. However, their activities stimulated the westering urges of more conventional people who became the second critical wave of Manifest Destiny. Joel and Mary Walker in 1840 and the fifty emigrants who followed them to the Pacific in 1841 were mainstream people. If they got in trouble with the Indians, British or Mexicans, there would be immediate, apolitical sympathy and pressure brought to bear on the government to assist and protect them, for the sake of the national honor if nothing else.

There were always strong Manifest Destiny men in high office—often including the presidency—but their expansionist tendencies were frequently curbed by the influential Little America body of opinion. Advocates of the latter position saw no reason to speed up the Americanization of the continent (which, after all, was inevitable) by engaging in risky diplomatic or military maneuvers or to spend public money in support of the movement. Their opposition was so effective that with few exceptions—notably the filibustering activities of Andrew Jackson—the architects of Manifest Destiny did not find it politically prudent to initiate overtly imperialistic actions. However, they were willing to encourage the private westering enterprises of the citizenry. In the main they did so with regular blasts of promigration, chauvinistic rhetoric, but on occasion they were able to initiate supportive and symbolic public works projects. Sending out George Sibley and his men in 1825 to "survey" the well-traveled Santa Fe Trail was an example of this tactic.

In regard expansion to the Pacific coast, it was apparent by 1840, when Joel and Mary Walker headed in that direction, that the inevitable would occur as soon as a few more emigrant families could be nudged into Oregon and California. In 1842, again largely through the efforts of Senator Thomas Benton, the Machiavelli or at least Patrick Henry of Manifest Destiny, John Charles Frémont was first dispatched to the west to act as a nudging instrument. Overtly and covertly Frémont's mission was almost identical to Sibley's earlier one. Officially he was ordered to survey the wagon road across the plains to the South Pass. There was even less need for this work than there had been on the Santa Fe Trail since by 1842 the South Pass road had been traveled by first furmen and then the first emigrants for fifteen years. In regard to actual trail work, Frémont did much less than Sibley because it interested him less and there was less to do.

Though never spelled out, the implicit purpose of his assignment was to increase public interest in the migration by making the west seem like a desirable place to go. In this, Frémont was much more successful than Sibley had been, for he was, as Sibley was not, a genius at creating symbols and using them to stimulate the public imagination. In time he was to be called the Great Pathfinder, but more accurately he was the Great Publicist of the West. In this capacity he may have had more influence than any other single man on the overland migration of the 1840s and 1850s. Temperamentally Frémont was well suited for this work. By dramatizing the West, he was able to do the same for himself, and he was a notable glory hound. It is tempting to speculate that if Frémont was not born for this calling, he was at least strongly inclined toward it by the circumstances of his birth. His mother, Anne Whiting, was the daughter of a socially prominent Virginia family. She had married young and respectably but, it seems, unhappily. In 1811, without benefit of divorce, she ran off with a handsome but penniless French émigré, Charles Frémon. This caused much scandalized talk in well-bred southern circles, and there was more when John Charles Frémon (he was later to add the terminal *t*) was born, technically a bastard, in 1813.

With their son, the Frémons wandered about the South, keeping boardinghouses and giving dancing lessons, but never completely living down their past. John Charles grew into an intelligent, good-looking youth with fine manners and an obsessive desire to win attention and approval from respectable people. He entered Charleston (South Carolina) College as a sixteen-year-old and there made a reputation as a quick, though not scholarly, student. Also in this period, he found his first important patron, Joel Poinsett, a nationally prominent South Carolina politician, who had served as the U.S. ambassador to Mexico in the 1820s. In 1836 Poinsett became the Secretary of War and among other things organized the Army Corps of Topographical Engineers. He remembered the agreeable young man from his hometown and obtained an appointment to the corps for Frémont, even though these assignments were considered exceptionally choice and were being hotly competed for by West Pointers.

Frémont did his first field work in the upper Mississippi Valley under the supervision of Joseph Nicollet, then the most distinguished formal topographer in the country. When they were finished, Frémont returned to Washington and, by day, diligently worked with Nicollet on the preparation of the survey report. During the evenings he cut a dashing figure in Washington's high society. Shortly he met, fell in love with, proposed to and was accepted by Jessie Benton, the beautiful and accomplished fifteen-year-old daughter of no less a personage than Senator Thomas Hart Benton of Missouri. The senator was enraged by the prospect of his daughter's marrying an impecunious young officer of dubious parentage. Jessie Benton, however, was as formidable a person as her father. Confronting the Lion of the West, she said of her intended as the biblical Ruth had of hers, "Whither thou goest, I will go; and where thou lodgest, I will lodge." The senator was able to recognize a *fait accompli* when he met one and acquiesced. After Frémont had become his son-in-law, Benton decided he might as well make use of him in the interests of Manifest Destiny. Thus it was that as the commander of a unit of the Topographical Engineers, Frémont was in Independence in May 1842, preparing to leave for the South Pass.

There he first met Walker, who was later to mention briefly that Frémont had offered him the job as chief guide for the survey party. Walker, however, was already planning to go back to the mountains with his wife. He declined the post and recommended young Kit Carson, also in Independence at the time, for the job. Frémont said nothing about this but did write that he needed a guide and was looking for Andrew Drips, Walker's old friend, the AFC partisan, but could not find him. Thereupon he was approached by Carson, who said that he thought he "could guide him to any point he would wish to go." Frémont said that since he did not know the young man, he would seek references as to his abilities. He did and was sufficiently impressed to hire Carson.

The job was a godsend for Carson, who was at the moment broke and without other prospects. Also, it was an excellent choice from Frémont's standpoint. Beyond the fact that Carson was well qualified to guide such an expedition as this, he was better suited to satisfy Frémont's temperamental requirements than Walker or another of the more senior mountain men would have been. This point was well made by Carson's most scholarly biographer, Harvey Lewis Carter:

> He [Frémont] spoke very favorably of the knowledge and experience of Thomas Fitzpatrick and Joseph R. Walker, who were considerably older men than Carson, and more distinguished in the fur trade than Carson had been. The difference in age [and, as Carter elsewhere suggests, accomplishment] made it hard for Frémont to warm up to them. He always referred to them as Mr. Fitzpatrick and Mr. Walker, but he seldom referred to Mr. Carson. It was just plain Carson or, more often, Kit. The more firmly established place that the older men had held in the fur trade also made them less adaptable than Carson. Fitzpatrick and Walker had been leaders and found it difficult to follow a younger man. Carson had not been a leader and was only three years older than Frémont.

Simple congeniality aside, Frémont may have recognized from the beginning—he was very shrewd in such matters—that Carson would serve very well so far as the real purpose of the mission was concerned —that is, publicizing and romanticizing the West. Up to that point Carson had been only a field hand among the frontiersmen, but the young man's accomplishments and adventures, though not known to the public, were real and numerous. Also, he was an attractive and modest fellow who provided Frémont with fine raw material for creating the new Daniel Boone. There was another advantage to Carson. Since he was unknown when Frémont found him, he could be built up and praised to the sky without fear that he would steal the exploring scene from the Pathfinder. In contrast, had Frémont followed Walker, Fitzpatrick or Drips to the South Pass, his own reputation would have been diminished because they were already celebrated figures.

The two young men seemed well pleased with their situation and each other as they set off onto the plains in the early summer of 1842. Frémont, leading his first independent expedition, said of himself that he was full of "the true Greek joy in existence—in the gladness of living." The book he later published still evokes those feelings, being filled with sketches of Frémont and Carson enjoying the marvelous scenery, galloping about the prairies on hunts, meeting grand Indians and all the while being serious explorers.

There was in the party a quite different, very unromantic, in fact, dour young man. This was Charles Preuss, a German emigrant who had been hired as a topographer. He had taken the job because of financial need but found the work interesting enough. However, early on he decided his leader was a posturing, lightweight popinjay. Preuss also was keeping a journal, but a very private one (it was written in German and not published until 1958). One of the first entries, that of June 6, 1842, is a fair example of Preuss's opinion about his leader. "Annoyed," he grumbled, "by that childish Frémont."

Understandably, since Preuss did nearly all the technical survey work, Frémont was very pleased with him and described him flatteringly as a loyal topographic man Friday. During the next six years the two men were to make three western expeditions together, and their disparate journals are often hilarious when read side by side. Some of the more entertaining and instructive entries were made in August of that first summer, when Frémont decided he would like to become the first man to climb the highest peak in the Rockies. By then they were in the Wind River mountains of Wyoming. Frémont arbitrarily selected a nearby pinnacle and declared it to be indeed the highest of all the Rockies and the object of assault for the party. In fact, Frémont Peak, as it was to be named, is 13,765 feet in elevation; there are fifty-five higher ones in the west, and one is within five miles of Frémont's.

They started out early in the morning of August 13 through soft snow but did not, according to Preuss, feel much of the Greek joy in existence. "The leader, Carson," wrote Preuss, "walked too fast. This caused some exchange of words. Frémont got excited, as usual, and designated a young chap to take the lead—he could not serve as a guide, of course. Frémont developed a headache, and as a result we stopped soon afterwards, about eleven o'clock. He decided to climb the peak the next morning with renewed strength and cooler blood." The following day Frémont had a word with Preuss to the effect that the topographer's figures about the elevation must be incorrect. These were changed, and Preuss wrote with considerable irony: "It finally looked as if Frémont would be satisfied with the altitude I had established and would add five or six hundred feet in order to fix the assumed highest point."

Again Frémont began to feel unwell, so the hike was canceled for another day. On the fifteenth they finally reached the summit. "The highest rock," noted Preuss, "was so small that only one after the other could stand on it. Pistols were fired, the flag unfurled, and we shouted 'hurrah' several times."

Frémont's version was that after heroically struggling through ice and snow, working his way across a vertical precipice, "I sprang upon the summit and another step would have precipitated me into an immense snow field five hundred feet below. To the edge of this field was a sheer icy precipice; and then, with a gradual fall, the field sloped off for about a mile until it struck the foot of another lower ridge."

After warming up in this fashion, Frémont reared back and delivered himself a volley of prose which, when it was published—along with a sketch of him standing on the icy summit with Old Glory in one hand and a sword in the other—probably did more than any other single paragraph to make him famous. In retrospect, the passage may also have been the most important accomplishment of his first expedition. Said the Pathfinder:

> Here, on the summit, where the stillness was absolute, unbroken by any sound, and the solitude complete, we thought ourselves beyond the region of animated life; but while we were sitting on the rock, a solitary bee (*Bombus, the bumblebee*) came winging his flight from the eastern valley, and lit on the knee of one of the men. It was a strange place, the icy rock and the highest peak of the Rocky Mountains, for a lover of warm sunshine and flowers; and we pleased ourselves with the idea that he was the first of his species to cross the mountain barrier—a solitary pioneer to foretell the advance of civilization.

These stirring words were to have an extraordinary impact on the public imagination. One who testified to it was the poet Joaquin Miller, who said he first read the passage as an Indiana farm boy and was exhilarated by the vision of Frémont's men scaling "the savage battlements of the Rocky Mountains, flags in the air, Frémont at the head, waving his sword, his horse neighing wildly in the mountain wind, with unknown and unnamed empires on every hand. It touched my heart when he told me how a weary little brown bee tried to make its way from a valley of flowers far below across a spur of snow. . . . I was no longer a boy . . . now I began to be inflamed with a love for action, adventure, glory and great deeds away out yonder under the path of the setting sun."

The incident involving the "highest mountain in the Rockies" is instructive in regard to Frémont's character and style. The gesture—the flag flying, the little brown bee, the sword and the rest—was immensely successful. As it did young Joaquin Miller, it affected thousands of Americans, set them thinking about the West and migration. But the gesture—the ascent, even in a sense the mountain itself—was bogus. This constituted a consistent pattern of behavior which Frémont was to follow throughout his career. His deep need for instant glory and his fertile imagination made him a master at recognizing or arranging for heroic situations in which he was the center of attention. In the 1840s he conceived himself as a kind of super Frontier

Hero, trailblazer for all the people. Later he was to see himself as a financial tycoon on the order of John Jacob Astor, as a general such as William Tecumseh Sherman and even as a president like Abraham Lincoln. He was able to strike convincing poses appropriate for these roles, but he was no more these other things than he was a mountaineer. When the time came to translate the gestures into reality and accept the consequences of them, something in Frémont—judgment, confidence, nerve—always failed, and he was unmasked as a playactor, performing in a self-produced drama. So far as his part as the Great Pathfinder was concerned, this exposure did not come until late in the 1840s. In the early part of the decade he played it brilliantly, to the acclaim of the nation.

In March 1843 he presented the report of his first expedition to the Congress. The legislators were enthralled with it—little bee and all. They should have been, because it is still one of the liveliest government documents ever written and in terms of its purpose, publicizing the West, one of the most effective. Money was appropriated to print 10,000 copies, which were snapped up quickly by the public.

Immediately thereafter Frémont, an almost overnight celebrity, again went west. A number of the men from the year before, including Carson and Preuss, were engaged for the 1843 expedition. However, since it was intended to go all the way to Oregon, through less well-traveled country, Tom Fitzpatrick was added as the chief guide and field adjutant. Also, Frémont took along a twelve-pound brass cannon, which he had obtained by irregular means from an army depot. There was no possible use for it, and it was fired on only one occasion, at a herd of buffalo, but it looked and would read well. Frémont's military superiors were furious when they found out what he had done, but by the time they did he was well out on the plains and the symbolic fieldpiece could not be retrieved without an undignified and ludicrous scene. As for the men who had to trundle the cannon over the trails, Charles Preuss probably expressed the sentiments of most of them when he wrote: "If we had only left that ridiculous thing at home."

Late in September 1843, after Walker had dined with Theodore Talbot and gone on with his wagons, Frémont reached Fort Hall. From there the surveyors traveled to Oregon, following much the same route used by Joel and Mary Walker in 1840 and by about 1,000 other emigrants who preceded the Pathfinder. Then Frémont took the expedition into the Sierra. Essentially this was another gesture-making exercise but a much more reckless one than climbing Frémont Peak, for they experienced considerable hardship in the deep snows. Eventually Fitzpatrick, Carson and Godey extricated the party. When they recovered from the ordeal, they left California and thus in May came to Mountain Meadows, where they were "rescued" by Walker.

After Frémont had departed Bent's Fort in July 1844, Walker sold his California horses either there or in Santa Fe. Then he rode north and spent the rest of the traveling season with the emigrants. (That year 1,475 overlanders made the trip to Oregon, and 53 to California.) By July 30 Walker reached Fort Laramie and there agreed to lead a caravan, which Andrew Sublette had piloted that far, on to Fort Bridger. The party had been organized by "Col." Cornelius Gilliam, a Missourian who, according to his son, Washington, was an old friend of Walker's. Washington Gilliam, one of several diarists in the train, wrote that "the noted mountaineer, Mr. Joseph Walker made a very acceptable guide for us."

The most detailed record of the journey was kept by the Reverend Edward Parrish, who, accompanied by his family, was going to Oregon from Ohio as a settler, not as a missionary. Parrish's diary indicates that the party had been quarrelsome from the beginning. Before they reached Laramie, these overlanders convened a kangaroo court to try and punish one of their members who had threatened another with a rifle. Also, one man and one woman who had started with them had died of disease, and all had suffered from the customary ailments, hardships and depressions. They gave Walker no trouble for the first week or so but began to grumble when he halted them on the Sweetwater River and took some of the more able men out to hunt buffalo. Those who remained in camp did not like the dirty work of butchering and drying the meat brought in by the hunters. Then another emigrant group which had been behind them caught up and passed them. This annoyed them for competitive reasons. "After the bustle and success in getting away ahead, we were ordered to camp till tomorrow to cure the meat we have, and to give Walker a chance to kill more, as he has not enough, it seems," griped Parrish. "It is now stated that the Captain [Gilliam] will not wait after to-day." However, Walker was able to hold them, with the warning that once they left the Sweetwater, there was no assurance that they would find more buffalo or much game of any sort. Three days later they began a difficult ascent of the Wind River mountains, and were cheered to find the wagon train which had passed them earlier in the week had itself halted and was waiting specifically for them. "They [the rival party] say they do not desire to go before, but wish to avail themselves of the experience of our pilot, Mr. Walker," wrote Parrish with evident satisfaction.

The complaints resumed when their pilot led them over several shortcuts on which they had to brush out the trail ahead of them. "The people are getting tired of leaving the road to follow Captain Walker in new routes, and I think they will quit it. This afternoon [August 27] looks like rain. My family are sick, Jackson, Marinda and Elizabeth Ellen. My health is better." The people continued to follow Walker despite the grousing, and he led them safely to Fort Bridger, where they arrived on the last day of the month. By then Parrish had reflected on the trip and was grateful for what Walker had done. "The water and grass are fine. Captain Walker kindly conducted us to the place of encampment and then returned to his own wigwam among his own Indians of the Snake nation. It is said he has several squaws, whether servants, concubines or wives, I know not. Mr. Walker has taken some pains to pilot this company from Fort Laramo to Fort Bridger."

Parrish may have been right about Walker's female companions, for polygamy was respectable among the Snakes. However, those who contributed more detailed reports on his family life never indicated there was more than one wife. Parrish may not have understood that among these people it was customary for younger sisters to live with married ones and earn their keep by helping with domestic chores. Or Parrish may—as so many easterners and especially men of the cloth were—have been titillated when he started thinking about the sex lives of the mountain men. Probably with some relief, Walker left the Gilliam-Parrish caravan, which eventually reached Oregon. He stayed that winter in the Green-Bear river vicinity with his wife and her people.

By the next summer, 1845, the effects of the previous emigration and, to no small extent, Frémont's first report were evident. Some 3,000 emigrants were on the trails. This was enough to set the official, so to speak, wheels of Manifest Destiny rolling. In May the War Department decided the overlanders required or provided justification for military action. Colonel Stephen Kearny and five companies of dragoons were therefore ordered to spend the summer patrolling the Santa Fe and Oregon trails. This, it was thought, was a sufficient force to show the flag to the plains tribes and keep them in line. It apparently was, for there was very little Indian trouble, only four whites and one red being killed that summer because of each other.

Walker left the mountains in late May for Fort Laramie, packing a load of furs which he had collected during the winter. On the way he met the first of these military units, heading west on a patrol to the South Pass. He stayed at Laramie only a few days, and then rode west again. On the Platte River he found and camped the night of July 8 with the same company of dragoons, now on their return ride. One of the officers in the detachment was Captain Philip St. George Cooke. He was an aristocratic Virginian, a professional by-the-book soldier who was later to become the army's leading expert on drill field maneuvers, but never much more. Being a spit-and-polish southerner, Cooke was unsettled by the bizarre appearance and colors of Walker's irregulars. However, there is a hint of envy in the entry which the elegant Captain made in his journal for that day, a strong suggestion that he found the man himself impressive:

> This afternoon Mr. Walker, whom we met at Independence Rock, visited our camp: he has picked up a small party at Fort Laramie; and wild-looking creatures they are—white and red. This man has abandoned civilization,—married a squaw or squaws, and prefers to pass his life wandering in these deserts; carrying on, perhaps, an almost nominal business of hunting, trapping and trading—but quite sufficient to the wants of a chief of savages. He is a man of much natural ability, and apparently of prowess and ready resource.

The wild-looking creatures made a swift ride to Fort Bridger. A few days out they picked up a small emigrant party which included one Joel Palmer, who said he was gratified to meet and be escorted by the "celebrated mountaineer Walker." Together they got to Bridger's post on July 26 and found a mob of overlanders resting up from the first leg of their journey and getting ready for the next one. One party was trying to shift some of the baggage it had carried in wagons to pack animals and was having a great deal of trouble with the job. In the group was a diarist named Jacob Snyder, who made an entry on July 28: "Completed our arrangements and started at 3 o'clock. We were very much indebted to Capt. Walker & Mr. Vaesus [Louis Vasquez, Bridger's partner] for their kind attention & assistance, this mode of travel being entirely novel to us, but to old mountain men none other need be recommended."

Walker remained around Fort Bridger for several weeks and then started toward the southwest with his wife and other members of his Snake family, to meet John Charles Frémont east of Salt Lake.

After returning to Washington from Bent's Fort in the summer of 1844, Frémont had prepared another public report on his travels. By the next spring, when he commenced to organize his third expedition, his reputation was so great that a Missouri newspaper editorialized that if he had wanted 1,000 men, "he could have procured them easy." However, he recruited only fifty men, eight of them Delaware mercenaries. Some, including Theodore Talbot and Alex Godey, had been with him before, but there were some able and interesting newcomers. Charles Preuss, the sour German, was replaced by Edward ("Ned") Kern, a well-educated and adventurous Philadelphian who had begged his idol, Frémont, for the chance to accompany the expedition as topographer and official artist. Lieutenant James Abert of the Topographical Corps was an excellent engineer, but he went only as far as Bent's Fort. There he was detached to make an independent survey of western Oklahoma and Texas. Another member of the company was Lucien Maxwell, a sometime Santa Fe trader and mountain man who later, in association with the Bents, was to obtain a famous million-acre grant in New Mexico. Finally, there was a young hand from Kentucky by the name of Thomas Breckenridge who left a very informal, irregular memoir about the trip, describing it from the standpoint of a man in the ranks. In addition to Frémont, Talbot and Kern kept more official journals.

Frémont's third expedition gathered in Independence, where Ned Kern began sketching. He found the community to be "a dirty place filled with Indians, Spaniards, Jews and all sorts and sizes of folk." From there they traveled along the Santa Fe Trail and at Bent's Fort picked up Kit Carson. Proceeding westward, the expedition reached Pueblo. At the time this was an infamous collection of huts and grog dens which had become a hangout for unemployed trappers, detribalized Indians, Mexican bandits and other southwestern undesirables. Among others, Bill Williams was using Pueblo as his civilized, so to speak, base of operations. He was at home when the expedition came through, and Frémont hired him as a guide, apparently feeling, as he had the year before, that he needed to back up Carson with a more experienced mountaineer. Indisputably Williams was very knowledgeable about the country to the west of Pueblo, but by then his drinking had become worse, and so had his temper. The latter very shortly created problems within the company.

Williams brought along his Ute wife, and Lucien Maxwell found her attractive. Maxwell, recalled Breckenridge, began calling on the woman in her tent "at very unfashionable hours and when Bill was not there." One night Williams came out to talk to Breckenridge, who was on guard duty. When their conversation was finished, Williams said he was going back to his tent. Having some idea of what might be going on there and "knowing the jealous and inflamable disposition of Old Bill," Breckenridge tried to detain him. Being unable to do so, the younger man went along with Williams. Maxwell was at the tent, though in respectable dress and posture. Nevertheless, "as soon as Old Bill saw him he brought his gun to his shoulder and drew a bead on him and there is no doubt but whart he would have killed him, had I not sprag forward just in time and struck the gun up, so the bullet passed through the top of the tent, it did not take Maxwell long to evaporate from that tent." Breckenridge said the matter was hushed up and he told Frémont, who apparently heard the shot in the night, that it was only accidental. However, Breckenridge concluded, "as long as Old Parson Bill and his squaw stayed with us Maxwell did not seem desirous of cultivating the acquaintance with the Williams family. Nor of persisting upon the family relations already established."

On the White River (a tributary of the Green in eastern Utah) the surveyors found Walker camped and waiting for them. They met, it seems, by prearrangement. Twice, earlier in the summer, once from Independence and again from Bent's Fort, Theodore Talbot had sent letters east in which he mentioned that they would later have the services of Walker, "the best man in the country." Also, in July, when Walker met Captain St. George Cooke on the Platte, he had told him that he was on his way to California. Whatever his agreement with Frémont, Walker apparently had multiple reasons for making the trip. When Breckenridge first met him on the White, he said the mountaineer had fifteen pack animals with him, "three very fine horses, as fine as would be found anywhere, and a fine lot of furs, beaver, otter, ETC." These he intended to sell in California. Breckenridge added that Walker's wife and "family" were with him.

Frémont immediately appointed Walker the chief guide. This annoyed Williams, who did not realize that he had been hired as an interim pilot. Shortly he began arguing with Walker about some minor trail decision. This surprised Breckenridge, who said it seemed to him that because of their long acquaintance and the fact that they both had their families with them, they should have been the "best of friends." However, he concluded that the real quarrel was not about the small matter at hand but reflected "jealousy or an old grudge." If he was right in this guess, the trouble may have started in 1833. Williams was perhaps the man Walker had disciplined or discharged from the expedition for killing the Indian on the Humboldt, the act which led to the massacre of the Diggers. A few days after he took charge, Walker had it out with Williams and apparently faced him down, for the latter went back in a sulk to his tent. The next morning the party awoke to find that during the night Williams had surreptitiously departed, taking with him two of Walker's best horses. "Walker," said Breckenridge, "had no idea of following him to get his horses, in fact there were few in those days that wanted to follow Old Bill for anything."

West of Salt Lake the expedition divided. Frémont, Carson and a dozen others took a swing to the south, while Walker guided the main body down the Humboldt River. At this time his wife and the other Snakes apparently returned to their home, for no further mention was made of their being in the company. Along the Humboldt, Walker held forth for the benefit of Kern and Talbot on the history, natural and otherwise, of the area—a subject about which he was one of the few white men who had any information. They camped one night at a small creek which Walker said he had named Walnut since, in 1833, his men had found several of these trees growing upstream along it. Kern, an enthusiastic naturalist, thought this might be the first discovery of this species in the desert. Later, when they came to the Humboldt Sink, Walker described the fight he had there with the Diggers, and they found some skulls they thought were remains of the Indians killed on that occasion.

At Walker Lake (as Frémont was officially to name this body of water) the two sections of the expedition rendezvoused, but they remained together only for a few days and then divided again. Frémont wanted to make a dash across the Sierra by ascending the Truckee River. However, it was mid-November, and Walker advised that if the entire expedition with its supply train attempted this route, there would be great risk of its being caught in the deep snows. Therefore, he took most of the men, his own and the expedition's pack animals south toward Walker Pass. After arranging for a meeting place in California, Frémont went off with a dozen men on his ride across the Sierra. He got through safely to Sutter's Fort after about three weeks, enjoying the good luck of an exceptionally mild winter in the mountains.

Being well supplied and able to travel rapidly, Walker and the others had a much easier trip along the Nevada-California border than had the emigrants he had led on this route two years before. At Owens Lake he told the men with him something about the difficulties of the wagon train and pointed out to them the place where the overlanders had cached their mill irons. (These were to remain there apparently until they rusted away, for nobody was ever known to have retrieved them.) Beyond the lake occurred what Thomas Breckenridge regarded as the only notable incident of this leg of the trip. "Among the foothills Capt. Walker who was out ahead succeeded in killing a large Mountain lion, which he brought in and we had a great supper off him, it was a change from our regular diet of mule and horse meat and very thin coffee." Many connoisseurs thought that excepting perhaps buffalo hump and tongue, puma steaks were the best feral food to be had in the west.

After crossing through Walker Pass, they traveled down the Kern River and on December 27 came to the south side of a marshy basin known as Tulare Lake. This is where they all thought they were to meet Frémont, and "according to my orders," noted Talbot, they stopped there to wait for him. There were many elk, deer, bear and waterfowl in the area, so they hunted and enjoyed themselves for a week or so. By mid-January they decided that either something had happened to Frémont or there had been a mix-up about the rendezvous point. Therefore, they started north, looking for the Pathfinder. By and by they met a former mountain trapper, Bill Fallon, a hulking man, commonly known as Le Gros. He told them Frémont had been in the area but had gone back toward Sutter's Fort. Being long acquainted with Le Gros, Walker rode back with him and a few days later found Frémont and took him to the others.

As it turned out, Frémont had followed the Kings River to the north side of the Tulare marshes and waited there, believing it was the place they had agreed to meet. Later he said that Walker, Talbot, Kern and the others either had misunderstood him or had simply become lost. Considering the records the various men left and, more important, their abilities, it seems much more likely that it was Frémont who went to the wrong place. Whatever the cause of the confusion, all the members of the expedition were reunited near San Jose in February 1846.

When he left Washington to commence his third expedition, Frémont had been instructed to make a reconnaissance along and westward of the upper Arkansas and Red rivers. These directions were vague enough so that he felt justified in pushing on immediately to California, even though no arrangement for his doing so had been made with the Mexican government. In California, Frémont explained that despite having strayed a bit, his was strictly a scientific expedition. Though dubious from the beginning about the sixty well-armed Americans under a Captain of the U.S. Army, the Mexicans granted the party permission to stay in California that winter. In fact, after reaching California, Frémont was almost exclusively preoccupied by political matters. Rumors that the United States and Mexico would soon be at war were circulating freely in northern California, where there were by that time some 500 American settlers. (The total non-Indian population of the entire state was only 7,000.) Many of them were in a very jingoistic mood, talking openly about overthrowing the Mexicans and establishing themselves as an independent republic until such time as they could join the United States. To what extent Frémont encouraged these revolutionists has remained a mystery, but he unquestionably was in frequent and cordial association with them. In consequence, the local military commander, Colonel José Castro, decided that the story about Frémont's expedition being a scientific one was very thin to false. In blunt terms, Castro ordered Frémont out of the state and began gathering regular and militia troops to enforce the demand. Frémont responded with a grand gesture. He took his sixty men to the top of Hawk's Peak in the Gabilan Mountains overlooking the Santa Clara Valley and erected a breastwork on this prominence. Then he unfurled Old Glory to, he said, the cheers of his men. From this position he began to strafe the Mexicans with barrages of belligerent rhetoric, saying among other things that "if attacked we will fight to extremity, and refuse quarter, trusting to our country to avenge our deaths."

Frémont, it seems, envisioned himself in the role of a gallant filibuster who would do in California what Jackson had done in Florida and Houston in Texas. The opportunity to act as such existed at that moment, but Frémont was not a Jackson or Houston. Very shortly he began to consider the consequences of the gesture. Without orders and as an active military officer, he had entered a foreign country and, beyond whatever other subversions he may have engaged in, committed what amounted to an act of war. These were not activities which a junior officer could easily explain to his superiors. More immediately, Frémont was worried about Colonel Castro, who had brought up some 200 troops and light artillery pieces below but never came within four miles of the American position.

Frémont remained on Hawk's Peak for three days, becoming increasingly nervous. Then the flag he had put up on a sapling pole accidentally fell to the ground. He took this as a very bad omen and immediately abandoned the position, hotfooting it, without interference from the Mexicans, to Oregon. He left without Walker, who severed his connections with Frémont on the spot and in, according to what he was later to say, a towering rage, rode south. Being a convinced Manifest Destiny man, Walker was no doubt in sympathy with the would-be California revolutionists, but his fury was of a personal sort. Because of Frémont, he, one of Andy Jackson's veterans, was put in the position of running from a rabble of Mexicans for whose military prowess he had very small regard. When a newspaperman later questioned him about the incident at Hawk's Peak, Walker was still very angry. In response, he said about Frémont the harshest things he was ever to say about any man. "Frémont," said the frontier Captain, "morally and physically, was the most complete coward I ever knew."

Walker was closely associated with two army officers on irregular missions, Bonneville and Frémont. His reactions to them are instructive in regard to the character of all three men. Bonneville, at least through Washington Irving, had some very unflattering things to say about Walker. However, perhaps because he realized why the public report of that expedition was written as it was, Walker was never openly critical of Bonneville. He made it clear he sometimes disagreed with that officer, but there was no suggestion that any grudge developed between them. They parted on good terms and, though disparate in personality, seemed to have respected each other as men.

In contrast, Frémont was effusive in praise of Walker. After their first trip together through the Great Basin in 1844, Frémont wrote of him that "he is celebrated as one of the best and bravest leaders who have ever been in the country." But Walker came to despise Frémont as he did no other man, for he thought him no man. "I would say," said Walker of the Pathfinder, "he was timid as a woman if it were not casting an unmerited reproach on the sex."

The End of the Mountains

After his escape from Hawk's Peak, Frémont spent a month cogitating in Oregon and then returned to California to take part in the opéra bouffe proceedings of the Bear Flag Rebellion. Following the official declaration of war between the United States and Mexico—which occurred in May—he marched south at the head of the so-called California Battalion made up of the remaining members of his surveying party and several hundred settler-insurrectionists. Eventually he joined with General Stephen Kearny, who, after capturing New Mexico, had invaded southern California with his regulars. Kearny found Frémont personally exasperating and insubordinate as a junior officer. Early in the winter of 1847 the general arrested the captain and sent him back to Washington to face a court-martial. Frémont was charged with disobedience of orders, mutiny and conduct prejudicial to military interests. The Pathfinder was found guilty on all three counts. Nevertheless, the court recommended leniency—largely it seems because of his political connections and public popularity—and that he be permitted to retain his commission. Frémont, however, rejected the offer and resigned from the army, convinced, as were many others, that he was the martyr of Manifest Destiny.

Walker also left California but in a manner of his own choosing. After the angry breakup with Frémont he came down from Hawk's Peak and, without being hindered by Mexican troops, rode on to Gilroy, north of San Juan Bautista. There he visited with the founder of the community, John Gilroy, the British sailor whose acquaintance he had first made in 1833. Also, Mr. and Mrs. Julius Martin, the couple he had come to admire while piloting their wagon train in '43, owned a ranch adjacent to Gilroy's. It seems likely that on his way north in

January to find Frémont, Walker left the pack animals and furs he had brought across the Great Basin with these old friends. At Gilroy he was joined by his nephew Frank McClellan, who had been in California since '43 but by then was anxious to return to Missouri to visit his family. In the latter part of March the two of them left for Los Angeles.

Neither the threat of war nor his part in Frémont's escapade was of much concern to Walker's acquaintances in the Mexican business community, for he sold his beaver and otter pelts without difficulty and immediately began investing the proceeds in horses and mules. Using Chino Ranch, west of Los Angeles, as a base, he accumulated a herd of some 500 animals and in early May started driving them east toward the States. In addition to Frank McClellan, he had seven hands with him. Two, Walter Reddick and Charles Taplin, had been at Hawk's Peak and presumedly left with him. The other man whose name is remembered was Solomon Sublette, youngest brother of the famous Missouri fur trading family.

By then the three older Sublette brothers, Bill, Pinckney and Milton, had died, and the fourth, Andrew, was suffering from consumption, the disease which had killed Bill. The family's fortunes and influence were greatly diminished, and Solomon, always something of a ne'er-do-well, had been drifting about the West. In 1845 he traveled from Missouri to Bent's Fort to California and spent most of the winter of '46 at John Sutter's post. There he earned a reputation as a noisy drunk and bully. Among others, he made a very poor impression on ,William Leidesdorff, recently arrived at Sutter's from Germany:

> There are several of the new emigration in town among them one great Blaggard a Mr. Subliz. On Christmas even him and five or Six others came to my house about eleven o clock. I was fast a sleep. They fired a gun off, an made a great hurahing in the corador. I got up and asked who they were, and got no answer, so I was afraid to open the door. At last one of the[m] answered friends. I answered tham, that If they could not give there names that I would no open the door, and if they had come to get liquor that I had none in the house. They then walked away. After awhile, this Mr. Subliz returned alone, and abused me shamefully, telling me that he had struck terror through all the towns he had been at, and would strike terror through me before he left this town. He finished by throwing two large stones on the roof of my house, one of which I exspected would come through the roof being so large. This is one of the last party which is said to be such fine people, and a man that I have no acquaintance with whatever.

Having found no employment and overstayed his welcome at Sutter's, Sublette wandered south and met Walker, who, perhaps as much in memory of his brothers as anything else, agreed to let Solomon work his way east as a wrangler. They took the herd out of California through Cajon Pass and from there turned northward, following the wagon trail Walker had blazed to the Humboldt. In mid-June they arrived at Fort Hall. Richard Grant was still in charge there but held no grudge against Walker or McClellan because of the quarrel over supplies for the emigrant train in '43. Walker therefore halted for a week at the Hudson's Bay post to recruit the stock after the trip across the mountains and desert. Sublette, Reddick and Taplin, in a rush to get home, were paid off and left directly for Missouri. Walker originally planned to go there himself to sell the horses, but information he received at Fort Hall changed his mind.

The first of the emigrants (there were to be nearly 3,000 in '46) were already on the trails. So were General Kearny and various other military detachments, marching toward New Mexico and California. McClellan said that he and his uncle decided that since all these travelers were going to need horses, it would be more convenient to dispose of their stock on the plains than to trail the herd back to Missouri. Therefore, when the animals were rested, they started toward Fort Bridger. Arriving there in early July, they found this small ramshackle post had become by mountain standards a metropolis, with some 1,000 overlanders, traders and Indians congregated around it. "Circles of white-tented wagons may now be seen in every direction, and the smoke from the camp-fires is curling upwards, morning, noon and evening," said one of the emigrants, Edwin Bryant, who arrived shortly after Walker and McClellan. "An immense number of oxen and horses are scattered over the entire valley, grazing upon the green grass. Parties of Indians, hunters, and emigrants are galloping to and fro, and the scene is one of almost holiday liveliness. It is difficult to realize that we are in a wilderness, a thousand miles from civilization. I noticed the lupin, and a brilliant scarlet flower, in bloom."

There were 300 or 400 Snakes camped nearby, and Walker moved in with them and his wife, whom he had not seen since the previous October. But during the next month, which he spent in the area, he was often occupied with the affairs of the emigrants, among whom he was a great figure. "Everyone here was well acquainted with Captain Jo," recalled young Frank McClellan. In the crowd were some old friends from Missouri, including his former political associate the ex-Governor Lilburn Boggs. Even those who knew him only by reputation hunted up the "celebrated mountaineer" to seek his advice about trails to the west. Information on this subject was in particularly great demand and short supply since many of the overlanders were milling about Bridger's post because they were very uncertain about how and where to proceed from there. The principal cause of the confusion was the aforementioned Lansford Hastings.

After having made his first crossing in 1842 under the guidance of Tom Fitzpatrick, Hastings had become an emigration promoter, publicizing the virtues of first Oregon and then, when better opportunities occurred there, California. He had written a popular emigrants' guidebook and gone to the East Coast to lecture to groups of prospective overlanders. In his book and speaking engagements, Hastings suggested that rather than follow the established trail from Bridger to Fort Hall and thence to the Humboldt, California-bound emigrants would do much better to go directly west from Salt Lake to the Sink and then across the Sierra into the Sacramento Valley. The route, he said, was very easy and 200 miles shorter than that via Fort Hall. By following this trail, which became infamously known as the Hastings Cutoff, overlanders could travel from Salt Lake to San Francisco Bay in a month, its promoter predicted, and would find good water and pasture all along the way. When he first began touting his cutoff, Hastings had no personal knowledge of the country he was recommending, but the route looked on a map to be plausible. From Hastings's standpoint the paramount advantage was that if it were passable, this road would lure emigrants away from Oregon and bring them directly into the Sacramento area, where he had real estate and other interests which would benefit from an influx of newcomers. During the winter at Sutter's Fort he had confidently predicted that 20,000 overlanders would arrive during the next year.

Since it promised so much, the Hastings Cutoff caused considerable excitement among those, as, for example, the Donner party, who were preparing in the east to go to California that year. Having received information about this interest, Hastings decided that it would be a good idea to examine the route about which he had written and spoken so convincingly. In the late spring of 1846 he left from Sutter's Fort to travel it, going east. He started the trip with James Clyman, the veteran mountaineer who had first come west with Ashley in 1823. Their party was made up of single men, mounted on good horses, unencumbered with domestic baggage. Even so, they found the trip strenuous and much slower than Hastings had guessed it would be. Clyman had never before been in that part of the Great Basin, but he had more than twenty years' experience in western travel and survival. After a time he concluded that recommending this route to family groups, inexperienced people, driving wagons was very wrong-headed, if not immoral. Therefore, he left Hastings and made his way northward to

Fort Hall over the old trail. Hastings with half a dozen men pushed on to Salt Lake and then to Fort Bridger. Though he found the route much harder to travel than to write about, he made no mention of the difficulties and continued to praise it to overlanders he encountered. As a result, many of the emigrants were in a quandary, their desire to shorten the hard trip to California being in conflict with their suspicions and fears about a trail which had not previously been used by wagons. One of the first to look up Walker and ask his opinion was Edwin Bryant.

> I was introduced to-day to Captain Walker, of Jackson county, Missouri, who is much celebrated for his explorations and knowledge of the North American continent, between the frontier settlements of the United States and the Pacific. Captain W. is now on his return from the settlements of California, having been out with Captain Frémont in the capacity of guide or pilot. He is driving some four or five hundred Californian horses, which he intends to dispose of in the United States. They appear to be high-spirited animals, of medium size, handsome figures, and in good condition. Captain W. communicated to me some facts in reference to recent occurrences in California, of considerable interest. He spoke discouragingly of the new route via the south end of the Salt Lake.

Bryant was traveling with a small party of well-mounted single men and therefore decided to risk the desert shortcut, but he was sufficiently impressed by Walker's advice to leave letters for friends in wagon parties that were still on their way to Bridger. He warned them to avoid Hastings' route and stick to the Fort Hall trail. One to whom Bryant wrote was a man named Reed, who was then coming on with the Donner party. Reed never got the note since Louis Vasquez, the man with whom it had been left, intentionally did not deliver it. To their everlasting discredit, Vasquez and his partner Bridger helped Hastings tout his cutoff that summer for the most venal of reasons. A new shortcut branching off from the main trail north of their post had recently been blazed. It led the emigrant caravans directly to Fort Hall without passing Vasquez's and Bridger's establishment. In contrast, there was no way to use the Hastings Cutoff without passing Fort Bridger. Coveting the overland business, the partners did not themselves criticize the new route and, at least in the case of Bryant, suppressed criticism others made of it.

Bridger and Vasquez were long-time associates of Walker, but he had no interest in promoting their business in this matter and continued to be "discouraging" about the cutoff when asked. One of the emigrants, A. J. Grayson, had personally queried Hastings (who came to and left Fort Bridger before Walker arrived) about the route but was still doubtful about it and the character of its promoter. "I for one," wrote Grayson, "consulted Capt. Walker, who happened to be at Fort Bridger, and well acquainted with both routes, and also a man whom I could believe; so I took his advice and went the old trail."

It was also at Fort Bridger that Walker met the McBride party, which included fourteen-year-old John, the future Congressman, who left an awed description of the dress, stature and style of the "noted trapper." While young John gawked at this "perfect prince of the wilderness," his father and Walker, who had been friends in Missouri, talked about the emigration. Even though the McBrides were bound for Oregon and therefore not directly concerned with the dispute about the Hastings Cutoff, Walker had some advice for this party. He suggested that they think about settling along the Great Salt Lake. Beyond the obvious, that this would shorten their trip by more than 700 miles, he said that in his opinion the land there was as good as or better than that in Oregon and they could have their pick of it since there were no other competing settlers. (The Latter-day Saints were already planning to make Utah the corner stake of their new Zion but would not arrive until the next year.) McBride was sufficiently interested to take a side trip, his son riding with him, to the lake and was extremely impressed with the prospects. However, they eventually decided for Oregon because there were established settlements there—the condition which to Walker's way of thinking was a principal drawback to the place.

Another young man who met Walker at Fort Bridger was Heinrich Lienhard. With a young friend, he had come from Switzerland to find adventure and fortune in the Wild American West. As working hands they had joined a twenty-six-wagon overland caravan in Independence. Though they spoke very little English, the Swiss boys were strong and adaptable. They made a good crossing of the plains and, according to Lienhard's excellent diary, were constantly exhilarated by the strange new country. At Bridger, Lienhard camped near the Indian-trader section of that temporary community. "In the larger tent, the hunters squatted in a circle Indian fashion, and were occupied with the comfortable task of drinking and chatting. Their leader seemed to be a tall, handsome fellow, some forty years old, by the name of Walker. Since I was afraid that I might disturb them in an important council meeting, I immediately moved away in spite of Mr. Walker's friendly invitation to sit down."

It seems a pity that Lienhard was so shy, for he was a resourceful, gritty young man of the sort Walker often recruited and took pains to tutor in frontier ways. (In California Lienhard became a valuable employee and trusted friend of his compatriot John Sutter.)

Walker disposed of most of his horses to the emigrants, Indians and traders at Fort Bridger but in early August moved on with about 100 remaining head toward Bent's Fort, where he expected to do business with the army. East of Bridger he passed the Donner party and was told that they were heading for the Hastings Cutoff. As he had the others, Walker warned them against this route, but this party paid no attention to him and in fact resented the advice. Though probably not to his face, they called Walker "a Missouri Puke" and went on their way—forty-four of them to their deaths on Hastings' trail.

Walker arrived at Bent's Fort during the last week of August and found that Kearny with most of the Army of the West had passed by ten days earlier en route to New Mexico and California. However, a detachment of Missouri militia, under the command of Sterling Price, was expected to arrive shortly. Walker determined to wait for this column, setting up camp eight miles upstream from the busy fort in a place where he was able to find better pasture for his animals. When they were established, Frank McClellan decided to ride on to Missouri. He took with him some of the profits which had already been realized on the expedition. The agreement was that he would use them to buy trade goods and with them would return early the next summer and meet his uncle. Walker, after finishing his business at Bent's Fort, would go back to spend the winter in the mountains with his Snake people.

Neither of the Bent brothers was at the post when Walker arrived. William had left to guide Kearny to Santa Fe. Charles had gone separately to New Mexico, where, after its conquest, he was appointed the civilian governor of the territory. The fort was left in charge of Marcellus St. Vrain, younger brother of the Bents' long-time partner, Ceran. Marcellus had always been a restless young man, with no great interest in the routine business of the company, and found staying home and taking care of the store excruciatingly tedious. Therefore, when Walker told him that antelope were plentiful around his camp and invited him to come out for sport hunting, Marcellus accepted eagerly so as to "obtain relief from the close confinement of the fort." The game was abundant, as promised, but Marcellus found the sand-flies were so fierce that he "little enjoyed the pleasure of hunting." Deciding he would rather be bored than bitten to death, he returned after spending a week as Walker's guest.

There was another restless and even more confined young man at the fort, Lieutenant James Abert, an officer in the Topographical Corps. After having started out with Frémont in the summer of 1845 and then going off to make his successful independent survey in Oklahoma and Texas, Abert had returned to the States. When war was declared, he had been assigned to Kearny's command and had left from

Missouri with it. However, on the plains he was laid low by an almost fatal attack of malaria. By the time the army reached Bent's Fort, Abert was much too weak to ride, let alone fight, and so was left behind there. By late August he was beginning to recover but was feeling very frustrated because he was still too feeble to go on to Santa Fe, where his brother officers were finding glory and advancing their professional careers. To pass the time and build up his strength, he began taking short therapeutic walks around the fort. During these, Abert, who had a vast and intelligent curiosity about western natural history, collected, attempted to identify and sometimes sketched animals, vegetables and minerals he encountered. He also made notes about the dress, language and customs of the Indians, mostly southern Cheyenne, who lounged about the place.

When Walker heard from St. Vrain that Abert was at the fort and ailing, he sent in a haunch of fresh venison for the lieutenant. Then he rode in to pay him a visit. Though they had not met previously, they got along very well. (As was the case with his own nephews, Zenas Leonard, Joe Meek, Kit Carson and many others, Walker seems to have been able to deal with younger men in an easy, nonpatronizing manner. They in turn were pleased and flattered to be treated as friends and equals of such a celebrity. Frémont was the obvious exception to this pattern.) Their conversations were botanical and zoological and, according to his journal, considerably cheered Abert. Among other things, Walker told him "that the box-elder, 'acer negundo' furnishes a sap which is highly saccharine, and when the hunters are in want of sugar, they collect some of the sap of this tree, and by boiling it form a very good molasses, which answers as an excellent substitute."

In addition to many other species of wildlife, Abert had become interested in the prairie dog, which "is well known, yet the skins are rarely to be met with in cabinets of Zoology." Abert wanted a study skin, but those brought to him previously had been ruined as collector's items because the hunters had shot them with rifles. Walker promised when he returned to his camp to try to get him an intact prairie dog by pouring buckets of water down a burrow and grabbing the rodent when it emerged. The incident suggests a scene more warm than ludicrous—of burly Walker, the "renowned" explorer, Indian fighter, etc., down on his knees in all his buckskin finery, trying to lay his hands on a rodent to satisfy the sick soldier. It provides a good counterbalance to commoner and gaudier recollections of such men and their times.

Walker may not have had time actually to catch and deliver a prairie dog, for the natural history pursuits of both men were interrupted on September 8, when the first outriders of Sterling Price's column came to the fort. Walker moved down from his camp to meet the troops following them. Abert said that he assumed his new friend "will, doubtless, dispose of them [his remaining horses and mules] to the Volunteers with great advantage, both to himself and to the troops, as their horses are completely broken down by the march across the desert . . . and their owners, now fatigued with marching on foot, will not stand upon trifles as to the price of a fresh animal."

Abert did not stay around to observe the transactions. Price's couriers remained only the night and the next day rode on to Santa Fe. Abert, unable to bear inaction any longer, went with them, accompanied by Marcellus St. Vrain, who was in the same frame of mind. Price's main column arrived during the next week, and they were indeed footsore, so Walker no doubt did dispose of his animals to advantage. Doing so could not have occupied him much beyond the first of October. Thereafter, and for nearly six months, he again disappeared so far as any surviving records are concerned. Probably he went back to the mountains, as he had told Frank McClellan he would. If so, he made an odd return trip to New Mexico late in the following winter, being met on March 27, fifty miles or so east of Santa Fe, by Solomon Sublette.

Sublette was riding hard for Fort Leavenworth on the Missouri River, carrying official government dispatches from Santa Fe. After having left Walker at Fort Hall the previous June, he had gone back to Missouri and there secured a position as a military courier. In early January Sublette had made an outbound trip from Leavenworth to Santa Fe. He had been delayed by an insurrection of local Mexicans and Pueblo Indians in Taos (during which Charles Bent was killed), and it had taken him seventy days to reach the New Mexican capital. After waiting there for less than a week, he had started back on the trail. Walker, who had no pack animals or furs with him, decided to go on to Missouri with Sublette. They, and two other men, made an extraordinary ride, covering the 800 miles to Leavenworth in twenty-three days. It was regarded as a feat, "comparable to anything on record," a Missouri newspaper later commented about their trip.

From Leavenworth, Sublette continued to St. Louis while Walker went to nearby Independence. There the local newspaper, *The Expositor*, put out an extra edition because "Capt. W. came in with an express from Col. Doniphan's Regiment." (Alexander Doniphan's command was made up largely of volunteers from the western part of the state, and thus the local interest was very high.) Under a boldface headline, "Important From Santa Fe and Chihuahua—Glorious Victory," *The Expositor* passed along to its readers Walker's news—and no doubt improved on it somewhat in an account of the Battle of

Chihuahua. According to the paper, "our boys poured in a volley of Artillery upon them [4,300 Mexicans, said *The Expositor*, but this proved to be a Joe-Meek-type figure] . . . when the Mexicans fled . . . they did not call a halt at Chihuahua but kept up running as if Old Nick had been bringing up the rear."

At the end of the stirring story, *The Expositor*'s editor added a confused but well-intended note about the messenger who had delivered at least the bare bones of it. "Capt. W. has been in Mexico for the last 15 years. He is an old man, looks hearty and hale, and we have no doubt he could stand more hardship than two-thirds of our young men. Our thanks for his kindness in giving us the particulars."

Frank McClellan was in St. Louis that April, buying trading supplies for the year. He came back to Independence, planning to organize his packtrain and set out immediately for the mountains, where, according to the agreement they had made at Bent's Fort in the fall, he expected to meet Walker. Therefore, when he returned home, he recalled later, he "was no little surprised" to find his uncle there. If anyone knew why Walker had so suddenly and completely changed his plans, it must have been McClellan, but he said nothing about it. Rather, he unpacked the trade goods and waited on his uncle.

Walker still had a few old friends, notably Zenas Leonard, in the area, but many had died or emigrated to the Pacific coast. By then a considerable number of nieces and nephews, many of whom he scarcely knew, were in the area, but of his own generation, members of the family who had come out from Tennessee, only three were left: his brother Sam and his wife, Barbara, and his brother-in-law Abraham McClellan, who had largely retired from business and politics. Big John Walker had died in 1845, and his three sisters, Jane, Susan and Lucy, who had come to Missouri were also deceased. Even so, Walker remained in Jackson County that spring and throughout most of the muggy Missouri summer, doing, it seems, very little.

Commencing in the fall of 1846, the next year was a peculiar one for Walker, during which he behaved in very uncharacteristic ways. He had disappeared from Bent's Fort in the middle of the excitement of the Mexican War. If he had gone back to the mountains, as he told McClellan he would, he came out of them abruptly and, as he never had before, without a load of furs. He met Solomon Sublette on the Santa Fe Trail almost as though he were a hitchhiker, made the hell-for-leather ride to Fort Leavenworth and then sat in idleness in Missouri for five months. While he was there, at least one of his nieces formed the impression that he was thinking of settling there permanently and retiring from frontier life.

All this suggests that something ailed him or a great change had occurred in his life. Perhaps he was sick, had suffered an accident or was simply feeling his years, for he was nearing fifty. However, the extraordinary ride he made with Sublette and the testimonial offered by the local newspaper editor about his physical condition indicate otherwise. Furthermore, after this odd period Walker resumed his energetic style of life and for the next fifteen years was involved in a series of ventures which required great physical and mental vigor. There is no substantiating comment from McClellan or anyone else who might have known the facts, but Walker behaved as a man might who was partially incapacitated because of a great disappointment or loss. This may well have been the case, and 1847 may have been a year of mourning for him.

After July 1846, when a number of the emigrants saw Walker at his tepee amongst the Snakes at Fort Bridger, no one ever reported meeting Walker with his Indian wife or family. It is possible that he simply left them. Some mountaineers did so, abandoning their Indian women and children when they came back to the settlements. More commonly they did not, William Bent, Jim Bridger, Tom Fitzpatrick, Andrew Drips, Joe Meek, Kit Carson, Doc Newell, Bill Craig and many others being examples of men who continued to recognize, support and show affection for the women they married and the children they fathered while living with the tribes. Given his character and the fact that he was proud of his wife, it seems much more likely that Walker lost rather than left her. If this occurred, it probably did sometime between October 1846, when he left Bent's Fort, and March 1847, when he intercepted Solomon Sublette on the Santa Fe Trail. Life in the west was then generally short and risky, especially for women. The Snakes and the Sioux were, for example, at each other's throats throughout most of 1846. However, it seems that if his wife and children had been killed or captured by raiders, stories would have been told about the incident and Walker would have reacted more violently than he did. A much greater danger than warfare was disease, specifically at that time Asiatic cholera, which, having been introduced by white emigrants and traders, was sweeping through the tribes and decimating them. The next year nearly half the southern Cheyenne, including several of William Bent's relatives, died during a two-week cholera epidemic.

It was during the summer of 1847, at a family gathering in Jackson County, that Walker remarked that he found white people "too damn mean" and was going back to live with the Indians. In fact, he never again lived with the Snakes who had been his people for nearly fifteen years, or with any other tribe. Given his previous life-style, it is difficult to imagine that this was a matter of choice. A more plausible explanation for his behavior that year is that sometime in the winter in the mountains he buried those with whom he had been most intimate in his middle years, returned to find he had few affectionate ties left to the society of his youth and was for a time affected by feelings of loss and loneliness. That he was never known to make mention of such a tragedy is not necessarily proof that it did not occur. He was an extremely reticent man in ordinary circumstances, and there are many indications that grief would have made him more so, that he was the kind to keep and endure sorrows deep within.

In late August Walker told McClellan he was ready to go. Lucy McClellan, a niece, wrote to one of her cousins that her uncle and brother were going to make only a short trip to the mountains to attend to some business and would be back in Jackson County before Christmas. Frank McClellan understood that they were going to ride straight through to California. If this was the case, they were leaving so late that they could scarcely hope to avoid heavy snow in the passes of both the Rockies and Sierra, odd, fatalistic behavior for Walker, who had always been such a prudent, knowledgeable traveler. Also, McClellan elsewhere disposed of the goods he had purchased the previous spring in St. Louis and whatever they had in mind, they were not equipped to trade in the conventional way in the mountains. There is a distinct impression that Lucy and Frank McClellan had different ideas about the trip because their uncle was uncertain about what he was going to do and even about where he was going.

They left Missouri—Walker would never return—on September 2. With them went another nephew, Sam's twenty-two-year-old son, James (usually called Jeemes), who was making his first trip west. Once they got started, they moved along at a good pace and on the Vermilion River on September 15 overtook Andrew Goodyear and four other men, who had left Independence several days before them. Goodyear was on the plains for the first time, but his brother, Miles, was a veteran mountain man, and Andrew was bringing supplies for a small trading post Miles had built on the Weber River, just east of Salt Lake near the present city of Ogden. Since Goodyear had a wagon, the two small parties joined forces, though the union slowed down the Walkers and McClellan. By early November they were only 100 miles east of Salt Lake but were stopped by heavy snows in the Uinta Mountains. Leaving the wagons and pack animals, Goodyear with another man, Thomas Sprague, decided to push ahead with only horses to his brother's trading post. Walker remained behind with his nephews and Goodyear's supplies. When Goodyear left, they backtracked for eighty miles to Henry's Fork on the Green River and wintered there, near the site which twenty-two years before William Ashley had selected for the first fur rendezvous. On this occasion Walker and his two nephews had the area entirely to themselves. They made rough lean-to shelters and passed the time trying to keep warm and hunting as the weather permitted. It was a makeshift Bonneville type of camp, the worst Walker ever made. Also, it was the only winter in a decade he spent in the Rockies without his wife or the comforts provided by a Snake village. Jeemes Walker found his first mountain experience unpleasant and said they "passed a forlorn and desolate Winter."

In early May, when the snows had melted sufficiently, Tom Sprague returned from Goodyear's post with provisions. He and Walker's two nephews had had enough of being cooped up and left almost immediately for Fort Laramie. After their winter they looked and could not resist playing the part of real, old-time mountain men. The first emigrants they met were greatly impressed with their fringed greasy buckskins, long hair and stories about being snowbound in the wilderness camp. At Laramie the three young men joined one of the wagon caravans as hands and hunters and went on to California. Walker stayed in the mountains for a few more months, doing no one now knows what, but by the end of July he was on the Green River not far from Fort Nonsense, which by then had fallen into ruins. There he met another nephew, Mike McClellan, Frank's older brother, who was traveling in an overland train with his wife and children. The company was under the direction of an old friend, Joe Chiles, who was taking his last emigrants to California. Chiles immediately arranged for Walker to guide the wagons across the new cutoff to Fort Hall, which avoided the detour to Fort Bridger. The diarist in the party was Richard May, who made an entry on July 26 about their famous pilot:

> Left camp earlier than common and traveled 18 miles. At our noon halt Joseph Walker, the noted mountaineer met us. He is a very fine looking man, the very picture of health, and discourses well on most topics. He conducted us through a pass in these mountains by which means we avoided a very steep hill both up and down. Mr. Walker appears to be about 45 years of age and steps off with the alacrity of a youth but this much may be said of any one that has lived in these mountains a few years. To see the life the buoyancy of a mountaineer would astonish the most of men. They tell me there is more real pleasure in one year in the mountains than a whole lifetime in a dense settled country.

It was the last time anyone reported seeing Walker in the central Rockies. After having spent, according to May's calculations, twenty lifetimes in those mountains, in the Absaroka, on the Snake plateau, along the Bear, Green and Wind rivers, the pleasure seemed to have gone out of the country for him. Walker stayed with the wagon train for only a day. After seeing them safely across the cutoff, he rode on alone. By a route on which he met no more journalists, he came in the early fall to California, which was to be his base during the rest of his life.

Two close former associates, if not friends, Bill Williams and John Charles Frémont, also departed from the mountains a few months after Walker. However, no one gave them such an admiring salute as Walker received from Richard May. Both left in disgrace, Frémont alive and Williams dead.

After being court-martialed for his part in the annexation of California and resigning from the army, Frémont was desperate to recapture the glory he had known as the daring young Pathfinder of the West. Restoring this reputation was also in the interests of his father-in-law, Thomas Benton. By way of assisting in the matter, the Senator put Frémont in touch with a group of financiers who were investigating the possibilities of a transcontinental railroad. Frémont told them that a line following straight across the West along the 38th parallel would make an ideal route. Some initial questions were raised about the southern Colorado and Utah sections. There the parallel traversed both the formidable Sangre de Cristo and San Juan mountain ranges and the homelands of the Ute. Though he had never been in that area, Frémont said that neither the terrain nor the Indians presented serious difficulties. To prove that the 38th parallel route was practical in any season for construction crews and, after them, rail travel, he offered to lead an expedition through this country in the dead of winter. His self-promotional talents had not declined, and the investors agreed to finance the demonstration.

Frémont assembled a party of thirty-two, including some of the men from his previous expeditions: Alex Godey, Thomas Breckenridge, Charles Preuss and Ned Kern. In addition, having heard so much about the Pathfinder from Ned, two of Kern's brothers, Benjamin, a physician, and Richard, also a topographer, joined the expedition. However, the party initially had no legitimate guide since Godey, though by then a veteran mountaineer, was not familiar with the terrain of southern Colorado. At Bent's Fort, which they reached on November 10, 1848, Frémont offered the job to several frontiersmen wintering there. All of them turned him down on the ground that trying to force a passage through the Sangre de Cristo so late in the season was a harebrained to suicidal scheme. Frémont ignored the warnings, his desire to vindicate himself as an explorer and leader having imbued him with, if not new courage, a dangerous sort of bravado. On the twenty-first, the expedition came to Pueblo and in the dives of that renegade community found Crazy Bill Williams, as he was then almost universally called. Williams said he could and would lead them through the mountains, even though it could be clearly seen that the foothills were already snow-covered. Because of age—he was then sixty-one—and, more important, dissipation, Williams was not the man he had been even a few years before. His drinking problem had become worse, and his activities largely involved getting together the wherewithal to support the habit. Had Frémont made inquiries about a guide to hell, Williams would no doubt have jumped at the opportunity if the wages had given him money for whiskey. There was a story about his flopping into Bent's Fort on his bony nag, screaming to Charles Bent, "Roll out the barrel, old hoss. I'll kill it or it'll kill me." On that occasion he had killed it, but the booze was indirectly responsible for the fact that when Frémont found him, he was recovering from a gunshot wound in the arm.

After Walker had displaced him as Frémont's guide in 1845 and run him out of their camp on the White River, Williams had gone back, leading two of Walker's best horses, to live with his wife's people, the Utes. In 1847 he had come down from the mountains to Taos, packing a load of furs belonging to members of the tribe and which he had agreed to sell for them. He did so but immediately drank up the proceeds. The binge had been a famous week-long one, during which, among other things, he bought bolts of dry goods and unrolled them in the streets of Taos because it entertained him to watch the poor Mexican women fighting over the cloth. When he sobered up, he realized it would be very unwise for him to try to rejoin the Utes. However, because of his long association with them, an opportunity arose for him to make some additional drinking money by guiding federal soldiers who had been ordered to make a punitive strike against the tribe. Leading these troops against the people who had so long been his, Williams received the wound he was nursing when Frémont came to Pueblo.

By December 6 the expedition was in the Sangre de Cristo and in trouble because of the depth of the snow and severe cold. Williams shortly became confused, as Frémont would later claim, or came to his senses, according to the reports of other surviving members of the party. In any case, he began to hedge on his promise to lead them directly across the mountains and suggested that if they were going to continue west, they should drop down into New Mexico and pursue a more southerly and temperate route. Frémont, however, was intent on making the 38th parallel gesture, so the party stayed on its predetermined course. Thereafter the men began to weaken rapidly. Williams, who had lost much of the strength and endurance for which he had been famous on the frontier for nearly forty years, was in very bad shape when they reached the crest of the Sangre de Cristo the week before Christmas. "That old fool Bill lay down and wanted to die, just at the summit. Many animals perished here," wrote Charles Preuss.

On December 27 the reality of their situation began to penetrate Frémont's fantasies. He dispatched Williams, despite his infirmities, Tom Breckenridge and two other men to return to Taos to find help. The others waited in a blizzard-swept camp, their strength steadily declining because of the cold and lack of food. After two weeks Frémont's nerve broke. Taking a small party of the fittest men and what supplies they could carry, he started out for the settlements, telling the others to take care of themselves as best they could, but if they wanted to see him again, they had better "be in a hurry about it, as he was going on to California" (if and when he reached Taos).

Thereafter it was every man for himself, with Frémont rapidly improving his position. On the way out he passed the first relief party, which had gone only about fifty miles. One of the four men had died, and the other three were greatly in need of help themselves; but Frémont, according to Breckenridge, did not offer any. However, as he was later to say, he did see signs which led him to believe that Williams had eaten part of the dead man. Breckenridge and the others who finally came out of the mountains made no mention of this, but Williams during the few remaining months of his life—and thereafter in some frontier histories—was to be labeled a cannibal. Frémont came to Taos on January 27. He stayed long enough to send off letters to the East, saying the whole thing had been the fault of the senile, man-eating Williams. Then he left for California, traveling on the warm-weather route through southern Arizona. He left behind, permanently, eleven of his men, who froze or starved to death in the mountains. More would have almost certainly died except that Alex Godey, the veteran of Walker's first trip through the Sierras in 1833, organized a pack-train in Taos and went back to rescue them. Returning to civilization, Frémont made an incredible statement about the expedition, which stands as a classic example of the dementive power of vanity. Said the Pathfinder, "The result was entirely satisfactory. It convinced me that neither the snow of winter nor the mountain ranges were obstacles in the way of a road."

Others thought differently. Ned Kern, who had followed Frémont faithfully and regarded him as a hero up to that time, became determined to expose him and said the "criminal egotism" of the leader had led to the tragedy. After word about the disaster in the Sangre de Cristo spread, most of the veteran mountaineers came around to Walker's simpler opinion that Frémont was "a complete coward, morally and physically."

In March, when the snows had somewhat melted and they had recovered their strength, Bill Williams and Dr. Benjamin Kern went back into the mountains to salvage the scientific instruments, notes and supplies which had been abandoned. The two were never seen again, but in time stories drifted down from the hills that made it possible to piece together what happened to them. They were apparently caught by the Utes, and Kern was killed in the skirmish. Williams, the one-time boy preacher of St. Charles, Missouri, was taken prisoner and executed as a traitor to his people.

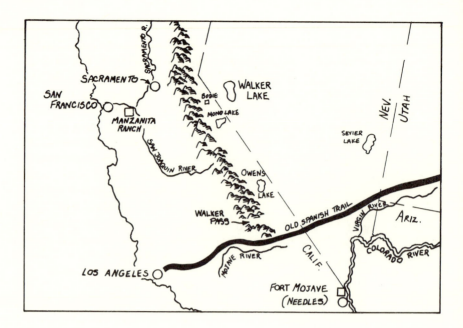

A Californian

While Walker and his two nephews were enduring the winter of 1848 in their rough camp on Henry's Fork, there occurred only nine days apart two events in California which changed that territory very suddenly and drastically. On January 24 James Marshall, a carpenter employed by John Sutter, discovered gold near Sacramento. On February 2 the Treaty of Guadalupe Hidalgo was signed, certifying the military victory of the United States over Mexico and transferring California along with other properties from the loser to the victor.

Of the two, the former had the greater immediate impact on life in California. Had gold not been discovered, the Americanization of the state would probably have proceeded at a pace and in a manner similar to that which occurred in New Mexico. There the population of Anglo residents built up rather slowly and was assimilated into the previous culture, creating a Mexican-American society. However, because gold was discovered, California became a thoroughly American territory almost overnight and officially a state, the most important west of the Mississippi, only two years after it was acquired. By the end of 1849 nearly 100,000 new emigrants had arrived from the United States, and by 1852 the Anglo-American population was about a quarter of a million, whereas a decade before there had only been some 7,000 residents of European origin in the province. Because of this influx, the influence of the Hispanic past and the remaining Mexican residents became instantly insignificant.

The first waves of gold seekers had begun to wash over California by the time Walker arrived there from the mountains in the fall of 1848. However, he was immune to the fever that infected them and thought no better of laboring with a pick and pan than he had of other repetitious work. So far as he was concerned, the most immediate consequence of the gold rush was that it dramatically improved the livestock market in which he had been trading most of his life. Therefore, he set about organizing a family business to take advantage of the opportunity. His nephews Jeemes Walker and Frank and Mike McClellan had come across the overland trails that summer, and his brother Joel and his family arrived in California from Oregon at about the same time as Walker did. Joel, settling down for good, took up a ranch in Napa County, north of the Sacramento, and it is probably there that the brothers were reunited after a separation of sixteen years. Joel's eldest son, John, was twenty-five years old and with his cousins Jeemes and Frank and Mike entered into an arrangement with their uncle for the purpose of hauling freight and delivering beef, riding and draft animals to the miners. The nephews represented the firm at the diggings, while their uncle was the buyer and trader. He purchased a ranch near his old friends the Julius Martins in the vicinity of Gilroy and used this as a holding place and feedlot for his stock. He bought from ranchers in southern California with whom he had been dealing for a decade. The animals were trailed north to Gilroy, where they were picked up by the nephews.

Walker was on a buying trip in the Los Angeles area in April 1849 when he met Tom Breckenridge and received an eyewitness report about Frémont's debacle in the Sangre de Cristo. Breckenridge was still suffering from this disaster, especially in a financial way. He had left New Mexico with Frémont, and en route Frémont had promised that in California he would see that Breckenridge was at least reimbursed for the personal gear he had had to abandon in the mountains. However, once in the Los Angeles area, Frémont had said he was in a great hurry to look at some mining property he had acquired in Maricopa County, and he left without paying Breckenridge even his wages.

Like nearly every other man in the state, Breckenridge had gold fever, but his reduced circumstances presented him with the problem of how to get from southern California to the diggings. Therefore, he was very glad to meet Walker and said he thought the pleasure was mutual. "Each had to recite his experiences since our last meeting. I gave him a full account of my trip which had just ended. Walker after looking over my poney said 'Tom you can never ride that critter to Sutter's Fort' . . . and he gave me a very good horse." (Breckenridge had very moderate luck in the gold fields, earning only enough to pay his way home to St. Louis the next year.)

As was the case with many suppliers, the Walkers and McClellans did better from the gold rush than did most of the would-be miners. In addition to the livestock and hauling business, the four nephews had capital and the inclination to take flings at other ventures around the camps. Mike McClellan and John Walker opened the first hotel in Sacramento, the Missouri House, a canvas and plank affair, and operated it for a few months before selling out in the late summer of 1849. Frank McClellan and Jeemes Walker traded in claims and did some part-time prospecting and digging. All four were eventually able to acquire sizable tracts of land in northern California and settled down as ranchers and farmers, while continuing to deal occasionally in livestock with their uncle.

Walker himself never or very seldom went near the mining camps but, from the early 1850s onward, was generally referred to in the California press—which took considerable interest in his activities— as a prosperous rancher. However, he was not a rancher in the conventional sense, leaving the land at Gilroy and several other properties he owned to the regular management of others. Trailing herds seems to have been the only part of the work which much interested him, and he was seldom at any of the ranches long enough to become often involved in the routine chores of feeding, branding, rounding up or mending fences. As he had throughout his life, he used his livestock business in California to obtain the means to pursue, and perhaps as an excuse for, his wilderness ventures. Whatever it was which seems to have sapped his vigor and spirit in 1847 and 1848, it passed or was cured. After establishing his new and profitable base in California, he turned again to unknown regions—the source of his abiding delight.

In January 1851 Walker set off on an extended trip into an area which had fascinated him for three decades, the southern Great Basin and Colorado Plateau. This was by then the last extensive tract of largely unknown land in the West, and the *San Francisco Herald*, on his return, ran a long (5,000-word) series of articles about the journey. The unnamed reporter who interviewed Walker wrote, by way of hyping his story: "The most implicit confidence may be placed in all his [Walker's] statements. He is entirely free from that habit of romancing and exaggerating which we often find among great travellers." The writer unfortunately was not free from the jargon and hyperbole we often find among journalists. Nevertheless, overlooking some of his asides and creations, the articles in the *Herald* provide the only account of one of Walker's expeditions presented essentially from his own point of view.

Walker said that he undertook the trip as a private exploration, to look for a more direct trail between Los Angeles and the Santa Fe-Albuquerque area, the principal American settlements in the southwest. At the time there were two routes, established years before by traders, between the two localities. The northern one, usually called the Old Spanish Trail, twisted from Santa Fe through southern Colorado, then made a large northern loop that took it almost to Utah Lake before it turned southwest again and crossed into California through the Mojave Desert. The southern, or Arizona, route proceeded from El Paso through Tucson and Yuma. The country in between these caravan trails—that is, western New Mexico and nearly all of central and northern Arizona—was seldom entered by whites. Walker, beginning in 1837, had explored parts of it but had never made a single traverse between the Colorado and Rio Grande. He said simply that he had always been interested in seeing if such a straight-line route was practical.

Secondly, Walker said that he had wanted to visit the Moqui Indians, as the Hopi were then called by whites. He had met these people briefly in previous years, thought them exceptionally interesting and wanted to become better acquainted. The *Herald* reporter took it from there, writing: "We believe that Capt. Joe Walker is the only white man in this country that has ever visited this strange people." The journalist was wrong: From the days of the first Taos trappers the mountain men had had occasional dealings with the Moqui. Also, these were the people Joe Meek had watched being massacred by the band of free trappers who had left Walker's expedition in the spring of 1834.

Walker crossed the Sierra, as he usually did, through his own pass. He had with him seven men, including his nephew Jeemes, who was eventually going to visit his parents in Missouri but had decided to take the long wilderness detour with his uncle. The other six men were never mentioned by name, nor is it made clear whether they came along for the adventure or had simply been engaged by the Walkers as safari hands. From Walker Pass they descended to the Mojave, the intermittent desert river, the outlet of which was still a geographical mystery. Walker said that on his previous "tramps" in and out of the Great Basin, he had followed the Colorado to above the point where it was joined by the Virgin and had never seen any sign of the Mojave flowing into it. The party followed the valley for more than 100 miles, backtracking along parts of the trail Jed Smith had used in 1826.

Though the riverbed was often dry, Walker had no trouble finding water. "Being well acquainted with 'signs,'" wrote the *Herald* man, "he found water sufficient, although oftentimes he had to dig down in the sand, where a novice would have passed the spot without any idea that water could be had. Springs were occasionally met with, which bubbled up, clear as crystal, ran for a little distance and disappeared again in the sands."

They then turned away from the dry riverbed, and Walker concluded that if the Mojave joined the Colorado, it must do so underground rather than on the surface. This was not a bad guess, for subsequently hydrologists determined that the river finally ended in the sinks around Soda Lake. The party cut across the desert south of Death Valley and reached the Colorado "considerably worn out." They recruited their horses and traded for provisions at a Mojave village, where "Captain Walker saw among them the largest pumpkins he had ever met with." They swam their horses across the Colorado just below the mouth of the Virgin and continued east into Arizona, traveling between the Grand Canyon and the Mogollon Rim, making short exploratory side trips along the way. In the San Francisco peaks, north of Flagstaff, they rode through impressive conifer forests, the largest stands of Jeffrey pine on the continent. Coming out of the woodlands, they made a discovery which obviously delighted Walker, a complex of ancient ruins which he said were far more extensive and better preserved than anything of this sort he had seen before in New Mexico or southern Arizona. They stopped for several days of archaeological exploration and found places where it seemed as if the ancient structures and even the rocks on which they were built had been sered from some enormous source of heat. "It was no ordinary conflagration," Walker told the reporter, "but must have been some fierce furnace-like blast of fire, similar to that issuing from a volcano, as the stones were all burnt, some of them almost cindered, others glazed as if melted. A storm of fire seemed to have swept over the whole face of the country, and the inhabitants must have fallen before it."

From the description it is clear they were in the vicinity of Sunset Crater, northwest of Flagstaff, where a considerable number of Indians had been forced to abandon their homeland because of a series of volcanic eruptions between A.D. 1000 and 1200. Much of this area is now set aside as national park land because of its spectacular lava fields and prehistoric ruins—phenomena which Walker and the others were possibly the first white men to have seen.

(His activities on this trip, his lectures to his trappers in 1833 about earthquakes and astronomy, the conversations with Theodore Talbot, Ned Kern and James Abert about topographical, botanical and zoological matters suggest that Walker was a keen and reasonably well-informed amateur natural historian. It is another side of his personality which remains obscure so far as written records and recollections are concerned, but he may have shared some of the passions of men like John James Audubon, Thomas Nuttall and George Catlin. As was the case with them, some of his wanderings may have been motivated because he was so greatly curious about so many natural phenomena.)

Proceeding east from Sunset Crater, Walker crossed the Little Colorado, then turned north to the Moquis, with whom he spent a very instructive and apparently agreeable week. "We have rarely listened to anything more interesting," enthused the journalist about Walker's account of his stay in the mesa-top villages. Walker was very taken by the architectural works of these Indians, how defensible their communities were ("perfectly secure from the attacks of the fierce tribes who live to the north and east of them"—the Utes, Navajos and Apaches), their agriculture, arts, crafts and especially their character:

> They are scrupulously honest . . . valuable articles may be left exposed and they will not touch them. Many of the women are beautiful, with forms of faultless symmetry. They are very neat and clean, and dress in quite a picturesque costume of their own manufacture. They wear a dark robe with a red border, gracefully draped so as to leave their right arm and shoulder bare. They have most beautiful hair, which they arrange with great care. The condition of a female may be known from her manner of dressing the hair. The virgins part their hair in the middle behind, and twist each parcel around a hoop six or eight inches in diameter. The effect is very striking. The married women wear their hair twisted into a club behind.
>
> The Moquis farm in the plain by day and retire to their villages on the mountain at night. They irrigate their lands by means of small streams running out of the sides of the mountain. Sometimes when it fails to snow on the mountains in the winter, their crops are bad. For this reason they always keep two or three years' provisions laid up, for fear of famine. Altogether, they are a most extraordinary people, far in advance of any other aborigines yet discovered on this continent.

Even after one allows for the journalist's fairly ripe prose, there is a strong suggestion that it would not have taken very much for Walker to have left his business in California and the white settlements in general and once again gone back to live with Indians. However, he eventually ended his visit to the engaging Moquis, continued eastward and "struck the Rio Grande, as he intended, at Albuquerque." Jeemes Walker and some of the other men then went back to Missouri, arriving in June. Walker, however, traveled to Santa Fe and spent the summer in that vicinity, where he had a number of old friends, including Kit Carson, Lucien Maxwell, the St. Vrains and William Bent. He also looked into the local livestock market but did not find it attractive. In November he started back to California with a small company, traveling on the established southern caravan trail. By then his arrivals and departures were sufficiently newsworthy as to be treated somewhat like those of ocean-going vessels. The long series on his explorations in Arizona and New Mexico was published later, but immediately on his return home, the *Los Angeles Star* noted in its news columns of December 13, 1851:

> Captain Joe Walker, the renowned mountaineer, has arrived from New Mexico with a company of twelve men. Capt. W. went to N.M. with the intention of procuring sheep for the California market, but finding they sustained too high a price to render the speculation profitable, he returned without them. A portion of the company who went to N.M. with Capt. W. proceeded to the Eastern states. Capt. W. reports 2 droves of sheep numbering altogether 12,000 on the road to Calif. Capt. W. had a slight skirmish with the Apaches, but saving that, had no trouble with the Indians.

Stories about strange places and people are eternally interesting, but Walker's travels in 1851 received more than customary attention in the press because they bore directly on one of the major public issues of the day: the location of the transcontinental railroad. When Joel and Mary Walker started west in 1840 as the first of the overland wagon emigrants, there was already speculation that someday a rail line might link the Pacific coast to the eastern United States. By 1850 rail and construction technology had so advanced that there was no doubt such a road could be built. However, where it should be located was a matter of very hot and general dispute. Particularly in the west, where communities were separated by extensive unsettled regions, it had become apparent that cities and even states which had convenient access to the railroad would grow and prosper, while those which did not would not. In consequence numerous lobbyists began pushing for routes which would favor their particular localities or special economic interests.

Topographical and engineering, as well as political, problems complicated the matter of locating the first transcontinental line. Though nearly 100,000 overlanders had made the trip to the Pacific coast by 1850, most of the interior of the west between the edge of the plains and the coastal range was not much better known than it had been in

1833, when Walker first crossed to the Sierra. The emigrants had stayed on a few well-beaten trails. To a large extent, federal military and surveying parties had been occupied with assisting and protecting the emigrants. The technology existed for laying a railroad, but there was a paucity of information about where it might be most easily and economically built. Consequently, Walker, by then one of the last and most respected of the trappers and traders who knew the country beyond the trails, suddenly found himself in great demand as a geographical consultant. Both those who were legitimately interested in finding the best route and those who wanted one that was best for them began to seek him out in the early 1850s. In the former category was Richard Kern, who, unlike his brother Ben, had survived Frémont's attempt at railroad exploration in 1848. Kern, himself a topographer, had for very good reasons decided that the 38th parallel route which Frémont and Benton backed was not suitable. He favored a more southerly line, which followed the 35th parallel from Albuquerque to Los Angeles, passing through the country Walker had explored in 1851. In 1852 Kern solicited Walker's opinions. These he incorporated in a report which he sent on to William Gwin, California's senior U.S. senator. After giving a general description of the 35th parallel route, Kern added:

> Of the country between the Little Colo. and Walker's Pass, no exploration has been made except by Walker, an old and experienced guide and mountaineer. He has crossed it several times, and assures me it was the shortest and most practicable route he ever traveled—always finding an abundant supply of wood, grass and water . . . He says the most difficult part of the whole distance is in the mountains (already mentioned)—[the Continental Divide] between Zuñi and the Rio Grande—this to my own knowledge is of but little consideration.

For obvious reasons of self-interest, the citizens of Albuquerque strongly favored the same 35th parallel route recommended by Kern. Reporting on sentiments in the community, a local correspondent for the *New York Herald* (who from the sound of it may have doubled as the secretary of the Albuquerque boosters' association) filed a dispatch in November 1852.

> We want Congress to give us money to build a penitentiary for the accommodation of our thieves—a very large house, about one mile long and half a mile wide. We want Congress also to to have explored for us all that portion of our Territory lying between the Rio Grande and the Pacific. This is all a *terra incognita*. Enough only is known of it to convince us that here exists an admirable route for the wagons and carriages of the

emigrants, and also for a railroad, should the Government ever conclude to favor the making of one, by exploring the country and opening the way. Unfortunately, there is but one man who is well acquainted with the route, and that is the celebrated Capt. Joseph Walker, the discoverer of the route. He is now a wealthy resident of California.

Shortly thereafter Captain John Pope of the U.S. Topographical Engineers Corps (later and unfortunately the commanding Union general at the Second Battle of Bull Run) was quoted in San Francisco papers as also supporting the 35th parallel rail route. He said he formed this opinion because of his own surveys in the area and on the basis of conversations he had had with Walker. In the late winter of 1853 a group of California politicians invited Walker to speak about rail routes at the State Capitol. He appeared on March 24. The chairman of the session, J. M. Estill, forwarded a copy of the testimony to the president of the Senate, with this note:

> The Committee on Public Lands having been instructed to obtain all the information in their reach, relative to the topography of the country between San Francisco and the Mississippi valley, and its adaptation to Railroad purposes, have, in accordance with their duty, addressed letters to various individuals from whom information of an important character was expected, but after a careful comparison of it all, find it only corroborates that obtained from Captain Joseph Walker, of Gilroy, California, and which is respectfully submitted. Your committee deem it important to state that Captain Walker has been a trapper and trader for eighteen years throughout the whole country which he has so carefully described. He is the brother of the Hon. J. P. Walker, member of the Constitutional Convention from the district of Napa, and has a character for veracity equal to any gentleman in our State.

Walker's four-page statement offered two routes which he thought would be suitable for rail lines because of the grades involved and the availability of wood and water. Both left California through Walker Pass. The more southerly one followed the 35th parallel across Arizona and New Mexico to Santa Fe. (From there on, across the plains, Walker was of the opinion that it made little difference where the tracks were laid, as, in fact, it did not, except to the communities competing for them.) As an alternative he suggested a route that would run from Walker Pass north along the eastern Sierra and from there up the Humboldt to Salt Lake, following approximately the trails he had blazed in 1834 and first used for wagons in 1843.

Walker described the terrain and other natural features along the two routes in great detail. Whether his remarks were made extemporaneously or were read from a prepared text, they were obviously those of an articulate, if terse, man with orderly habits of mind. Nothing in the statement suggests the rambling, backwoods, campfire style of communication. As a matter of historical interest, this testimony is by far the most extensive surviving record in which Walker speaks for himself without being interpreted or paraphrased by one sort of journalist or another.

Portions of routes he proposed were used for rail lines, but none was laid through Walker Pass, the common point in both routes. As things developed, after the Civil War, neither of his suggestions proved politically and economically attractive. Also, when professional surveyors were finally able to get into the field, they found the 35th parallel and Owens Valley-Humboldt lines presented construction problems which in the 1850s were not apparent to Walker or anyone else. Nevertheless, the routes have remained logical and serviceable ones for overland travel. Both trails blazed in the first half of the nineteenth century now lie largely beneath the beds of state and national highways.

Somewhat as had been the case in the 1840s, when overland emigrants had sought his advice about wagon trails, Walker, in regard to the railroad issues, seemed satisfied to give his opinion and let others do what they would with it. He never joined a particular railroad lobbying group, and after 1853 he returned to his private geographical ventures, which could be pursued only on horses and mules.

Upon leaving his uncle in Santa Fe, Jeemes Walker had returned to Missouri and remained there until the spring of 1852. Jeemes was a dutiful son. Between 1847, when he went west for the first time and 1851, he made three trips home. On one of them he traveled with his cousin Frank McClellan by ship to Panama, across the isthmus by rail, by ship again to New Orleans and then by steamboat up the Mississippi and Missouri rivers. During the course of the visit his parents decided to relocate in California, where most of the other family members had settled. They left Independence in the spring of 1852 in a twenty-four-wagon caravan, with Jeemes serving as both captain and pilot. In addition to his parents, he had with him his younger sisters, Annie and Jane, and two teen-age cousins, Lucy and Mary Ann McClellan. The McClellan girls were particularly pleased to be going. Their father, Abraham, had died two years earlier, and the girls had become depressed by the prospect of being left in Missouri when, as Lucy wrote an Alabama kinswoman, "everyone has gone to California."

Frank McClellan came east from California to meet his sisters and the others at the Bear River. With the two cousins, by then experienced frontiersmen, in charge, the party made a smooth crossing. However, during its course Sam Walker became ill and died of the bloody flux. Remarkably, considering how many of them were involved, he was the only Walker to die while westering during the nineteenth century. His family buried him in an unmarked grave at the Humboldt Sink, which had been since the fall of 1833 a particularly ill-fated place for Walkers. Jeemes and Frank McClellan brought the rest of the party through safely. Barbara, the newly made widow, and the girls stayed with Walker at his Gilroy ranch for a time. Jeemes, now the head of his branch of the clan, set about acquiring property on the northwestern slope of Mount Diablo, a few miles inland from Martinez, a small waterfront village on Suisun Bay. When he had a house ready, he brought his mother and sisters to live with him, and a few years later he took a wife, another emigrant from western Missouri. During the remainder of the decade the family bought more land, at $10 per acre, and eventually had a ranch, which they called Manzanita, of about 1,500 deeded acres. Their "Captain Uncle Jo" almost certainly helped with the financing, having the means and inclination to do so. He took a protective interest in his sister-in-law Barbara, whom he had known since they were children in Tennessee, and, with no living children of his own, came to regard Jeemes Walker almost as if he were a son. Walker sold his own property near Gilroy in 1855 or thereabouts and moved north to Manzanita Ranch. Thereafter this served as his base for livestock trading and nomadic wilderness ventures.

Though Walker personally did no mining, finding or taking others to mining areas was a suitable objective for travel and exploration. In 1855 he led a company across the Sierra to prospect in the Mono-Walker lakes region, which he had discovered in 1833. They located promising ore, and within a few years two moderately prosperous districts, Bodie and Esmeralda, were established in the area. Walker however, stayed for less than a year and was gone before the camps were built.

In 1858, according to newspaper reports, he had started for Arizona on another expedition of unspecified purpose. However, on the west side of the Colorado he had a "fracas" with the Mojave Indians, in which a man named Lyon was seriously wounded. To get medical attention, Walker returned to Los Angeles, where Lyon died, the only man, so far as authentic records go, who was ever killed while following Walker. He went back to the Colorado in 1858 as a guide for a military party under the command of Colonel William Hoffman. Hoffman had been ordered to march from Fort Tejon, near Los Angeles, with fifty men, to discipline the Mojaves. Once this was accomplished, he was to establish a permanent post, Fort Mojave, on the Colorado River, near the present community of Needles, from which the military could keep a watch on the tribe.

Walker led them across the desert to Fort Yuma on the lower Colorado and then, in January 1859, up the river toward the Grand Canyon. Hoffman and his troops were astonished by the knowledge and skills of their veteran guide, who seemed to them to be a figure out of the mythic past. One of the men in the command later provided a California newspaper with information about the campaign:

> The old man [Walker] had been down the Colorado on an occasion twenty or more years prior . . . and had never been up it. Nevertheless he would make an accurate map each morning of the country to be marched over during the day, showing where the mountains approached the river, and where the valley widened; where sloughs or tributaries made in, marking the halting place for the night, and giving a description of its appearance and extent. Furthermore, he would say, "There is grass and wood in those mountains off there, with water flowing to the northward"—or whichever way it went.

The second guide with Hoffman was William Goodyear (a brother of Andrew, who had traveled west for the first time in 1847 with Walker). In 1859 Goodyear himself was regarded as a crafty frontier veteran by the young troopers, and he did nothing to disabuse them. As the company proceeded farther upriver, it began to skirmish with the Mojave, and Goodyear was determined to act as casually and coolly as did Walker during these engagements. One night, after a sharp exchange during the day in which Goodyear had been nicked by an arrow, he and Walker spread their blankets somewhat apart from the soldiers and went to sleep. "So much used were we both to such little affairs, that I do not believe we should have awakened at all, had we not been called." Goodyear fairly yawned as he recollected the incident. However, about midnight he and Walker were roused by a sentry, who said he thought he heard Indians in the bushes.

"Joe says," said Goodyear, "Bill, get up and see what it is. My eyes are not as good in the night as yours."

Goodyear rolled out of his blankets, looked around, found a sulking Mojave, dispatched him with one shot (presumedly there was a full desert moon) and came back to bed. The next day the Mojaves attacked in force, but, said Goodyear, "as our rifles could throw a bullet more than twice as far as any arrow could be thrown, the battle was rather a source of amusement to us, than of terror. . . . Old Joe Walker practiced with our Hawkins rifles and revolvers, as he said 'just to keep his hand in.' " At the end of the day some sixty Mojaves were dead, bringing the campaign to a close.

Goodyear, among others, noted that Walker's eyes were not as sharp as they had been, and during the remainder of his life his vision worsened. However, as the Mojave expedition indicated, he was otherwise remarkably fit for a man in his sixties. His spirit was obviously at least as willing as his flesh. Leaving Hoffman and his men to build the fort on the Colorado, Walker returned to Manzanita Ranch. Sometime during the next year he began planning his last private expedition, one which was in some respects to challenge him as a leader more than had any previous one and provided an extraordinary climax for his fifty-year frontier career.

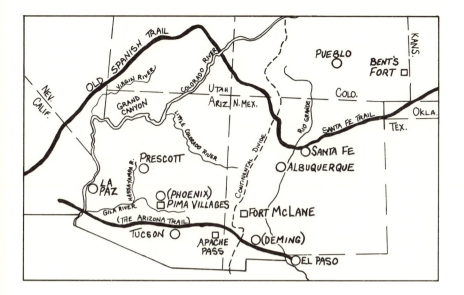

Mangas

The Civil War and the attendant turmoil halted railroad planning and field surveys for almost a decade. One consequence was that the country between the Rio Grande and Colorado rivers, which had in 1852 been described as a terra incognita by the *New York Herald* correspondent, remained that until the mid-1860s. Because it was so poorly known, bizarre stories about what this extensive territory might contain naturally continued to circulate. One of these, which he helped originate, was responsible for Walker's final expedition.

Except that he was a trapper who went with Walker to Arizona in 1837–38, very little is remembered about a man named Jack Ralston. Sometime after leaving Walker, he went to Canada and worked as a hunter and trapper for the Hudson's Bay Company. In 1857 he returned to the States, ending up in southern Oregon at a small gold field. Seeing, for the first time, gold nuggets, Ralston told his story. He said that when he was in Arizona with Walker, the party had been traveling across the dry plateau directly above the gorge of the Little Colorado River. Needing water, Walker and the others had started picking their way down a cliff to the river. Ralston was left in a ravine to guard the horses. While waiting and idly poking around in the rocks, he found a few lumps of an odd, yellow, metallic-looking substance. When the others returned, he showed it to them. "It was examined by all and

247

thought to be curious but none knew what it was, and [it] was used as pocket pieces until lost or thrown away," so he recalled twenty years later.

This was not surprising behavior at the time since fur was regarded as virtually the only commodity of great value which could be found and taken out of the western wilderness. The trappers were as a rule ignorant and not greatly curious about minerals. Even had they found and identified rich deposits, it would have done them little good because of the expense and difficulty of carrying ore to the settlements over hundreds of miles of primitive trails. Not until after the California gold rush of 1849—and the improvement of transport—did prospecting and mining become large enterprises in the west. Then old furmen like Ralston began to remember, and to be interrogated by others, about precious metals they had found, or thought they found, years before.

When he saw some samples of gold in Oregon, Ralston said this was exactly what the pocket pieces had been. At least one of those who heard Ralston's story took it seriously. This was George Lount, a thirty-two-year old Canadian who had emigrated to Michigan as a teen-ager. After working for a time as a merchant seaman, he had gone to California and then to Oregon, looking for gold. In the latter diggings he had done moderately well and decided to invest some of his profits in an expedition to investigate Ralston's claims. However, before he could, Ralston, who would have guided him, died. Nevertheless, Lount thought that he had received accurate enough instructions from Ralston to enable him to find the place on the Little Colorado by himself. In 1858 he attempted to do so but was not enough of a frontiersman for the job. He, his brother and two or three other men started east from Los Angeles but got no farther than the Mojave Desert. There they became lost, and Lount's brother was killed by Indians. Deciding he needed expert assistance, Lount then traveled to northern California, looking for Walker, whose name he had received from Ralston. Meeting, the two men had, said Lount, a long conversation. Walker confirmed Ralston's story, saying that what they had picked up on the Little Colorado was much like what he had seen miners bring out of the California diggings. Lount then inquired if Walker would be willing to lead a party to the site. Whether or not there was gold on the Little Colorado had obviously been a matter of indifference to Walker. As recently as 1851—by which time he had learned, if he had not known before, what gold looked like—he had been close to the place where Ralston had made his find and had not bothered to do any prospecting. However, the chance to make another expedition into the territory which had long fascinated him was attractive, and he accepted Lount's proposal.

Lount recruited seven other miners willing to take the risk. Walker added another of his nephews, Jeemes' younger brother Joseph Rutherford Walker, to the party. (Bearing the same name as his uncle, this nephew was later thought, mistakenly, by some in Arizona to be Walker's son.) They left through Walker Pass and on the far side of it met twelve more prospectors, who were there for reasons unrecorded. Since their own group was dangerously small, Walker and Lount told these men about the purpose of the expedition and invited them to join it; they did. Crossing the Colorado below the Virgin, as he had in 1851, Walker led the prospectors directly to the gulch on the Little Colorado where Ralston had found the peculiar rocks twenty-three years before. All seemed satisfied that they were in the right location, but either what Ralston had found was not gold or, if it was, there had only been a few nuggets washed down the river from elsewhere. In any event, there was no more, and the prospectors were of the opinion that they were not in gold-bearing formations. They were correct, and no notable discoveries were ever made in the area.

After exploring adjacent canyons, the party left the Little Colorado in the late fall, going first to Albuquerque and then on to Colorado. They remained near Denver for six months before returning to New Mexico late in the summer of 1862. There was then no diarist in the group, but members of it were later to say there were two principal reasons for this detour and long stay in Colorado. Several years before, gold in modest quantities had been discovered in several areas between Denver and Pikes Peak. The quantity and quality of ore had been greatly exaggerated, but such was the nature and prevalence of gold fever at the time that nearly 100,000 would-be miners had swarmed into Colorado between 1859 and 1861. Being in the vicinity, and as hopeful and credulous as all prospectors, Walker's men wanted to explore the new fields for themselves. Secondly, Union and Confederate armies were maneuvering and fighting in New Mexico throughout the winter and spring of 1862. Especially because many of his prospectors were southern by birth, if not sympathy, Walker thought it prudent to get his armed civilians out of the combat zone.

Hostilities had commenced shortly after Christmas of 1861. During the previous fall General H. H. Sibley of the Confederacy had collected 2,300 troops: some defecting federal regulars; nearly all the Texas Rangers, the already famous border patrol; and a number of veterans of the Mexican War. With these men Sibley had taken and used El Paso as a staging area. From there he had sent 100 troopers directly west to Tucson. They occupied that community to the general satisfaction of its American population, which was solidly prosouthern. With his main force, Sibley crossed into New Mexico in early January and marched northward up the Rio Grande toward Albuquerque and Santa

Fe. He was opposed by Colonel E. R. S. Canby, whose troops were superior in numbers but inferior in quality, being mostly hastily recruited militia, strengthened by only a few companies of regulars. For three months, Sibley and Canby chased each other about the Rio Grande Valley with very little consequence except for the 500 men who died in the skirmishes. After some initial success Sibley was defeated at Glorieta Pass near Santa Fe, an engagement grandly called the Gettysburg of the West. Being unable to maintain their supply lines, the Confederates retired from the southwest in midspring, never to return.

The New Mexican campaigns sufficiently alarmed federal strategists so that 1,500 fresh troops were raised in California and sent east under the command of General James Carleton. Walker had first met him twenty years earlier, when Carleton had been a dragoon lieutenant serving with Philip St. George Cooke on Indian patrols in the plains. The two had encountered each other occasionally since that time and became congenial acquaintances, a fact which was to be of some significance in the affairs of Walker and his prospectors during the next year. The California Column, as Carleton's command was named, arrived in Tucson on April 15. They brushed aside the company of Confederates stationed there and restored Arizona (which for practical purposes consisted of Tucson and its environs) to the Union. They then continued on to Santa Fe, where Carleton replaced Canby as the commander of the Department of New Mexico, which included Arizona. To deal with any lingering Confederate supporters and with the Navajo and Apache, both of whom were on the warpath, and because it seems to have suited his authoritarian temperament, Carleton immediately declared a state of martial law in the territory. This remained in effect throughout the Civil War, during which Carleton was the principal administrator of both the military and civilian affairs in the American southwest.

The fighting in New Mexico and Arizona was brief and trivial so far as the main events of the Civil War were concerned. However, it left an uncommon amount of bitterness in its wake. As in border states such as Missouri and Arkansas, the contending "armies" had been largely composed of local residents. Many of them had been feuding, long before the war broke out, about matters of purely local concern. When the brief military actions were concluded, the troops returned to civilian life, in which they often found dealing with their former opponents both necessary and aggravating. The ex-Confederates were bitter because they had lost. The Union men tended to crow about their triumphs and to conduct witch hunts aimed at exposing and penalizing southern sympathizers.

For reasons which were literally fantastical, Walker was caught up in the post-fighting hysteria. A freewheeling journalist and fire-eating Unionist by the name of A. F. Banta was working in 1861 in Albuquerque. There he discovered and later published the "true story" in regard to the Walker party. They were not, said Banta, prospectors but Confederate soldiers. The plan had been that while Sibley invaded from the east, Walker would cross the Colorado, he and his twenty men forming the western half of a vast pincers movement which would nip off the Department of New Mexico from the Union and attach it to the Confederacy. However, arriving on the Little Colorado and learning that Sibley was not holding up his strategic end, Walker—whom Banta described as a "natural commander of men"—had retreated to Colorado to reassess his position. After doing so, he returned to Arizona (to jump ahead in narrative sequence) with the intention of leading an insurrection which would seize that territory for the South and make Walker the Confederate General of the West. All this, said Banta, would have happened had not General Carleton cleverly placed a spy, one A. S. Benedict, within Walker's ranks. Benedict supplied Carleton with intelligence which permitted the Union commander to place his 3,000 troops in positions where they were able to frustrate Walker. As for how he learned of all this, Banta explained, "I was in Albuquerque at the time; the country was under martial law; Lt. Johnson was Provost Marshal; H. S. Johnson published the Rio Abajo Press; he was on the 'inside' in matters military, and I worked in the office, so I too, was on the 'inside.' Nuff sed."

Before Banta told his story, there may have been nobody in the Department of New Mexico except him who thought there was such a plot. Neither Walker nor any of his men ever gave indication that they knew they were Confederate commandos, nor acted as if they were. Nor did Carleton or any other federal officials deal with them as if they were. Carleton, in fact, extended many courtesies to Walker and, a year later, made an unsolicited blank-check sort of offer to assist him and his men. Benedict did join Walker when he returned from Colorado and went with him to Arizona. However, beyond personal ones, his reason for doing so was to let Carleton and some of his friends in Santa Fe know immediately if Walker's prospectors found gold so that the federal officials could get in on the ground floor of the enterprise as private investors.

As for Walker himself, he never made any reference to Banta's story or, for that matter, any involving the Civil War. This is not particularly surprising since he was an apolitical man who seldom displayed great interest in the issues (excepting Manifest Destiny) which exercised the residents of the settled regions. He had lived as a boy and a young man in east Tennessee and western Missouri—neither hotbeds of secessionist sentiment—but for nearly half a century he had been, by choice, a westerner. By then all his immediate family was living in California, and whatever, if any, ties he had with the South were weak.

Most of his adult life was spent on the fairly cosmopolitan frontier, among other and mixed bloods and whites from every state in the Union. It is very difficult to imagine him as a passionate racial bigot or a Yankee-hating southern xenophobe. There is no evidence that he was.

The true story behind Banta's story seems to have been that the author had a journalist's penchant for appearing to be an insider and the imagination which enables dedicated conspiracy hunters to add two and two and get a total of five. Sibley and Walker had arrived in the southwest at about the same time. Walker had a southern drawl. His men were armed. Carleton was interested in the party. Benedict went with it and wrote letters back to Santa Fe. There was a war going on. Banta was a patriot. It all fit together. Nuff sed.

In the late summer of 1862 Walker, with twenty-five men, left the Colorado diggings where the party had been prospecting and staying out of trouble for the previous six months. (Some of the original members had gone back to California, and new men had been added.) Their intention was to travel, by way of the New Mexican settlements, to northern Arizona and look for gold there. Shortly after they crossed Raton Pass on their way south, they were joined by another recruit, a desperate and exhausted young man, Daniel Conner, who appeared unexpectedly out of the wilderness. At least from the standpoint of posterity he was a valuable addition, for Conner appointed himself as the historian of the expedition and served as such for the next two years and, in a sense, until his death in 1920.

Conner had been born and grew up in Kentucky. He attended college for a year in Indiana but had dropped out of school and gone to Colorado for gold. Like many others there, he had found none and survived by doing occasional farm and ranch work, hunting and not eating well in the mountains. When hostilities commenced in the east, he was open in expressing his support for the southern cause. In the late winter of 1862 he and about 100 like-minded miners, under the influence of martial and other spirits, had declared themselves to be a "Confederate regiment." They had gone off to an isolated valley, Mace's Hole, southwest of Pueblo, and made a great show of drilling, did much talking about seizing federal forts and riding south to reinforce General Sibley. Nothing came of this. Hearing something of the matter, the commander of a detachment of federal troops in the area dispatched a half company to Mace's Hole to investigate. As they approached, the Confederate Regiment immediately and unceremoniously disbanded, the putative rebels scattering, in every-man-for-himself, the-devil-take-the-hindmost formations. With little else to occupy them after the defeat of Sibley, Union troops, with enthusiastic assistance from bellicose civilian sympathizers, began a vigorous search for these failed secessionists. Depending upon the circumstances, those caught were imprisoned, shot or hanged.

Conner had been on the run, hiding in the mountains and with a few friends he could count on, for most of the summer. By the end of September his position was very uncomfortable. Winter was coming, and he had neither the experience nor supplies to remain in the wilderness. If he stayed in the settled areas of Colorado, he was certain he would shortly be found or betrayed. However, as a single man and a fugitive he had very little chance of crossing the plains to Missouri, where he could disappear into the civilian population. The only other possibility was New Mexico; but martial law prevailed there, and the territory was crawling with Carleton's troopers.

Early in October the harassed Conner showed up at a tavern-livery near Pueblo which was kept by a man named Jim Gray who had previously befriended other refugees from the Confederate Regiment. Conner arrived after dark and went to the back door of the establishment. This was fortunate since the front was occupied by a squad of feds investigating the proprietor. Gray was able to slip away from them for a moment and hurriedly told Conner to go to the shack, a mile away, occupied by one of his Mexican braceros. He was to wait there until Gray could come talk to him. Gray was not free until after midnight, and when he arrived, he brought Conner a meal and some mixed information. The bad news was that the troops knew Conner was nearby, had a description of him and orders to shoot him on sight. Gray was of the opinion that if Conner was still in the area after the sun came up, he would not live to see that phenomenon again.

The good news was that Gray thought he knew how Conner could get out of not only his immediate difficulties but Colorado as well. The day before, the celebrated Captain Joseph Walker had passed by with his band of prospectors. Gray suggested that if Conner could catch them, he might be able to join and more or less lose himself in this company. It was the best opportunity for escape that had presented itself to Conner, and he immediately asked which trail Walker had taken. This gave Gray a chance to deliver himself of a famous line. He said that if Conner hoped to catch up, he would have to take to the mountains, for "Captain Walker does not follow trails. He makes them."

Conner was gone before dawn. He rode for two days, stopping only to water his horse and take catnaps. On the third evening he found the prospectors and was taken into the camp to be questioned by the captain. Having left Colorado as Daniel Ellis Conner, he introduced himself simply as Daniel Ellis. Among those present who had joined the party in Colorado were several who had known Ellis-Conner there, so an alias could not have deceived anybody for very long. However, he continued to go by the name of Ellis for the next several years. All this was apparently of no concern to Walker, who sized him up as a promising man and allowed him to join the expedition with no questions asked about his politics or status in Colorado.

As a fugitive Conner had one final scare. While in Colorado, Walker, always prudent in such matters, had obtained a pass from the military authorities which identified his party and permitted it to travel freely in that territory. After crossing Raton Pass, he decided to go to Santa Fe and get a similar document for the Department of New Mexico. This alarmed Conner and perhaps several of the others, but they had little choice but to go along. At a camp eight miles north of Santa Fe the prospectors were met by a company of federal cavalry. The officer in charge halted, in "big style" reported Conner, twenty feet in front of Walker and demanded that he and his men identify themselves and take oaths of allegiance on the spot. Walker responded in somewhat larger style:

> Our old captain asked why Carleton didn't come out, and continued coolly, "I expected him, after receiving word to that effect. I have known Carleton for many years and have had many games of euchre with him, but had I known that he was not coming I should not have waited here nearly a week for a pass simply because I can take these men and pass anywhere in this wilderness without fear or favor. I only waited here to be courteous to my old friend."

Conner did not report whether or not a pass was obtained or Carleton and Walker met, but shortly thereafter they left the area. For as long as they remained in the Department of New Mexico, they were never interfered with or challenged again and, in fact, were generally treated with great deference by the military. Conner was not only grateful but very impressed by the way his old frontier captain had outfaced the young cavalry officer, and as his "history" shows, he came increasingly to regard Walker with a respect that approached hero worship. After the expedition was concluded, Conner wrote of his relationship with Walker: "I was but a boy and he kept me out of dangerous places without letting me know it or even know how it was done. I feel constrained to say that he was very nearly the best friend I ever had and certainly as true and by nature as well fitted for that delicate and pure relationship as any man."

After the episode outside Santa Fe, being no longer worried about the law, Conner became more serious about his self-assigned duties as the scribe of the party. However, in this respect he was no Zenas Leonard. He was less informative than Leonard about the overall conduct and purposes of the expedition, much weaker in regard to names, dates and geography, more prone to pass off hearsay as fact and to self-glorification. However, he was a keen observer and, if lacking a strong narrative sense or style, very good at reporting isolated incidents and details. Because of this ability and his admiration for the man, Conner provided the only lengthy description of Walker in day-to-day action as a leader. Better than any other, Conner's account helps explain why Walker was often and successfully followed and so long and widely regarded as a "natural commander of men."

In this regard Conner had splendid material. During the next eighteen months Walker, despite being sixty-five years old and troubled with failing eyesight, put on a virtuoso performance which displayed all the skills and knowledge he had acquired during the previous half century. Beyond being Walker's last one, this adventure was also in a sense the final, true field demonstration of the body of frontier expertise Americans had commenced acquiring in approximately 1732, when John Walker of Wigton, Scotland, arrived in the wilderness of western Virginia and founded the Creek Nation.

Leaving Santa Fe, the party followed the Rio Grande Valley, passing through the scattered settlements along the river. Walker used the period to conduct what amounted to training exercises for the men, the majority of whom were new ones who had joined in Colorado or thereafter. (By then there were thirty-seven in the company.) Nearly all of them were under thirty-five and relative newcomers to the west, who had spent most of their time there in mining camps. Because of this experience or the generally belligerent atmosphere engendered by the Civil War, they were rough and had itchy trigger fingers. This was particularly true in regard to Indians, whose extermination they regarded as not only a necessary but righteous act. However, their first-hand knowledge of the tribes was minimal, and their general wilderness experience was comparable to that of a company of overland emigrants.

In consequence Walker found it necessary to give them instructions in matters that would never have needed to be mentioned in a fur brigade thirty years before: how to set up defensible camps, identify quicksands, pack mules properly and the importance of keeping them together. Conner, for example, noted that Walker expected them to travel in a tighter order than even the military used. The Captain himself was always at the head of the column, the other men—with pack animals spaced between them—following in a tight single file. The formation, if maintained, prevented straggling and allowed Walker to read trail signs before they were obliterated. They themselves left a very narrow trail with few distinct signs from which anyone following could determine the size and composition of the party. The advantages were not, however, immediately apparent to some of the green hands, and during the first few weeks Walker found it necessary to keep at them continually, commanding, "Catch up, catch up."

They camped at Fort Craig, the last military post on the river below Albuquerque, and as a gesture of hospitality the commanding officer sent them five gallons of whiskey. Conner says that "Walker took in that situation easily," but when the drinking was finished, he told the men they were about to enter real Indian country and therefore would begin a new routine so far as their camps were concerned. Cooking fires would be laid in the middle of the camp. The men would spread their blankets, with their saddles near them to provide cover, in a circle around the fires, far enough back from the light so that they would not present silhouetted targets. All the mules and horses were to be side-lined (hobbled) each night and left to graze beyond the men. On the outer perimeter shifts of armed guards would remain on patrol throughout the night.

Since these arrangements made considerable extra work and because they had seen no Indians—and many of the men had never met any wild ones—there was some grumbling and shirking. One man reported for guard duty with his blanket and crept off in the bushes to continue his sleep. Conner himself let a mule stray because he was engrossed by an eclipse of the moon, the first he had ever observed. Conner said that the Captain was very "displeased" by this carelessness. Three days beyond Fort Craig they received an object lesson in the value of such precautions. About midnight several Apaches slipped through the sentries and fired a quick volley, attempting to stampede the stock. Because of the arrangement of the camp, the animals hobbled away from the shots into the ring of sleeping men, and therefore, none were lost; but the Indians escaped unseen. Walker was out of his blankets immediately and was furious that his guards had been so lax. Conner recorded:

> He caught George Lount putting a charge in his gun and halted, and the following conversation took place.
>
> "Why Mr. Lount, didn't I give orders particularly that all the guns should be loaded tonight?"
>
> "Yes sir, but I cleaned my gun just before dark and thought that I would wait for it to get dry before reloading it."
>
> "Does it take your gun half the night to dry after cleaning it?"
>
> "No, reckon not that long."
>
> "Well, why didn't you reload it?"
>
> "I didn't think that there was any use of it, because I thought there was no danger here."
>
> "No danger, no danger," broke in the old Captain, "no danger—I have seen a great many no danger men since I have been

in the mountains and I have yet to see the first one that is worth a d--n for anything. You are always in danger in an Indian country."

After laying out Lount, Walker doubled the guard, as much for instructional purposes as anything else, and then went back to sleep. The next day they began to see signal smokes on the ridges, and Walker explained to them that this was the Indian telegraph. There were few days during the next three months when they did not see some of these smoke messages. Though they were seldom met in person, the prospectors came to realize they were being kept under constant surveillance by the warriors of Mangas Coloradas, the great chief of the Mimbreño Apaches.

The Mimbreños in particular and, in general, the Apache (a loose confederation of tribes related by language and custom who occupied most of south-central New Mexico and Arizona) were at the time the most dangerous Indians in the southwest so far as whites were concerned. The nation had migrated from the plains some 200 years before. Finding the desert and rough canyon country poor for agriculture and even hunting, they had devised an economy which was principally based on armed robbery. Initially they had preyed on more sedentary, agricultural tribes in the region, the Zuñi, Hopi, Pima and Papago. However, after the coming of the Spanish they found the European settlements to the south were both richer and safer to attack than the Indian ones. For more than a century they had raided deep into Sonora-Chihuahua and Sinaloa. (In 1850 Apaches had razed Mazatlán on the Pacific coast.) They took what they needed in the way of supplies, women and children for the slave markets, weapons, ammunition and particularly horses.

Their own land did not permit them to maintain the huge horse herds that were the pride and glory of the plains tribes, nor did they value them as did Indians to the east and north. The horse for the Apache was a disposable tool. When one was used up, they discarded it and took another from the Mexicans. Also, as the American military were to discover, they were not so dependent either physically or psychologically on horses as were the plains warriors. When the occasion demanded, they were willing to fight and travel on foot, and in the rough canyon country they remained almost as mobile as they were when mounted. The Spanish and, after them, Mexicans had attempted to deal with the Apache problem in various ways: by fortifying their communities, sending out patrols, offering bounties on scalps and paying protection money to the tribes. None of these responses was very successful. The Europeans had to defend an enormous area against small bands of raiders who knew the country much better than they did and who could retreat into mountain sanctuaries which the whites were seldom strong enough to invade.

The Apaches had little to do with Americans during the first half of the nineteenth century. The few they met were transient and well-armed trappers, traders and military parties, who provided much less attractive prey than their traditional Mexican victims. However, in the 1850s American ranchers and other settlers began arriving in the newly acquired territories of southern Arizona and New Mexico. They had sufficient trouble with and fears about the Apaches so that troops were sent to the area and stationed in scattered garrisons to protect American residents and travelers. The beginning of the Civil War brought more serious hostilities. In immediate and desperate need of regulars, Union commanders transferred most of the frontier troops, including nearly all those in the sparsely settled Southwest, to the East. The Apaches, whose predatory traditions and successes had made them an especially hubristic people, were of the opinion that their own activities had forced the soldiers to flee. With the departure of the troops the Apaches turned on the remaining civilians for profit, to settle old scores and with the general intention of ridding their country of all whites. They came close to doing so in 1861 and the early part of 1862. Travel and trade across the southern caravan route were brought almost to a halt, and American residents were forced to flee from isolated settlements and take refuge in a few defensible communities such as Tucson and Mesilla in southern New Mexico.

The Apaches had things very much their own way until the spring of 1862, when the California Column crossed their territory en route to Santa Fe. In an attempt to halt this march, Mangas Coloradas, the only Apache chief with sufficient influence and reputation to conduct joint operations with other tribes, met the California Column at Apache Pass in southeastern Arizona. With about 200 warriors, his own Mimbreños and some Chiricahuas led by his son-in-law, Cochise, Mangas fought well. However, after a six-hour battle in the narrow defile he was forced to retreat when Carleton's men brought up a mountain howitzer, a weapon which the Apaches had never encountered before and were unable to defend themselves against. Mangas was wounded, and his Mimbreños carried him to Janos, a Mexican town southwest of El Paso. The warriors occupied the community and secured the services of the local physician, who was told that if Mangas did not live, he and all the citizens of Janos would be killed. Mangas recovered and Janos was spared.

Carleton was well aware of the intentions of the Apaches and the threat they presented. However, on taking command of the Department of New Mexico, he found that the Navajos had, like the Apaches, broken loose after the cavalry garrisons had been transferred to the east. Since they were much closer to Santa Fe and Albuquerque, the two principal American settlements in his territory, Carleton chose to deal with the Navajos first and picked Kit Carson to lead the expedition against them. Carleton's Indian policy was direct and brutal—so much so that even in the midst of the Civil War it was to become something of a national scandal and earned Carleton the reputation of being a frontier monster. His orders in regard to the Navajos were: "The Indians are to be soundly whipped without parleys or councils . . . All Indian men of that tribe are to be killed whenever and wherever you can find them. The women and children will not be harmed, but you will take them prisoners. . . . I think that this severity in the long run will be the most humane course that could be pursued toward these Indians."

Carson, never an Indian hater, openly objected and refused to carry out some of Carleton's more genocidal schemes. However, Carson had always been a man who respected authority. He accepted the assignment and succeeded in destroying the Navajo nation to an extent and by means that seemed, during the few remaining years of his life, to bother his conscience. Later Carleton was to try to use the same tactics against the Apaches, but with less immediate success (those tribes continued to resist for nearly twenty-five years). However, in 1862, after Walker and his men had left Fort Craig, they were more or less on their own, for the bulk of the troops which Carleton could spare for Indian fighting had been assigned to the Navajo campaign.

By the time Walker turned west from the Rio Grande, Mangas's wounds had healed and he had returned from Janos to New Mexico. He was determined to make an object lesson of the white prospectors, who were the first sizable civilian party that had attempted to pass through the territory since the general Apache uprising. Mangas's intention to do so and Walker's to resist created one of the most prolonged and tactically interesting actions ever conducted between white irregulars and Indians. The figure is overused in military affairs, but in this case the contest between these two veterans—very equal in age and experience—was in fact similar to a chess match between masters. It was played for three months across most of the southern half of New Mexico with living pieces and for the highest stakes.

Walker's objective was to get through the Mimbreño stronghold— along the Continental Divide—and into central Arizona. Mangas wanted to stop him, either by inflicting such harassments and casualties that he would turn back or by simply rubbing out the whole company. Both wanted to achieve these mutually exclusive ambitions with as little loss of life as possible on their own side. Contrary to later fictions to the effect that the white-red wars were conducted with suicidal recklessness, both Indian and white leaders were very protective of their men. They never had many of them, and those they led were usually friends and relatives, not nameless, expendable soldiers.

Walker's company was outnumbered but never it seems by more than two or three to one. Again, the vision of "hordes" of Indians attacking in continuous waves is largely mythic. All the western tribes were relatively small. At the time the Mimbreños probably had no more than 200 warriors in the entire nation, and having other uses for them, Mangas could never bring all his braves against Walker at the same time. Nevertheless, if the Apaches could get the whites into close quarters, their superiority in numbers was sufficient to give them a considerable advantage. Also, for hand-to-hand fighting their weapons—they were armed with bows, lances and a few muskets taken from the Mexicans—and skills were at least equal to those of the whites. However, at long range, the superior rifles and marksmanship of Walker's men gave them the advantage. The men they had at their disposal, and their arms, dictated the tactics of Walker and Mangas. So long as they stayed in the open, the whites were relatively secure and their sharpshooters could inflict occasional casualties. Mangas, on the other hand, was continually trying to lure Walker into situations suitable for an ambush and was also continually harassing his camps by sending in scouts at night to reduce his strength by taking livestock or careless men.

Finally, both Mangas and Walker realized that the latter, if he was to do what he wanted—get west—sooner or later had to come in out of the open—i.e., find and use a pass across the Continental Divide. When he did, he would be in the position Mangas wanted him. In consequence, almost as if his company were a sailing vessel, Walker, throughout the fall of 1862, tacked up and down New Mexico, staying to the east of the mountains but looking for a way through them, feinting and maneuvering in an attempt to make his break. But he was always dogged by the Mimbreños. Conner's narrative is so jumbled that this extraordinary duel cannot now be re-created in a day-to-day, place-to-place way. However, Conner did contribute enough vignettes of individual actions and incidents to give a sense of the general style of the campaign:

> We found the Indians too strong for us in this continuous and apparent endless expanse of terribly broken country. Serious obstacles were continuously confronting us, necessitating a slow and uncertain progress. We found a long sharp ridge and took up our march to its top. It was rocky and craggy and covered sparsely with low chaparral. A sharp, precipitous ravine divided this ridge from a similar one, which was occupied by a

strong force of Indians. The occupants of both ridges traveled nearly all day parallel with each other and kept up an irregular skirmish across this nearly impassable ravine, all day.

They had the advantage of their ridge as a breastwork for their footmen, but we could not always keep our mules out of sight behind our ridge and therefore had some of them wounded, but the wounds of our men were inconsiderable. We had the advantage of better and heavier guns and therefore the responsibilities on each side were somewhat equal. . . .

Time and again they would have our party surrounded entirely and we would pass out of their lines upon the highest ground which lay in our direction, and sometimes succeed without firing a shot. . . . Capt. Walker kept them laying plans for two weeks without giving them any satisfaction. They would fortify a gap and wait for us, but we would never go through the right one. They would lay in wait at the limited watering places, but we would camp in a dry desert or on a dry hill for the night and get water as we crossed it in the daytime. If we became entangled in rough and craggy places so near night that we could not find an open place to occupy, we would huddle together on the summit of a little peak until daylight.

We knew that our defeat meant destruction and therefore held the enemy aloof by adhering to an open country. The Apache thought that he would out general us in the end and therefore contented himself for a long while with setting cunning traps and making feints to annoy. They would steal around the guardsmen at night and raise quietly from behind a rock or ridge or bunch of bushes, while holding a "bouquet" of brush in the left hand and before the face, so as not to be noticed, until their gun, which was extended through the bouquet was discharged. . . . The ever industrious John Apache, as he is called on the border, was hovering at the edge of the little plain amongst the rocks of the foothills, in force. Their object was to stampede the stock first and then shoot as many men in the melee as might be convenient. But the first motion was discovered by one of our dogs in time to countervail their calculations.

The two dogs were an unnamed brindle bull and a shepherd called Curly, "a lithe animal of a grisly, gray color [that] could hardly be seen at a little distance early in the morning or late in the evening." In addition to serving as guard, the two dogs provided some recreation. When they were able to, the men trapped coyotes and, after hobbling or hamstringing them, threw them to Curly. "Our cruel and mischievous fellows would keep these animals fighting as long as Curly could hold out and then let the old brindled bulldog finish the wolves which was always done with dispatch."

In addition to attempting to catch him in narrow passes, Mangas during these maneuvers was constantly trying to force Walker to travel through the worst possible country, where his men could not hunt and their horses and mules would be weakened by lack of forage and water. Approaching the present site of Deming, New Mexico, they were driven into exactly such a place in late November, a creosote- and yucca-covered barrens, through which they traveled for two days without water. Walker, however, remained confident. He told them that many years before (presumedly in 1837–38) he had been in this country and found a good spring. According to his recollection, it was halfway up the side of a ridge and was marked by a prominent, perpendicular formation of rock which stood above the water. He thought it was nearby. If they found it, the spring would provide them with water; and the particular ridge would give him a means of orienting himself so as to determine better their position in relation to the Continental Divide.

On the morning of the third waterless day, Conner said, "there was much anxiety felt, if not expressed, as to our old Captain's doubtful guess at the true position of a spring that he had only seen once, in such a rugged country as this, and that, too, after the expiration of thirty years." At noon Walker halted and told them that he now thought they were within five miles of the spring. He detailed Conner and four other men to go ahead on foot (their horses were then too weak to make much speed) according to the directions he gave them. They were warned if they located the water not to go near it because it was bound to be watched by Apaches. Conner and the other scouts found the spring precisely where Walker told them to look. However, they were so thirsty that they went directly to it and "got a big drink, contrary to orders." Almost immediately the wisdom of the Captain's advice was demonstrated, "for on raising the hill toward the highland in the direction that we had come, a long-ranged volley was sent after us from the rocks at the foot of the mountain. We were not hit and hurried on to meet the party, which we did. . . ."

Conner then gave some indication of the kind of discipline Walker had established within the company. Though they had come very close to being bushwhacked by John Apache, their concern when they came up to the main party was with what Walker might do if he discovered they had ignored his orders. "We failed to tell Captain Walker that we had gone to the spring and drank, and after thinking it over, we begun to fear that we had left our tracks in our haste, to detect our disobedience." However, Walker had more pressing matters on his mind. Approaching the ridge, he sent out a party of skirmishers to clear out the Apache guards. Even after this had been accomplished, he did not permit the men to get their drinks. Instead, he drove the animals ahead and watered them so that if the Apaches returned in force and they had to abandon the position, at least the stock would be in better condition. When the horses and mules were finished, the men finally were allowed to go to the spring. By then the animals had so trampled the ground around the water hole that not even Walker could find the signs the disobedient scouts had left. "All's well that ends well," wrote the relieved Conner.

After recruiting the animals for a day or so, Walker picked up the old overland caravan route and made an attempt to make a quick break to the west toward Apache Pass. However, shortly they saw a signal smoke which aroused their suspicions since it rose not from a ridge, as was customary, but from thickets along the trail. Investigating, they found "three white men, who it seemed had been crazy enough to attempt a passage over this 'Southern Route' alone, to California. They were hanging by their ankles all in a row to a horizontal piñon limb. Their hands were tied behind them and their heads hung to within a foot of the ground and a little fire had been built directly under each head. They were dead and the skin and their hair was burned off of their skulls, giving them a ghastly appearance as they swung there perfectly naked."

There is no indication in Conner's history that Walker had any further problems with sleeping guards, stragglers or general discipline. By erecting this grisly no trespassing sign, Mangas informed the whites that again he was ahead of them. Walker concluded that with only 37 men he stood no chance of fighting his way through Apache Pass, which Carleton with 1,500 troops had had difficulty forcing only six months before. Therefore, he changed direction once again and started riding northwest, still following along the eastern side of the Continental Divide, still looking for a way through it and still trailed by Mangas. In January 1863 in the vicinity of the present Silver City, they came to Fort McLane, one of the frontier posts which had been abandoned when the garrison troops had pulled out of the Southwest two years before. Some of the buildings and corrals were still standing. To let his animals rest and the men take cover from the winter weather which had become bitter, Walker halted there for a time.

At McLane, Walker reassessed his strategy. During the previous three months he had not lost a man, and only two or three had been wounded, none seriously. (It seems from Conner's account that perhaps six Apaches had been killed.) However, they were not much nearer central Arizona than they had been in October, and it appeared they might spend the rest of their lives maneuvering as they had during the fall. Therefore, Walker told the company they would try a new and very bold plan. By some means he had learned that Mangas Coloradas and a band of his warriors were also in winter quarters—

twenty-five miles to the north at Pinos Altos, a former mining camp which had been abandoned because of repeated Apache raids. Walker proposed to send a small detachment of men there to capture Mangas himself. If successful, they would hold him as a hostage, returning him to the Mimbreño if and when the tribe let them pass unmolested to the west. Conner made absolutely no explanation of why this plan suddenly occurred to Walker. Also, there was no mention of why anyone thought it would work, why, after three months of marching and countermarching aimed at keeping the Apaches at least at rifle-shot distance, they thought they could walk into the stronghold of the Mimbreños and casually seize their chief. However, this is what they did. Walker detailed a dozen men, including Conner, for the raid. They were led by Jack Swilling.

An early historian of Arizona remarked that Swilling was "the typical desperado of the old-time days," and the description seems to be fair. Later in that territory he was to be a miner and rancher. However, he became more famous as a gunslinger, an alcoholic and, by his own admission, a morphine addict. He committed a series of cold-blooded murders, but the community and the law excused them on the grounds that Swilling became homicidal only when he was roaring drunk or under the influence of harder drugs. More important, he killed only Indians, Mexicans and Chinese. However, eventually Swilling robbed a stagecoach with white passengers and gold and for this act was arrested and locked up in the federal prison at Yuma. He died there, it was said, in agony caused by his enforced withdrawal from morphine.

Like many of the western badmen of the latter half of the nineteenth century, Swilling was an embittered ex-Confederate. He had been a lieutenant in the troop Sibley had dispatched to occupy Tucson in 1861. When Carleton's California Column dispersed this force, Swilling simply stopped being a soldier and a Confederate. However, for some reason, perhaps because there was more southern sentiment in Arizona than in Colorado, Swilling did not have to hide and run as did Daniel Conner. In fact, several weeks after the reoccupation of Tucson he was employed by the federal garrison as a civilian teamster. Later he drifted on to New Mexico and joined Walker's expedition shortly after Conner. As further evidence of his peculiar powers of command, Walker, according to Conner's report, had no difficulty controlling Swilling. When the time came to make the raid against Mangas, it is not surprising that he should turn to him, for this was an enterprise, if ever there was one, which called for the skills and nerve of a desperado.

Again with unexplained ease, Swilling and the others found and approached the Apache camp. Swilling left the rest of the men in the

cover of some brush and advanced alone. Mangas and two of his counselors came forward to meet him, while a number of Apache warriors
remained hidden in the rocks nearby. Swilling, wrote Conner, "though
six feet tall, looked like a boy beside Mangas [whose height was reported to be somewhere between six-four and seven feet]." Swilling
reached up and put his hand on the chief's shoulder, and at this signal
Conner and the others rose and trained their rifles on him. Speaking
Spanish, Swilling told Mangas that he was to come with him and if
either he or any of his men made a false move, they were dead. Mangas
dismissed the two warriors with him, saying to them, "Tell my people
to look for me when they see me." The whites then explained Walker's
plan to him: that if the party were allowed to pass safely through the
Mimbreño country, Mangas would then be released. That Mangas,
one of the ablest men the Apaches ever produced, while surrounded by
his own warriors could be taken in this fashion is, to say the least, surprising—so much so that it would seem Conner, who was the only reporter, either did not know the full story or chose not to tell it. Simply
as a guess—but one which fits the circumstances—Walker, the army
or someone may have previously taken hostages important to Mangas,
perhaps a wife or children. Mangas allowed Swilling to approach and
came out to negotiate about these captives.

When Swilling returned to Fort McLane, he found that Colonel
John West, the officer Carleton had assigned to keep an eye on the
Apaches while Carson was conducting the Navajo war, had arrived
with a company of troops. West immediately demanded that the civilians turn Mangas over to him. Having neither means nor perhaps inclination to resist the order, Walker agreed to it. The prospectors and
soldiers camped adjacent to each other, and that night both parties
posted guards to patrol their respective areas. Conner had the midnight
duty and walked his beat along the perimeter of the military camp. He
said that there were six sentries posted, two of whom stood directly
over Mangas. The Apache chief lay by a fire on a blanket, "with his
trinket under his head for a pillow. I noticed," continued Conner, "that
the soldiers were annoying Mangas in some way and they would become quiet and silent when I was about approaching the fire, keep so
until I again walked off in the dark on my beat. . . . I could see them
plainly by the firelight as they were engaged in heating their fixed
bayonets in the fire and putting them to the feet and naked legs of
Mangas. I didn't appreciate this conduct one particle, but said nothing
to them at the time and really I had some curiosity to see to what extent
they would indulge it. . . . I was about midway of my beat and approaching the firelight, just when Mangas raised himself upon his left elbow
and began to expostulate in a vigorous way by telling the sentinels in
Spanish that he was no child to be playing with. But his expostulations

were cut short, for he had hardly begun his exclamation when both sentinels promptly brought down their minnie muskets to bear on him and fired, nearly at the same time through his body."

Conner reported that the next morning, as the men gathered around to view the body of the famous Apache, "A little soldier—calling himself John T. Wright—scalped Mangas with an Arkansas toothpick [bowie knife], borrowed from Bill Lallier, the soldier's cook." Mangas was then buried, but a few nights later the body was exhumed so that the army surgeon, a Dr. Sturgeon, could remove the skull. This, because of its extraordinary size, he later shipped east to a scientific institution.

In his report to the War Department, Colonel West said only that Mangas had been captured and that during the night he had made three attempts to escape. On the final one he was shot by the guards. No mention was made of the prospectors, the scalping or the anthropological interests of Dr. Sturgeon. When Conner read the army's version, he said, and was to continue to insist throughout his life, that it was untrue. Later a member of West's command, Clark Stocking, contributed his own recollection, and it supported Conner. Stocking said that early in the evening Colonel West personally took aside the men who would be on guard duty that night and talked to them about Mangas: "Men, that old murderer has got away from every soldier command and has left a trail of blood for 500 miles on the old stage line. I want him dead or alive tomorrow morning, do you understand, I want him dead."

Arizona

After the death of Mangas, Colonel West sent troops to Pinos Altos, where they killed some twenty Apaches waiting for the return of their chief. While this was happening, Walker quickly moved his men out of Fort McLane, over the Burro Mountains and through the Continental Divide. Though things had not worked according to the original plan, his tactical assessment that Mangas was the key to the situation was correct. Thereafter his party had no particular trouble with the demoralized Mimbreños. They stopped for a time to explore the upper waters of the San Francisco River and then went on to Tucson, where they arrived in April. The Apache wars had reduced this community to a beleaguered population of fewer than 500, and the prospectors were unable to buy supplies there. After staying only a day, they continued on toward the Pima villages located on the Gila River near where Phoenix was to be established later.

The Pimas were an industrious agricultural people who consistently maintained good relations with the whites, principally because they found them useful allies against the Apaches, their hereditary enemies. After bartering for food with the Pimas, Walker led the party up the Hassayampa River in a northeasterly direction. Above the Pima villages they passed into a region occupied by a mixed population of Mojaves and Tonto Apaches, among whom a principal chief was Irotaba (or Iretaba), of the former tribe. After the defeat of the Mojaves by Hoffman's troops whom Walker had guided in 1859, Irotaba had kept a sullen peace with the whites and largely restricted his activities to the east side of the Colorado, where he met few of them. Though not a warrior comparable to Mangas Coloradas, he was regarded as still a clever and potentially dangerous leader. After traveling several days up the Hassayampa, the prospectors encountered Irotaba in person. The chief had with him, along with his wife, a young Mojave (the prospectors named him Charley) who was one of the few members of the tribe who spoke English. With Charley acting as an interpreter, Irotaba stayed with them for a week and proved to be useful, pointing out springs and pastures for their animals. Not far from the present town of Wickenburg, at a good campsite where there was water in the intermittent Hassayampa, Irotaba said he wanted to halt and parley. Standing beside Walker, who had removed his saddle and was using it for a seat, Irotaba, said Conner, "delivered in a yell, a string of gutturals that resounded all through these cañons, gorges and craggy mountain sides. . . . After quite a pause he raised one arm aloft and steadily held it there while his eyes were fixed steadily upon a high object up in the mountain. . . . He stood thus for some moments like some crazy practitioner in witchcraft."

Shortly thereafter some forty Mojave-Apache warriors materialized from the rocks so suddenly that Conner said he did not know "how they came." After getting over their surprise and digesting the fact that they had been under surveillance, probably for as long as they had been following the river, some of the men noted with interest that besides being "black and nearly naked," Irotaba's men were poorly armed. Therefore, one of the prospectors, who apparently represented the majority opinion, announced, "These naked, barbarous wretches sneak out of their holes as insidiously as so many rats, and are not entitled to a consideration more dignified than that which is accorded to the rats and mice about the city livery stable." He went on to say, according to Conner, that "the rifle and six-shooter were the proper implements with which to make such treaties."

Walker, however, was still very much in command. "Here," reported Conner, "our old mountain captain put an end to all objections by quietly saying, 'Be easy, be easy, for the more you become acquainted with these savages, the more you will respect their demands, and we will put off all rifle negotiations as long as possible, for I fear they may come too soon for us at best.' "

Walker made his opinion stick and, after calming his men, commenced making medicine with Irotaba. He said, through Charley (who Conner thought was not an honest interpreter), that they were a peaceful party, hunting gold, for which the Mojaves and Apaches had no use. Their intention was to continue up the Hassayampa, and they would neither provoke hostilities nor do the Indians any harm. In translated reply, Irotaba said that the upper Hassayampa was a terrible place (in fact, it was regarded as prime hunting country) and that he would personally show the whites much better land to the west, along the Colorado River. Walker said that for reasons of their own they wanted to continue along the Hassayampa. Irotaba said that if they did, he and his men might fight. Walker informed him, in effect, so be it, telling Charley to tell Irotaba that "if they begin to steal our mules or shoot our men, we will quit hunting gold and go to hunting Indians."

Irotaba refused to negotiate further, and the matter rested, though the Indians stayed around the camp, peacefully, for the remainder of the day. In the evening they disappeared as suddenly as they had arrived, taking with them, it was later discovered, all of the company's reserves of tobacco—not an inconsiderable loss, the men felt. There being no way they could catch the elusive Indians, the prospectors continued up the Hassayampa, smokeless and ready for rifle negotiations. However, they were left undisturbed for the time being. Ascending feeder streams which flowed down from Spruce Ridge, five miles or so south of the present town of Prescott, they began about May 1, 1863, to find gold in quantities. The prospectors in the crowd were of the opinion that almost anyplace on those tributaries a man could make between $50 and $100 a day from a placer claim.

The discovery was not a lucky one in the sense of being accidental. From the time the men left Colorado nearly nine months before, throughout the duel with Mangas, they had been determined to get into central Arizona. Once there, Walker had led them on a beeline to the high tributaries of the Hassayampa without any dawdling about to prospect elsewhere. Furthermore, Carleton, Benedict and others in New Mexico had been aware the previous summer of the general destination of the expedition and became interested in it, Banta's conspiracy theories notwithstanding, because they believed there was an excellent chance that Walker and his men would find gold. The puzzle is why they had not done so earlier, since in 1861, while proceeding east from California, the party had passed within 100 miles of Spruce Ridge. On that occasion they did not stop to investigate the area, and it took them nearly two years of hard, dangerous travel to get back to it. Neither Conner nor others who left briefer recollections of the expedition dealt directly with this obvious question. The only explanation which appears to fit the circumstances is that after the disappointment on the Little Colorado in the fall of 1861, Walker, who, as Zenas Leonard remarked, "never done anything by halves," became a more interested and better informed prospector. Having learned something about the properties of gold-bearing formations in the Colorado fields, he told the men he could lead them to promising ones on the upper Hassayampa, a district he had visited many years earlier. They trusted him, as so many others had, and their faith was justified in the spring of 1863.

There was another curious and related matter having to do with the founding of the gold fields around Prescott. The only other white reputed to have been previously familiar with that part of the country was Powell Weaver. It was later claimed by others (but not the two principals) that he had been with Walker on the 1833 expedition to California and again with Walker and Ralston in northern Arizona in 1837–38. Even if not, Weaver had drifted into the southwest after the fur trade changed in the late 1830s. He was an often irascible loner on the order of Bill Williams and thereafter became a desert rat, wandering about in southern California, Arizona and adjacent parts of Mexico. Because of his association with Spanish-speaking settlements, he came to be called Paulino—and then Pauline in English. During the six-month journey of the Walker party, rumors of its progress and purpose began to circulate in the outside world. Early in 1863 a group of California prospectors decided to act on them and at Fort Yuma obtained the services of Pauline Weaver as a guide. From there they went to the Pima villages and then also turned up the Hassayampa. Exactly three weeks after Walker's prospectors had made their strike along the streams of Spruce Ridge, Weaver's group arrived in the vicinity of what is now Wickenburg, fifty miles to the southeast, and found gold in paying quantities. Again, they did not flounder about but proceeded more or less directly to the site of their first diggings. Like Walker, Weaver, once he became interested, was apparently able to recall precisely where it was he had seen gold-bearing country long before.

Walker's prospectors were afire to start getting rich. However, as he had with the emigrant caravan in 1843, which was in a similar mood immediately after crossing Walker Pass, their leader restrained them, pointing out that they were by no means home free. The most pressing concern was that they were very low on supplies. (Among other things, Walker who was a habitual pipe smoker must have missed his tobacco.) Their long-range problem was that they were in Indian country, 250 miles from the nearest white settlements and military post. Though they had temporarily outfaced Irotaba, Walker was of the opinion they had not seen the last of him. Also, having ascended high up on the Hassayampa, they had entered country directly under the control of the Tonto Apaches, considered more dangerous than the Mojaves.

They dealt with the supply situation by returning to the Pima villages in the latter part of May and obtaining provisions there. Also, both Walker and Benedict left messages, to be carried east by the first white travelers, for friends and officials in New Mexico. To substantiate the information about the new gold field they had discovered, Walker sent along a sample nugget. After returning to the mountain, the party did some additional exploring and prospecting. Camped in approximately the location of the present courthouse square in Prescott, they had a small encounter with the Apaches which confirmed Walker's warnings that they must continue to be vigilant. While they were cooking their evening meal, several Apaches arrived in, wrote Conner, "very ugly humor and one very black and painted warrior made a savage speech to them." Contemptuously this warrior walked past the whites' cooking fire, kicking at their pots. "Capt. Walker seized him by his long hair and pushed him back with a little petulant order to stay out of the way. He leaned toward the Captain and brought a deep prolonged 'ugh' as though much insulted." There was, however, no more trouble at that time.

On the eastern side of Spruce Ridge, they found what seemed to be even better gold prospects along a stream they named the Lynx because one of the men was jumped by a cat there. Hunting, water and forage were good in the area, and it was a defensible spot. A permanent camp, which was immediately named Walker, was established there. They then commenced to organize themselves as a governing body for the new mining district. Unanimously Walker was nominated as the "President" of the community, but he declined the job. However, he remained indisputably in command of the party and, rather than relax discipline, increased it, a remarkable accomplishment considering that the men were fairly twitching with gold fever. "With implicit confidence in the judgment and prudence of Captain Walker," wrote Conner in a passage that might have been taken from Leonard's journal of thirty years earlier, "the men obeyed his orders without question under any and all circumstances. To be sure of the safety of the animals of the herd, extraordinary precautions were observed by having six men always on guard—day and night. . . . This work—added to all other camp duties—made up a continuous round of never-ending labor—extremely nervous —yet all accomplished without friction or impatience."

Though the residents of the fortified camp did not know it, assistance and reinforcements were on the way. The letters which Benedict and Walker sent from the Pima villages arrived in New Mexico in June and created an immediate sensation. Benedict had written directly to his uncle Kirby, then the chief federal judge in the territory. Kirby Benedict resigned from the bench and organized a company to exploit the discoveries in Arizona. No less enthusiastic (and a clandestine investor in Benedict's enterprise) was General James Carleton. He immediately sent a dispatch to Washington addressed to Major General Henry Halleck, the chief of staff of all Union military forces. He told

Halleck that the Arizona country was "teeming with millions on millions of wealth," which would inestimably benefit the entire war effort. Also, suggested Carleton, since his territory had suddenly become such a valuable one, it would be appropriate if his command were increased:

> If I only had one more good regiment of California Infantry, composed, as that infantry is, of practical miners, I would place it in the Gila country. While it would exterminate the Indians, who are a scourge to New Mexico, it would protect people who might wish to go there to open up the country, and would virtually be a military colony when the war ended, whose interests would lead the officers and soldiers to remain in the New El Dorado.

Then Carleton wrote to Walker, calling him "My dear Captain." Congratulating him on the "wonderful discovery" he and his men had made, Carleton diffidently asked him—"if you can do so"—to return to Santa Fe and guide federal troops and surveyors to the new diggings. (Walker did not, but there were never any hard feelings about the matter.) Carleton went on to say that the Navajo campaign was going so nicely that Walker and his men did not have to worry about that tribe raiding in their direction. Also by way of assistance, Carleton said he was establishing a new fort, Canby, on the New Mexico-Arizona border, which he suggested would be the easiest place for "your people to get supplies. . . . The sutler there will doubtless have a large stock of goods, and I will tell him about keeping on hand such articles of prime necessity as you all might require. I send you a map of the country, so that you may know about where Fort Canby will be situated."

Then Carleton rather coyly added, "I send you another similar map, on which you can trace your new gold fields." The General concluded:

> If I can be of any service to yourself or party, it will afford me pleasure to help you. If I can help others to a fortune, it will afford me not quite as much happiness as finding one myself, it is true—but nearly as much. My luck has always been not to be at the right place at the right time for fortunes. I have been a little too far ahead, or else a little too much behind, for that. Yourself and your party deserve success for your industry and perseverance. Hoping that each of you will receive abundant reward for your past toil and hardships and danger, I am, captain, very respectfully, Your Obedient Servant, James H. Carleton, Brigadier-General, Commanding.

Nothing in either the contents or the tone of Carleton's long, effusive letter suggests Walker, Banta's Confederate General of the West, had aroused in Carleton anything except avarice.

As promised, Carleton dispatched a small detachment of troops to the new diggings, but without a guide they became lost and did not arrive until midsummer. Near Prescott they established a permanent bivouac, which later became Fort Whipple, but the nature of the country was such that they were largely occupied in maintaining themselves. Walker, at least, had a poor opinion of their abilities as Indian fighters. On one occasion, when he was going off on a reconnaissance of his own, he left Conner and several other of his men, camped with some soldiers, to guard his mules. Before leaving, he "warned us privately not to trust our mules with the soldier's herd . . . that the soldiers were too d--ned careless and then he continued to say that Uncle Sam was better able to lose his stock than our party, and that on his return, if he found us alive, he wanted [to] find those mules safe also." When he returned, the men and mules were in good order. Conner was pleased to report that they had indeed been raided by the Apaches. Alert, as they had been taught to be, the civilians had kept their stock safe from the Indians, but the soldiers, asleep or otherwise occupied in their tents, had lost a dozen animals.

Through the fall and early winter of 1863, while Walker continued to command the camp, its population was increased by the arrival of the first gold rushers from elsewhere. By Christmas time there were so many newcomers that there was no need or way to maintain the semi-military arrangements. Walker relinquished his responsibilities with apparent relief and, in doing so, delivered one of the crust-breaking comments for which, through long experience, he had developed a nice touch. "Captain Walker," recalled Conner, "was delighted and disbanded the expedition [the thirty-seven men who had been under his direct authority] with the remark that—'We opened the door and held it open to civilization, and now civilization will do the rest.' "

The Congress established Arizona as a territory, separate from New Mexico, in February 1863. During the months following, President Lincoln appointed a set of officials for it: a governor, John Goodwin; three federal judges, Joseph Allyn, William Howell and William Turner; a secretary of state, an attorney general, a surveyor, an Indian superintendent, a marshal and some lesser officeholders. These dignitaries, accompanied by military escorts, left Missouri in October 1863. Originally their intention was to make Tucson the seat of territorial government, but the excitement caused by Walker's new El Dorado caused them to change this plan. (By the end of 1863 there were 1,000 residents in the vicinity of the diggings, which only a year before had been unexplored.) Therefore, it was decided that Prescott— which officially became such in May 1864—should be territorial capital. After a slow trip Governor Goodwin and civil authority arrived there on January 17, 1864.

Civilization was a different matter. Even in comparison with other early mining communities, the camps around Prescott were rough and wretched. Among other things, the place was permeated by racism of the most blatant and vicious sort. Included in the first ordinances passed by the miner-citizens was one which prohibited "Asiatics and Senoranians [i.e., Mexicans]" from filing claims, working or living in the district. This was later amended because the exclusion of the latter proved inconvenient, both Mexican laborers and traders being useful to the miners. Therefore, a committee was established to determine "who are and who are not Mexicans." Desirable "Senoranians" were certified as Spanish.

The bigotry was at least even-handed. A prospector identified by Conner only as Tat came into a local saloon one evening and found some of the black soldiers who were stationed at Fort Whipple. He requested that they "pull off their hats and drink 'like Niggers all ought to do.'" Thereupon he pulled out a gun and with it killed one of the troopers. Tat escaped Prescott but was later murdered in Tucson by, it was generally believed, another soldier. The attitudes and behavior of the early miners became traditional in Prescott, which well into the twentieth century prided itself, informally, on being the "Only white man's town in Arizona."

The situation with the Indians was worse. After the original expedition had disbanded, Conner remarked that "the Indians discovered that there was not a Capt. Walker at the head of all this immigration." Conner's meaning was that without the frontier wisdom of Walker, the whites began to suffer from Indian depredations, but in fact, it was the tribes who suffered more than the whites from the lack of a Walker. The Tontos were neither sufficiently numerous nor well organized to mount a frontal assault. However, they commenced to harass the camps and occasionally to pick off their residents. Among the whites, public opinion became solidly genocidal. Given the spirit of the place, it would probably have been the same even if the Apaches had made no forays. Conner, who was more liberal-minded than most, casually remarked that "it was a rigid rule all over the country to shoot these savages on sight." *The Arizona Miner*, a weekly newspaper established in Prescott in 1864, put the matter succinctly in an editorial: "We see no other remedy—than to exterminate nearly if not the whole race of savages on the Pacific coast, and the sooner this is accomplished the better for the whole country."

The *Miner* during the mid-1860s was one of the most bellicose journals ever published in this country. Beyond the Indians themselves, the editors of the paper were constantly and greatly exercised by Eastern humanitarians and liberal "picture magazines [*Harper's Weekly* was a frequent target for their invective] who theorize about the 'principles of humanity,' and indulge in speculative dreams concerning the 'gradual civilization' of the noble red man." The *Miner* was particularly fearful that "humanitarian twaddle" would restrict the military and bring about situations in which "If an Indian scalps an American soldier, outrages and then burns at the stake an American woman, or brains an American baby, [the government will] give him some beads and a new scalping knife, and let him go. It is this sort of tomfoolery that costs the lives of so many innocent women and children and brave soldiers every year." The *Miner* concluded: "The Indian race has served its day and generation, and will eventually be studied upon earth as an extinct species of man, as naturalists now study the Saurians and reptiles of the Jurassic age, among animals. They ought soon to be exterminated."

There were few early issues of the *Miner* in which there were not accounts of violent encounters with the local Indians. These communiqués were of two general types. One standard report had to do with a miner, or two or three of them, valiantly dispatching a dozen or more Apache warriors. However, their efforts never seemed to be enough, for the other common class of stories in the *Miner* was accounts of bloodthirsty savages massacring peaceful whites. The great majority of the victims were single women and children. Cumulatively the *Miner* reports suggest that northern Arizona was inhabited by thousands of Apache males and at least as many white women—mostly blond virgins—and infants.

In reality, there were probably no more than 500 Indians, of all ages and sexes, in the vicinity of Prescott, and hunting them down became something of a blood sport, the pleasures of which were enhanced by the conviction that bagging savages contributed to the spread of civilization. Jack Swilling was to build on his reputation as a desperado by killing Apaches around Prescott, but another member of the former Walker party, King Woolsey, an Alabaman of small stature but vicious spirit, was to become the most famous and respectable Indian fighter. His most notable victory was in 1864, when, under the guise of conducting peace negotiations, he presented a band of Apaches with a present of flour which had been laced with strychnine. Though the subsequent body count could not be exactly determined, it was generally thought that twenty-four of the savages were eliminated in this fashion. Woolsey was thereafter known as Colonel and became a considerable local hero.

As had been so often the case, Walker, having "opened the door" for civilization, seemed to lose interest in the Arizona settlements which he had made possible. He kept a cabin on Lynx Creek but after 1864 used it as a layover place between his travels, which once again became his principal activity. In the summer of 1864 he guided Governor Goodwin and other territorial officials on a tour of the Little Colorado basin. Later in the year he went back to California and spent several months at Manzanita Ranch. Returning to Prescott, he made a series of private explorations, accompanied by Conner and some other of the more inquisitive of his "old" men. On the most extensive of these outings, he again visited the country along the south rim of the Grand Canyon, a wilderness about which he had been insatiably curious since the 1830s. During this trip the small party had some minor trouble with the Apaches but extricated themselves by means of the old frontier skills rather than the new ones, such as King Woolsey was devising.

In regard to the Indians, it is difficult to imagine Walker being in sympathy with the murderous opinions and practices that prevailed in Prescott. However, his fame was such that he was permitted certain eccentricities in this regard. When he was in the area, he was treated reverently as the grand old man of Arizona. To have come with him into the country in '63 was a matter of considerable status in the community, so much so that, as Conner sarcastically commented, a good many hundreds of people, beyond the original thirty-seven, were, as time passed, to claim this honor.

Shortly after they had arrived, Governor Goodwin and Justice Allyn, among others, made a courtesy call on Prescott's living legend. Allyn was a diarist and recorded the occasion: "Six miles of climbing brought us to Captain Walker's camp. . . . After resting a few minutes, we started to call on Capt. Walker, whose cabin was across the creek a short distance. I had met the old gentleman before at the post when I first arrived, and he greeted me kindly. Presenting the rest of our party to him, we entered his cabin, and after a toddy the conversation became brisk."

Allyn said Walker reminded him more of Gideon Welles, the Secretary of Navy in the Lincoln cabinet, "than any man I have ever seen; he has the same beard, wears glasses, and his height and build is that of Mr. Welles. In manner he is not unlike him. Capt. W. has spent his life in the mountains, and knows them as well, if not better, than any man living. His memory is wonderful of the geography and topography of portions of the country he has not seen for thirty years." A few months later Allyn was to meet Walker and Pauline Weaver together and, in a letter home, comparatively commented about the two historic mountaineers: "I have described Capt. Walker to you before: a cool, reticent, courteous man, careful what he says, and impatient of contradiction. Captain Weaver, from California, a man older than Walker [in fact he was two years younger] . . . is the opposite of Walker in every respect; garrulous to a fault, tells large stories until he has the reputation of a sort of Arizona Münchhausen, impulsive, and with a failing memory."

As time passed, making ceremonial visits and references to these pioneers became *de rigueur* for Arizona politicians. One of them was Richard McCormick, who replaced Goodwin as governor and, in this capacity, delivered a rousing Fourth of July address in 1866. He thought better (or thought it was politic to appear to do so) of Weaver than did Justice Allyn, and in his address he jointly extolled the two old mountain men as the Washington and Jefferson of the territory.

"Walker and Weaver had crossed and recrossed the continent, trapped on every stream, bartered and fought with every tribe of Indians, and imperilled their lives a hundred times, before Frémont had left Charleston College," orated McCormick, making a comparison that must have especially pleased Walker. "The real pioneer is seldom a man of words or seeker for notoriety. I have for several years been anxious to obtain from our own most noted pioneers, Walker and Weaver, the story of their eventful lives, and I am satisfied that few explorers have experiences so rich in interesting incident and valuable observation, or ones more worthy of public preservation."

Governor McCormick was forced to conclude rather lamely, saying that in regard to the biographies of the two famous pioneers, he had "succeeded to this time in obtaining only the merest outline of the same." He was never able to advance this historical project, for shortly Pauline Weaver died and Walker left Arizona for good, thus frustrating the governor, as he had so many other inquiring reporters.

Manzanita Ranch

The lives of an inordinate number of the leaders and heroes of the westering movement ended badly. Some died young, violently and with little dignity. More, in a sense, lived too long, so long that their skills and experiences became irrelevant and their accomplishments and glories were forgotten or ignored. They lingered on as relict curiosities or embittered misfits unable to cope with the passing of the frontier, the values and way of life that it had permitted and encouraged. Meriwether Lewis, who of all of them was perhaps most haunted by the sense that the opening of the West was both a glorious and a tragic happening, was murdered by land pirates or committed suicide in a hovel on the Natchez Trace when he was thirty-five years old, only two years after he had returned from his single great exploration. Charles Preuss, the able pessimist who did so much of Frémont's cartographic work, hanged himself on an apple tree in the suburbs of Washington because, wrote Jessie Frémont, "his glad, free days in the open were over." At forty years of age, at Fort Laramie, Lucien Fontenelle, the AFC partisan who led Bonneville such a merry chase in the 1830s, died either directly by his own hand or as a result of *mania a potu* ("drunken madness"). Jed Smith, Henry Vanderburgh and Henry Fraeb were cut down in their primes because they became too careless and arrogant in their dealings with the Indians. Jim Beckwourth, the blood brother of the Crows, lived on until after the Civil War but was reduced to cadging drinks in Denver dives. He made a final trip back to the Absaroka, but there it is thought he was executed, as was Bill Williams, and for the same reason, because his former people were convinced that he had betrayed them.

Jim Bridger was ignominiously driven from his trading post in Utah by the Mormons, having to hide two days in the brush to escape the irate Saints. Thereafter he scouted occasionally for the cavalry but was increasingly treated as a figure of fun by younger officers who teased him into telling what they regarded as his tall stories. He spent his last years in a small house in Kansas City, nearly blind, pottering about the neighborhood with a stick, or, as recalled a compassionate neighbor girl, "He would sit on the porch, resting his chin on his cane, with his face towards the West—a lonely figure. He liked to talk about his life on the Plains, and I remember his saying once, at a time when his eyesight was almost gone, 'I wish I was back there among the mountains again—you can see so much farther in that country.' "

Joe Meek, the blithe spirit of the mountain men, held minor political offices in Oregon but came to despise white society for the way it discriminated against his Nez Percé wife and their children. He died in poverty and bitterness. Charles Bent, newly appointed territorial governor of New Mexico, was dragged from his house, killed and scalped in the street during the brief Taos revolt. William Bent, in either a fit of rage or melancholy, burned down the great adobe fort-castle he and his brother had built on the upper Arkansas. Later his sons by his beloved Cheyenne wife were hunted down as renegades, while Bent himself was kept under military guard so that he could not warn either them or the Cheyenne of the impending Sand Creek massacre.

Lansford Hastings, the confidence man of the emigration, died while trying to establish a colony of unreconstructed Confederates in Brazil. The courageous Alex Godey, who had crossed the Sierra with Walker in 1833 and was the only hero of Frémont's debacle in 1848, retired from the mountains to Sacramento. There, while watching a traveling circus, he was scratched by a caged tiger and died of blood poisoning. Daniel Conner worked for many years as a maintenance man in a small California town. After he was fired from that job and until the end of his life—he lived until 1920—he tried to support himself by selling accounts of the adventures he had had fifty years before in New Mexico and Arizona.

Perhaps the longest and saddest decline of all was suffered by John Charles Frémont, who more than any of the others had hoped to be the American Hero. For a time he was able to trade (as did others) on his reputation as the Pathfinder. When California became a state, he was appointed a U.S. senator. He ran as a presidential candidate on a splinter Republican ticket in 1856 and again in 1864. During the Civil War he was reinstated in the army as a major general. He made a fortune in real estate. But he was always undone by the flaws of character which were his fate. He never won an election or a battle, lost his fortune and was removed from his Civil War command, came to be generally regarded as a conniving politician, an unscrupulous speculator and an incompetent, timid soldier. He died old, alone and destitute in a Manhattan boardinghouse, where he had been attempting to earn a living as a hack writer.

There were, of course, exceptions—William Clark, William Ashley, Zenas Leonard, James Clyman, Benjamin Bonneville—men who retained their dignity and the respect of others until the end. Walker, as in so many other matters, was among the most notable of them. He was active on the frontier for longer than any but, as a result of good sense and luck, was able to leave it at a time and in a manner of his own choosing. He spent his last years about as well as a man can hope to: in good health, except for failing eyesight; in comfortable circumstances; surrounded by a loving family and friends; widely honored and respected for how he had lived and what he had accomplished.

Walker stayed in Arizona until the summer of 1867, when he made his final wilderness trip, accompanied only by Daniel Conner. The two of them traveled north toward the Grand Canyon and then, needing supplies, continued on to La Paz, a river port on the Colorado. A small incident occurred in La Paz which Walker found embarrassing. Having bought hay for their mules from an Indian, he paid with what looked to him, with his fuzzy eyesight, to be a silver dollar. However, later examining his purse, he found that he had in fact given a $20 gold piece. Therefore, he went in search of the hay seller. When he found him, the Indian readily gave up the coin, saying, wrote Conner, "Me know it, too much-e—me no steal—me no want to steal." This relative facility with English caught Walker's attention, and he finally recognized the man as the young Mojave who had served as Irotaba's interpreter in 1863. Walker brought up the subject of their last meeting.

"Charley, you know me?"

"Yes, yes, me know Captain Walker."

"Well, Charley, I thought you said that you didn't steal. I suppose you have forgotten that you and Irotaba and the black warrior and squaw stole our smoking tobacco on the night you all slipped off from us on the Haviamp?" Charley protested that the others, not he, had taken the tobacco. The exchange was a good-humored one, and they parted friends.

Shortly after they had left La Paz, heading back to Prescott, Conner suffered a painful camp accident, badly gashing his foot with an ax. A day or so later his mule strayed and, though limping, he went after it because Walker could not see well enough to trail the animal. Conner discovered that the mule had been picked up by a small band of Mexican *pistoleros* who were waiting a short distance from camp to waylay whoever came after the animal. The bandits were from Sonora and had ridden north for a bit of rustling in the Anglo mining camps. When Conner caught up with them, they were not particularly alarmed by a gringo on only one good foot. Their initial inclination was to keep the mule, take anything else Conner had of value and dispatch him. However, Conner gave them pause by pointing out that in a fracas it was most likely that one of them would at least be wounded, that encumbered and incapacitated, the robbers would have to travel slowly, that they would probably never make it back to Sonora because he had a party of well-armed friends nearby who would ride them down and avenge him. To dramatize this bluff, Conner pulled out his pistol and fired a warning shot, hoping for the best.

Walker's vision was poor, but his instincts were still good. He sent off a volley of rifle fire in the general direction of the commotion, and it was enough to make the bandits accept Conner's bluff. Without discovering that the support party consisted of one, nearly blind old man, they returned the mule and rode off in the opposite direction. "His timely shot was all that saved me," a grateful Conner later wrote in his report of the encounter. Back in their camp, Walker told Conner that "the little incident caused him more trouble for a short time than any other had for years. To send me [Conner] on so uncertain an errand with such an ugly wound and yet be unable to go himself he considered a very unsatisfactory state of affairs."

They rode back, without further incident, to the Prescott camps, and Conner received treatment for his lacerated foot. Walker, proud and pragmatic to the end, decided that if he could not see well enough to make change or fend off a few horse thieves, the time had come to retire. While he was winding up his business in Prescott, there arrived a San Francisco newspaperman who had set out some weeks before to report on the gold fields. The man had had a harrowing experience. Entering Arizona, he lost his way and wandered for eight days, finding only grass to eat and dew to drink. Finally, choking on his thirst-swollen tongue, raving from exhaustion and panic, he stumbled into an Apache camp. The Indians assumed the journalist was demented. This was fortunate for him since the Apaches were traditionally solicitous of lunatics. They fed him and, after he had rested, sent him on his way to the mining camps. In Prescott the journalist recovered physically, but he was extremely eager to leave Arizona as soon as he could find somebody to show him the way. Walker, having completed his arrangements, agreed to take the man with him. Daniel Conner, his foot partially healed, escorted his old leader on the first leg of his last journey. Sadly Conner parted from him at the crossing of the Colorado, saying, of his Captain and friend, that "this was the kindest man I ever knew."

From the Colorado, Walker, accompanied by the shaken journalist, continued westward through the Mojave, following trails he could no longer clearly see but had known longer and better than any other white man. It was a fitting mode of departure, for he left this small remaining piece of the frontier as he had entered the great wilderness fifty years before—as a guide. The journalist never got around to writing this particular story, and he presumedly took public transportation as soon as they found any. However, Walker had stock with him and rode on up the San Joaquin Valley toward Manzanita Ranch, the family base. He arrived there for the last time in the late fall of 1867.

Manzanita Ranch was located on the northwestern slopes of Mount Diablo in Contra Costa County, the across-the-bay region east of San Francisco. By the time Walker returned to it the family holding, in addition to the 1,500 deeded acres, included grazing rights to several thousand more acres of adjacent open range. There were stands of pine in the upper pastures, while below, a series of prairielike benches and gentle valleys were set with groves of oak and manzanita. This parkland extended northward to Suisun Bay, a complex of marshy lagoons below the junction of the San Joaquin with the Sacramento. The land was well watered by springs and from streams flowing down Diablo. The sea fogs did not usually rise so high as the upland ranch, but it was close enough to the coast to benefit from the moderating ocean breezes. The air was clear, and the sun warm almost all the year. Practically and in a sense metaphorically, this across-the-bay country made a very appropriate retirement place for a man like Joe Walker, of a sort that many old frontiersmen deserved but very few found.

Even today in suburban residential neighborhoods, on some of the remaining agricultural lands, along occasional undeveloped sections of the waterfront, an attractive tawny sheen gilds this country. A century ago, from midsummer, when the grasses, oak foliage and marsh sedges began to harden, until spring, when the new growth appeared, much of Contra Costa must have been of a soft golden cast, peculiarly suited in a symbolic way for this particular place. For three centuries Americans, generically speaking, had been yearning for and struggling toward the Ultimate West. As they did so, they invariably colored it gold on the maps of their imaginations: the golden cities of Cíbola, the lost mountain of gold, golden fields of grain, golden eagles, ages, spikes, gates and girls. Located on the extremity of the continent, hard against the Pacific and directly under the setting sun, bountifully endowed and prettily tinted by nature, the across-the-bay country into which Walker rode to retire came as close to approximating the mythic True Golden West as any place ever did or probably ever will.

Manzanita Ranch, which the family commenced acquiring in the 1850s, was one of the showplaces of the area largely because of the efforts of James Walker, the "young Jeemes" of the emigrant trails. While developing it, he employed six full-time plowmen to break and disk the valley land and turn it into grain fields. When they arrived in the Missouri wilderness with a bundle of apple scions, the Walkers had a reputation as being knowledgeable orchardists, and James continued this tradition. Sending wagons south, he obtained apple, peach and walnut trees and grape cuttings from the old Spanish mission gardens below San Jose. These plantations flourished, and later a small winery, the first in Contra Costa County, was built on the property. However, it remained principally a stock ranch. There were hogpens and sheepfolds, 100 head of Walker cattle and fifty horses grazing on the Diablo pastures. The range animals bore a curious brand, the outline of a drawn Cherokee bow. It had been designed in Tennessee and was carried across the continent on the flanks of Walker stock.

The first house on the property was a double log cabin, similar in design to those which other Walkers had put up in the Appalachians and Missouri. However, when the ranch prospered, James built a larger grander family home, a more western-style place with a veranda facing Suisun Bay. After the new house had been completed, the original cabin and several other bunkrooms were used for the help: cowboys, orchard workers, mechanics and a Chinese cook, Charley. Two of the hands, Feliz Pena and Pete Carpenter, are remembered by name. Both had interesting histories closely tied to that of the family.

Pena was an Indian, probably a Papago or Yaqui. He had been stolen as a child by raiding Apaches and sold as a slave in Santa Fe. In 1851 he somehow came to the attention of Walker and his nephew James, who arrived in that town after concluding their explorations in the country between the Colorado and Rio Grande. Pena told them that his owner was a cruel man and that his own life was a miserable, painful one. He begged the gringos to take him with them, promising that he would be a good and faithful worker. The Walkers were moved by his story and either bought or simply liberated Pena. He went on with James to Missouri and the next year made the trip with the family to Contra Costa. There he married a woman from one of the California tribes, reared a family on Manzanita Ranch and remained with the Walkers, as a free man, for the rest of his life.

The man who was called Pete Carpenter while he lived with and worked for the Walkers was in fact a Chouteau, a member of the great Franco-American merchant clan. The Chouteaus made their start in the fur trade in the eighteenth century and expanded their activities until, by the 1830s, they were the most affluent and influential family in St. Louis. Like other furmen, the Chouteaus, when amongst the tribes, had taken Indian women but, unlike many of their Anglo colleagues, regarded them as concubines or "country wives," in a phrase of the time. When it came time to make real marriages, they found wives in the polite, usually Gallic society of St. Louis or New Orleans. However, because of tribal liaisons of which no particular secret was made, there were many Chouteaus, by name and otherwise, of mixed color scattered throughout the Mississippi and Missouri valleys.

Though he became a nonperson so far as the family was concerned, Pete Carpenter was the son of Pierre Chouteau, who, as the head of the clan in the mid-nineteenth century, bought the western division of the American Fur Company and became one of the first indigenous St. Louis millionaires. Pete (very likely christened Pierre) was apparently a wild young man who spent much of his time in the Indian country of Oklahoma living with the Osage, among whom he had blood relations. Sometime in the 1870s at a drunken frolic he killed, or so he thought, one of his red kinsmen in a knife fight over a girl. With the help of his powerful white family he was able to escape before either the law or revengeful tribesmen caught him. To protect himself and the Chouteau name, he was sent—as Pete Carpenter—directly to California and the Walkers, who had been acquainted with the Chouteaus for nearly half a century. Ironically, Carpenter was later to learn the man he thought he had murdered in Oklahoma had in fact recovered, and the only charge against him was brawling, regarded then as a trivial offense. However, Carpenter retained the alias and after a time left Manzanita Ranch, married and settled down to become a respectable California citizen. Except for the Walkers, nobody was aware of Carpenter's true identity while he lived. However, after his death a daughter, having had hints or sensing that there was some mystery about the origins of her father, became interested in solving it. Eventually she came to the descendants of James Walker, among whom the story of Pete Carpenter had survived and was treated as a confidential matter. Since none of the principals was then living, the daughter was told who her father had been and why he had come to California.

James Walker and his wife, Mary (a Vaughan, whose people had also come from Tennessee by way of Missouri), had three children, John, Barbara and Josephine. As an indication of how well Manzanita Ranch was doing, a young New England woman, Flora Kendall, was added to the household after the children were of a suitable age. She was a well-educated, apparently spirited but impecunious woman who had gone west to improve her position and seek adventure. Miss Kendall's status at the ranch was somewhere between that of an employee and permanent houseguest, and her function was to tutor the children and give them music lessons until they were old enough to go off to a private military school or female seminary.

The youngest daughter, Josie, was named after her famous uncle, who, after he returned from Arizona to live permanently at the ranch, served and was remembered by the children as a surrogate grandfather. They took walks together about the property, the two little girls each holding one of his big hands, sat by his chair on the veranda as he gravely discoursed on subjects suitable for young ears. When he came in from the frontier for good, he put aside the exotic beaded and embroidered buckskins he had customarily worn there and dressed usually in a suit with a high-collared shirt and tie, as was appropriate for a gentleman of the settlements. It was also remembered he spent many hours on the porch with a book, his vision, no longer suitable for the wilderness, being sufficient for reading with the aid of spectacles.

Barbara Walker, Sam's widow and James's mother, was also a permanent resident at the ranch. Her daughters, Annie and Jane, who had made the overland crossing from Missouri in 1852, remained in their brother's household until they married and then settled nearby. Frank McClellan and his family had their own ranch only five miles from Manzanita. Across the Sacramento in Napa County, Joel Walker and his sons and daughters had establishments equal in size and prosperity. All in all, there were about 100 Walkers, McClellans and Toomys living along the river, and they made frequent visits, some lasting for several months, back and forth between their respective homes. The veranda of the Manzanita ranch house was a favorite gathering place, and on it was a sheltered corner where the elders of the clan—Joel, Joe and their sister-in-law Barbara—could sit, take the sun, talk and smoke. (Like many Appalachian-bred women of her day, Barbara Walker enjoyed her pipe as much as any man.) Only vague, many times handed-down accounts of the stories they told survive, but the conversations must have been remarkable. Even then it would have been difficult—and very shortly impossible—to bring together three people who had done so much pioneering as these Walkers. They had been children together at the turn of the nineteenth century in Tennessee, playing on the outfields of a blockhouse built as protection against Shawnee and Cherokee raiders. Thereafter they had spent most of their lives westering, had persevered and come finally into a place and circumstances very close to the visionary ones which had lured thousands of their contemporaries westward—and some hundreds of them to early graves.

They are so long gone and said so little about themselves when they were alive that they cannot be remembered idiosyncratically: what they looked like; how their voices sounded; what, as they recollected their experiences, made them laugh; which of their acomplishments they were proudest of or what they regretted. But even in the abstract there is something inexpressibly poignant about the thought of these three old people sitting on the sunny porch of a fine ranch house, overlooking a beautiful property in the farthest corner of the most Golden West. It is as if they are figures appearing at the end of a long, sometimes confusing and violent dream, who signify that it has a happy and triumphant ending.

Both Joel and Barbara Walker received considerable public attention for being among the last and most admirable of the surviving pioneers, but perhaps less than they deserved or would have had not "Captain Uncle Jo" been such a great celebrity. "The name of Captain Walker is known in every household in the state," editorialized a no doubt exaggerative journalist, who was among a number of the same calling who visited and respectfully recorded his impressions of the old Frontier Hero. The last of these interviewers, a correspondent for the *Napa County Reporter* by the name of George Gift, appeared in August 1876. The better to carry out his assignment or to save on expenses, Gift camped out for several days at Manzanita Ranch. Between sessions with the Captain he very much enjoyed the attractive place and the hospitality of James Walker.

There never was—and perhaps never will be again—in the United States such a good year as 1876 for historical journalism, which is what Gift had in mind. During the Centennial, reflections about and pride in the national accomplishments were general. There were virtually no doubts, such as those which would surface by the Bicentennial, about the propriety of what had been done or the prospects for the future. Historic euphoria was rampant, especially in the West, where the memory of the glorious conquest of the continent was very fresh and often personal. George Gift also had what journalists now call a current news peg as a reason for the interview. A few weeks previously the Sioux and Cheyenne had rubbed out General George Armstrong Custer and 225 of his troopers in Montana. This was by far the biggest news story of the Centennial summer, but it was treated as an accidental disaster—on the order of a terrible train wreck or tornado—not as a serious national setback or crisis. By then everybody, including Sitting Bull and Crazy Horse, knew who had won the West. Custer's calamity simply drew a thrilling red line of emphasis under the self-congratulatory mood of the year and served as a reminder of the great risks which had been so boldly taken during the first century. To tie his local story into this national one, Gift asked Captain Walker, renowned among other things for his prowess as an Indian fighter, what he thought about recent events on the Little Bighorn.

Walker said that they were not surprising since for as long as he could remember, federal troops had performed indifferently on the plains. "Soldiers," he remarked, "are well enough to mount guard and to make a show on dress parade but are poor things when Indians are to be fought." (In the west before the Civil War the frontier irregulars had contemptuously called the soldiers Neddy boys—*Ned* being the country word for pig—and laughed at them because they were so dependent upon their slow-moving supply wagons and wretched salt pork.) As for the Sioux, whom various military and political analysts had suddenly begun touting as the world's best light cavalry, Walker was also skeptical. "They are numerous and therein only are they formidable," he told the interviewer. "I have always considered them as inferior to many other tribes, man to man. They will fight, but still they are not to be feared by men who understand Indian fighting, if the numbers are anything like equal. I have fought better Indians than the Sioux, with the odds five to one against me, and the position of their own choosing." He concluded by making a small joke, using an expression from the middle border of the Appalachians. "I still wear my hair," he pointed out to the journalist by way of establishing his credentials in the matter. There were so many Indians for him to remember: William Weatherford and his Red Sticks at Horseshoe Bend; Francisco Largo on the Cimarron; the Blackfeet interrupting the game of old sledge on the Madison; the primitive, always troublesome Paiutes at the Humboldt Sink; Walkara's Ute raiders; the gentle Moqui; the Sioux on the buffalo range who had lifted Henry Fraeb's hair when he became careless; and the Snakes, his own people.

Having disposed, so to speak, of General Custer, Gift brought up another sometime military man, John Charles Frémont, who remained a figure of interest and controversy in California. The name of the man he had so long and thoroughly despised could still strike sparks. "Frémont," Walker scoffed. "They tell me that Stonewall Jackson whipped him in a battle; it was no credit to him for an old Squaw could whip Frémont."

Thereafter the interview trailed off, and by evidence of what he later wrote, Gift was reduced to ticking off episodes in his subject's career which he would briefly confirm or deny. The writer later apologized to his readers for the lack of traditional tales of glory and gore by explaining that "the old chief was too feeble to talk much." However, as his previous sharp comments about the federal military, Indian warfare and Frémont indicated, Walker had not completely sunk into mumbling senility. Gift was simply brought up short, as so many other would-be storytellers had been, by Walker's refusal to contribute to frontier fictions which were already replacing the facts.

The correspondent dealt with the difficulty as other scribes had. He remarked that while Captain Walker was "probably the most distinguished of the mountaineers who had become famous for their western explorations," these were so numerous that for the moment he could only list them. Sometime, the hero permitting, Gift hoped to treat them in the detail they deserved. The writer never got a chance to do so. Walker died on October 27, 1876, at Manzanita Ranch, from nothing more or less, it seems, than having lived long enough. The notes the last interviewer had made served as the basis for a front-page obituary, which appeared in the *Napa Reporter* and was widely copied by other papers in California, Arizona and New Mexico.

Walker was buried at Martinez, the Contra Costa County seat, in a plot which James Walker had purchased the year before in Alhambra Cemetery. It is located on a hill above Suisun Bay, very nearly the westernmost point in the United States where a man could then be laid to final rest. Shortly after the burial James Walker set a headstone on his Captain Uncle Jo's grave. It was inscribed as the deceased had directed and constituted as much of a biographical statement as he is ever known to have made. It read:

BORN IN ROAN COUNTY, TENN—DEC 13, 1798
EMIGRATED TO MO—1819
TO NEW MEXICO—1820
ROCKY MOUNTAINS—1832
CALIFORNIA—1833
CAMPED AT YOSEMITE—NOV. 13, 1833

Only a man of strong historic sense and pride could have ordered such an epitaph. He had done this and that, had the sort of adventures that people had always been trying to get him to yarn about. But when it came to the end and was time to write on stone, Walker was certain about what had been important. He had made, sometimes led, the great westward hop, skip and jump of the American people from the Appalachian ridges to the True West.

In the last line he did permit himself a bit of personal comment, but even that was so restrained as to be almost unrecognizable as a brag. He did not add, as most would have, that he was the very first to see that marvelous valley of the Sierra which may still be the most wondrous one we have. There is a feeling that Walker presumed that anyone who had a sense of history would be able to imagine what it must have been like to camp at Yosemite in the fall of 1833. Therefore, people could form some notion of the kind of man he had been and what was important to him.

THE END

Addendum: Of Dreams

I am not a believer in tales about, much less in the existence of, conventional ghosts—wispy beings who hang about graveyards, attics and basements, moaning cryptically and nursing ancient grievances. It seems to me that if there were such ethereal veterans amongst us, they would dress better, live in more attractive places and be much more instructive conversationalists. On the other hand, I am convinced, as this book should indicate, that we, the quick, are influenced by the thoughts, actions and personalities of the dead. There is nothing spooky about this observation, which is simply a restatement of the generally accepted proposition that we are to a considerable extent the product of our history.

I am also of the opinion that emanations from the past are often strong or at least more easily detected when one is in places or doing things which were of interest to particular people from the past. By way of a homely example, an old farm in the Pennsylvania Blue Ridge has been home base for our family for twenty-five years. On it is a spring, walled with stone. This part of the country was settled in the eighteenth century by Scotch-Irish frontier people, so it is possible that the spring was first dug and rocked in more than 200 years ago. It is a pretty but aggravating hole since ground water from the mountain persistently works its way behind the wall and every ten years or so causes a partial collapse. There is probably some clever engineering technique which would solve the problem more or less permanently. However, as archaeological evidence indicates, the custom has been to rebuild the stone wall as necessary. The first time I had occasion to do so, I came to a point in the job where I needed a trapezoidal-shaped rock to fill in a niche. Kneeling in the mud, which is the only way this work can be done, I felt, sharply, a stone under one knee. When it was grubbed loose, it fit the gap nicely, having served that purpose for a good many years, perhaps for several centuries. I have no idea who it was who first found this particular rock in the field or nearby stream bed and lugged it to the spring, but I feel a certain intimacy with and understanding for him because we are members of a historical relay team. I know a bit about him and the others because we have met, so to speak, over that rock and spring. For the same reasons, I can make some guesses about and am interested in those who will probably join the relay later.

This sort of thing is a very soft approach to history, much more sensual than cerebral, and is not a substitute for formal research. It serves more as an aid to the imagination and has sometimes so served, it seems to me, in my pursuit of Joe Walker. This work was commenced on the above-mentioned place in the Appalachians and, perhaps to an extent I do not comprehend, because of that place. Much of the archival type of research was done in Missouri because that is the location of some splendid collections having to do with the western frontier. But living there also made it convenient to float down the Big Muddy in a canoe, poke about in the remains of Fort Osage, ride and walk along what was once the Santa Fe Trail. Most of the book was written in the old bunkhouse of a ranch which is eight miles from the next nearest habitation, 6,000 feet up in the Huachuca Mountains of southern Arizona. It is a place I knew and liked long before I was seriously interested in Walker, and it has many attractions other than being a good place to write a book about him. But it is that, too. He may have been on this mountain in 1838 or 1862, but if not, he was on many that were like this one, the Huachucas having changed very little since his time.

Investigation by environmental osmosis generally is something which simply occurs sometimes. However, during this undertaking there was one occasion when it was employed deliberately and with curious results. I have a good friend by the name of John Thomson, who has been a companion in several peculiar quests. Among others, we spent a summer in the Barren Lands of Canada trying to follow the trail used in 1819—and very rarely since—by Sir John Franklin, the doughty British explorer of the high Arctic. These great northern plains are still as uninhabited and unused as they were in 1819 and for centuries preceding. They are a long way from Walker country geographically but perhaps closer in nature than any other contemporary place in North Ameria. Often as I read and thought about him entering into the Great Basin, I have thought of the Great Barrens and imagined that I had a better sense of what he had experienced because of my experience there.

In any event, John became interested in Joe Walker and, because he is also a Californian and a mountaineer, particularly interested in the route Walker used when he first crossed the Sierra in 1833. This is a problem which has engaged several others and probably will never be completely solved because Zenas Leonard's account of the expedition is a sketchy, impressionistic one. However, matching Leonard's descriptions of physical features against large-scale topographic maps, John eventually plotted a route which represents as good a guess as can be made as to where Walker made his crossing. Late in the summer he and I left from the Nevada side of the Sierra to walk some eighty miles of this hypothetical route. Near the crest we camped in a patch of open grass which lay between the edge of a snowfield and the shore of a small mountain lake. Naturally we talked about Walker and the others. I said that if I could meet him, there were three questions I would ask— ones that I was convinced could never be answered by conventional research. I wanted to know what he had done as a Taos trapper in the 1820s, what his relationship with Benjamin Bonneville was, and about his Indian wife. We talked until we were too cold to sit up longer and then got into our sleeping bags. Thereafter an incident occurred which is most simply called a dream, though it had—and has in my remembering it—a quality unlike that of any previous dream I had had. I appeared, by unknown agency, in the public room of an old tavern I had known in Missouri. There were half a dozen men and two women in the room, dressed as working people did in the early part of the nineteenth century. One of the women was tending the bar, and the other one was leaving the room by a side door which was being held open for her by a tall, massive man. As she left, he said, "I will see you in a short while, Barbara." His back was turned toward me, but I had the intuitive feeling that the man was Joe Walker and the woman was his sister-in-law, Barbara. So far as the man was concerned, this was shortly confirmed. When he turned back into the room, his face was that of Walker's as I had seen it in the portrait by Alfred Jacob Miller.

The woman behind the bar said, indicating me by a gesture, "Joe, this is the man I told you about, the one who has been asking questions." Walker and the others in the room looked at me quizzically. In the course of various journalistic assignments, I have been in other places— a burned-out ghetto apartment in the South Bronx, a leper colony in the Pacific, an Inuit village in the Arctic—where I had feelings similar to those I had in that room. I did not have the sense that anyone was particularly hostile, but that judgment about me was waiting to be made, that it was imperative that I explain myself and my purpose immediately. Because I was such a stranger, this did not seem easy to do. Speaking directly to Walker, I said hesitantly, "I don't know exactly how to say this, but I am not from your time. I lived, or I live, later than you did."

Walker nodded as if to help me along and said, "I understand that." I felt very grateful for his understanding and was struck, as I remembered others had been, by how kind he seemed. The other men gathered around us and gave the impression that they regarded me as unusual but not incredible. Walker introduced me to all of them, and I shook hands with each of the men. At the time I recognized all their names, but when the time passed, I could remember only that of one of them, George Nidever. Awkwardly trying to make conversation, I said, "I know you. I have seen records about you."

One of the men behind me laughed and said, "If you have records about him, he will go to jail." It was a pleasantry aimed, it seemed, at putting me more at ease.

Walker asked, "What is it you want?"

"I am interested in things you did and would like to ask some questions."

Walker gave an encouraging nod, but I was very rattled and, rather than proceeding in a logical sequence, commenced with my second question: about Bonneville. "There was a man who wrote"—and I paused, trying to express myself diplomatically but being unable to do so, blundered ahead—"after you were dead." I paused again, fearing I said the wrong thing.

"That is alright," said Walker, smiling at my confusion and indicating that the word I had used was not offensive, just as a leper had told me that word was one which could be politely used in conversation with those afflicted with the disease.

"He wrote," I went on with relief, "that you were a partner of Bonneville's."

"That is not exactly as it was," Walker answered crisply. "When I returned from Santa Fe, I had money in gold, but there was sickness in my family, as you know. [I thought of both his sister Susan and brother Big John, but did not want to interrupt with a digressive question.] I had other uses for the gold and did not choose to invest it with Benjamin Bonneville. I was the partisan. Lieutenant William Montgomery introduced me to Benjamin Bonneville." While I was trying to frame my next question, Walker said, "This is not a good place to make private conversation. There is a better place we can go to talk quietly if you wish to do so."

I said that I did. He turned to the door, indicating I should follow him. However, as soon as we were outside in the night, he disappeared suddenly and completely. I was enraged, not at him but at myself for losing sight of him and also because I had conducted such a clumsy interview. Giving vent to my frustration, I shouted, "Shit." By then I had entered another realm of time or consciousness because this yell woke John. As we both sat up in our sleeping bags, we startled a large mule deer which had apparently been browsing near our camp. The deer bounded across the foot of John's bag, close enough so that we could see him clearly in the darkness.

I then immediately told John this story and thus was able to preserve it before it became garbled as dreams or whatever do. When I was finished, John said, "I think that deer was probably Joe Walker." Then he asked me what I was going to do next. I said I was going to go back to sleep and try to find my man. I did sleep, but it was uneventful. (Several times during the next year I had similar vivid historical dreams or rather, as I remembered them, fragments of dreams that had no narrative and did not make much sense. There were several more glimpses of Barbara Walker and a rather scary one of a man I supposed was Bill Williams. However, Walker himself never returned.)

The next morning John and I, of course, talked it all over again. He said he had not gone to sleep easily. "You convinced me. I thought sure he was going to come back. If he did, I thought I should get up, but I didn't have my pants on. I didn't want to meet a man like Joe Walker in my underwear, but it was too cold to get up and put them on, so I just worried about it."

I said that I thought the most curious thing was the mention of the name of Lieutenant William Montgomery. By then my wife and I had completed most of the research for this book, and I did not recall ever having heard of anyone, past or present, by that name. Two days later we came to Yosemite Valley and a telephone, and I immediately called Ann, retold the story and asked if she knew anything about William Montgomery. The name was as new to her as it had been to me.

Our home in Pennsylvania is not far from the Army War College and historical library which are located in Carlisle. When I returned from California, Ann and I visited the military reference collections. I told the archivist that during the course of working on a biography of Walker I had come across (no explanation was given of how) the name of a Lieutenant William Montgomery. I asked if we could determine whether such an officer served on the early frontier. The archivist shortly turned up the information that a Lieutenant William Montgomery, a West Pointer, had served at Fort Leavenworth in 1827 and thereafter at several other border posts, where he would have been from time to time a messmate of Benjamin Bonneville. Leavenworth was only a few miles upstream from Independence, where Walker, in 1827, was the sheriff. It seems impossible that two men of roughly the same age, both concerned with frontier affairs and living in such a sparsely settled area,

were not acquainted. However, additional conventional research failed
to establish any documentary link between the two.

William Montgomery aside—I have no good explanation for him—I
do not think it is particularly startling that visions of Joe and Barbara
Walker or even George Nidever and Bill Williams should pop into my
head. These people were and have remained much on my mind, and
that is an organ or instrument which is notorious for playing tricks on
its titular owners.

My interest has been special, and therefore, special effects can be
reasonably expected. However, it seems to me that dreams, of both the
nighttime and daytime variety, about western history are a common
American phenomenon, one of our most commonly shared imaginative
experiences. They occur generally and persistently for the same reasons
the one described occurred to me, because collectively we are perhaps
still more preoccupied with these matters than any other historical ones.
Our art, literature, music, language, dress and many other cultural concerns testify to the extent of this interest in the early west. That this
period should so fascinate us is not surprising. Those times and the
people of them were adventurous and picturesque. Most important,
the occupation of the continent is commonly, if subliminally, regarded
as our most notable and successful national accomplishment. The inclination to remember and dream about ourselves when we seemed to
be at our best is understandable.

I have entered the name of Lieutenant William Montgomery in the
notes appended to this book as though it were a legitimate reference.
However, that was done—as the explanation about the curious way in
which this information was acquired should make clear—as a kind of
joke to entertain myself and perhaps others. Absolutely no other references are taken from such sources. This is mentioned because I think
that we often forget or are unable to separate fancy from fact when it
comes to our western experience. Our interest is so obsessive and the
fantasies that rise from the interest are so vivid that we are prone to
believe and act as if our dreams represent reality.

Among other things, we have fantasized so greatly about our frontier
past that we sometimes appear to have difficulty accepting the fact that
we have not been a frontier people for more than a century and cannot
and should not behave as if we were. More than nostalgia is involved,
for out of this confusion about reality and illusion has evolved an en-
demic American ideology which might be called the Frontier Response.
Its existence, the passion it inspires and the influence it has on us are
currently more obvious than they have been at any time during the

preceding half century. The ideology is rooted in the belief that the West, particularly the trans-Mississippi territories, was won by a small, easily identifiable, specially endowed group: by white men of Anglo origins, who were supported by their obedient women and children. As a class they were bold, aggressive, competitive, pugnacious, impatient and acquisitive. Direct, physical, forceful and violent action was esteemed as an effective, manly response to challenges. Being confident about the innate superiority of their own kind, they were intrinsically racist, xenophobic and paternalistic. There was an anarchistic distrust of laws and other social contracts (excepting their own) which were often regarded as devices for handicapping the most able so as to confer undeserved opportunities and rewards on their inferiors.

Since, so runs the Frontier Response, the West was won and the nation made strong, prosperous and stable by these people and attitudes, we should continue to respect and follow them. At the heart of the ideology is the notion that if we have the wisdom and fortitude to act as Scotch-Irish frontiersmen did, most of our contemporary problems and frustrations will be resolved. The negative expression of this faith is that we have gone to hell in a handcart, become a weak, confused, corrupt people because we have turned from the old ways, rejected the authority and values of the class of white men who are the inheritors of the traditions, if not always the genes, of the frontiersmen.

Somewhat like those supporting the divine rights of royalty, it is a theory based on self-interest, wrapped in many layers of fantasy. The frontier disappeared a century ago, and no evidence or logic makes it reasonable to assume that responses which were valid then still are. Furthermore, this ideology evokes not a real but a largely invented past. It is a dreamlike creation compounded of fragments of fact rearranged in surrealistic patterns and of many pure fictions which owe less to nineteenth-century history than to twentieth-century western novels and, particularly, movies. The acceptance of this ideological frontier and the mythic response to it as realities constitute a pervasive and dangerous derangement.

Not long ago President Reagan had occasion to address some of his political supporters on the subject of opposition to his policies having to do with inflation, taxation and other economic matters. Giving advice on how best to deal with these opponents, the President remarked, "I say draw sabers and charge." It is a metaphor straight out of the fantastic western past in which the cavalry charge was the classic frontier response and the one largely responsible for the winning of the West. In fact, the maneuver was seldom used, and when it was, by officers who could not stifle their medieval fantasies, the results were usually disastrous for the chargers. Military surveyors and explorers were the army men who made the most significant contribution to the westering movement. The men with the sabers were not much of a factor until the last decade or so of the enterprise, when they were brought in to police the demoralized tribes. Even then they performed indifferently.

As for the Indians, the implied objects of the saber in all such allusions, they were not outcharged, and their prowess, tactics and morale seldom proved to be inferior to those of their opponents. In fact, the most surprising thing about the so-called Indian wars is how long and successfully the tribes resisted. They were not cut down by the saber but ground down by history. Because of the way the two cultures had evolved, the warriors were too individualistic, too primitive technologically and far too few for the outcome to have been any different from what it was. Nevertheless, the cavalry charge and all it implies continue to be used as a true metaphor and as a symbol for an effective, desirable response to confrontational problems, personal and social, domestic and foreign. It has, for example, been observed that Vietnam was regarded in many quarters as an Indian war, that we were humiliated because the Sioux won and we did not charge hard enough with the modern equivalent of sabers.

As it has evolved into ideology, the Frontier Response extols the most hubristic elements of the western movement. These elements existed, hubris being a prominent characteristic of the original Scotch-Irish emigrants. However, as the migration moved on, the most successful westerners were generally those who controlled or evolved away from these tendencies. Overland companies, for example, the members of which were able to create and accept communal discipline, invariably made better crossings than those who were only collections of bickering, competing individuals. As a leader of voluntary parties, Walker was among the most effective of the genuine frontiersmen. His prowess and expertise were, of course, significant, but more notable was his extraordinary ability to get people to cooperate for the common good. The journals and recollections of those who rode and walked with him give no sense that his authority was based on fear: that he could and might smash the head or put a bullet in the body of those who crossed him. He was followed, it seems, because he was known to be a prudent, fair-minded, humane man. Most importantly, his response to the real frontier worked. People who went with Walker got to where they wanted to go, alive and well.

In the dream scenes of the ideological frontier, the man with a gun is a central figure, and the central fact is that the West was taken at gunpoint. The men with the guns, the Jack Swillings, King Woolseys, Bill Williams, Custer with his saber and Frémont with his brass cannon, were there, but in fact, as opposed to fiction, they were relatively small, unimportant figures on the periphery of the scene. Much larger and more in the foreground of any true group portrait of the winners of the West are George Sibley, the idealistic frontier viceroy; Abraham McClellan, the town builder, his wife, Jane, the orchard planter, and her brother Big John, the whittler on white oak trees; Zenas Leonard and his mates, awed by Yosemite, the great sequoias and the beached whale; Joe Meek, blowing a year's pay on finery for Mountain Lamb, his Shoshoni wife; Myra Eells in her sewing circle with the Indian matrons; Thomas Jefferson Farnham, the utopian; Adolph Wislizenus, the physician-naturalist; Willard Smith, the diffident architect; Tom Fitzpatrick, William Bent, Pierre Jean De Smet, valiantly trying to preserve at least the dignity of the doomed horse Indians; Nancy Kelsey, walking barefoot out of the Sierra with her infant daughter in her arms; Pierson Reading, reveling in fields of prairie flowers; William Baldridge, defending the abused Miss Eyers; Jeemes Walker, taking Feliz Pena out of slavery; Daniel Conner, losing a mule while marveling at the eclipse of the moon—and so many other sensible, decent men and women who became more so in response to the challenge of the real frontier.

Very close to the center of the scene must be the burly figure of Joe Walker, "the best man in the country," so many thought. Walker—the crust breaker, taking his existential delight in the unknown regions for fifty years; the sheriff who did not kill or bully; lecturing his trappers on the nature of meteorite showers; considering the habits of prairie dogs with Lieutenant James Abert; speculating on the origins and ends of ancient civilizations; a host in himself to trusting emigrants; man of the Snakes, friend of the gentle Moqui, honorable opponent to Mangas; desperately trying to instruct the stone age Paiute on the properties of rifles; standing on the last frontier as virtually the last of the frontiersmen, restraining men hot to massacre the black Mojave, saying, "Be easy, be easy, for the more you become acquainted with these savages, the more you will respect their demands and we will put off all rifle negotiations as long as possible"—was as much as anyone ever was a westering man. Yet rarely and reluctantly was he the man with the gun.

It is indicative of the real westering values that Walker and a few uncommonly good men like him, not the uncommonly bad men, were admired in their own time as the genuine Frontier Heroes. They personified the strengths and virtues of the historic frontier and still can be recollected, even dreamed about with pride and pleasure. It is the fantastic frontier and the phantasms that roam it which haunt and trouble us.

Cave Canyon, the Huachuca Mountains, 1982

Notes

Full bibliographical information for sources cited here is in the bibliography, p. 319.

Page 5. WALKER'S SIZE. He was frequently described by contemporaries as over six feet tall and 200 pounds. The passport for him secured by Benjamin Bonneville in 1832 lists Walker's height as six feet four inches.

Page 6. DESCRIPTION OF DRESS AND APPEARANCE. McBride, pp. 317–18.

Page 7. WALKER'S NAME. In the surviving documents in which Walker signed his name or where it was used formally it always is Joseph R. Walker. The evidence is overwhelming that the middle name was Rutherford, not Reddeford, as it appears in scores of histories published after his death. A famous Scottish ancestor was the Reverend Samuel Rutherford (see page 25). In America virtually every generation of the family has included some members who bear the given name Rutherford. During Walker's lifetime at least two boys, a nephew and the son of a Missouri neighbor (see page 186), were named for him, both as Joseph Rutherford. In January 1873 John McPhearson, a poet-journalist-pioneer, who had been well acquainted with the family since at least 1848, when he crossed the plains with two of Walker's nephews, published, under the pen name Juanita, a series of sketches about the Walkers in the *Oakland* (California) *Transcript*. Three of these six articles were concerned with the adventures of Walker, whom McPhearson formally interviewed at the family ranch. McPhearson introduced his subject as Joseph Rutherford Walker (*Oakland Transcript*, January 15, 1873).

As for how he became Reddeford, Walker died on October 27, 1876, at the ranch in Contra Costa County. A week later the *Contra Costa Gazette* (November 4, 1876) published an obituary in which the deceased was referred to as Joseph Reddeford Walker. Very likely the writer heard the name from a family member, then spelled it phonetically and incorrectly. It would have been an easy error to make, for the Scotch-Irish, southern

Appalachian drawl can be hard to understand. For example, the Scotch-Irish who settled a town in central Missouri intended to call it Raleigh, after the North Carolina community. However, it seemed to others that they spoke of it as Rolla, which became and remains its name.

Douglas Watson lists the obituary among his sources and gives Reddeford as the middle name of his subject. Having no other biographical source, subsequent writers followed Watson's lead. It is a good example of how hardy, once planted, historical error can be. I am pleased to root out this one, but it is no reason for gloating. Though I obviously hope not, it is possible that similar errors exist in this book.

Page 7. THE SEMIFICTIONAL BIOGRAPHY. Percy Booth, a Los Angeles industrialist, became curious about Walker because he says that business often took him through the Sierra pass named for the man. Finding little information available, Booth commissioned Douglas Watson to prepare a biography. Watson did, and the book was titled *The West Wind*. One hundred copies were privately printed and copyrighted by Booth in 1934. Watson attached a short list of sources but did not key them to the text or document the text in other conventional ways. I have not used Watson as a source, excepting where other references substantiate his work.

Page 8. THE LOST JOURNAL. While living at Manzanita Ranch in the 1870s, Walker was a grandfatherly figure for the three children of his nephew James. One of these children, Barbara, remembered the story of the lost journal and related it to her son, C. M. Walker, now a resident of Sacramento, California. (C. M. Walker, born in 1899, is a great-grandson of both Joel and Samuel Walker, brothers of Joe Walker.) He kindly shared this family recollection and several others with me.

Pages 9–10. CONNER'S RECOLLECTION. Conner manuscript. Huntington Library.

Page 10. FRÉMONT RESCUE. Frémont (*Report of*), p. 271.

Pages 10–11. WALKER'S RESPONSE. *Santa Rosa* (California) *Daily Democrat*, November 20, 1876.

Page 13. BEVERLY. Arnow, p. 91.

Page 16. SCOTCH-IRISH. Several works dealing with the history of the Scotch-Irish are listed in the bibliography. I most frequently referred to Leyburn.

Page 19. PENNSYLVANIA GAZETTE. Leyburn, p. 170.

Pages 19–20. JAMES LOGAN. Leyburn, pp. 190–93; Baldwin, p. 128.

Page 21. PRAYER. Baldwin, p. 119.

Page 24. EARLY WALKER FAMILY HISTORY. The monumental genealogical work of White provides most of the information about the family in Scotland and the first three generations of American Walkers. This has been supplemented by family diaries in the possession of Mrs. Mary Moore Mason of Rockbridge County, Virginia. Mrs. Mason is a ninth-generation descendant of the original emigrants, John and Katherine Walker, and resides on the site where the Creek Nation (see page 29) was established in the 1730s.

Page 24. JOHN AND KATHERINE WALKER. White, p. 283.

Page 26. INDENTURED SERVANTS. Leyburn, p. 176.

Pages 27–28. JACK HAYES. White, p. 468; Woodruff.

Page 29. FIRST CABIN. White, p. 283, 468–69.

Pages 29–30. BENJAMIN BURDEN. White, pp. 482–83; Summers, p. 42.

Page 31. AXES. Baldwin, pp. 35–37.

Page 32. SPLIT RAILS. Dick, pp. 103–104 and 304.

Page 32. CORN AND CLEARINGS. Dick, pp. 98–100.

Page 32. BEARSKIN. Arnow, p. 100.

Page 32. TURKEYS. Dick, pp. 35 and 287.

Page 33. RIFLES. Arnow, pp. 89 and 99.

Pages 33–34. WALKER RIFLES. White, pp. 169, 170 and 282. As for the piece displayed in the museum of Washington and Lee University, the contemporary curator of that collection has a recollection that once, long before his time, there was such a rifle. However, a search of the premises and records in the summer of 1981 produced no trace of it.

Page 34. CREEK NATION FORT. Woodruff; Mason diaries.

Page 35. THE PERFECT UNDERSTANDING. Moore, p. 50.

Page 35. WHITE-INDIAN FATALITIES. Don Russell, pp. 47 and 61; Unruh, pp. 184–85.

Pages 36–37. CHEROKEE INCIDENT. Van Every (*Forth*), pp. 152–56; Summers, pp. 67–73.

Page 37. RANGER JOHN. Woodruff. White, pp. 477–84, also records military service of Walkers.

Page 37. JOHN ECHOLS. Summers, pp. 62–64.

Pages 37–38. POINT PLEASANT. Van Every (*Forth*), pp. 352–55; Arnow, p. 139; Summers, pp. 144 and 249.

Page 38. DEATH OF RANGER JOHN. White, p. 6.

Page 38. ABDUCTION OF WILLIAM WALKER. White, p. 12.

Pages 39–40. APPS VALLEY "MASSACRE." This became something of a legendary frontier tale. There are several versions. I used those appearing in White (commencing on p. 131) and Summers, pp. 116, 382–85.

Pages 41–42. RETURN OF JAMES MOORE. White, p. 135.

Page 43. "WHITES ARE TOO DAMN MEAN." Willis family letters. W. F. Willis, July 28, 1848.

Page 45. EARL OF DUNMORE. Van Every (*Forth*), pp. 322–23.

Page 47. LONG HUNTERS. Summers, pp. 114–15; Arnow, p. 164.

Page 48. SAMUEL WALKER'S WILL. White, pp. 260–61.

Page 48. JOSEPH WALKER, SR., IN TENNESSEE. Alda Walker letter.

Page 49. BIRTH OF WALKER CHILDREN. For information about the family in the latter part of the eighteenth century, White depended heavily on records left by Joel Walker, the youngest brother of Joseph Walker, Sr. However, Joel Walker moved to the Ohio Territory in the 1790s and apparently lost track of his brother and his family. Therefore, White's information is garbled in regard to them. Contemporary family historians have sorted out most of what would seem to be the facts in regard to the vital statistics of Joseph Sr.'s children. Samuel, listed in White as the oldest brother, was probably the youngest one since he was the last to leave for Missouri and his children were the youngest in the next generation. Joel Walker, in his memoir, indicates that his brother Joe, the Frontier Hero, may have been born in Virginia rather than in Tennessee. The best evidence to the contrary is Joe Walker's tombstone, which gives his place of birth as Roan[e] County.

In the *Contra Costa County* [California] *History*, Purcell states that according to "Walker family tradition," Big John Walker died at the Alamo, another brother, William (or Ike) was killed by the Mormons in Utah and Joe Walker and all his brothers and sisters were, through their mother, nephews and nieces of the famous Shawnee chief Tecumseh. In fact, John Walker, according to the records of Jackson County, Missouri, died there in 1845. There are no records about the Mormon incident or for that matter of a fourth brother. Records of Goochland County, Virginia, clearly indicate that Susan Willis Walker was a planter's daughter, white and English. Contemporary family members whose recollections extend back to the early part of this century say that there was a Walker in the generation before them who "told big stories and drank." They think such tales may have started with him. Douglas Watson picked up the stories about the Alamo and Mormon murder. Therefore, they have been erroneously included in some subsequent histories, including *The Trailblazers*, in which I first wrote about Joe Walker and his family.

Page 50. THE REVEREND SAMUEL CARRICK. White, p. 178.

Pages 50–51. HOUSTON. James (*Houston*), pp. 19 and 25.

Page 54. JACKSON-BENTON DUEL. James (*Jackson*), pp. 152–58; Baldwin, pp. 238–39.

Page 55. WALKER BROTHERS WITH JACKSON. In his memoir Joel Walker describes his service. He makes no reference to Joe, but he was an extremely laconic man. In his biography he mentions his famous brother only twice and never mentions any of his other brothers. Joe Walker is never known to have said anything about his service in the Creek War, but again he had very little to say about many of his adventures. However, in the National Archives is a document in which Joseph Walker of Roane County empowers one William Brown, an attorney of Kingsport, Tennessee, to collect the back pay owed him for service with "Colonel John Brown's Rigament of mounted gunmen of Volunteers on an expedition against the hostile Creeks." This is dated January 16, 1815. There was in Roane County no other Joseph Walker of the right age to have ridden with John Brown.

Pages 55–56. BROWN'S ADVANCE. Hartsell, p. 145.

Page 56. HORSESHOE BEND. James (*Jackson*), pp. 170–72. The account of the meeting between Jackson and Weatherford was given later by a junior staff officer. The language of the conversation sounds more like that of Sir Walter Scott than Andrew Jackson, but the sense of the passage is plausible.

Page 57. SEMINOLES. Peters gives a general account of these wars, and James (*Jackson*), pp. 285–318, describes the campaign of 1817–18. Joel Walker recalled his part in it in his memoir, *Pioneer of Pioneers*. This was dictated, to R. A. Thompson, when Walker was eighty years old. However, it is generally very accurate at least in regard to those sections which can be checked against other sources.

Page 58. WALKER IN THE SOUTHWEST AS A TEENAGER. *Napa* (California) *Reporter*, November 18, 1876.

Page 58. WALKER AND MISSOURI STEAMBOATS. James O'Meara, p. 352. James O'Meara was a Copperhead, a pugnacious and often scurrilous journalist. However, he was acquainted with Walker and was obviously a great admirer of his, being among those who contemplated but never completed a Walker biography. In the *Santa Rosa* (California) *Daily Democrat*, November 20, 1876, an obituary states that Walker made his memorable ride on the first steamer, the *Expedition*, in 1822. This is inaccurate since the *Expedition* first ascended the Missouri in the summer of 1819, wintered near Council Bluffs and descended in March 1820. See Atherton, p. 463, and Hubbell, p. 373. The *Daily Democrat* in the same article says Walker first came to Missouri in 1818. Lacking better evidence, I have accepted the inscription on Walker's tombstone as the most authoritative source: that he came to Missouri in 1819 and left for New Mexico in 1820.

Page 59. THE SLAVE HARDY. Juanita, January 29, 1873.

Page 59. MCCLELLAN'S REAL ESTATE TRANSACTIONS. Deed books of Roane County from Woodruff.

Pages 60–61. THE GREAT MIGRATION. Dan Clark, pp. 6–14; Hafen and Rister (*Western America*), p. 143. Unruh, p. 120.

Page 60. MISSOURI EMIGRATION—1819. Violette, p. 51.

Page 61. FRANKLIN. Robins (October 1953), pp. 60–65.

Page 61. MISSOURI WEATHER—1819. Sibley papers.

Page 64. HISTORY OF FORT OSAGE. Gregg ("Osage").

Page 66. MARY SIBLEY. Gregg (*Santa Fe*), p. 15; Chiles ms.

Page 67. SIBLEY AND THE OSAGE. Wilcox, pp. 24–27.

Page 68. SIBLEY AND WALKERS. Sibley papers.

Page 68. AZUBAH CHILES. Wilcox, p. 46.

Page 70. TO TEXAS. Joel Walker, p. 5.

Page 71. JOE WALKER TO SANTA FE. Juanita, January 15, 1873; James O'Meara, p. 353.

Page 71. SPANIARDS AND SIOUX. Irving (*Bonneville*), p. 17.

Page 71. BEAUTIFUL DAUGHTER. Pattie, pp. 48–50.

Pages 71–72. WALKER IN NEW MEXICO. Among those who suggest that Walker remained in the mountains 1820–22 are: Stone, pp. 35–36; Weber, p. 100; and Cleland (*Reckless Breed*), p. 276.

Page 73. BAIRD AND CHOUTEAU PARTIES. Duffus, pp. 59–61.

Pages 73–74. EZEKIEL WILLIAMS. Voelker, p. 17.

Page 74. MERIWETHER. Duffus, p. 65; Meriwether, pp. 85–96.

Pages 74–75. JAMES AND FOWLER PARTIES. Duffus, pp. 70–74.

Page 75. FOWLER. Fowler, pp. 3–4.

Pages 75–76. BECKNELL EXPEDITION. This expedition has been treated by several authors, writing in the *Missouri Historical Review*. Included are: Gregg (Vol. 34, No. 4); Stephens (Vol. X, No. 4 and Vol. XI, No. 3); Becknell (Vol. IV, No. 2). Also, Cleland (*Reckless Breed*), p. 277, and Duffus, pp. 68–69.

Page 76. CASH SHORTAGE. Sibley papers—letter to Dr. Dorsey.

Pages 76–79. WALKER-COOPER PARTY. Cooper (in the *History of Howard and Cooper Counties*, p. 152) and Walker left memoirs about the trip. Both claimed to be the principal leader but otherwise agree about the details. Walker's account is more extensive, and I have used that. However, as Cooper and much circumstantial evidence make plain, Walker was mistaken about the year of the expedition. It occurred in 1823 rather than 1822. Considering that he dictated his memoir nearly sixty years later, the error is understandable.

Page 79. BAIRD-CHAMBERS. Golley.

Page 80. TRAPPING ON GREEN RIVER. Becknell, p. 82.

Page 80. SANTA FE SURVEY. In *The Road to Santa Fe*, Gregg has published the original reports and journals of Sibley, the other commissioners and chief surveyor, along with her own excellent commentary. Gregg is the source, unless otherwise noted, for this account of the survey.

Page 81. BILL WILLIAMS. Biographical material about Williams is provided by Favour, Hafen (*Mountain Men*) and W. T. Hamilton.

Page 86. BREAKING THE CRUST. James O'Meara, p. 354.

Page 87. SANTA FE TRAIL JOBS. Gregg (*Santa Fe*), pp. 177–78.

Page 87. JACKSON COUNTY COURT. *History of Jackson County*, p. 102.

Page 88. WALKER LANDS. Township deed books at Jackson County courthouse.

Page 89. NAMING JACKSON COUNTY. Juanita, January 15, 1873; James O'Meara, p. 354.

Pages 89–90. ORGANIZATION OF JACKSON COUNTY AND FIRST ELECTION. *History of Jackson County*, pp. 101–31.

Page 90. "NEVER A BRAGGART." Wilcox, p. 43.

Page 90. CRIMINAL CASES. Records of the Circuit Court of Jackson County, 1827–29. These records were made in a ledger now (1981) preserved in the chambers of Paul E. Vardeman, presiding judge of the Circuit Court of the Sixteenth Judicial District of Missouri. During a renovation of the Independence courthouse, Judge Vardeman came upon a pile of paper trash which had been collected for the incinerator. Rummaging through it, he found this ledger in which the proceedings of what was then the westernmost court in the United States are described in a very informal and nonlegal style. I am indebted to Judge Vardeman for salvaging this interesting document and making it available to me.

Page 91. GOUGING. Dick, p. 140.

Page 92. DUEL WITH THE INDIAN CHIEF. Ruxton, p. 88.

Page 93. 1827 JAIL. *History of Jackson County*, pp. 638–39. The jail was Walker's home while in Independence and not a very comfortable one. In 1828 it became so infested with fleas that a herd of sheep had to be driven through it to collect and remove the parasites.

Page 93. KIT CARSON. Carter, pp. 39–40.

Page 93. MISSOURI COURTROOMS. McCurdy, pp. 2–5.

Pages 93–94. SHERIFF'S ACTIVITIES. Records of the Circuit Court of Jackson County, 1827–29.

Page 94. LIQUOR CONSUMPTION. Rorabaugh, pp. 7–12 and 113–18.

Pages 94–95. HANNA. Records of the Circuit Court of Jackson County, 1827–29.

Page 95. WALKER'S HORSE TRADING. Juanita, January 15, 1873.

Page 97. LIEUTENANT MONTGOMERY. See page 293.

Page 97. HOUSTON'S MARRIAGE. Agnew, p. 77.

Page 97. WALKER-BONNEVILLE MEETING. Juanita, January 15, 1873.

Page 97. BONNEVILLE. Irving (*Bonneville*), Editor's Introduction. Irving's *Adventures of Captain Bonneville* was reissued in 1961 and edited by Edgeley W. Todd. Todd's excellent introduction provides biographical information about Bonneville and an account of the preparations made for the Bonneville-Walker expedition.

Page 98. BONNEVILLE AS AN UNDERCOVER AGENT. Carl Russell, p. 15. In regard to the "spy theory," also see Cleland (*Reckless Breed*), pp. 278–79; DeVoto (*Across the Wide Missouri*), pp. 58–60; and Goetzmann (*Exploration and Empire*), pp. 148–50.

Page 99. BONNEVILLE-IRVING LITERARY ARRANGEMENTS. McDermott, pp. 459–67.

Page 101. WALKER AS A STOCKHOLDER. Juanita, January 15, 1873.

Page 104. BONNEVILLE EXPEDITION. Irving's *Bonneville* is the only complete published description of this expedition and therefore provides the base for this account. Where information is taken from other sources they are noted.

Page 105. IRVING ON BEE HUNTERS. Irving (*A Tour on the Prairies*), pp. 50–55.

Pages 106–110. FUR TRADE. The literature on the Rocky Mountain fur trade is extensive. I most often referred to Chittenden, DeVoto (*Across the Wide Missouri*), Goetzmann (*Exploration and Empire*) and Phillips.

Page 110. GODIN. On May 22, 1836, Antoine Godin was invited to the camp of some Blackfoot trappers who said they had furs to trade. Negotiations took place near Fort Hall on the Snake River. The traders sat in a circle around which a ceremonial pipe was passed. When it reached Godin, one of the Blackfeet drew a hidden gun and shot him. As Godin was dying, one of his assailants took out a knife and carved his forehead with a sign indicating he was a traitor to his race. (Hafen, *Mountain Men*, vol. 2, p. 178.)

Page 111. WALKER ON FORT BONNEVILLE. Juanita, January 16, 1873.

Pages 112–113. FORT NONSENSE. Ferris, p. 165.

Page 113. WALKER AND FREE TRAPPERS. DeVoto (*Across the Wide Missouri*), p. 55.

Page 113. THE MISERABLE CAMP. Ferris, p. 147; Juanita, January 16, 1873.

Page 115. WALKER TO MADISON RIVER. Juanita, January 16, 1873.

Page 115. OLD SLEDGE. Irving (*Bonneville*), p. 87; James O'Meara, p. 356.

Page 115. CHRISTMAS, 1833. Ferris, p. 152.

Page 115. WALKER'S BRIGADE. Juanita, January 16, 1873.

Page 116. FUR TALLY. Gowans, pp. 118–19.

Page 116. WALKER'S SPRING HUNT. Ferris, p. 164; Juanita, January 16, 1873.

Page 118. PASSING THE LIQUOR. Irving (*Bonneville*), p. 149.

Page 119. THE LAST GOOD YEAR. Gowans, p. 118. Gowans (pp. 102–22) provides a good record of the rendezvous of 1833, including excerpts from the diaries and memoirs of those who attended it.

Page 120. "THAT AR ENGLISHMAN." Ruxton, p. 10.

Page 120. "THE BIRDS BEGAN TO SING." Victor, p. 110.

Page 121. BONNEVILLE REPORT. Irving (*Bonneville*), p. 381.

Page 122. LEONARD BIOGRAPHY. Leonard, p. xviii. This material is provided by John C. Ewers, in his introduction to the 1959 edition of Leonard's journal. Leonard describes his adventures in the west up to the time of joining Walker on pages 1–63.

Page 123. "MR. WALKER." Leonard, p. 64.

Page 124. PREPARATION FOR EXPEDITION. Leonard, p. 65; Victor, p. 144; Nidever, p. 34.

Pages 124–125. BONNEVILLE'S INSTRUCTIONS. Irving (*Bonneville*), p. 162.

Page 125. PASSPORT. On June 30, 1966, while visiting the National Archives, Mrs. Ethel Walker Lindsay, one of the Walker family genealogists, found Walker's passport: number 2567 as listed by the State Department. It was issued at the request of Bonneville on January 23, 1832, and mailed to Missouri (according to Register of Letters received by the State Department—Vol. 7., January 23, 1832—National Archives). Mrs. Lindsay requested and received a photostatic copy of the document, which is now in my possession. The passport was executed by a clerk who did not have the most legible of hands. Therefore, in hopes that several words which on the photostatic copy were hard to decipher might be easier to read on the original, I asked Margaret Walmer, a professional researcher, to make a trip to the Archives and reexamine the document. Mrs. Walmer found the file purportedly holding the Walker passport (and others issued between 1817 and 1834) was missing. She asked the attending archivist about this, and he said that he had no idea where it was. She then said, "Doesn't it bother you that I have a client who has a copy, originally made here, of a document which you have lost?" He just smiled and said, "No," reported Mrs. Walmer. This is not to suggest that there is an ongoing

150-year-old conspiracy to hide the true relations of Walker and Bonneville. However, because of the obvious importance of this passport in regard to the matter, it seems to be worth reporting in detail. The visa for the passport was later provided by J. María Montoya, the Mexican chargé d'affaires in Washington; see Hafen (*Old Spanish Trail*), p. 242.

Pages 126–127. JED SMITH. See Morgan (*Jedediah Smith*) for an account of Smith's career.

Page 128. MEEK-WALKER. According to Victor, p. 144, when Joe Meek joined the expedition, he thought it was going only to the Great Salt Lake; the decision to continue to California was made later. If so, Meek's understanding was contrary to that of all the other men who participated and commented on the journey. It is difficult to see how such a routine trip could have inspired Meek to comment that the making of it would be "a feather in a man's cap." Also, there is reason to doubt that Meek was as ignorant of the planned destination as his biographer said he was. As many other references indicate, Victor had read Irving's account and accepted it as the official record of the expedition. Elsewhere Victor tends to present Meek so that his words and deeds agree with conventional historical works. This incident seems to be an example of that practice.

Page 128. THE CALIFORNIA EXPEDITION. Leonard's is the only extensive account of the expedition and, unless otherwise noted, mine is based on his. To the extent it can be checked, Leonard's report, considering the circumstances under which he made it, is very accurate. However, there was some confusion—either Leonard's or his original editor's—on dates. Leonard had the expedition leaving the Green River about two weeks later than it actually did according to the recollections of others and interior evidence provided by his journal. I have extrapolated from the journal itself and used what seems like more reasonable dates than those sometimes given by Leonard.

Page 128. EXPLORING SALT LAKE. Irving (*Bonneville*), p. xlii; Juanita, January 16, 1873; James O'Meara, p. 357.

Pages 128–129. WALKER'S SWIM. *Lewiston* (Idaho) *Morning Tribune*, March 3, 1918.

Page 130. BILL WILLIAMS. Craig in his recollection (*Lewiston Tribune*) says that Williams was with the party. Favour, William's principal biographer, has accepted this and proceeds as if Williams were present at least until they recrossed the Sierra in 1834. However, Tom Fitzpatrick, a notably veracious man, wrote in November 1833 to his partner Milton Sublette that Williams was acting as a guide for a Rocky Mountain Fur Company brigade trapping that fall on the lower Green River. (See Hafen and Ghent, *Broken Hand*, p. 132.) What may have happened is that Williams started out with Walker—which is all that Bill Craig actually said of him—left the party in the early fall and returned to guide Fitzpatrick's men. A plausible reason for his departure is that he took part in the ambush of the Paiutes on the Humboldt and was discharged by an angry Walker or so severely reprimanded that Williams left in a sulk. Under somewhat similar circumstances Williams was to do the same a decade later. (See page 212.)

Page 132. IRVING'S VERSION. Irving (*Bonneville*), pp. 283–86.

Page 133. EATING WORMS. Frémont (*Narratives*), pp. 248–49.

Page 134. AMBUSH OF INDIANS. Nidever, p. 33; Leonard, p. 75.

Page 137. METEORITE SHOWER. Hill, p. 75; Leonard, p. 90; *Santa Rosa* (California) *Daily Democrat*, November 20, 1876. Walker requested that his tombstone be inscribed to indicate that he had camped at Yosemite on November 13, 1833. If so, this would have been the day after the meteorite shower, the date of which was recorded throughout the Northern Hemisphere. Leonard, however, says that they were already in the San Joaquin Valley when this occurred. Also, they could not have heard the sounds of surf, which Leonard described, if they had been camped where and when he wrote they were. Whatever the sequence, there is absolutely no reason to doubt that they did and saw what Leonard claimed. Among others, the National Park Service has investigated the matter and concluded that Walker and his men were the first whites to see Yosemite Valley, and a memorial to them stands in Yosemite Park.

Pages 139–147. WINTER IN CALIFORNIA. The activities of the party during the winter of 1833–34 and their return to the mountains the following spring are described by Leonard, pp. 99–133.

Page 142. JOE MEEK IN CALIFORNIA. Victor, pp. 149–51.

Page 143. "NOT WANTONLY PRODIGAL WITH GOLD." James O'Meara, p. 362.

Page 145. THE FREE TRAPPERS IN ARIZONA. Victor, p. 153.

Page 147. BONNEVILLE, 1833–34. Irving (*Bonneville*), pp. 219–74.

Page 148. BONNEVILLE AND SQUAW. *Santa Rosa* (California) *Daily Democrat*, November 20, 1876. This article, an obituary, was written by R. A. Thompson, an associate editor of the *Democrat* who had interviewed Walker before his death. The remark about Bonneville and the squaw is given as a direct quote from Walker. Thompson was well acquainted with the family, and it was he who persuaded Joel Walker, in 1878, to dictate his memoirs. (See James O'Meara, p. 362, on Thompson.)

Page 148. BONNEVILLE'S REACTION. Irving (*Bonneville*), pp. 95–96.

Pages 150–152. TRAPPING IN 1834–35. Leonard, pp. 135–59.

Page 152. LEONARD EPILOGUE. Introduction (Ewers) to Leonard, pp. xviii–xx.

Pages 154–155. NEWELL AND MEEK. Gowans, p. 257; Victor, p. 264. The words attributed to Meek sound suspiciously like those of Mrs. Victor, a romantic historian-journalist. The sense of them seems accurate.

Page 156. CALIFORNIA TRADE. Breckenridge, pp. 42–43.

Page 157. BUYING MEEK'S FURS. Vestal, p. 229; Victor, p. 251.

Page 157. WILLIAMS-BECKWOURTH. Lavender, p. 213.

Page 158. MEEK-FARNHAM. Vestal, p. 240.

Page 158. MEEK-WALKER. Victor, p. 257.

Page 158. FORT DAVY CROCKETT. Hafen ("Fort Davy Crockett"); Wislizenus (*Journey to*), p. 129.

Pages 158–159. WALKER AND RUSTLERS. E. Willard Smith, pp. 266–67; Victor, p. 260.

Pages 159–160. WALKER-WALKARA. Ferris, p. 210; Hill, p. 136; Lawrence, pp. 19–22.

Page 161. DENIG. Walter O'Meara, pp. 182 and 289.

Page 162. "DO WHITE PEOPLE HAVE ANY WOMEN?" Walter O'Meara, p. 17.

Page 163. BLACKFEET. Walter McClintock, pp. 69–70.

Page 165. MEEK AND MOUNTAIN LAMB. Victor, p. 176.

Pages 165–166. INDIAN WIVES. Irving (*Bonneville*), p. 113.

Page 165. BONNEVILLE'S "BELLES." Walter O'Meara, pp. 140 and 186.

Page 167. MILLER ON WALKER PORTRAIT. Miller, p. 78.

Page 168. WALKER'S WIFE. Wislizenus (*Journey to*), p. 84.

Page 168. WALKER-WISLIZENUS. Wislizenus (*Journey to*), p. 135.

Page 169. RECHERCHÉ FEAST. Miller, p. 78.

Page 169. MISSIONARY WIVES. Eells, pp. 77–79.

Page 170. VISIT TO SIX MILE CHURCH. This story was reported by Alda Walker in a letter to Audrey Woodruff (December 3, 1965), a copy of which was made available to me by Mrs. Woodruff. Mrs. Walker had received the information, including the quoted material, in correspondence from G. Poe Smedley. Though they made later efforts to contact Smedley, neither Walker nor Woodruff was able to do so. Nor have I.

Page 171. ARIZONA IN 1837. *History of Arizona Territory*, p. 207; Farish, Vol. II, p. 241; Ruxton, p. 92.

Page 171. TRAVELING WITH SQUAW. Breckenridge, p. 43.

Page 172. WALKER'S INTEREST IN COLORADO RIVER. E. Willard Smith, p. 268; Talbot (*Journals*), p. 48.

Page 172. VIRGIN RIVER. *San Francisco Herald*, November 28, 1853.

Page 173. FRAEB AND STEARNS. Hafen (*Old Spanish Trail*), p. 184.

Page 174. PREPARATIONS FOR OVERLAND TRIP. Joel Walker tells, in his terse way, the story of the emigration of his family. Where other sources are used in this account they are noted.

Page 175. AFC CARAVAN. Barry, p. 392.

Page 176. CARSON ON DE SMET. Carter, p. 71.

Page 176. INDEPENDENCE ROCK. Field, p. 176.

Page 177. MEEK, NEWELL AND CRAIG. Victor, p. 279–80.

Page 177. WEARY MISSIONARIES. *History of Sonoma County*, p. 482.

Page 177. INDIAN TROUBLES. Clyman, p. 156; Lindsay papers.

Page 177. RECEPTION BY METHODISTS. Bancroft (Vol. 29, *History of Oregon*) p. 242; Sonoma County Historical Society publication, 1979, No. 1); Victor, pp. 282–83.

Page 178. ASAHEL MUNGER. Bancroft (Vol. 29, *History of Oregon*), p. 240.

Page 178. EMPLOYMENT BY EWING YOUNG. Lindsay papers compiled from Albert Cooke family papers, December 1, 1975.

Page 179. SUBLETTE-VASQUEZ. E. Willard Smith, p. 265.

Page 180. RECEPTION IN CALIFORNIA. Hafen (*Old Spanish Trail*), p. 242.

Page 180. RAID OF THE RUSTLERS. Hafen (*Old Spanish Trail*), pp. 240–44.

Page 181. WALKER-STEARNS. Cleland (*Cattle on*), p. 186.

Page 181. WALKER'S PURCHASES. Hafen (*Old Spanish Trail*), p. 184.

Pages 182–183. BARTLESON PARTY. Bidwell ("First Emigrant Train"), pp. 106–30; Hafen and Ghent (*Broken Hand*), pp. 172–85; Stewart, pp. 5–29.

Page 183. FRAEB'S FIGHT. Hafen (*Mountain Men*, Vol. 3), pp. 137–39.

Page 184. BARTLESON'S WHISKEY. Bidwell, ("First Emigrant Train"), p. 119.

Page 184. INDIAN TROUBLES. Barry, pp. 432, 434 and 439.

Page 185. CROSSING PLAINS IN 1841. Rufus Sage, a young Connecticut travel writer making his first trip west with the trader Lancaster Lupton, reported meeting, in October, a party that sounds very much like that of the Walkers. The group was headed for Missouri, "taking a large drove of horses and several domesticated buffalo with them." Sage heard that the horses were from California and might have been among those rustled by Phil Thompson earlier in the year. This raid had by then become so famous that there was a tendency to believe every California horse was part of the booty. There is no record of Walker's having previously disposed of the animals he obtained legitimately in California, and these could have been his. However, Sage mentioned no names. He was very green and in awe of real mountain men, shy, it seems, about talking to them. Also his trail boss, Lupton, may not have encouraged his men to chat casually with strangers. Lupton was a notorious whiskey merchant and, though Sage did not know it at the time, bootleg booze was hidden in many of the packs. See Sage, p. 137.

Page 186. WALKER PARTY. The account I have given of the travels of the Walkers in 1841–42 is based on circumstantial evidence and deduction. It cannot be certainly documented, but I think it is plausible for the following reasons: Walker is reported to have made two trips back to Jackson County after he left with Bonneville in 1832. The last was made in 1846–47. The details and the fact that he was alone can be documented—see page 226 and accompanying notes. The first trip was made with his wife—see page 170—but those who remembered it did not give a date for this visit. However, since Walker's activities in all the other winters between 1832 and 1847 are accounted for, it must have been in 1841–42.

If they traveled as was customary, the Walkers would have gone east in the fall and returned to the mountains in the spring of 1842. Two reporters, both of whom were acquainted with Walker, wrote that in May 1842 he met John Charles Frémont in Missouri. See Conner (*Confederate*), p. 75, and *Napa County Reporter*, November 18, 1876. As for the fight with the Sioux, Walker (*Napa County Reporter*) mentioned only that he had had one but did not give any dates. Again, on the basis of what is known about his activities, the summer of 1841 seems to be the most likely time for this to have taken place.

Page 187. WIND AND AIR TRAVEL. Unruh, p. 100.

Page 188. GUIDE FEES. Unruh, p. 110; WALKER'S FEE: *History of Napa and Lake Counties*, p. 389.

Pages 188–189. OREGON-CALIFORNIA. Unruh, pp. 92–93.

Page 189. OVERLAND ACCIDENTS. Unruh, pp. 404–13.

Page 190. COMPLAINTS OF WALKER PARTY MEMBERS. Boardman and Reading, excerpts from their journals.

Page 190. JOYS. Reading, p. 169.

Page 191. ACCIDENTS WITH FIREARMS. Unruh, pp. 410–14 and 517.

Page 191. HASTINGS. Hafen and Ghent (*Broken Hand*), p. 180.

Page 192. DRY MEAT AND COFFEE. Boardman, p. 108.

Page 193. MISS EYERS. *History of Napa and Lake Counties*, pp. 387–90.

Page 193. GRANT'S DINNER. Talbot (*Journals*), pp. 47–48.

Page 195. WALKER A HOST. Stewart, p. 47.

Page 195. MARTIN-MCCLELLAN. Talbot (*Journals*), pp. 48–49.

Pages 195–197. WALKER WAGON PARTY. Stewart, pp. 36–52.

Page 196. TRADING HORSESHOE NAILS. *Santa Rosa* (California) *Daily Democrat*, November 20, 1876.

Page 197. MRS. MARTIN. C. M. Walker recollection.

Page 198. TRAIL HERD IN 1844. Bancroft (*History of California*, Vol. IV), p. 392, and *Santa Rosa Daily Democrat*, November 20, 1876.

Page 198. MARAUDING SAVAGES. Frémont describes his rescue by Walker in *Report of Exploring Expedition*, pp. 269–71.

Page 199. GOOD SORTS. Frémont (*Report of*), p. 272; Preuss, p. 132.

Page 200. BUENAVENTURA. Frémont (*Narratives of Exploration*), pp. 372–73.

Pages 200–201. DANGERS PAST. Frémont (*Report of*), p. 288.

Pages 202–203. FRÉMONT EARLY CAREER. Nevins (*Frémont*), pp. 1–26.

Page 203. WALKER-FRÉMONT MEETING. This is mentioned by Conner, (*Confederate*), p. 75, and by George Gift (*Napa County Reporter*, November 18, 1876). Conner says Walker was offered $5,000 to guide Frémont, but this is unbelievable given the going rates for this sort of work. Conner, somewhat like Joe Meek, was weak on large figures. Gift says that Walker was actually engaged by Frémont, but not liking the young officer's general arrogance, Walker withdrew before the expedition left Missouri.

Page 204. FRÉMONT-FITZPATRICK-WALKER. Carter, p. 7.

Page 205. CHILDISH FRÉMONT. Preuss, p. 3.

Page 205. SCALING FRÉMONT PEAK. Frémont (*Report of*), pp. 62–71; Preuss, pp. 37–47.

Page 206. "THE SAVAGE BATTLEMENTS." Joaquin Miller, pp. 42–3.

Page 207. "RIDICULOUS CANNON." Preuss, p. 83.

Page 208. WALKER JOINS GILLIAM PARTY. Gilliam, p. 205.

Pages 208–209. FORT LARAMIE TO FORT BRIDGER. Parrish, pp. 98–105.

Page 210. COOKE-WALKER. Cooke, p. 389.

Page 210. AT FORT BRIDGER. Palmer, p. 33; Snyder, p. 243.

Page 210. FRÉMONT'S MEN AT INDEPENDENCE. Hine, pp. 8–14.

Page 212. MAXWELL–WILLIAMS–WALKER. Breckenridge, pp. 42–45.

Page 212. MEETING WITH WALKER. Talbot (*Soldier*), pp. 13 and 32.

Page 212. WALKER AND WILLIAMS QUARREL. Breckenridge, p. 46.

Pages 213–214. WALKER PARTY TO CALIFORNIA. Breckenridge, p. 49; Hine, pp. 326–27; Talbot (*Soldier*), pp. 327–28.

Pages 214–215. FRÉMONT IN CALIFORNIA TO HAWK'S PEAK. Nevins (*Frémont*), pp. 217–33.

Page 215. WALKER LEAVES FRÉMONT AND COMMENTS. Lovell, p. 87; *Napa County* (California) *Reporter*, November 18, 1876.

Page 216. FRÉMONT ON WALKER. Frémont (*Report of*), p. 153.

Page 218. MCCLELLAN-WALKER. Juanita, January 26, 1873.

Page 218. "GREAT BLAGGARD." Nunis ("The Enigma"), pp. 342–43.

Page 219. FORT HALL AND FORT BRIDGER. Bryant, p. 144; Juanita, January 29, 1873; Nunis ("The Enigma"), p. 345.

Page 220. HASTINGS CUTOFF. Bancroft (*History of California*, Vol. IV), pp. 396–99.

Page 221. BRYANT AND REED. Bryant, p. 143; Unruh, p. 252.

Pages 221–222. WALKER AT FORT BRIDGER. Hill, p. 144; McBride, pp. 317–19; Lienhard, p. 94.

Page 223. WALKER-DONNERS. DeVoto (*Year of*), p. 319.

Page 223. AT BENT'S FORT. Abert (*New Mexico*), pp. 9–25; also Abert (*Western America*), p. 23 (the latter is a slightly different version of the former); Juanita, January 29, 1873.

Page 225. SUBLETTE-WALKER RIDE. Sublette Papers, Solomon Sublette letter, May 1, 1847.

Page 225. WALKER DISPATCH. The story in *The Expositor* was reprinted in the *Liberty* (Missouri) *Weekly Tribune*, April 24, 1847, and the excerpts are taken from that publication.

Page 226. MCCLELLAN IN MISSOURI. Juanita, January 29, 1873.

Page 228. LUCY MCCLELLAN. Willis letters, July 28, 1848.

Page 228. LEAVING MISSOURI, MEETING GOODYEAR. Barry, pp. 714–15.

Page 228. WINTER OF 1847–48. Barry, p. 714; Juanita, January 4 and 29, 1873; *History of Contra Costa County*, pp. 607 and 687.

Page 229. EMIGRANTS—1848. Bayley (ms.); May (ms.—entry July 26, 1848).

Page 230. FRÉMONT AT BENT'S FORT. Lavender, p. 307.

Page 231. WILLIAMS. Lavender, pp. 153–54, 306–08.

Page 232. "OLD FOOL BILL." Preuss, p. 145.

Page 232. FRÉMONT TO CALIFORNIA. Preuss, p. 148.

Page 232. SATISFACTORY RESULTS. Hine, p. 61.

Page 233. DEATH OF WILLIAMS. Favour, pp. 206–07, provides two different accounts of the killing of Williams by the Utes, which probably occurred on March 14, 1849. One suggests it was a planned murder for revenge, while the second indicates that Williams was rubbed out in an open fight. A third version was given by a mountaineer named Oliver Wiggins, who said he was told by two Ute chiefs, "Colorow" and "Washington," that the tribe had "executed" Williams. In 1910, when he was eighty-seven years old, Wiggins told this story to Edwin Sabin, a reputable biographer of Kit Carson. Sabin related it to Joseph Hill of the Bancroft Library in a letter dated September 21, 1933 (Hill Collection File No. 1, Bancroft Library). When it came to stories about his adventures and prowess, Wiggins told many outrageous stretchers but was more reliable if he was not personally involved. His account tends to verify one of those offered by Favour. The Utes indisputably had a motive for executing Williams.

Page 233. NED KERN. Preuss, p. xxviii.

Page 235. LIVESTOCK TRADING. There are references to the business enterprises of the Walkers and McClellans in Lindsay papers; Hill, p. 147; Lovell, p. 97. Also, I am indebted for family recollections of these activities supplied by C. M. Walker.

Page 235. MEETING BRECKENRIDGE. Breckenridge, p. 21.

Page 236. RANCHES. Walker "took up" (whether as owner or leaser is not clear) at least three ranches in California between 1849 and 1855. In addition to the one at Gilroy, he had a property near Soledad (*Daily California Chronicle*, April 16, 1856) and another some thirty miles west of Sacramento. He was met at this latter place in November 1849 by Jacob Gruwell, who had suffered terribly on an overland trip from Salt Lake. Gruwell was destitute, staggering along on foot, trying to find his relatives. As he had Breckenridge, Walker aided him, giving him a "fine mule & rigging—a generous act," said Gruwell. (See Hafen, *Journals of Forty-Niners*, p. 30.)

Page 236. WALKER ENTERPRISES. In 1850 James Walker and Frank McClellan made a visit to their families in Missouri, going by ship to New Orleans and riverboat up the Mississippi and Missouri to Independence (see page 243). While on the river packet *Ne Plus Ultra*, Frank McClellan was robbed of $11,400 in gold, according to a news item which appeared in the April 5, 1850, issue of the *Liberty* (Missouri) *Tribune*. Unfortunate as he may have been on this occasion, the incident suggests that McClellan and therefore his cousins and uncle did very well in California during the early years of the gold rush.

Pages 236–240. SAN FRANCISCO HERALD REPORT. The account of Walker's trip appeared in a four-part series: September 25, October 9, November 28 and 30, 1853. James O'Meara (p. 362) wrote that an assistant editor, A. J. Moulder, was responsible for the feature, but whether as an editor or writer, O'Meara does not make clear. No by-line appeared with the articles. There is probably an important error in the reports, i.e., about when Walker made the trip. *History of Contra Costa County*, pp. 687 and 690, states that Walker and his nephew James departed for Arizona and New Mexico in January 1851. However, the *Herald* (November 28) mentioned rather casually that the party left in February 1850. Joseph Hill (p. 149) considered this matter and concluded, "But despite the definite statement [the 1850 date given in the *Herald*] I am inclined to think 1851 is the correct date." I am inclined to agree with Hill. Beyond the information in the *History of Contra Costa County*, interior evidence supports this opinion. James Walker did arrive in Missouri in the early summer of 1851, according to a letter written by Lucy McClellan in July of that year (Willis family papers). Joe Walker was in New Mexico in the summer of 1851 and returned to California that fall (see page 240). It is possible that he made two such trips in successive years, but there are no references to a second one, and the logistics would have been difficult.

As to why the *Herald* waited a year and a half (or two and a half years) after his return to print the story, the news business was more leisurely— as well as more casual about facts—then than now. Having heard the story, Moulder or someone else may have dawdled in preparing it but got cracking because of its connection with the railroad route question (see page 240), which by 1853 had become one of great public interest.

Page 240. WALKER'S RETURN TO CALIFORNIA. The story in the *Los Angeles Star* was reprinted in the *San Francisco Herald* on December 19, 1851. However, when Walker actually returned to his home in northern California is not made clear.

Page 241. KERN-GWIN. Lovell, pp. 102–03.

Page 241. ALBUQUERQUE DISPATCH. Reprinted in *San Francisco Daily Herald*, February 12, 1853.

Page 242. WALKER'S RAILROAD REPORT. Adler and Wheelock, pp. 30–34.

Pages 243–244. JAMES ("JEEMES") WALKER. Accounts of his return to Missouri in 1851 and overland trip to California in 1852 are found in Willis family papers; *History of Contra Costa County*, pp. 452 and 687; Juanita, January 4 and 29, 1873. SAMUEL WALKER'S DEATH: Woodruff. In the Willis family letters there was mention that Samuel Walker was "very unwell" in 1848.

Page 244. ACQUIRING MANZANITA RANCH. *History of Contra Costa County*, p. 687. Later land purchases are recorded in the Contra Costa County deed book, Vol. 1, pp. 193–95. It is the recollection of descendants of James Walker, that Joe Walker moved his base of operations to Manzanita Ranch in the mid-1850s.

Page 244. MONO LAKE AND FRACAS WITH MOJAVE. *History of Contra Costa County*, p. 690.

Pages 244–245. WITH COLONEL HOFFMAN. Abbot, pp. 312–19; *Napa County* (California) *Reporter*, November 18, 1876.

Pages 245–246. FAILING EYESIGHT. When they met in 1848 near Los Angeles, Thomas Breckenridge said (p. 21) that Walker was "nearly blind" because he had been wounded by a "poisoned arrow," delivered by unidentified Indians. Considering what Walker was to do during the next seventeen years, it seems Breckenridge overstated his handicap. The poison arrow story sounds like a fabrication. There were rumors widely circulated, by whites, that Indians, especially the Apaches, used this technique, but virtually no proof of it. Daniel Conner (*Walker*, p. 350), who was with Walker in the 1860s, commented on the matter: "I do not suppose that there is one single instance of a responsible man ever charging an Apache Indian with ever having used a poisoned arrow or lance." It seems most unlikely that had Walker been such a victim, Conner would not have mentioned it. Breckenridge, who wrote long after the fact, may have heard that Walker was growing blind and for purposes of his story, which he was trying to sell to magazines, predated the affliction to 1848 (the last time Walker and Breckenridge met) to be able to work in a poisoned arrow. Also, the *Daily California Chronicle* (San Francisco) reported on April 16, 1856, that Walker's "sight has become unfortunately affected by the hardships of his mountain campaigns; but his ordinary health is good. [He] is still fond of hunting and exploring the frontier country."

Page 247. WALKER-RALSTON-LOUNT. Allyn, pp. 72–73; *History of Arizona Territory*, p. 207; James H. McClintock, p. 302.

Page 249. FORMATION OF PARTY. Barney Collection.

Page 249. LEAVING WAR ZONE. Allyn, p. 72.

Pages 249–250. WAR IN NEW MEXICO. *History of Arizona Territory*, pp. 69–80.

Page 250. WALKER-CARLETON. Cooke and therefore Carleton met Walker twice while on patrol in 1845 (see page 210).

Pages 250–251. BANTA'S CONSPIRACY STORY. Barney Collection.

Page 252. LEAVING COLORADO. Sam Miller (Barney Collection), one of the original prospectors, states that twenty-five men left Colorado. The number was to fluctuate during the next months as some of the original group left and recruits were added in New Mexico and Arizona. However, there were never more than forty men in the party.

Pages 252–254. CONNER'S ESCAPE. Conner (*Confederate*), pp. 167–69, and Conner (Walker), p. 3. For the various Conner publications and manuscripts see bibliography. Unless otherwise indicated, I have used Conner's *Joseph Reddeford Walker and the Arizona Adventure*.

Page 254. CHALLENGED BY CAVALRY. Conner, p. 13.

Page 254. "I WAS BUT A BOY." Conner, p. 201.

Pages 256–257. NIGHT RAID ON CAMP. Conner, pp. 20–21.

Pages 257–259. APACHES. The material on the Apaches and the career of Mangas prior to 1863 is taken principally from Worcester.

Pages 260–264. DUEL WITH MANGAS. Conner, pp. 21–32.

Pages 264–265. JACK SWILLING. Wallace, pp. 16–19.

Page 265. CAPTURE OF MANGAS. Conner (Prescott Collection, pp. 39–40.)

Page 266. DEATH OF MANGAS. Conner, pp. 38–39.

Page 266. LITTLE SOLDIER—JOHN WRIGHT. Conner (Prescott Collection), p. 41.

Page 266. CLARK STOCKING. Conner, p. 39.

Pages 267–268. MEETING IROTABA. Conner, pp. 87–90.

Pages 269–270. DISCOVERY OF GOLD. Benedict Collection, letter from A. S. Benedict to Kirby Benedict, May 21, 1863.

Page 271. APACHE AT CAMPFIRE. Conner, p. 111.

Page 271. CONFIDENCE IN WALKER. Conner (Prescott Collection), p. 36.

Page 272. CARLETON CORRESPONDENCE. Farish, Vol. 3, pp. 4–5; Keleher, pp. 339–40.

Page 273. CARELESS SOLDIERS. Conner, p. 48.

Page 273. EXPEDITION DISBANDED. Conner (Prescott Collection), p. 36.

Page 274. ARRIVAL OF GOVERNOR. Allyn, pp. 24–25.

Page 274. RACIAL ORDINANCES. Barney Collection.

Page 274. TAT. Conner, p. 243.

Pages 274–275. INDIAN EDITORIALS. Excerpts from the *Arizona Weekly Miner*: December 15, 1866; July 27, 1867; August 17, 1867.

Page 275. STRYCHNINE. Another version of the story (see Conner, pp. 170–75) was that Woolsey lured the Apaches to a parley and murdered them during the negotiations. However, Browne, pp. 120–24, and James McClintock, Vol. I, pp. 185–86, report that strychnine was used. It may have been that by the time Conner wrote his history, it was no longer good form to boast about poisoning Indians.

Page 276. WALKER VISIT TO CALIFORNIA—1864. *Arizona Weekly Miner*, May 11, 1864.

Page 276. EXPEDITION WITH "OLD MEN." Conner, pp. 145–47.

Pages 276–277. WALKER-WEAVER-ALLYN. Allyn, pp. 72–74 and 84–85.

Page 277. MCCORMICK SPEECH. *Arizona Weekly Miner*, July 11, 1866.

Page 278. PREUSS SUICIDE. Preuss, p. xxix.

Page 278. BRIDGER. Alter, p. 339.

Pages 280–281. CONNER-WALKER TO LA PAZ. Conner, pp. 193–201.

Page 282. WALKER LEAVING ARIZONA. Conner does not date this incident, and it is possible to read his story and conclude that it occurred as early as 1864. However, Walker was definitely in the Prescott area in the summer of 1865 (*Arizona Daily Miner*, December 29, 1876), and it would seem from Governor McCormick's speech (see page 277) that he was there in the summer of 1866. Several of the interviews and obituaries which appeared in 1876 said that Walker had been living in Contra Costa County at Manzanita Ranch for ten years. Also, in 1871 a census (Great Register) of Contra Costa County was published. It lists Walker as first being a permanent resident of the county in 1867. His occupation is given as "old pioneer." Conner himself left Arizona in September 1867. He, Walker and the journalist traveled together as far as the Colorado River. There it seems likely (though Conner did not give details) they parted, Conner going on to the Los Angeles area, Walker to Manzanita Ranch and the journalist no doubt to a good hotel.

Pages 282–283. MANZANITA RANCH. Descriptions of the ranch are given by Juanita, January 4 and 12, 1873. More information was provided by C. M. Walker. In his boyhood (he was born in 1899) Manzanita Ranch had not changed greatly from the 1870s. Mr. Walker heard the stories about Flora Kendall, Pete Carpenter and Feliz Pena from his mother, aunts and uncles who were young contemporaries of the people involved.

Pages 286–288. THE LAST INTERVIEW. *Napa County* (California) *Reporter*, November 18, 1876. The *Contra Costa* (California) *Gazette*, November 25, 1876, gave the information that George Gift was the author of the article in the *Reporter* and had interviewed Walker during the previous summer.

Page 288. GRAVESTONE. Several photographs (see Farquhar, p. 35) were made and published of the original stone. However, sometime prior to 1935 this marker was damaged and replaced by one on which the information about Walker was abbreviated, possibly to accommodate more information about the memorialists. It reads:

Capt. Joseph R. Walker
    Pioneer
Camped in Yosemite Nov 13 1833
Born Roan County Tenn Dec 13 1798
Died Oct 27 1876
Dedicated by
Mt. Diablo Parlor No 101
Native Sons of the Golden West
and Las Juntas Parlor No 221
Native Daughters of the Golden West
    July 1935

Page 295. PRESIDENT REAGAN. *Time* magazine, March 22, 1982, p. 34.

Bibliography

Abbott, John S. C. *Christopher Carson.* New York: Dodd, Mead & Company, 1873.

Abert, James William. *Abert's New Mexico Report: 1846–47.* Albuquerque: Horn & Wallace, 1962.

————. *GUADAL P'A: The Journal of J. W. Abert, from Bent's Fort to St. Louis in 1845.* Canyon, Texas: The Panhandle-Plains Historical Society, 1941.

————. *Western America in 1846–1847: The Original Travel Diary of Lieutenant J. W. Abert, Who Mapped New Mexico for the U.S. Army.* San Francisco: John Howell Books, 1966.

Adler, Pat, and Wheelock, Walt. *Walker's R.R. Routes—1853.* Glendale Calif.: La Siesta Press, 1965.

Agnew, Brad. *Fort Gibson.* Norman: University of Oklahoma Press, 1980.

Allyn, Joseph Pratt. *The Arizona of Joseph Pratt Allyn: Letters from a Pioneer Judge.* Edited by John Nicolson. Tucson: University of Arizona Press, 1974.

Alter, J. Cecil. *Jim Bridger.* Norman: University of Oklahoma Press, 1962.

Arizona Miner (Prescott), July 11, December 15, 1866; July 27, August 17, 1867.

Arnow, Harriette Simpson. *Seedtime on the Cumberland.* New York: The Macmillan Company, 1960.

Atherton, Lewis E. "Missouri's Society and Economy in 1821." *Missouri Historical Review* 65 (July 1971): 450–77.

Baldwin, Leland D., ed. and comp. *The Flavor of the Past.* Vol. 1. New York: Van Nostrand Reinhold Company, 1968.

Bancroft, Hubert Howe. *The Works of Hubert Howe Bancroft.* Vol. 1: *1834–1848.* Vol. 29: *History of Oregon.* San Francisco: The History Company, Publishers, 1886.

————. *History of California,* Vol. 4. San Francisco: A. L. Bancroft & Company, 1884.

Banta. Banta papers, Arizona Historical Society Library, Tucson.

Barney, James M. "History of the Walker Party." Barney Collection, Arizona Historical Society Library, Tucson.

Barry, Louise. *The Beginning of the West: 1540–1854.* Topeka: Kansas State Historical Society, 1972.

Bayley, T. "Recollections of Early Days in El Dorado County." Manuscript in Bancroft Library.

Beall, Thomas J. "Recollections of Wm. Craig." *Lewiston* (Idaho) *Morning Tribune,* March 3, 1918, p. 8.

Becknell, William. "The Journals of Capt. Thomas [William] Becknell." *Missouri Historical Review* 4 (January 1910): 65–84.

Beckwourth, James P. *The Life and Adventures of James P. Beckwourth.* Edited by T. D. Bonner. New York: Alfred A. Knopf, 1931.

Benedict, Albert Case. Benedict Collection, Arizona Historical Society Library, Tucson.

Bidwell, John. *Echoes of the Past.* New York: The Citadel Press, 1962.

———. "The First Emigrant Train to California." *Century* 41 (ns19) (November 1890): 106–30.

Billington, Ray Allen. *The Westward Movement in the United States.* Princeton: D. Van Nostrand Company, Inc., 1959.

Boardman, John. "The Journal of John Boardman." *Utah Historical Quarterly* 2 (October 1929): 99–121.

Bogue, Allan G.; Phillips, Thomas D.; and Wright, James E., ed. *The West of the American People.* Itasca, Ill.: F. E. Peacock Publishers, Inc., 1970.

Breckenridge, Thomas. Breckenridge manuscripts, untitled and undated. Joint Collection: University of Missouri, Western Historical Manuscript Collection—Columbia/State Historical Society of Missouri Manuscripts.

There are two typescript copies of original manuscripts, one of eighty-two pages and the second of thirty pages. The former is an autobiographical account of Breckenridge's adventures while a member of the third and fourth Frémont expeditions. The second is a third-person version of the same events and obviously represents an attempt by Breckenridge or somebody else to condense the autobiographical material for magazine publication. This may have been done in the 1890s since in August 1896 *Cosmopolitan* magazine published an "as told to" story by Breckenridge about the fourth expedition. The longer manuscript, which was the only one used here as a source, deals principally with the events of the Bear Flag Rebellion, the war between the United States and Mexico in California and the arrest of Frémont. Breckenridge is very unreliable in regard to these happenings, consistently and greatly exaggerating the importance of his own role in them. Beyond self-glorification he was motivated by the desire to substantiate claims he made for a military pension. However, it seems to me that the earlier part of the narrative—in which he reports on the travels of Frémont and Walker before they reached

California—is much more plausible. In this section Breckenridge writes more as a detached observer without any obvious self-serving purpose. The language and sense of the incidents he describes ring true, and where his recollections can be checked against other sources they seem to be quite accurate.

Brewerton, George Douglas. *Overland with Kit Carson*. New York: Coward-McCann, Inc., 1930.

Browne, J. Ross. *A Tour Through Arizona, 1864, or Adventures in Apache Country*. Tucson: Arizona Silhouettes, 1951.

Bryant, Edwin. *Rocky Mountain Adventures*. New York: Worthington Co., 1888.

Byrd, William. *The Secret Diary of William Byrd of Westover, 1709–1712*. Edited by Louis B. Wright and Marion Tinling. Richmond, Va.: The Dietz Press, 1941.

Carleton, Lt. J. Henry. *The Prairie Logbooks*. Chicago: The Caxton Club, 1943.

Carson, Kit. *Kit Carson's Autobiography*. Edited by Milo Milton Quaife. Lincoln: University of Nebraska Press, 1966.

Carter, Harvey Lewis. *'Dear Old Kit': The Historical Kit Carson*. Norman: University of Oklahoma Press, 1968.

Chiles, Mary Sue. "A Brief History of the Six Mile Territory." Manuscript in Joint Collection: University of Missouri, Western Historical Manuscript Collection—Columbia/State Historical Society of Missouri Manuscripts.

Chittenden, Hiram Martin. *A History of the American Fur Trade of the Far West*. Vols. I and II. Stanford, Calif.: Academic Reprints, 1954.

Clark, Dan Elbert. *The Middle West in American History*. New York: Thomas Y. Crowell Company, 1937.

Clark, Thomas D. *Frontier America*. New York: Charles Scribner's Sons, 1959.

Cleland, Robert Glass. *The Cattle on a Thousand Hills*. San Marino, Calif.: The Huntington Library, 1951.

———. *This Reckless Breed of Men*. New York: Alfred A. Knopf, 1950.

Clyman, James. *James Clyman, Frontiersman*. Edited by Charles L. Camp. Portland, Oregon: Champoeg Press, 1960.

Conner, Daniel Ellis. *A Confederate in the Colorado Gold Fields*. Edited by Donald Berthrong and Odessa Davenport. Norman: University of Oklahoma Press. 1970.

———. *Joseph Reddeford Walker and the Arizona Adventure*. Edited by Berthrong and Davenport. Norman: University of Oklahoma Press, 1956.

Conner devoted the latter part of his life to writing about the adventures of his youth on the southwestern frontier. Except for a few articles in small California newspapers, he was unable to publish any of these stories during his lifetime. After his death (in 1920) most of his manuscripts and correspondence about his histories found their way into three collections: the Huntington Library; Arizona State

Library (Phoenix); and the Sharlot Hall Historical Society (Prescott, Arizona). Working principally with the Arizona State material, Berthrong and Davenport edited and published the two volumes of Conner's writings.

In my account of the Walker party in New Mexico and Arizona, I have relied mainly on the *Walker* volume. Where this has been supplemented with unpublished material from Conner manuscripts and correspondence in other collections, these sources have been noted.

Contra Costa Gazette. November 4, 1876.

Cooke, Philip St. George. *Scenes and Adventures in the Army.* Philadelphia: Lindsay & Blakiston, 1857.

———. Whiting, William Henry Chase; Aubry, Francois Xavier. *Exploring Southwestern Trails, 1846–1854.* Edited by Bieber and Bender. Glendale, Calif.: The Arthur H. Clarke Co., 1938.

DAR, Kansas City Chapter. *Vital Historical Records of Jackson Co., Mo.* Collected, compiled and published by DAR, Kansas City Chapter. Kansas City, Mo.: DAR, 1933–34.

DeVoto, Bernard. *Across the Wide Missouri.* Boston: Houghton Mifflin Co., 1947.

———. *The Course of Empire.* Boston: Houghton Mifflin Co., 1952.

———. *The Year of Decision: 1846.* Boston: Houghton Mifflin Co., 1942.

Dick, Everett. *The Dixie Frontier.* New York: Octagon Books, 1974.

Duffus, R. L. *The Santa Fe Trail.* New York: Tudor Publishing Co., 1930.

Eells, Myra F. "Journal of Myra F. Eells Kept While Passing Through the United States and over the Rocky Mountains in the Spring and Summer of 1838." *Transactions of the Seventeenth Annual Reunion of the Oregon Pioneer Association for 1889*, pp. 54–88a.

Elliott, T. C. " 'Doctor' Robert Newell: Pioneer." *The Quarterly of the Oregon Historical Society*, 9 (June 1908): 103–26.

Ellison, William Henry. *The Life and Adventures of George Nidever.* Berkeley: University of California Press, 1937.

Ellsberry, Elizabeth Prather, comp. *Marriage Records of Lillard & Lafayette County, Mo., 1821–1850.* Chillicothe, Mo.: typescript, 1959.

Estergreen, M. Morgan. *Kit Carson.* Norman: University of Oklahoma Press, 1962.

Farish, Thomas Edwin. *History of Arizona.* Phoenix: Filmers Brothers Electrotype Co., Vols. I–III, 1915–16.

Farquhar, Francis P. "Walker's Discovery of Yosemite." *Sierra Club Bulletin*, 27 (1942): 35–49.

Favour, Alpheus H. *Old Bill Williams: Mountain Man.* Chapel Hill: University of North Carolina Press, 1936.

Ferris, Warren Angus. *Life in the Rocky Mountains.* Salt Lake City: Rocky Mountain Book Shop, 1940.

Field, Matthew C. *Prairie and Mountain Sketches.* Norman: University of Oklahoma Press, 1957.

Fiske, John. *Old Virginia and Her Neighbors.* Cambridge, Mass.: The Riverside Press, 1897.

Ford, Henry Jones. *The Scotch-Irish in America*. Princeton: Princeton University Press, 1915.

Foreman, Grant. *Pioneer Days in the Early Southwest*. Cleveland: The Arthur H. Clark Company, 1926.

Fowler, Jacob. *The Journal of Jacob Fowler*. Edited with notes by Elliott Coues. New York: Francis P. Harper, 1898.

Frazer, Robert W. *Forts of the West*. Norman: University of Oklahoma Press, 1965.

Frémont, John Charles. *The Expeditions of John Charles Frémont*. Edited by Mary Lee Spence and Donald Jackson. Urbana: University of Illinois Press, 1970.

——. *Narratives of Exploration and Adventure*. Edited by Allan Nevins. New York: Longmans, Green & Co., 1956.

——. *Report of the Exploring Expedition to the Rocky Mountains*. Ann Arbor, Mich.: University Microfilms, Inc., 1966.

Garrard, Lewis H. *Wah-To-Yah and the Taos Trail*. Edited by Ralph P. Bieber. Glendale, Calif.: The Arthur H. Clark Company, 1938.

Gilbert, Bil. *The Trailblazers*. New York: Time-Life Books, 1973.

Gilliam, Washington Smith. "Reminiscences of Washington Smith Gilliam." *Transactions of the 31st Annual Reunion of the Oregon Pioneer Association for 1903*, pp. 202–20.

Goetzmann, William H. *Army Exploration in the American West: 1803–1863*. New Haven: Yale University Press, 1959.

——. *Exploration and Empire*. New York: Alfred A. Knopf, 1971.

——. *The Mountain Man*. Cody, Wyo.: Buffalo Bill Historical Center, 1978.

Golley, Frank B. "James Baird, Early Santa Fe Trader." *Missouri Historical Society Bulletin* 15 (April 1959): 171–93.

Gowans, Fred R. *Rocky Mountain Rendezvous*. Provo, Utah: Brigham Young University, 1975.

Gregg, Kate L. "The History of Fort Osage." *Missouri Historical Review* 34 (July 1940): 439–88.

——, ed. *The Road to Santa Fe*. Albuquerque: University of New Mexico Press, 1952.

Hafen, LeRoy R. "Fort Davy Crockett, Its Fur Men and Visitors." *The Colorado Magazine* 24 (January 1952): 17.

——. "Mountain Men—William Craig." *The Colorado Magazine* (September 1934): 171–76.

——. *Hafen Collection of Americana*. Provo, Utah: Brigham Young University, 1962.

——, ed. *The Mountain Men and the Fur Trade of the Far West*. 10 vols. Glendale, Calif.: The Arthur H. Clark Company, 1965–72.

——, and Hafen, Ann W., eds. *The Far West and the Rockies Historical Series*. 15 vols. Glendale, Calif.: The Arthur H. Clark Company. *Old Spanish Trail*. Vol. 1, 1954.
To the Rockies and Oregon: 1838–1842. Vol. 3, 1955.
Journals of Forty-Niners. Vol. 15, 1961.

————, and Ghent, W. J. *Broken Hand.* Denver: The Old West Publishing Company, 1931.

————, and Rister, Carl Coke. *Western America.* New York: Prentice-Hall, 1941.

————, and Young, Francis Marion. *Fort Laramie and the Pageant of the West, 1834–1890.* Glendale, Calif.: The Arthur H. Clark Company, 1938.

Haines, Francis. "Pioneer Portraits: Robert Newell." *Idaho Yesterday* 9 (Spring 1965): 2–9.

Hamilton, William T. *My Sixty Years on the Plains.* Edited by E. T. Sieber. Columbus, Ohio: Long's College Book Co., 1951.

Hart, Freeman H. *The Valley of Virginia in the American Revolution: 1763–1789.* Chapel Hill: University of North Carolina Press, 1942.

Hartsell, J. "The 'J. Hartsell Memora': The Journal of a Tennessee Captain in the War of 1812." Edited by Mary Hardin McCown. The East Tennessee Historical Society's Publications 11 (1939): 93–115; 12 (1940): 118–46.

Hastings, Lansford W. *The Emigrants' Guide to Oregon and California.* Princeton: Princeton University Press, 1932.

Henson, Pauline. *Founding a Wilderness Capital: Prescott, A.T. 1864.* Flagstaff, Ariz.: Northland Press, 1965.

Hill, Joseph J. "Capt. Joe Walker—Mountain Man, Trapper, Trader, Guide. 1798–1876." Manuscript in Hill Collection at Bancroft Library, Berkeley, Calif.

   The late Joseph Hill was the assistant librarian of the Bancroft Library and a prominent western history scholar. He worked on this Walker biography for a number of years prior to his death, but the 200 pages in this collection are not a final draft, many of the chapters existing only in outline or note form.

Hine, Robert V. *Edward Kern and American Expansion.* New Haven: Yale University Press, 1962.

History of Arizona Territory—1884. San Francisco: Wallace W. Elliott & Co., 1884. Flagstaff, Ariz.: Northland Press, 1964.

History of Contra Costa County, California. San Francisco: W. A. Slocum & Co., 1882.

History of Howard and Cooper Counties. St. Louis: National Historical Company, 1883.

History of Jackson County, Missouri. Cape Girardeau, Mo.: Ramfre Press, 1966 (reprint of 1881 edition).

History of Napa and Lake Counties. San Francisco: Slocum, Bowen & Co., 1881.

History of Sonoma County. San Francisco: Alley, Bowen & Co., 1880.

Holmes, Kenneth L. "The Benjamin Cooper Expeditions to Santa Fe in 1822 and 1823." *New Mexico Historical Review* 38 (April 1963): 139–50.

————. *Ewing Young.* Portland, Ore.: Binford & Mort, Publishers, 1967.

Hubbell, Captain W. D. "The First Steamboats on the Missouri." Edited by

Vivian K. McLarty. *Missouri Historical Review* 51 (July 1957): 373–81.

Hulbert, Archer Butler, ed. *Southwest on the Turquoise Trail.* Published by The Stewart Commission of Colorado College and The Denver Public Library, 1933.

Illustrated Historical Atlas of Jackson Co., Missouri—1877. Reprinted by Jackson Co. Historical Society, 1976.

Irving, Washington. *A Tour on the Prairies.* New York: Pantheon Books, 1967.

————. *The Adventures of Captain Bonneville, U.S.A.* Norman, Okla.: University of Oklahoma Press, 1961.

Jackson, Orick. *The White Conquest of Arizona.* Los Angeles: The Grafton Co., 1908.

James, Marquis. *The Life of Andrew Jackson.* Indianapolis and New York: The Bobbs-Merrill Company, 1938.

————. *The Raven: A Biography of Sam Houston.* Indianapolis: The Bobbs-Merrill Company, 1929.

Johnson, Overton, and Winter, William H. *Route Across the Rocky Mountains.* Readex Microprint Corporation, 1966.

Journal of the Pioneer and Walker Mining Districts: 1863–65. Arizona Statewide Archival and Records Project, Historical Records Survey Project, August 1941.

Juanita. Author of a series of articles appearing in the January 4, 12, 15, 16, 29 and 30, 1873, issues of the *Oakland* (California) *Transcript.*
    Juanita was the pen name of John C. McPhearson, a free-lance journalist, poet, historian and, by report, notable drinker. (McPhearson died in 1881 in San Francisco as a result of falling off a railroad trestle which he was attempting to cross while intoxicated.) McPhearson emigrated to California from Missouri in 1848, making the overland crossing in company with Walker's three nephews, James, Frank and Mike McClellan. He remained a family friend for the rest of his life. Of all the professional journalists who wrote about Walker, McPhearson was probably the best acquainted with him. The Juanita series was based on a series of interviews he conducted while visiting Manzanita Ranch in the summer and fall of 1872.

Keleher, William A. *Turmoil in New Mexico: 1846–1868.* Santa Fe: The Rydal Press, 1951.

Kercheval, Samuel. *A History of the Valley of Virginia.* 3rd ed. Woodstock, Va.: W. N. Grabill, Power Press, 1902.

Kern, Edward. "From Walker Lake to Walker Pass with Frémont's Third Expedition: The Travel Journal of Edward Kern." Edited by Meri Hanson. *Nevada Historical Society Quarterly* 21 (Spring 1978): 56–65.

Korns, J. Roderic. *West from Fort Bridger.* Salt Lake City: Utah State Historical Society, 1951.

Lamar, Howard R., ed. *The Reader's Encyclopedia of the American West.* New York: Harper & Row, Inc., 1977.

Lavender, David. *Bent's Fort*. Garden City, N.Y.: Doubleday & Co., Inc., 1954.

Lawrence, Eleanor. "Wakara, Napoleon of the Desert." *Touring Topics* 24 (May 1932).

Leonard, Zenas. *Adventures of Zenas Leonard, Fur Trader*. Edited by John C. Ewers. Norman: University of Oklahoma Press, 1959.

Lewiston (Idaho) *Morning Tribune*. Article by T. J. Beall. March 3, 1918.

Leyburn, James G. *The Scotch-Irish*. Chapel Hill: University of North Carolina Press, 1962.

Liberty (Missouri) *Weekly Tribune*. April 24, 1847; April 5, 1850.

Lienhard, Heinrich. *From St. Louis to Sutter's Fort, 1846*. Norman: University of Oklahoma Press, 1961.

Lindsay, Ethel Walker (Mrs. Edward T.)

   Mrs. Lindsay (Santa Rosa, California), a great-granddaughter of Joel and Mary Walker, generously shared genealogical notes and records and was an especially valuable source regarding the activities of the Walkers in Oregon and northern California.

Lovell, Merton N. "Joseph R. Walker, Mountain Man and Guide of the Far West." A thesis submitted to the Department of History, Brigham Young University, Provo, Utah, June 1959.

McBride, John R. "Pioneer Days in the Mountains." *Tullidge's Quarterly Magazine* 3 (July 1884): 311–20.

McClintock, James H. *Arizona*. Chicago: Clarke Publishing Co., 1916.

McClintock, Walter. *Old Indian Trails*. Cambridge, Mass.: The Riverside Press, 1923.

McCurdy, Frances. "Courtroom Oratory of the Pioneer Period." *Missouri Historical Review* 56 (October 1961): 1–11.

McDermott, John Francis. "Washington Irving and the Journal of Captain Bonneville." *Mississippi Valley Historical Review* 43 (December 1956): 459–67.

McPhearson, John C. See Juanita.

Martin, Paul S., and Plog, Fred. *The Archaeology of Arizona*. Garden City, N.Y.: Doubleday, 1973.

Mason, Mary Moore Montgomery.

   Mrs. Mason has in her possession a number of diaries written by members of the Walker family in the eighteenth and nineteenth centuries, and she permitted me to read these and to record, on tape, passages pertaining to this work. These tapes are now in my possession.

May, Richard M. "Journal of Richard M. May." Manuscript in Bancroft Library.

Meek, Stephen Hall. *The Autobiography of a Mountain Man: 1805–1889*. Pasadena: Glen Dawson, 1948.

Meriwether, David. *My Life in the Mountains and on the Plains*. Edited by Robert A. Griffen. Norman: University of Oklahoma Press, 1965.

Merk, Frederick. *Manifest Destiny and Mission in American History*. New York: Vintage Books, 1966.

Miller, Alfred Jacob. *The West of Alfred Jacob Miller (1837)*. Norman: University of Oklahoma Press, 1951.

Miller, Joaquin. *Overland in a Covered Wagon*. Edited by Sidney G. Firman. New York: D. Appleton and Co., 1930.

Missouri Intelligencer. May 28, and July 23, 1819.

Missouri Pioneers. County and Genealogical Records. Compiled and published by Miss Nadine Hodges and Mrs. Howard W. Woodruff.

Moore, Arthur K. *The Frontier Mind*. Lexington: University of Kentucky Press, 1957.

Morgan, Dale L. *Jedediah Smith*. Lincoln: University of Nebraska Press, 1953.

————, ed. *Overland in 1846*. Georgetown, Calif.: The Talisman Press, 1963.

Napa County Reporter. Walker obituary written by George Gift. November 18, 1876.

Nevins, Allan. *Frémont: Pathmarker of the West*. New York: Frederick Ungar Publishing Company, 1961.

Nidever, George. *The Life and Adventures of George Nidever (1802–1883)*. Edited by William Henry Ellison. Berkeley: University of California Press, 1937.

Nunis, Doyce Blackman, Jr. *Andrew Sublette*. Los Angeles: Glen Dawson, 1960.

————. "The Enigma of the Sublette Overland Party, 1845." *Pacific Historical Review* 28 (November 1959): 331.

O'Meara, James. "Captain Joseph R. Walker." *Oregon Historical Society Quarterly* 16 (December 1915): 350–63.

O'Meara, Walter. *Daughters of the Country*. New York: Harcourt, Brace & World, Inc., 1968.

Palmer, Joel. *Journal of Travels over the Rocky Mountains*. Cincinnati: J. A. & U. P. James, 1847. Readex Microprint Corporation, 1966.

Parkman, Francis. *The Oregon Trail*. New York: Dodd, Mead & Company, 1964.

Parrish, Rev. Edward Evans. "Crossing the Plains in 1844." *Oregon Pioneer Association Proceedings—16th Annual Reunion*, 1888, pp. 82–121.

Pattie, James Ohio. *The Personal Narrative of James O. Pattie, of Kentucky*. Readex Microprint Corporation, 1966.

Peters, Virginia Bergman. *The Florida Wars*. Hamden, Conn.: Archon Books, 1979.

Phelan, James. *History of Tennessee*. Cambridge, Mass.: The Riverside Press, 1889.

Phillips, Paul Chrisler. *The Fur Trade*. 2 vols. Norman: University of Oklahoma Press, 1961.

Porter, Mae Reed, and Davenport, Odessa. *Scotsman in Buckskin: Sir William Drummond Stewart and the Rocky Mountain Fur Trade*. New York: Hastings House, 1963.

Poston, Charles D. *Building a State in Apache Land.* Tempe, Ariz.: Aztec Press, 1963.

Potter, Alvina N. *The Many Lives of the Lynx.* Prescott, Ariz.: 1964.

Preuss, Charles. *Exploring with Frémont.* Translated and edited by Erwin G. and Elizabeth K. Gudde. Norman: University of Oklahoma Press, 1958.

Purcell, Mae Fisher. *Contra Costa County History.* Berkeley: Gillick Press, 1940.

Ramsey, J. G. M. *The Annals of Tennessee (Ramsey's Annals of Tennessee).* Kingsport, Tenn.: Kingsport Press, Inc., 1967.

Reading, Pierson B. "Journal of Pierson B. Reading, Written During His Journey from Westport, Missouri to Monterey, California in 1843." *Quarterly of the Society of California Pioneers* 7 (September 1930): 148–98.

Records of Lillard and Lafayette County, Mo.: 1821–1850. State Historical Society of Missouri, Columbia.

Rittenhouse, Jack D. *The Santa Fe Trail: A Historical Bibliography.* Albuquerque: University of New Mexico Press, 1971.

Robins, Ruby Matson, ed. "The Missouri Reader." *Missouri Historical Review.* Part I: 45 (October 1950): 1–11. Part XIII: 48 (October 1953): 59–70.

Rorabaugh, W. J. *The Alcoholic Republic.* New York: Oxford University Press, 1979.

Russell, Carl P. *Firearms, Traps and Tools of the Mountain Men.* Albuquerque: University of New Mexico Press, 1967.

Russell, Don. "How Many Indians Were Killed?" *The American West* 10 (July 1973): 42–63.

Ruxton, George Frederick. *Life in the Far West.* Edited by LeRoy Hafen. Norman: University of Oklahoma Press, 1951.

Sage, Rufus B. *Rocky Mountain Life; or, Startling Scenes and Perilous Adventures in The Far West.* Boston: Estes and Lauriat, 1880.

San Francisco Herald. December 19, 1851; February 12, September 25, October 9, November 28 and 30, 1853.

Santa Rosa (California) *Daily Democrat.* November 20, 1876.

Sibley, George. "Common-place Book, No. 1." Sibley Manuscripts, Missouri Historical Society, St. Louis.

Sitgreaves, Captain L. "Report of an Expedition down the Zuni and Colorado Rivers." U.S. Engineering Dept., Washington, 1853.

Smith, E. Willard. "Journal of E. Willard Smith While with the Fur Traders, Vasquez and Sublette, in the Rocky Mountain Region, 1839–1840." *Oregon Historical Society Quarterly* 14 (September 1913): 250–79.

Smith, Henry Nash. *Virgin Land: The American West as Symbol and Myth.* Cambridge, Mass.: Harvard University Press, 1950.

Snyder, Jacob R. "The Diary of Jacob R. Snyder, Written While Crossing the Plains to California in 1845." *Quarterly of The Society of California Pioneers* 8 (December 1931): 224–60.

Sonoma County Historical Society "Bulletin." Number 1, 1979.

Stephens, F. F. "Missouri and the Santa Fe Trade." *Missouri Historical Review*. Part 1: 10 (July 1916): 233–62. Part 2: 11 (April–July 1917): 289–312.

Stercula, Beverly Margaret. *Heads of Families: 1830 Census of Missouri.* Fullerton, Calif.: Genealogems Publications, 1966.

Stewart, George R. *The California Trail.* New York: McGraw-Hill Book Company, 1962.

Stone, Irving. *Men to Match My Mountains.* Garden City, N.Y.: Doubleday and Company, Inc., 1956.

Storrs, Augustus, and Wetmore, Alphonso. *Santa Fe Trail: First Reports: 1825.* Houston: Stagecoach Press, 1960.

Sublette, Solomon. Sublette Papers, Missouri Historical Society, St. Louis.

Summers, Lewis Preston. *History of Southwest Virginia, 1746–1786, Washington County, 1777–1870.* Richmond: J. L. Hill Printing Company, 1903.

Talbot, Theodore. *The Journals of Theodore Talbot: 1843 and 1849–52.* Edited, with notes, by Charles H. Carey. Portland, Ore.: Metropolitan Press, 1931.

———. *Soldier in the West.* Edited by Robert V. Hine and Savoie Lottinville. Norman: University of Oklahoma Press, 1972.

Trenholm, Virginia Cole, and Carley, Maurine. *The Shoshonis.* Norman: University of Oklahoma Press, 1964.

Turner, Frederick Jackson. *The Frontier in American History.* New York: Holt, Rinehart and Winston, 1920.

Unruh, John D., Jr. *The Plains Across.* Urbana: University of Illinois Press, 1979.

Van Every, Dale. *A Company of Heroes.* New York: William Morrow and Company, 1962.

———. *Forth to the Wilderness.* New York: New American Library, 1962.

Vestal, Stanley. *Joe Meek: The Merry Mountain Man.* Lincoln: University of Nebraska Press, 1952.

Victor, Frances Fuller. *The River of the West.* Hartford, Conn.: R. W. Bliss & Co., 1870. Reprinted by Long's College Book Company, Columbus, Ohio, 1950.

Vineyard, Arva Lee (Mrs. John), comp. and pub. *Deed Books A, B, C of Jackson County, Mo.* Independence, Mo.: 1969.

———, comp. and pub. *Original Land Entries of Jackson Co., Mo.* Independence, Mo.: 1971.

Violette, E. M. "Early Settlements in Missouri." *Missouri Historical Review* 1 (October 1906): 38–52.

Voelker, Frederic E. "Ezekiel Williams of Boon's Lick." *Bulletin of Missouri Historical Society* 8 (October 1951): 17.

Wagoner, Jay J. *Arizona Territory: 1863–1912.* Tucson: University of Arizona Press, 1970.

Walker, Alda (Mrs. John M.). Letters to Audrey Woodruff.

Walker, Joel P. *A Pioneer of Pioneers.* Los Angeles: Glen Dawson, 1953.

Wallace, Andrew. "John W. Swilling." *Arizoniana* 2 (Spring 1961): 16–19.

Ward, John William. *Andrew Jackson: Symbol for an Age*. London: Oxford University Press, 1953.

Wasson, Joseph. *Bodie and Esmeralda*. San Francisco: Spaulding, Barto & Co., 1878.

Watson, Douglas. *The West Wind: The Life Story of Joseph Reddeford Walker*. Los Angeles: Johnck and Seeger, 1934.

Weber, David J. *The Taos Trappers*. Norman: University of Oklahoma Press, 1971.

White, Emma Siggins. *Genealogy of the Descendants of John Walker of Wigton, Scotland, with Records of a Few Allied Families: 1600–1902*. Kansas City, Mo.: Tiernan-Dart Printing Co., 1902.

Wilcox, Pearl. *Jackson County Pioneers*. Independence, Mo.: 1975.

Willis Family Letters. Joint Collection: University of Missouri, Western Historical Manuscript Collection—Columbia/State Historical Society of Missouri Manuscripts.

Wilson, Iris Higbie. *William Wolfskill*. Glendale, Calif.: The Arthur H. Clark Company, 1965.

Wislizenus, F. Adolphus. *A Tour to Northern Mexico*. Glorieta, N.M.: The Rio Grande Press, Inc., 1969.

———. *Journey to the Rocky Mountains, 1839*. St. Louis: Missouri Historical Society, 1912.

Woodruff, Audrey (Mrs. Howard W.). Walker family records.

    Mrs. Woodruff of Independence, Mo., is a distinguished genealogist whose husband is a descendant of John and Katherine Walker, the emigrants from Wigton, Scotland. Mrs. Woodruff kindly made available family records and genealogical material in her possession.

Worcester, Donald E. *The Apaches*. Norman: University of Oklahoma Press, 1979.

Young, Otis E. *The West of Philip St. George Cooke: 1809–1895*. Glendale, Calif.: The Arthur H. Clark Co., 1955.

Yount, George C. *George C. Yount and His Chronicles of the West*. Edited by Charles L. Camp. Denver: Old West Publishing Company, 1966.

Index

Abert, Lt. James, 210–11, 223–5, 238
Absaroka, 150–2, 156, 230, 278
Adams, David, 116, 150
Adams, Joseph Rutherford Walker, 186
Adams, William, 186
Agriculture, 14, 15–16, 18, 32, 35, 47, 68–9
Ailstock, Lucian, 70
Alabama, 53, 54
Albuquerque, N. Mex., 237, 239, 241, 249, 250–1
Allande, Pedro María de, 73
Allein, Joseph, 25
Allyn, Joseph, 273, 276–7
Ambrister, Robert, 57–8
American Fur Company (AFC), 98, 108–17 *passim*, 151, 154–7, 161, 169, 175, 284
Anderson, Lewis, 198
Año Nuevo Point, 201
Apache Indians, 4, 156, 239, 240, 250, 256–9, 267, 281, 283; Chiricahua, 258; Mimbreño, 257, 258–67; Tonto, 267–8, 270–1, 273, 274–5, 276
Appalachian frontier, 14; Indians of, 4, 14, 19, 20, 22, 27, 34–46, 52–6, 63, 104; Scotch-Irish on, 4, 16, 21–44, 48, 289, 295, 296; treaty line on, 45–6
Apps Valley, 38–40, 41, 43
Arapaho Indians, 109, 121, 134, 150, 156, 164, 183
Arbuckle, Col. Matthew, 98
Arbuthnot, Alexander, 57–8
Arikara Indians, 106, 107, 116, 122, 162
Arizona, 232, 242, 273, 288; Civil War in, 249–50, 264; gold in, 4, 9, 247, 252, 269–74; Indians of, 145, 257–8; racism in, 274–5; Walker's exploration of, 4, 171–2, 237–40, 244
Arizona Miner, The, 274–5
Arkansas, 64, 95, 250

Ashley, William, 107–8, 125, 150, 153, 154, 177, 220, 229, 280
Astor, John Jacob, 98, 99, 108, 154, 207
Audubon, John James, 239
Austin, Moses, 70, 143
Austin, Stephen, 70, 143

Baird, James, 73, 79
Baldridge, William, 193, 297
Bandini, Juan, 181
Bannock Indians, 128, 156
Banta, A. F., 250–2, 269, 272
Baptists, 170, 186
Bartleson, John, 182–4, 187, 188–9, 190–1, 196
Becknell, William, 75–6, 80, 85, 117
Beckwourth, Jim, 9, 150, 155–7, 278
Benedict, A. S., 251, 269, 270–1
Benedict, Kirby, 271
Bent, Charles, 223, 225, 231, 279
Bent, William, 43, 155–7, 162, 223, 227, 240, 279, 297
Benton, Thomas Hart, 54, 80–1, 83, 86, 93, 102, 202, 203, 230, 241
Bents, the, 156, 161, 211
Bent's Fort, 10, 156, 200–1, 208, 211, 218, 223–4, 226, 230–1
Beverly, Robert, 13–14
Bidwell, John, 182, 184
Bighorn, 151–2
Billy the Kid, 91
Blackfoot Indians, 106–7, 108, 109–10, 114–15, 116–17, 119, 122–3, 150, 155, 156, 163, 287
Blackwell, Jefferson, 122
Black Wolf, 39–40, 41, 43
Boardman, John, 192–3
Boggs, Lilburn, 88–9, 92, 102, 179, 219
Bonneville, Capt. Benjamin Louis Eulalie de, 96–7, 128, 165–6, 200, 280; fur trapping expedition of, 97–121 *pas-*

sim, 124–6, 147–53 *passim*, 185, 186, 215, 278, 291, 292; and Washington Irving, 99–100, 103, 104, 105, 114, 116, 124–6, 132–3, 148–9, 165, 215
Boone, Daniel, 4, 7, 61, 143
Bowie, Jim, 91
Braddock, Gen. Edward, 36
Bradshaw, John, 139–41, 148, 201
Breckenridge, Thomas, 9, 156, 171, 211–13, 230, 232, 235–6
Bridger, Jim, 4, 7, 9, 43, 96, 107–8, 114–15, 117, 125, 128, 155–6, 161, 173, 175, 179, 181, 188, 192, 221, 227, 278–9
Brown, John, 54–6
Brown, Joseph, 83, 84, 86
Brown's Hole, 157, 158, 172, 179, 180, 181
Bryant, Edwin, 219, 221
Buenaventura River, 128, 199–200
Burden, Benjamin, 29–30
Burris, Henry, 89
Byrd, William, 33

Calhoun, John, 62–4
California, 89, 100, 101, 112, 126–7, 172, 173, 179; Frémont in, 198, 207, 214, 217, 232, 279; gold in, 143, 234–6, 244, 248; Indians of, 130, 137, 139, 140, 141, 143, 144; and Mexican War, 217, 219, 223, 234; under Mexico, 125, 126, 139, 140–3, 149, 156, 180–1, 189, 201, 214–15, 218, 235; migration to, 88, 144, 178–9, 181–3, 186–7, 188–9, 191–7, 202, 208, 220–3, 229, 234–5; U.S. interest in, 140, 201, 214–15; Walker settled in, 7, 230, 235, 244, 282–8; Walker's expedition to, 4–5, 11–12, 122, 123–44, 149, 152, 175, 176
California Trail, 197
Campbell, John, 24–5, 29
Campbell, Mrs. John (Elizabeth Walker), 24
Canby, Col. E. R. S., 250
Carleton, Gen. James, 250–2, 253, 254, 258–9, 263, 264, 265, 269, 271–3
Carpenter, Pete, 283–4
Carrick, Barbara, 51
Carrick, Samuel, 50–1, 58
Carrick, Mrs. Samuel (Annis), 51, 58, 88
Carrick, William, 51
Carroll family, 15
Carson, Kit, 4, 7, 9, 10, 43, 93,145,155–6, 159, 164, 166, 176, 199–201, 203–5, 207, 211, 212, 224, 227, 240, 259
Carter, Harvey Lewis, 204
Cass, Lewis, 98
Castro, Col. José, 214–15
Catlin, George, 239
Cerré, Michael, 103, 106, 111, 121, 148, 149, 185
Chambers, Samuel, 73, 79
Champlain (partner of Williams), 74
Charley (cook), 283
Charley (interpreter), 268–9, 280

Cherokee Indians, 14, 16, 23, 27, 28, 34, 36–7, 38, 40, 41, 44, 49, 50, 51, 52, 53, 97, 285
Cheyenne Indians, 105, 121, 150, 156, 157, 160, 162, 166, 183–4, 192, 224, 227, 279, 286
Chihuahua, Mex., 73, 160, 225–6, 257
Chiles, Azubah, 68, 183
Chiles, Joe, 183, 188, 189–90, 191, 194–6, 229
Chinook Indians, 164
Cholera, 227
Chouteau, Auguste, 73
Chouteau family, 283–4
Church of England, 18
Civil War, 97, 106, 242, 247, 249–52, 255, 258, 259, 264, 272, 279–80
Clark, Harvey, 175–6
Clark, William, 4, 64, 114, 166, 280
Clark, William, 39–40
Clearfield Republican, 152
Clemson, Capt. Eli, 64
Clyman, James, 107, 177, 220, 280
Cochise, 258
Colonists, 13–16, 20–3, 26, 34
Colorado, 73, 200, 237, 249, 252–3, 254, 264, 269
Comanche Indians, 52, 75, 127, 145, 184
Comcomly, 164–5
Confederate Army. *See* Civil War
Congregationalists, 175–6
Conner, Daniel, 9–10, 11, 252–6, 260–76 *passim*, 279, 280–1, 297
Cooke, Capt. Philip St. George, 209–10, 212, 250
Cooper, James Fenimore, 28
Cooper, Stephen, 76–7, 79
Cornplanter, 38
Coulter family, 49
Council Bluffs, Mo., 64, 74
Council Grove, 84, 85
Courts: in Missouri, 89, 90, 93–5
Cowen, Andrew, 38
Cowen, Mrs. Andrew (Ann Walker), 38
Cowie, Tom, 198
Craig, Bill, 9, 124–5, 127–44, 154, 159, 176–7, 179, 227
Crazy Horse, 286
Creek Indians, 36, 52, 53–6, 57
Creek Nation, 29–34, 38–40, 41, 52, 56, 62, 255
Creek War, 54–6
Crockett, Davy, 4, 11
Crow Indians, 105, 107, 116, 121, 150–1, 156, 161, 162, 166, 278
Custer, Gen. George A., 286–7, 296

Dawson, Fleurnaye, 198
Dawson, Nicholas, 190
Deer Little Woman, 161
Delaware Indians, 38, 41, 104, 109, 111, 112, 184, 210
Demere, Capt. Paul, 36–7
De Mun, Jules, 73
Denig, Edwin, 161–2

Denver, Colo., 249, 278
De Smet, Pierre Jean, 176, 182, 297
Digger Indians, 130, 133, 212, 213
Donelson family, 49
Doniphan, Col. Alexander, 225
Donner party, 191, 220–1, 223
Drips, Andrew, 109, 114, 117, 162, 168, 170, 175, 203, 204, 227
Dunkleberry, Amos, 37, 41
Dunmore, John Murray, earl of, 45–6, 60

Earps, the, 91
Easton, Rufus, 66
Eaton, John, 98
Echols, John, 37, 41
Education: on frontier, 50
Eells, Cushing, 169
Eells, Mrs. Cushing (Myra), 169–70, 171, 297
El Paso, Tex., 237, 249
Emigration: growth in, 58–60, 186–8, 201–2, 207–9, 219, 234–5, 240–1; promoters, 185–8, 190, 220–3; western society altered by, 184–6; see also Wagon trains
England. See Great Britain
Estill, J. M., 242
Evans, Martha, 40, 41–2
Expositor, The, 225–6
Eyers family, 193

Fairfax family, 15, 30
Fallon, Bill, 214
Farnham, Thomas Jefferson, 158, 297
Ferris, Warren, 112–17 passim, 160
Field, Matt, 9
Figueroa, José, 141, 142–3
Fink, Mike, 91
Fitzpatrick, Broken Hand (Tom), 7, 96, 107–8, 114, 115–16, 117, 150–1, 156, 182, 184, 190, 199–200, 204, 207, 220, 227, 297
Flathead Indians, 107, 109, 120, 156, 182
Florida, 53, 57–8, 215
Fontenelle, Lucien, 110–11, 112, 113, 114, 185, 278
Fort Boise, 194, 195
Fort Bridger, 208, 209, 210, 219–23, 229
Fort Canby, 272
Fort Craig, 256
Fort Davy Crockett, 157, 158–9, 172
Fort Gibson, 96, 97, 98, 100, 102–3, 125
Fort Hall, 154, 157, 176–7, 183, 193–5, 198, 207, 219, 220–1, 229
Fort Laramie, 188, 192, 208, 209, 210, 229
Fort Leavenworth, 225, 226, 293
Fort Loudoun, 36
Fort McLane, 263, 265, 267
Fort Mims, 53
Fort Mojave, 244
Fort Nonsense, 111–13, 117, 121, 154, 229
Fort Osage, Mo., 62, 64–5, 66, 70, 80, 81,
83, 85, 90, 103, 104, 111, 152, 170, 174, 183, 186, 290
Fort Strother, 54
Fort Tejon, 244
Fort Union, 108, 109, 110, 161
Fort Walla, 147
Fort Whipple, 273, 274
Fort Yuma, 270
Fowler, Jacob, 74–5
Fraeb, Henry, 155–6, 173, 175, 179, 181, 183–4, 188, 278, 287
Franklin, Benjamin, 23, 31
Franklin, Sir John, 290
Franklin, Mo., 61, 75, 76, 81, 88
Franklin Intelligencer, 81
Frazier (mountain man), 130
Frémon, Mr. and Mrs. Charles, 202
Frémont, Capt. John Charles, 202–3, 277; and California under Mexico, 214–15, 217, 230; in Corps of Topographical Engineers' expeditions, 10–11, 84, 193–4, 198–201, 202–8, 210–16, 223, 278, 296; court-martial of, 217, 230; explored route for railroad, 230–3, 235, 241, 279; obsessed with personal glory and reputation, 84, 198–201, 202, 204–7, 210, 230–3, 279–80; publicized the West, 202, 204, 206–7, 209; and Walker, 10–11, 198–201, 203, 207, 210–18, 221, 224, 233, 287
Frémont, Mrs. John Charles (Jesse Benton), 54, 203, 278
French, the, 15, 18, 27, 36
French and Indian War, 36, 45
Fristoe, Richard, 89
Frontier, the: agriculture, 32, 35, 47, 68–9; courts, 89, 93–5; entrepreneurs, 87–8, 96, 185, 187; journalists on, 8–12, 71–2, 91–2; politics, 87, 88–90, 101; restlessness of people, 46–7, 48; in 1700s, 13–14; society, 23, 50–3, 65, 97; tools and guns, 31–2, 33, 51; violence and crime, 90–1, 92–4, 102; see also Appalachian frontier; West, the
Frontier Heroes, 3–4, 12, 24, 206, 278–80, 286, 288, 297; see also Mountain men
Fur trade, 4, 15, 35, 45, 47, 62–3, 96, 98, 103, 248; competition in, 108–119 passim, 153–5; decline and change in, 153–5; and Indians, 15, 45, 62–3, 64–5, 104–23 passim, 149, 154–7, 161–2, 185; rendezvous system in, 107–8, 109–10, 112, 117, 119–22, 126, 127, 145, 148, 154–5, 162, 167, 175, 179, 229; Rocky Mountain, 72, 90, 98–122, 153–7, 161–2, 188; Santa Fe, 72–80, 90, 104, 188

Gantt, John, 122, 192
Gantt and Blackwell, 109, 122–3, 154
Georgia, 53
German emigrants, 16, 20, 21, 26, 34
Gift, George, 286–88
Gilliam, Cornelius, 208

Gilliam, Washington, 208
Gilroy, John, 140, 217
Gilroy, Calif., 217–18, 235–6, 244
Girty, Simon, 42
Glass, Hugh, 107
Glenn, Hugh, 74–5
Godey, Alex, 199, 207, 210, 230, 232, 279
Godin, Antoine, 110
Gold: in Arizona, 4, 9, 247, 252, 269–74; in California, 143, 234–6, 244, 248; in Colorado, 249, 252, 269
Gooch, William, 30
Goodwin, John, 273–4, 276–7
Goodyear, Andrew, 228, 245
Goodyear, Miles, 228–9
Goodyear, William, 245
Gordon (mountain man), 158–9
Grand Canyon, 238, 276
Grant, Richard, 193–5, 219
Gray, Jim, 253
Grayson, A. J., 221–2
Great Basin, 4, 10, 126, 156, 159–61, 172, 199–200, 216, 218, 220, 236–9, 290
Great Britain, 36, 37, 38, 52; colonists from, 13–15, 21, 22–3; fur traders, 27, 45–6, 104, 106; and lowland Scots, 16–19, 22–3, 25; in the West, 98, 99, 121, 140, 143, 147–8, 189, 201
Great Salt Lake, 124–5, 128, 148, 194, 200, 222
Great Valley, 27
Gregg, Jacob, 95
Gregg, Josiah, 95, 96; *Commerce of the Prairies*, 95
Gros Ventres Indians, 109–10, 123
Guns: on frontier, 33, 51, 296–7; and violence, 90–1, 94; on wagon trains, 190–1
Gwin, William, 241

Haddard, Will, 78
Halleck, Gen. Henry, 271–2
Hanna (slave), 94–5
Hardin, John Wesley, 91
Hardy (slave), 59
Harper's Weekly, 275
Harrison, Benjamin, 120
Hastings, Lansford, 191, 220–3, 279
Hastings Cutoff, 220–3
Hayes, Jack, 27–8
Hayes family, 49, 70
Head, Mark, 144, 145
Henry, Alexander, 164–5
Hoffman, William, 244–5, 267
Holmes, George, 120–1
Hopi Indians. See Moqui Indians
Horseshoe Bend, 55–6, 57, 89, 97, 102, 287
Houston, James, 51
Houston, John, 51
Houston, Sam, 43, 50, 51, 52, 55, 97, 102, 215
Houston family, 29, 49, 51, 101

Howell, William, 273
Hudson's Bay Company, 106, 108, 110, 127, 147, 154, 155–7, 178, 193, 194, 219, 247
Hunting, 47; as basis of Indian economy, 185–6; on expeditions, 127, 192–3, 208

Idaho, 71, 106, 130, 182
Indentured servants, 15, 26, 93
Independence, Mo., 4, 43, 88–95, 102, 175, 182, 187, 189, 203, 221, 222, 225, 226, 228, 243, 293; *see also* Jackson County, Mo.
Independence (steamboat), 58
Independence Rock, 176, 210
Indians, 62, 66–7, 72, 78, 98, 209; on Appalachian frontier, 4, 14, 19, 20, 22, 27, 34–46, 63; attacked wagon trains, 177, 179, 184, 190–1; customs and culture, 35, 41–4, 162–5, 185–6, 209; and fur trade, 15, 45, 62–3, 64–5, 104–23 *passim*, 149, 154–7, 161–2, 185; injustices against, 5, 41, 63, 161, 275, 297; and liquor, 93–4, 157; and missionaries, 169, 175–8, 182; prisoners of, 41–2, 184, 257; problems of, caused by western emigration, 184–6, 201; racism against, 35, 42, 63, 184–6, 274–5; rapport between whites and, 4, 5, 41–4, 150–1, 155–61, 185–6, 196, 199, 275; territory of, and Santa Fe Trail, 80, 83, 105; as wives to whites, 161–71, 284; *see also* Indian wars; *individual tribes*
Indian wars, 5, 49, 97; on Appalachian frontier, 4, 22, 35–41, 42, 43, 44, 52–6, 104; and U.S. Army, 231, 244–5, 250, 257–9, 265–7, 272, 273, 287, 296; western, 35–6, 231, 244–5, 250, 255–69, 270–1
Iowa, 62, 184
Ireland, 18–19, 24, 26, 30
Iroquois Indians, 14, 16, 23, 27, 34, 35, 36, 41, 44, 52–3, 104, 109, 110
Irotaba, 267–70, 280
Irving, Washington, 9, 71, 72, 91, 175; *Adventures of Captain Bonneville, U.S.A., The*, 99–100, 103, 104, 105, 114, 116, 124–6, 132–3, 148–9, 165, 215

Jackson, Andrew, 3, 36, 49, 53–8, 89, 97, 98–9, 101–2, 201, 215
Jackson, David, 108
Jackson, Thomas (Stonewall), 287
Jackson County, Mo., 95, 143, 186–8, 226, 227; courts in, 89, 90, 93–5; politics in, 87, 88–90; violence and crime in, 90–1, 92–3, 102; *see also* Independence, Mo.
James, Thomas, 74, 75
James I, King of England, 18, 19
Jandreau (emigrant), 177
Janos, Mex., 258
Jefferson, Thomas, 64, 65

Johnson, Lieutenant, 251
Johnson, H. S., 251
Johnson, Waldo, 93
Journalists, 8–12, 71–2, 91–2, 236–40, 250–2, 286–8

Kansas, 62, 64, 83, 95, 104
Kansas City, Mo., 62, 89, 279
Kansas Indians, 73, 84, 104
Kearny, Gen. Stephen, 209, 217, 219, 223
Kelawatset Indians, 127
Kelsey, Nancy, 183, 297
Kendall, Flora, 284–5
Kentucky, 47, 48, 49, 61, 74
Kern, Dr. Benjamin, 230, 233, 241
Kern, Edward ("Ned"), 210–14, 230, 232–3, 238
Kern, Richard, 230, 241
Kingston, Tenn., 49, 54, 58
Knox, James, 47
Knox, John, 17
Knoxville, Tenn., 48, 50

Lagoda (ship), 139–41
Lallier, Bill, 266
Lancaster, Pa., 13, 34
La Paz, Ariz., 280
Largo, Francisco, 78, 79, 287
Leidesdorff, William, 218
Leonard, Zenas, 9, 149–53, 186, 192, 224, 226, 254, 269, 271, 280, 297; Adventures of Zenas Leonard, Fur Trader, 152, 175, 291; on California expedition, 122–5, 127–47, 201
Lewis, Meriwether, 4, 64, 114, 166, 278
Lewis and Clark expedition, 4, 64, 106, 114
Lienhard, Heinrich, 222
Lincoln, Abraham, 3, 207, 273
Liquor: drunkenness on frontier, 93–4; sale to Indians, 93–4, 157
Little, Milton, 196
Little America party, 63–4, 80, 201
Little Bighorn, 286–7
Littlejohn, Philo, 175–6
Logan, James, 19–20, 26–7
Long Hunters, 47–8
Los Angeles, Calif., 126, 127, 156, 160, 173, 180, 181, 198, 218, 235, 237
Los Angeles Star, 240
Louisiana Purchase, 62, 64
Lount, George, 248–9, 256–7
Lovell, Merton N., 8
Lupton, Lancaster, 184
Lyon (on Walker expedition), 244

Mace's Hole, 252
Macomb, Gen. Alexander, 98, 112, 121
Malaria, 60–1, 192
Mangas Coloradas, 257, 258–67, 269, 297
Manifest Destiny, 80–1, 201–3, 209, 215, 217, 251
Manzanita Ranch, 244, 246, 276, 282–4, 288

Marsh, John, 143
Marshall, James, 234
Martin, Julius, 192, 195, 217, 235
Martin, Mrs. Julius, 192, 193, 197, 217
Martin family, 49
Marxists, 201
Maryland, 19, 24
Mather, Thomas, 81, 83, 85
Maximilian, Prince of Wied, 66
Maxwell, Lucien, 43, 211–12, 240
May, Richard, 229–30
Mazatlán, Mex., 257
McBride, John, 6, 222
McBride party, 6, 222
McClellan, Abraham, 58–9, 68–9, 70, 87–90, 95, 96, 101, 102, 186, 188, 226, 243, 297
McClellan, Mrs. Abraham (Jane Walker), 49, 58–9, 68, 226, 297
McClellan, Barbara, 49
McClellan, Frank, 188, 192, 195, 218–19, 223, 225, 226–7, 228–9, 234, 235, 236, 243–4, 285
McClellan, Lucy, 228, 243–4
McClellan, Mary Ann, 243–4
McClellan, Mike, 88, 229, 235, 236
McClellan family, 29, 49, 51, 70, 152, 243, 285
McClintock, Walter, 163
McCormick, Richard, 277
McDougall, Duncan, 164
McKnight, Robert, 73
McLoughlin, Dr. John, 178
Meek, Joe, 9, 120–1, 122, 124, 127–45, 154–5, 157–9, 164, 165, 166, 176–7, 179, 224, 226, 227, 237, 279, 297
Meek, Sam, 9
Meek, Stephen Hall, 124, 127–44
Meriwether, David, 74
Mesilla, N. Mex., 258
Methodists, 177–8, 182
Mexican War, 97, 217, 219, 223–6, 234
Mexico, 72–3, 74–5, 79, 98, 99, 160, 231, 237, 257–8, 260, 274, 280–1; California under, 125, 126, 139, 140–3, 149, 156, 180–1, 189, 201, 214–15, 218, 235; Mexican War, 97, 217, 219, 223–6, 234; and Santa Fe Trail, 81, 84–5
Mexico City, Mex., 73, 85
Miller, Alfred Jacob, 167, 168–9, 171, 291
Miller, Joaquin, 206
Mining prospectors. See gold
Minnesota, 62, 64
Missionaries, 169, 175–8, 182, 189
Missouri, 183, 225–8, 250, 251, 290; economic problems in, 76, 81, 88; emigration movement in, 186–8; movement to, and settlements in, 50, 58–70, 82; traders from, 73–80, 127; see also Jackson County, Mo.
Mitchell, Levin, 123–4, 127–44, 159, 180
Mojave Indians, 127, 238, 244, 245–6, 267–8, 270, 280, 297
Monroe, James, 62, 80

Montana, 106
Monterey, Calif., 140–1, 198
Montgomery, Lt. William, 97, 292–4
Montoya, J. Maria, 180
Moore, Alexander, 39
Moore, D. W., 152
Moore, James, 29, 38
Moore, Mrs. James (Jane Walker), 29, 38
Moore, James (son), 38–40, 48
Moore, Mrs. James (Martha Poage), 38, 40
Moore, James (grandson), 39, 41–2
Moore, Jane, 40
Moore, John, 40
Moore, Mary, 40, 41–2
Moore, Peggy, 40
Moore, Rebecca, 39
Moore, William, 39
Moore family, 49
Moqui Indians (Hopi), 237, 239, 257, 287, 297
Mormons, 92, 222, 279
Mountain Lamb, 165, 297
Mountain men, 9, 11, 91, 102, 127, 153–65, 200, 209, 210, 227, 229, 233, 237, 278–80, 288; expedition to California, 4–5, 122, 123–47, 176, 197, 199; and Rocky Mountain fur trade, 106–22 *passim*, 153–7; and wagon trains, 176–8, 179, 182
Munger, Asahel, 178
Murrell, John, 59–60

Napa County Reporter, 286, 288
Nashville, Tenn., 53
Navajo Indians, 156, 160, 171, 239, 250, 258–9, 265, 272
Nevada, 130, 156, 183, 198
Newell, Doc (Robert), 154–5, 157, 158–9, 176–7, 179, 227
New England, 31, 63
New Mexico, 71–80, 85–6, 91, 96, 117, 166, 171, 211, 240, 242, 254, 270, 271, 279, 288; Civil War in, 249–52; Indians of, 145, 257–69, 272; and Mexican War, 217, 219, 223–6, 234
New Orleans, La., 243, 284
New Orleans Picayune, 9
New York City, N.Y., 99, 103, 132
New York Herald, 241, 247
New York State, 14
Nez Percé Indians, 107, 109, 120, 147, 150, 156, 157, 182, 279
Nicollet, Joseph, 203
Nidever, George, 124–5, 127–44, 292, 294
Nidever, Mark, 134
North Carolina, 14
Nuttall, Thomas, 239

O'Connor, Joe, 93
Ogden, Peter Skene, 126
Ohio, 39, 48
Oklahoma, 62, 71, 95, 97, 134, 211, 223, 284

Old Spanish Trail, 181, 198, 237
Oregon, 106, 112, 198, 201, 207, 215, 217, 247, 248, 279; British in, 98, 99, 121, 147–8, 189; migration to, 88, 154, 176–9, 183, 186–7, 188–9, 191, 193, 202, 208–9, 220, 222; missionaries in, 169, 175–8, 182, 189
Oregon Trail, 9, 209
Osage Indians, 64, 66–7, 82–3, 88, 93–4, 170, 184, 284
Osage Trace, 61
Oto Indians, 168

Paiute Indians, 130–3, 146–7, 156, 160, 196, 287, 297
Palmer, Joel, 210
Palomares, Ygnacio, 180–1
Papago Indians, 257
Parkman, Francis, 9
Parrish, Edward, 208–9
Patterson family, 29, 49, 70
Pattie, James Ohio, 71–2
Pawnee Indians, 74, 76–7, 121, 151, 156, 184
Paxton family, 49
Pena, Feliz, 283, 297
Penn, William, 19–20
Penn family, 15
Pennsylvania, 14, 19–20, 24, 26–7, 29, 36
Pennsylvania Dutch, 16, 31
Pennsylvania Gazette, 19
Pensacola, Fla., 58
Philadelphia, Pa., 20
Philips (mountain man), 142
Pierre's Hole, 109–10, 114, 115, 118, 123
Pima Indians, 257, 267, 270, 271
Pinos Altos, 264, 267
Poage, Robert, 39
Poage family, 29, 39, 49
Poinsett, Joel, 84–5, 203
Point Pleasant, 37
Politics: in Missouri, 87, 88–90
Pope, Capt. John, 242
Porter, Rufus, 187
Powell, John Wesley, 172
Presbyterians, 17–18, 22, 25, 26, 34, 50, 169
Prescott gold fields, 4, 269–74, 281
Preuss, Charles, 204–5, 207, 210, 230, 232, 278
Price, Sterling, 223, 224–5
Protestants, 17, 176, 189; *see also individual religions*
Pueblo, Colo., 211, 231, 253
Pueblo Indians, 225

Quakers, 19

Racism, 91, 274; against Indians, 35, 42, 63, 184–6, 274–5
Railroad, 230–3, 240–3, 247
Ralston, Jack, 171, 247–9, 270
Reading, Pierson B., 190, 297
Reagan, Ronald, 295

Reddick, Walter, 218–19
Reed (emigrant), 221
Reeves, Benjamin, 81, 83, 85
Revolutionary War, 36, 38, 46, 48, 52
Richards (hired man), 39
Rocky Mountain Fur Company (RMFC), 108–9, 114, 116, 127, 151, 154, 173
Rocky Mountains, 14, 176, 205–6, 228–30, 288; fur trade, 72, 90, 98–122, 153–7, 161–2, 188
Roman Catholics, 18, 19, 176, 189
Rose, Edward, 107, 150
Russell, Carl, 99
Russia, 140, 143
Rutherford, Samuel, 25
Ruxton, George, 9, 91–2, 120, 161, 171; *Life in the Far West*, 92

Sacajawea, 166
Sacramento, Calif., 236, 279
Sage, Rufus, 9
St. Clair, Gen. Arthur, 35
St. Joseph, Mo., 187, 189
St. Louis, Mo., 60, 66, 79, 81, 88, 103, 107, 109, 121, 122, 154, 182, 225, 226, 228, 284
St. Louis Enquirer, 61
St. Vrain, Ceran, 156, 223, 240
St. Vrain, Marcellus, 223–4, 225, 240
Salmon River camp, 113, 115
Sand Creek massacre, 279
San Diego, Calif., 126
San Francisco, Calif., 178
San Francisco Herald, 236–8
Sangre de Cristo Mountains, 230, 231–3, 235
San Joaquin Valley, 12, 126, 137, 139, 144
San Jose mission, 141
San Juan Bautista mission, 140–1, 144
San Luis Obispo, Calif., 180
Santa Fe, N. Mex., 71–80, 85–6, 88, 96, 103, 104, 127, 143, 160, 181, 188, 198, 208, 223–5, 236, 240, 242, 249–50, 254, 259, 283
Santa Fe Trail, 4, 10, 72, 76, 79, 95, 127, 209, 211, 226, 290; survey of, 80–7, 90, 102, 105, 202
Say, Asa, 94
Scientific American (magazine), 187
Scotch-Irish clans, 16–26; on frontier, 4, 16, 21–44, 48, 289, 295, 296; in Missouri, 89, 92, 93–4, 96, 101
Scott, Katherine, 49
Seminole Indians, 57–8
Sevier, Nolichucky Jack, 49
Shawnee Indians, 27–8, 34, 37–40, 41, 44, 285
Shepherd, Maxwell, 170
Sherman, William Tecumseh, 207
Shoshoni Indians, 71, 116, 128, 130, 156, 164, 165, 297
Shotwell (emigrant), 191
Sibley, George, 64–9, 76, 89, 297; and Santa Fe Trail, 81, 83–7, 202

Sibley, Mrs. George (Mary Easton), 66
Sibley, Gen. H. H., 249–50, 251–2, 264
Sierra Mountains, 100, 126, 192, 196, 207, 213, 220–3, 228, 237, 244; Walker's expedition through, 4–5, 11–12, 122, 133–6, 143–6, 176, 197, 199, 288, 291
Simpson, John, 40
Sinaloa, Mex., 257
Sinclair, John, 193
Sioux Indians, 23, 106, 121, 150, 156, 159, 160, 162, 183–4, 186, 227, 286–7
Sitting Bull, 160, 286
Slavery, 61, 93, 94–5, 160, 171, 257, 283
Smallpox, 155
Smedley, G. Poe, 170
Smith, Alvin, 175–6
Smith, Jedediah, 5, 7, 96, 107–8, 126–7, 141, 142, 237, 278
Smith, Peg-leg, 9, 180
Smith, Willard, 172, 297
Snake Indians, 107, 116, 117–18, 120, 121, 150, 156, 159–61, 166, 167, 170, 176, 180, 181, 183, 188, 192, 209, 210, 212, 219, 223, 227, 229, 287, 297
Snyder, Jacob, 210
Society, 53, 63; colonial, 15–16, 23; frontier, 23, 50–3, 65, 97; western, altered by emigration, 184–6
Socorro, N. Mex., 171
Sonora, Mex., 257, 281
South Carolina, 14, 36, 203
Spanish: in America, 58, 70, 71–4, 79, 257
Spotswood, Alexander, 16
Sprague, Thomas, 228–9
Steamboats, 58, 88
Stearns, Abel, 173, 181
Stewart, George, 195
Stewart, William Drummond, 119–21, 167, 171, 176, 188, 192, 200
Stocking, Clark, 266
Sturgeon, Dr., 266
Sublette, Andrew, 96, 172, 179, 208, 218
Sublette, Bill, 96, 107–8, 109–10, 116, 117, 127, 188, 218
Sublette, Milton, 43, 96, 108, 109–10, 117, 218
Sublette, Pinckney, 218
Sublette, Solomon, 218–19, 225, 226–7
Sunset Crater, 238
Sutter, John, 143, 178, 222, 234
Sutter's Fort, 194, 195, 196, 213, 214, 218–19, 220, 236
Swilling, Jack, 264–5, 275, 296

Talbot, Theodore, 172, 193–5, 198, 207, 210–14, 238
Taos, N. Mex., 72, 78, 85, 96, 156, 160, 188, 225, 231, 232, 279
Taos trappers, 72, 75, 79, 106, 117, 166, 237, 291
Taplin, Charles, 218–19
Tat (prospector), 274
Tecumseh, 53, 160

Tennessee, 47–53, 251, 285
Texas, 50, 70, 97, 184, 211, 215, 223
Texas Rangers, 249
Thomas, Wind Wagon, 187
Thompson, Philip, 159, 172, 180
Thomson, John, 290–3
Todd, Richard, 89
Tomahawk rights, 20
Tools, frontier, 31–2
Toomy, Ambrose, 70
Toomy family, 29, 39, 49, 50, 70, 101, 285
Trade, 15, 27, 51–2, 64–5, 102; Santa Fe, 72–80, 86, 88, 90, 95, 96, 103, 127, 143; see also Fur trade
Tübatulabel, 144
Tucson, Ariz., 237, 249–50, 258, 264, 267, 273, 274
Tuolumne Canyon, 135, 136
Turner, William, 273
Twain, Mark, 12

Ulster, 18–19, 24, 26
Union Army. See Civil War
United States, 64–5, 66–7, 88, 156; Congress, 207, 241–2, 273; Frontier Response in, 294–7; and Manifest Destiny, 80–1, 140, 201–3, 209, 215, 217, 251; migration restriction of, 62–4, 72; survey of Santa Fe Trail, 80–7; see also Mexican War
U.S. Army, 95, 97–8; Corps of Topographical Engineers, 84, 193–4, 203, 211, 223, 242, 296; and Indian wars, 231, 244–5, 250, 257–9, 265–7, 272, 273, 287, 296; and Mexican War, 217, 219, 223–4; and wagon trains, 209–10, 241; see also Frémont, Capt. John Charles
U.S. State Department, 125
U.S. War Department, 98, 99–100, 103, 112, 121, 209, 266
Utah, 92, 130, 156, 222
Ute Indians, 10, 156, 159–61, 180, 198, 199, 211, 230, 231, 233, 239, 287

Vancouver, Can., 178
Vanderburgh, Henry, 109, 114, 115, 151, 278
Vasquez, Louis, 155–6, 172, 179, 188, 192, 210, 221
Vietnam, 296
Violence and crime: on frontier, 90–1, 92–3, 94, 102
Virginia, 14, 19, 27, 45, 52, 255; see also Appalachian frontier

Wagon trains, 174–9, 181–97 passim, 208–9, 219–23, 229, 240–1, 296; Indian attacks on, 177, 179, 184, 190–1; see also Emigration
Walkara, 160–1, 180, 199, 287
Walker, Alexander (son of original emigrant), 29

Walker, Alexander (nephew of original emigrant), 29
Walker, Annie, 243–4, 285
Walker, Barbara, 284–5
Walker, Elizabeth, 52
Walker, James (son of original emigrant), 29, 37
Walker, James (grandson of original emigrant), 49
Walker, James (Jeemes; nephew of Joseph), 228–9, 234, 235–6, 237, 239, 243–4, 283, 286, 288, 297
Walker, Mrs. James (Mary Vaughan), 284
Walker, Jane, 243–4, 285
Walker, Joel, 49, 51, 55–6, 57–8, 59, 66, 68, 69–70, 76–9, 85, 88, 89–90, 154, 235, 242, 285–6; emigrated to West, 174–80, 182, 183, 187, 189, 201–2, 207, 240
Walker, Mrs. Joel (Mary Young), 79, 154, 174–9, 182, 187, 201–2, 207, 240
Walker, John (original emigrant), 24–9, 33, 48, 50, 62, 255
Walker, Mrs. John (Katherine), 24–7, 29, 50, 62
Walker, John (son of original emigrant), 29, 37–8, 48
Walker, John (nephew of original emigrant), 29, 33
Walker, John (grandson of original emigrant), 49
Walker, John (brother of Joseph), 49, 51, 58, 69, 81, 83–5, 87–8, 186, 226, 292, 297
Walker, John (nephew of Joseph), 178, 235–6
Walker, John (son of Jeemes), 284
Walker, Joseph (son of original emigrant), 29
Walker, Joseph (grandson of original emigrant), 48–52, 58–9
Walker, Mrs. Joseph (Susan Willis), 48–52, 58
Walker, Josephine, 284–5
Walker, Joseph Rutherford, 4–5, 7-8, 24, 25, 49, 51–2, 58–9, 68, 69, 184, 186, 290–7; appearance of, 5–6, 49, 167; in Arizona, 4, 171–2, 237–40, 244, 269–77, 280; on Bonneville expedition, 4, 96–121 passim, 149–52, 166, 185, 186, 215, 291, 292; in Creek War, 55–6; on exploratory expeditions, 4–5, 52, 171–3, 236–9, 243, 246, 276, 280, 296, 297; and Frémont, 10–11, 198–201, 203, 207, 210–18, 221, 224, 233, 287; guided army, 244–6; guided prospectors, 244, 248–57, 259–76; and Indian wars, 4, 5, 255–7, 259–69, 270–1, 287; Indian wife and family of, 166–71, 181, 183, 186, 188, 203, 209, 210, 212, 219, 227–8, 229, 291; led party through Sierras to California, 4–5, 11–12, 122, 123–47, 149, 175, 176, 188,

197, 199, 288, 291; led wagon trains, 174, 188, 191–7, 208–9, 229–30, 297; marked Santa Fe Trail, 4, 10, 81–7, 102; mountain man, 4–5, 64, 102, 155– 62, 176, 226, 228–30, 288; natural historian, 224, 238–9, 241–3, 297; in New Mexico, 70–2, 74, 75–6, 77–80, 91, 96, 117, 166, 188, 225, 240, 288, 291; obscurity of, 6–12, 70–2, 76, 239; personality of, 8–12, 227–8, 239, 255; rapport with Indians of, 4, 43, 116, 132, 155–61, 171, 186, 239; reputa- tion of, 5–7, 91, 94, 101, 121–2, 136, 137, 159, 182–3, 186, 219, 224, 276, 280, 286, 297; settled in California, 7, 230, 235, 244, 282–8; sheriff of Inde- pendence, 4, 87–96, 102, 297; trader and fur trapper, 4, 51–2, 95–6, 102, 115–17, 150–2, 156, 179–81, 188, 198, 209, 217–25, 235–6

Walker, Joseph Rutherford (nephew of Joseph), 249
Walker, Louisa, 178
Walker, Lucy (Mrs. Ambrose Toomy), 40, 70, 226
Walker, Samuel (son of original emi- grant), 29, 37, 48
Walker, Mrs. Samuel (Jane Patterson), 48
Walker, Samuel (grandson of original emigrant), 38, 48, 49
Walker, Samuel (brother of Joseph), 49, 70, 186, 226, 228, 243–4
Walker, Mrs. Samuel (Barbara Toomy), 70, 226, 243–4, 285–6, 291, 293–4
Walker, Susan (Mrs. Lucian Ailstock), 49, 70, 226, 292
Walker, William, 38, 41
Walker, Mrs. William (Catherine Mon- tour), 41
Walker family, 4, 24–34, 37–40, 47, 48– 52, 58–62, 66, 67–70, 101, 152, 170, 175, 226–7, 235, 243–4, 280, 283, 284–8
Walker Lake, 133, 213, 244
Walker Pass, 144, 196, 213, 237, 242–3, 249, 270
Walton, Major, 195
War of 1812, 41, 53, 60, 62
Washington, George, 3, 55

Washington, D.C., 10, 99, 121, 125, 201, 203, 210, 214, 217
Weatherford, William, 53–6, 57, 102, 287
Weaver, Powell (Pauline), 124, 127–47, 171, 270, 276–7
Welles, Gideon, 276
West, Col. John, 265, 266
West, the, 15–16, 30, 104–5, 294; al- tered by emigration, 184–6; and Fron- tier Response, 294–7; government re- striction on migration to, 62–4, 72; movement to, 22, 40–1, 43, 48, 50, 58–64, 80, 86, 87–8, 106, 186–8, 201– 2, 207–9, 219, 234–5, 240–1; publi- cized by Frémont, 202, 204, 206–7, 209; railroad to, 230, 240–3, 247; see also California; Emigration; Frontier; Oregon; Wagon trains
Western Emigration Society, 187
Western Engineer (steamboat), 58
White Plume, 104–5
Wigton, Scotland, 24, 255
Willamette Valley, 177–8
Williams, Bill, 81–5, 123–4, 127–44, 155–6, 157, 180–1, 211–12, 230, 231– 3, 270, 278, 293–4, 296
Williams, Ezekiel, 73–4, 75
Williams, Joseph, 182
Williamsburg, Va., 30
Willis, William, 48, 49
Willis family, 70
Wislizenus, Adolph, 167–8, 297
Wolfskill, William, 75, 93, 126
Wood, John, 55
Woolsey, King, 275–6, 296
Workman, David, 93
Wright, John T., 266
Wyandotte Indians, 38, 41, 170
Wyeth, Nathaniel, 109, 154, 193
Wyoming, 106, 156, 205
Wyoming Valley, 35

Yellowstone (steamboat), 108
Yosemite Valley, 12, 135–6, 288, 297
Young, Ewing, 79, 126, 175, 178
Young, John, 88
Young, Martha, 174, 175, 178, 179
Young family, 49, 175
Yuma, Ariz., 237

Zuñi Indians, 160, 257